LOEB CLASSICAL LIBRARY

FOUNDED BY JAMES LOEB 1911

EDITED BY

JEFFREY HENDERSON

MAXIMUS OF TYRE

PHILOSOPHICAL ORATIONS

II

LCL 554

MAXIMUS OF TYRE

PHILOSOPHICAL ORATIONS

VOLUME II

EDITED AND TRANSLATED BY

WILLIAM H. RACE

HARVARD UNIVERSITY PRESS

CAMBRIDGE, MASSACHUSETTS

LONDON, ENGLAND

2023

LOEB CLASSICAL LIBRARY® is a registered trademark
of the President and Fellows of Harvard College

Library of Congress Control Number 2023002950
CIP data available from the Library of Congress

ISBN 978-0-674-99757-8

*Composed in ZephGreek and ZephText by
Technologies 'N Typography, Merrimac, Massachusetts.
Printed on acid-free paper and bound by
Maple Press, York, Pennsylvania*

CONTENTS

CONTENTS

ΜΑΞΙΜΟΥ ΤΥΡΙΟΥ
ΠΛΑΤΩΝΙΚΟΥ ΦΙΛΟΣΟΦΟΥ
ΤΩΝ ΕΝ ΡΩΜΗΙ ΔΙΑΛΕΞΕΩΝ
ΤΗΣ ΠΡΩΤΗΣ ΕΠΙΔΗΜΙΑΣ

THE DISCOURSES OF THE
PLATONIC PHILOSOPHER
MAXIMUS OF TYRE,
DELIVERED IN ROME
DURING HIS FIRST VISIT

ORATION 22

INTRODUCTION

The title in the manuscript is misleading. It is not the enjoyment (*euphrosynē*) of philosophical discourse that makes it superior to other forms of entertainment, but its healing power for the soul. However, that power is left vague, indeed questionable, at the end of the oration.[1] The metaphor of a "feast (*euōchia*) of words" dominates the entire discussion. It opens with Odysseus' praise of the feast Alcinous prepared for him, with its lavish board, flowing wine, and inspired singer, as "the very best thing" (§1). However, Odysseus cannot mean that this entertainment is actually the best, for he had already rejected the food of the Lotus-Eaters and the song of the Sirens. In fact, Homer was actually privileging the pleasure of melody for the ears over that of the food for the belly (§2). But what kind of melody brings proper pleasure to the ears? Not that from musical instruments, because it is irrational and contributes little to the soul's enjoyment. Words provide the proper feast for the ears: they are like food that is nourishing, whereas melody is like mere smell. The is-

---

[1] In §7 philosophers (Socrates, Plato, Xenophon, and Aeschines) and poets (Homer and Hesiod) are mentioned only in passing; any healing of the soul must come from the gods.

sue then becomes, what kind of words should be served at
a proper feast? Not those from the law courts, where truth
and justice are corrupted and falsified (§3). Not playacting
spectacles. Not oratory in assemblies, where Athenian
demagogues rant like drunkards (§4). Then what about
historical narratives? These are extremely pleasurable because they encompass so many events from all over the
world and allow the soul to experience, almost firsthand,
the events of the distant past (§5). Yet, the problem with
historical narratives is that they indiscriminately mix good
and evil. Indeed, history is so full of tragic events that its
fare is unwholesome;[2] in contrast, healthful discourse is
that served by Socrates, Plato, Xenophon, and Aeschines
(§6). So, forget about the Persian Wars and the plague and
address instead the strife and sickness in the human soul.
Who then will take command and heal it? This task, however, is beyond humans: it requires oracles and prayers for
the healing power of an Apollo or a Zeus (§7).

---

[2] Contrast the fulsome praise of history by Diodorus Siculus
at *Bibl.* 1.1.1–6, with its emphasis on the moral lessons of history.

ORATION 22

Ὅτι πάσης τῆς διὰ λόγων εὐφροσύνης ἡ διὰ
φιλοσόφων λόγων ἀμείνων

1. Διηγεῖται Ὅμηρος περὶ Ὀδυσσέως, ὅτι χήτει νεὼς
ἐπὶ σχεδίας πλέων, χειμῶνος ἐπιγενομένου, σκεδασθεί-
σης τῆς σχεδίας, νηχόμενος, ὑποβαλλούσης αὐτῷ
κρήδεμνον τῆς Λευκοθέας, ἐκπεσὼν εἰς τὴν Φαιάκων
γῆν, ἱκετεύσας βασιλικὴν παρθένον, κομισθεὶς ὑπ'
αὐτῆς εἰς τὸ ἄστυ, τυχὼν αἰδοῦς παρ' Ἀλκίνου, κοινωνεῖ τῆς ἑστίας τοῖς Φαιάκων ἀρίστοις, καὶ μετὰ
τοῦτο ἐνάρχεται τῶν πρὸς τὸν Ἀλκίνουν λόγων ὡδί
πως· "Ἀλκίνοε βασιλεῦ, καλὸν μὲν ἀκούειν ἀοιδοῦ
ἀγαθοῦ, οἷος οὗτος τὴν τέχνην θεῖος· τί γὰρ ἂν εἴη
χαριέστερον τέλος δήμου εὐθυμουμένου καὶ δαιτυ-
μόνων οἴκοι ᾠδῆς ἀκροωμένων, καθημένων ἑξῆς, καὶ
τραπέζης ἀφθόνου καὶ κρατῆρος μεστοῦ;" ἐρωτῶ δὴ
τὸν Ὀδυσσέα· "τί ἡγεῖ εἶναι τὴν εὐφροσύνην, ὦ σοφώτατε ἀνδρῶν; τράπεζαν μεστὴν κρεῶν καὶ σίτου
καὶ κρατῆρα πλήρη καὶ οἶνον διαχεόμενον, καὶ ἐπὶ
τούτοις ᾄδοντα ἀοιδὸν οἵας ἐκεῖνος ᾠδὰς ᾖδεν,

---

[1] The following is a synopsis of *Odyssey*, Books 5–8.

4

ORATION 22

That the enjoyment of philosophical discourse is superior to that of any other discourse

1. Homer tells how Odysseus,[1] when no ship was available, was sailing on a raft; how a storm came up and his raft was shattered, and how, as he swam for his life, Leucothea buoyed him up with her veil; and how, after being washed ashore on the land of Phaeacia, he supplicated a royal maiden for help, was escorted by her to the town, was respectfully received by Alcinous, shared a feast with the Phaeacian nobles, and afterward began his speech to Alcinous along these lines:[2] "King Alcinous, how good it is to listen to a fine singer,[3] divinely inspired in his art as this one is. For what could be a more consummate delight than having contented subjects and diners listening to a song in your palace, reclining in due order, with a bountiful board and a mixing bowl full of wine?" But my question for Odysseus is, "What exactly do you consider enjoyment to be, O wisest of men? Is it a table laden with meat and bread, a full mixing bowl, wine being poured all around, and, in addition, a singer singing songs like the one the bard sang about

---

[2] The following is a paraphrase of *Od.* 9.2–11.
[3] That is, Demodocus.

5

νεῖκος Ὀδυσσῆος καὶ Πηλεΐδεω Ἀχιλῆος,

ἢ αὖ κοῖλον ἵππον, ἔνθα εἰσδύντες οἱ ἄριστοι τῶν Ἑλλήνων, εἰς τὸ ἄστυ εἰσενεχθέντες, προχυθέντες τοῦ ἵππου, μεθύουσιν ἐπιθέμενοι, εἷλον τὸ ἄστυ;

τοῦτό τί σοι κάλλιστον ἐνὶ φρεσὶν εἴδεται εἶναι;"

2. Δεινός τις εἶ, ὦ σοφώτατε Ὀδυσσεῦ, ἐπαινέτης εὐφροσύνης δημωδεστάτης, οἵαν ⟨ἂν⟩[1] καὶ βάρβαρος ἀνὴρ ἐπαινέσαι καὶ ἄρτι ἐκ Βαβυλῶνος ἥκων, συνήθης πολυτελεῖ τραπέζῃ καὶ οἴνῳ χεομένῳ πολλῷ καὶ ᾠδῇ αὐτοσχεδίῳ· καὶ ταῦτα, ὡς φῇς, ὑπεριδὼν παρ' ἄλλοις τοῦ μελιηδέος λωτοῦ καὶ τῆς Σειρήνων ᾠδῆς.

Μήποτε οὖν ἔοικέν τι Ὅμηρος αἰνίττεσθαι ἄλλο κρεῖττον ἢ ὁποῖον τὰ ἔπη λέγει οὑτωσὶ ἀκούσαντι εὐθύς. τὸ γάρ τοι κειμένων σιτίων ἀμφιλαφῶν καὶ οἴνου πολλοῦ, ταῦτα μὲν ἐπιθεῖναι ταῖς τραπέζαις καὶ τὸν οἶνον τῷ κρατῆρι ἐγχέαι, ἐπαινέσαι δὲ τοὺς δαιτυμόνας ἐν τοσαύταις ἡδοναῖς ἀκροωμένους τοῦ ἀοιδοῦ σπουδῇ, εὐσχήμονά τινα ἔοικεν εὐωχίαν διηγεῖσθαι ἡμῖν, οἵαν μιμήσαιτο ἄν τις νοῦν ἔχων, μεταθεὶς τὰς ἡδονὰς ἀπὸ τῶν αἰσχίστων ἐπὶ τὰ κοσμιώτατα, ἀπὸ τῆς γαστρὸς ἐπὶ τὰς ἀκοάς. ἢ οὐδὲ τοῦτο ἀπόχρη, εὐωχεῖν τὰς ἀκοὰς εἰκῇ καὶ ἀνέδην,

αὐλῶν συρίγγων τ' ἐνοπῇ

[1] suppl. Trapp

---

[4] *Od.* 8.75. What follows is a synopsis of *Od.* 8.499–520.

the quarrel between Odysseus and Peleus' son
 Achilles,[4]

or again the one about the hollow horse that the best of
the Greeks entered, and how they were hauled into the
city, poured forth from the horse, attacked the drunk inhabitants, and captured the city?

Does this seem to your mind to be the very best
 thing?"[5]

2. O most wise Odysseus, you are one powerful eulogist
of a most vulgar form of enjoyment, one which would also
win praise from a barbarian newly arrived from Babylon,
accustomed to an extravagant board, copious wine being
poured out, and impromptu song. And yet you say all this,
while on other occasions, as you admit, you disdained the
honey-sweet lotus and the song of the Sirens.

Perhaps, then, it is likely that Homer is hinting at something greater than what these verses convey to someone
first hearing them. For in fact, when those lavish foods and
abundant wine were at hand, he simply placed the food on
the tables and poured the wine into the mixing bowl, but
went on to praise the diners, amid all these pleasures, for
listening attentively to the bard, thus making it likely that
he is describing for us a seemly kind of feast that any sensible man would imitate, by his transferring pleasures
from the basest of the senses to the most orderly one, that
is, from the belly to the ears. Or is not even this sufficient,
when the ears can feast randomly and glut themselves

on the sound of pipes and pan flutes

---

[5] *Od.* 9.11, substituting "your" (τοι) for "my" (μοι).

καὶ ἀνθρώπων ὁμάδῳ, ἀλλὰ κἀνταῦθα τέχνης δεῖ
κατακοσμούσης τὴν ἀκοῆς εὐωχίαν ἁρμονίᾳ δεξιᾷ.

3. Καὶ τίς ἂν ἡμῖν ἡ τοιαύτη ἁρμονία γένοιτο;
ἀγαπῶ μὲν γὰρ ἔγωγε τὴν ἐκ μελῶν ἡδονὴν προσιοῦ-
σαν ταῖς ἀκοαῖς ἢ δι᾽ αὐλῶν ἐμπνεομένων ἢ διὰ λύρας
κρουομένης ἢ δι᾽ ἄλλου του μουσικοῦ ὀργάνου δυ-
ναμένου χορηγεῖν καὶ ἐπιπέμπειν ἡμῖν προσηνὲς μέ-
λος· δέδια δὲ μὴ ταυτὶ τὰ μέλη ἡδονὴν μέν τινα ἔχῃ
κεκραμένην ὑπὸ τέχνης καλῶς, ἄσημα δὲ ὄντα καὶ
ἄλογα καὶ ἄφωνα μηδὲν μέγα τῇ ψυχῇ εἰς εὐφροσύνην συντελῇ. εἰ γάρ τις ἐθέλοι παραβαλεῖν τὴν ἐκ
μελῶν ἡδονὴν τῇ τῶν λόγων, ἐοίκοι ἂν ὁ μὲν λόγος
σιτίοις, τὸ δὲ μέλος ὀδμαῖς· ὧν τὰ μὲν εἰς ὑποτροφὴν
προσφορώτατα, ὀδμὴ δὲ καὶ ἐν ἡδονῇ[2] κιβδηλότατον
{ἐν}[3] χρῆμα καὶ ἐν τροφῇ ἀσθενέστατον. εὐωχητέον
οὖν τὰς ἀκοάς, τρέφοντας ὁμοῦ, τὰς μὲν ὀδμὰς ταύτας
τὰς ἐκ τῶν μελῶν παραπεμπομένους, τὰ δὲ ἐκ λόγων
σιτία προσάγοντας αὐταῖς.

Ἐπεὶ τοίνυν λόγῳ καὶ οὐκ ἄλλῳ τῳ χαίρειν εἰκὸς
δαιτυμόνας δεξιούς, τίνας καὶ λόγους αὐτοῖς παραθή-
σομεν φέροντες; ἆρα οἳ μὲν μιμοῦνται τὰς ἐν δικαστηρίοις ἔριδας καὶ φιλονικίας ⟨καὶ⟩[4] ἐπιτεχνήσεις
καὶ μάχας, κρατύνοντες μὲν τὰ ἄδικα, ἐπικοσμοῦντες
δὲ τὰ αἰσχρά, κιβδηλεύοντες τἀληθῆ, ὑγιὲς δὲ οὐδὲν

---

[2] ἐν ἡδονῇ Trapp: ἐνοδμὴ R
[3] del. Schenkl, Trapp
[4] suppl. Schottus, Trapp

and "the din of men,"[6] but in this case some further art is needed to bring order to this feast of the ears with its refined harmony?

3. So what might be the nature of this harmony of ours? I ask, because I myself welcome the pleasure of melodies coming to my ears, either from the playing of pipes, or the strumming of lyres, or from any other musical instrument able to produce and convey a pleasant melody to us. I fear, however, that although these melodies possess a certain pleasure that is well crafted by art, they nonetheless make no major contribution to the soul's enjoyment, because they are inarticulate, irrational, and unable to speak. For if someone should wish to compare the pleasure derived from melodies to that from words, then speech would come to resemble food and melody smell. Food is perfectly suited to provide nourishment, whereas smell is altogether deceptive in providing pleasure and utterly incapable of providing nourishment. Therefore we must feast the ears, but at the same time nourish them, by rejecting the "smells" of melodies and serving them instead the "food" of words.

Since then refined diners should take delight in speech rather than in anything else, what kind of words shall we serve up to them? Are they words that imitate the disputes, rivalries, verbal contrivances, and clashes that take place in law courts, words that validate unjust acts and dress up shameful ones, that falsify the truth and allow

---

[6] An adaptation of *Il*. 10.13, describing the festivity in the Trojan camp.

οὐδὲ ἄδολον, οὐδὲ ἐν τῷ φύσεως ἐπιχωρίῳ μένειν ἐῶντες, ἀλλ' αὐτὸ ἐκεῖνο οἷονπερ οἱ τῶν ἀνδραπόδων κάπηλοι, οἳ σώματα παραλαβόντες ἁπλᾶ ὑφ' ἡλίῳ καθαρῷ καὶ ἀέρι ἐλευθέρῳ τεθραμμένα, σκιατροφοῦντες ταῦτα καὶ λεαίνοντες λυμαίνονται αὐτῶν τὴν ἀπ' ἀρχῆς δημιουργίαν, ἣν ἡ φύσις αὐτοῖς περιέβαλεν κρείττονα τέχνης; τοιοῦτον γάρ τι ἀμέλει καὶ οἱ περὶ τὰς δίκας εἰλούμενοι δρῶσιν.

4. Ἀλλὰ τά γε τούτων μιμήματα πρὸς τῷ κίβδηλα εἶναι καὶ σκυθρωπὰ κομιδῇ καὶ εὐωχουμέναις ψυχαῖς οὐ πάνυ τι ἀκούειν ἐπιτήδεια. ὡς ἐγὼ οὐδὲ τὰ Αἰνιάνων θεάματα ἐπαινῶ, ὅσα ἐν πότῳ εὐφραίνονται Αἰνιᾶνες, οἱ μὲν δρῶντες, οἱ δὲ ὁρῶντες· ἄνδρες δύο μιμοῦνται μάχην ὑπαυλοῦντος ἄλλου· ὁ μὲν αὐτοῖν γεωργός τέ ἐστιν καὶ ἀροῖ, ὁ δὲ λῃστὴς καὶ ὅπλα ἔχει, κεῖται δὲ καὶ τῷ γεωργῷ τὰ ὅπλα ἀγχοῦ· ἐπειδὰν δὲ ὁ λῃστὴς ἔλθῃ, ἀφέμενος ὁ γεωργὸς τοῦ ζεύγους, δραμὼν ἐπὶ τὰ ὅπλα, συμπεσόντες μάχονται, παίοντες τὰς ὄψεις[5] καὶ μιμούμενοι τραύματα καὶ πτώματα, θεάματα οὐ συμποτικά.

Ἐπαινῶ πρὸ τούτων τὸν Περσικὸν νόμον τὸν ἀρχαῖον, δι' ὃν Πέρσαι τῆς ἐλευθερίας ἐπελάβοντο. ἀνέκειντο τοῖς Πέρσαις αἱ βουλαὶ εἰς τὰς εὐωχίας ὥσπερ τοῖς Ἀθηναίοις εἰς τὰς ἐκκλησίας, καὶ σπουδαστικώτερον ἦν συμπόσιον Περσικὸν ἐκκλησίας Ἀττικῆς· ἐκεῖ μὲν γὰρ νόμος κολάζων τὴν μέθην ἐπή-

---

[5] τὰς ὄψεις obel. Trapp

nothing to remain wholesome, genuine, or in its natural state? Such men are just like slave dealers who acquire sound bodies brought up in pure sunlight and open air, but then rear them indoors and make them soft, thereby ruining the original form with which nature endowed them and which surpasses the work of artifice. That is precisely the kind of thing these professional lawyers do.

4. But imitations of that kind, in addition to being fraudulent, are utterly dispiriting and completely inappropriate for feasting souls to hear. I also disapprove of the spectacles that the Aenianes enjoy when drinking,[7] in which some participate while the others look on, as two men imitate a fight, while a third plays accompaniment on a pipe. The one assumes the role of a farmer plowing, and the other of a rustler carrying weapons. Near the farmer lie his weapons, and when the rustler comes up, the farmer lets go of his team and runs for his weapons. When they come together, they fight, striking each other's faces and imitating wounds and falls—hardly a spectacle for a symposium!

To these I prefer the ancient Persian custom, by which the Persians won their freedom. They used to reserve their deliberations for feasts, just as the Athenians reserved theirs for assemblies, but the Persian symposium was a more serious affair than the Athenian assembly, because in the former a law prohibiting drunkenness actually

---

[7] The Aenianes are a northern Greek tribe; the account is an elaboration of Xen. *An.* 6.1.8–9.

γειρεν αὐτῶν τὰς ἀρετὰς τῇ εὐωχίᾳ,⁶ καθάπερ ἔλαιον πυρὶ⁷ ἐπιχέων τῇ ψυχῇ συμμέτρως, μὴ τελείως σβεννὺς αὐτῆς τὸ φιλότιμον, μήτε ἐξάπτων τῆς χρείας περαιτέρω· ἐνταῦθα δὲ οἱ νήφοντες οὗτοι δημαγωγοί, μηδενὸς αὐτοῖς ἐφεστῶτος νόμου κολάζοντος τὴν ἐξουσίαν τῶν λόγων, ἐξωρχοῦντο ἐν ταῖς ἐκκλησίαις πάσης μέθης ἀκολαστότερον.

5. Τὰ μὲν οὖν τῶν Περσῶν καὶ τὰ Ἀττικὰ ἐῶμεν, ἐπανάγωμεν δὲ αὖθις ἐπὶ τὰ ἡμέτερα. λόγοις τοιγαροῦν εὐωχητέον τὰς ἀγαθὰς ψυχάς, καὶ οὐ δικανικοῖς λόγοις, φησὶν ὁ λόγος. τίσιν μήν; ἆρα οἱ τὰς ψυχὰς ἐπὶ τὸν πρόσθεν χρόνον ἀναβιβασάμενοι παρέχουσιν αὐταῖς τὴν θέαν τῶν γενομένων πάλαι; προσηνὲς γὰρ ἡ ἱστορία καὶ τὸ μηδὲν καμόντα πανταχοῦ περιπολεῖν, πάντα μὲν χωρία ἐποπτεύοντα, πᾶσιν δὲ πολέμοις ἐκ τοῦ ἀσφαλοῦς παραγιγνόμενον, μῆκος δὲ ἀμήχανον χρόνον ἐν βραχεῖ ἀναλεγόμενον, πλῆθος δὲ ἄπειρον πραγμάτων ἐν ὀλίγῳ μανθάνοντα, τὰ Ἀσσύρια, τὰ Αἰγύπτια, τὰ Περσικά, τὰ Μηδικά, τὰ Ἑλληνικά· νῦν μὲν πολεμοῦσιν ἐν γῇ παραγινόμενον, νῦν δὲ ἐν θαλάττῃ ναυμαχοῦσιν, νῦν δὲ ἐν ἐκκλησίαις βουλευομένοις· μετὰ Θεμιστοκλέους ναυμαχοῦντα, μετὰ Λεωνίδου ταττόμενον, καὶ μετὰ Ἀγησιλάου διαβαίνοντα, καὶ μετὰ Ξενοφῶντος σῳζόμενον· ξυν-

⁶ τῇ εὐωχίᾳ R: τὴν εὐωχίαν Markland, Trapp
⁷ πυρὶ H, Trapp: πῦρ R

spurred on their virtues in the feast, by pouring ⟨wine⟩[8] on the soul in just the right proportions, like oil on a flame, so as neither to extinguish its combativeness entirely, nor to enflame it beyond usefulness,[9] whereas in the latter those sober demagogues, with no law laid down to restrict their license to speak, danced about in their assemblies more intemperately than any drunkard.

5. Let us then dismiss Persian and Athenian customs and return to our subject. So, our argument states that good souls must feast on words, but not on those of judicial speeches.[10] On which ones, then? Should it be those words that transport souls to a former time and allow them to witness events of long ago? Yes, history is indeed a pleasure, for it allows a person to travel anywhere without any effort, to observe all places, to be present at every battle from a position of safety, to compress an immense stretch of time into a brief period, and to learn of a vast number of events in a short time, be they Assyrian, Egyptian, Persian, Median, or Greek. At one moment he is present when they fight on land, at another when they battle at sea, and yet again when they debate in assemblies. He fights on board ship with Themistocles, stands in formation with Leonidas, crosses the sea with Agesilaus, and returns home safely with Xenophon.[11] He becomes one of

[8] The text is uncertain.

[9] At Hdt. 1.133.3–4 the Persians are said to deliberate when moderately intoxicated, but to make final decisions when sober.

[10] These were rejected in §3.

[11] References are to Herodotus' accounts of the battles of Salamis and Thermopylae and to events in Xenophon's *Agesilaus*, *Hellenica*, and *Anabasis*.

ἐρῶντα Πανθείᾳ, συνθηρῶντα Κύρῳ, συμβασιλεύοντα Κυαξάρει.

Εἰ δὲ καὶ Ὀδυσσεὺς σοφὸς ὅτι πολύτροπος ἦν καὶ

πολλῶν ἀνθρώπων ἴδεν ἄστη καὶ νόον ἔγνω . . .
ἀρνύμενος ἦν τε ψυχὴν καὶ νόστον ἑταίρων,

πολύ που σοφώτερος ὁ τῶν μὲν κινδύνων ἐξιστάμενος, τῆς δὲ ἱστορίας ἐμπιμπλάμενος. Χάρυβδιν ὄψεται, ἀλλ᾽ οὐκ ἐν ναυαγίῳ· Σειρήνων ἀκούσεται, ἀλλ᾽ οὐ δεδεμένος· Κύκλωπι ἐντεύξεται, ἀλλ᾽ εἰρηνικῷ. εἰ δὲ καὶ Περσεὺς εὐδαίμων ὅτι πτηνὸς ἦν καὶ περιεφέρετο ἐν τῷ αἰθέρι πάντα ἐποπτεύων τὰ ἐν γῇ παθήματα καὶ χωρία, πολὺ τῶν Περσέως πτερῶν ἡ ἱστορία κουφότερον καὶ μετεωρότερον· ἢ λαβοῦσα τὴν ψυχὴν περιφέρει πανταχοῦ, οὐκ ἀργῶς οὐδὲ ἠμελημένως δεικνύουσα, ἀλλὰ καὶ ἄνδρα γενεαλογεῖ·

Κροῖσος ἦν Λυδὸς μὲν γένος, παῖς δὲ Ἀλυάττεω, τύραννος δὲ ἐθνῶν·

Δάρδανον αὖ πρῶτον τέκετο νεφεληγερέτα Ζεύς·

Panthea's lovers, he joins Cyrus in the hunt, and he reigns
alongside Cyaxares.[12]

And if Odysseus was wise because he was versatile and
because

> he saw the cities of many men and learned their
> minds . . .
> striving to save his own life and bring his comrades
> home,[13]

how much wiser, I think, is someone who stays clear of
those dangers, and takes his fill of the historical account.
He will see Charybdis without being shipwrecked; he will
hear the Sirens without being tied up; he will meet the
Cyclops, but one that is peaceable. And if Perseus was
blessed because he had wings and could travel around the
sky and observe all the places and everything happening
on earth, then how much more easily and higher can history take us than Perseus' wings! History takes hold of the
soul and carries it around everywhere, not casually and
haphazardly pointing to things, but also tracing the origin
of men:

> Croesus was a Lydian by birth, the son of Alyattes
> and ruler over the nations;[14]

> cloud-gathering Zeus first begot Dardanus;[15]

---

[12] References to incidents in Xenophon's *Cyropaedia*.
[13] *Od.* 1.3 and 5.
[14] Hdt. 1.6.1.
[15] *Il.* 20.215. Dardanus was the progenitor of the Dardanians.

15

γενεαλογεῖ καὶ πόλιν·

Ἐπίδαμνός ἐστιν πόλις ἐν δεξιᾷ εἰσπλέοντι τὸν
Ἰόνιον κόλπον· προσοικοῦσιν δ' αὐτὴν Ταυλάν-
τιοι βάρβαροι·

ἔστι πόλις Ἐφύρη μυχῷ Ἄργεος ἱπποβότοιο·

γενεαλογεῖ δὲ καὶ ποταμόν·

ὃς ῥέων ἐκ μεσημβρίης πρὸς βορέην ἄνεμον εἰς
τὸν Εὔξεινον πόντον καλεόμενον ἐκδιδοῖ·

ὃν Ξάνθον καλέουσι θεοί, ἄνδρες δὲ Σκάμανδρον.

Τοῦτο τὸ ἄκουσμα ἐφήμερον ⟨ὃν⟩[8] τὸ τῶν ἀνθρώπων γένος καὶ φθειρόμενον ταχὺ καὶ ἀπολλύμενον
καὶ ὑπορρέον τῇ μνήμῃ σώζει καὶ τὰς ἀρετὰς φυλάτ-
τει καὶ τὰς πράξεις ταῖς δόξαις ἀθανάτους ποιεῖ. διὰ
τοῦτο ὁ Λεωνίδης ᾄδεται οὐχ ὑπὸ Λακεδαιμονίων μόνον τῶν τότε, καὶ ὁ Θεμιστοκλῆς ἐπαινεῖται οὐχ ὑπὸ
Ἀθηναίων ⟨μόνον⟩[9] ἐκείνων· μένει δὲ καὶ ἡ Περικλέους
στρατηγία καὶ νῦν ἔτι ἡ Ἀριστείδου δικαιοσύνη· δίδωσιν Κριτίας καὶ νῦν δίκην, φεύγει καὶ νῦν Ἀλκιβιάδης. συνελόντι δὲ εἰπεῖν, οἱ καθ' ἱστορίαν λόγοι
τῷ μὲν ἀνηκόῳ τερπνότατον καθ' ἡδονήν, τῷ δὲ εἰδότι
ἐπαγωγότατον κατὰ ἀνάμνησιν.

[8] suppl. Reiske, Trapp
[9] suppl. Markland, Trapp

as well as of cities:

> Epidamnus is a city on the right side as one sails into
> the Ionian gulf; its neighbors are the Taulantians, a
> barbaric tribe;[16]

> There is a city, Ephyre, in a corner of horse-pasturing
> Argos;[17]

as well as of rivers:

> the one that flows from south to north and empties
> into the so-called Euxine Sea;[18]

> the one the gods call Xanthus, but men call
> Scamander.[19]

Given that the human race is ephemeral, quick to deteriorate, perish, and pass away, it is this history that preserves its memory, safeguards its virtues, and makes its achievements live forever in glory. Thanks to it Leonidas is sung not only by his contemporary Lacedaemonians, and Themistocles is praised not only by the Athenians of his own time. Then too the generalship of Pericles lives on, as does the justice of Aristides still today. And still today Critias is punished; still today Alcibiades goes into exile. In a word, historical accounts are most delightful for the pleasure they bring to someone who has never heard them before, but are also most attractive for reminding someone of what he already knows.

[16] Thuc. 1.24.1.   [17] *Il*. 6.152.   [18] Adapted from Hdt. 1.6.1, describing the Halys River.   [19] *Il*. 20.74.

6. Τίς ἂν οὖν γένοιτο ψυχαῖς εὐωχία λόγων ταύτης προσηνεστέρα; χαλεπὸν μὲν εἰπεῖν καὶ ἀντιτάξασθαι πολλῷ καὶ γενναίῳ λογοποιῷ, ῥητέον δὲ ὅμως ὅτι καλὴ μὲν ὑμῶν ἡ ἁρμονία καὶ ᾄδεσθαι προσηνής, ἄλλο δὲ ποθεῖ ἡ ἐπιεικὴς ψυχὴ καὶ οὐχ οἷον παρέχεσθε ὑμεῖς. τί γὰρ σεμνὸν ἡ μνήμη τῶν πάλαι κακῶν τῷ μήπω μαθόντι ὅπως ταῦτα φυλακτέον; ἢ τί πλέον Ἀθηναίοις ἐγένετο διὰ τὴν ἱστορίαν τὴν Ἀττικήν; ἢ τί πλέον Ἁλικαρνασσεῦσιν διὰ τὴν ἱστορίαν τὴν Ἰωνικήν; ἢ τί Χῖοι διὰ ταύτην εὐδαιμονέστεροι;

Εἰ μὲν γὰρ ἀποκρίναντες τὰ καλὰ τῶν αἰσχρῶν, τὰ μὲν ἀπέκρυπτον, τὰ δὲ ἱστόρουν, ἦν ἄν που τῇ ψυχῇ ὄνησις κατὰ μίμησιν τῶν ἱστορημένων, καθάπερ ὀφθαλμοῖς κατὰ μίμησιν γραφῆς· νῦν δὲ ἀναμὶξ εἰσφύρεται πάντα ἐν τοῖς λόγοις καὶ πλεονάζει τὰ χείρω καὶ κρατεῖ τὰ αἰσχρά· καὶ τὸ πολὺ τῆς ἱστορίας πλεονέκται τύραννοι καὶ πόλεμοι ἄδικοι καὶ εὐτυχίαι ἄλογοι καὶ πράξεις πονηραὶ καὶ συμφοραὶ ἀγνώμονες καὶ περιστάσεις τραγικαί· ὧν σφαλερὰ μὲν ἡ μίμησις, βλαβερὰ δὲ ἡ μνήμη, ἀθάνατος δὲ ἡ δυστυχία. ἐγὼ δὲ ποθῶ πρὸς τὴν εὐωχίαν τροφὴν λόγων ὑγιεινῶν, καὶ ἀνόσου τοιούτου δέομαι σιτίου ἀφ' οὗ καὶ Σωκράτης ὑγίανεν καὶ Πλάτων καὶ Ξενοφῶν καὶ Αἰσχίνης.

---

[20] That is, from the histories of Thucydides, Herodotus, and Theopompus.

6. What feast of words could be more pleasing to souls than this? Now I find it difficult to speak in opposition to so many noble historians, but nonetheless I must say to them: "Your harmony is indeed beautiful and pleasant to be sung, but a reasonable soul longs for something other than what you offer." For what good is the record of age-old evils to someone who has not yet learned how to guard against them? Or what good did the Athenians gain from their Attic history, or the people of Halicarnassus from their Ionian history, or what made the Chians any happier for theirs?[20]

For if historians had distinguished good things from shameful ones, and had suppressed the ones and recorded the others, perhaps the soul would derive some benefit from the imitation of what was recorded, just as the eyes derive benefit from the imitation of a painting.[21] But as it is, everything is mixed together indiscriminately in their writings, and bad deeds outnumber good ones and shameful ones prevail. The great bulk of history consists of greedy tyrants, unjust wars, unwarranted successes, sordid deeds, cruel disasters, and tragic situations.[22] Imitating these is dangerous, and recalling them is harmful; the ill fortune they bring goes on forever. For my feast I crave the nourishment of healthful words, and I need such wholesome food as maintained the health of Socrates, Plato, Xenophon, and Aeschines.[23]

[21] Cf. *Or*. 26.5, where painters such as Polygnotus and Zeuxis do not paint haphazardly, but imitate true beauty.

[22] Contrast *Or*. 26.5–6, where Homer fosters an emulation of virtue by contrasting good and bad examples.

[23] Aeschines of Sphettus, a student of Socrates (quoted at *Orr*. 6.6, 18.4, and 38.4).

7. Ἐπιθυμεῖ ἡ ἀνθρώπου ψυχὴ καὶ δέδιεν καὶ λυπεῖται καὶ φθονεῖ, καὶ ἄλλοις συνέχεται παντοδαποῖς καὶ ἀλλοκότοις παθήμασιν· στάσιν ὁρᾷς πικρὰν καὶ ἀκήρυκτον· τοιοῦτόν μοι διηγοῦ τὸν πόλεμον, τὸν δὲ Μηδικὸν ἔα· ταύτην μοι διηγοῦ τὴν νόσον, τὸν δὲ λοιμὸν ἔα. εἰπὲ τίνι ἐπιτρέψω τὴν στρατηγίαν καὶ τὴν ἴασιν, Ἱπποκράτην δὲ ἔα τοῖς σώμασιν καὶ Θεμιστοκλέα τῇ θαλάττῃ· λέγε τὸν ψυχῆς ἰατρόν, λέγε τὸν στρατηγόν. κἂν ἀπορῇς ἀνδρῶν, ἐπὶ τοὺς θεοὺς ἴθι. ἔρου μὴ περὶ γῆς δῃουμένης, μηδὲ περὶ θαλάττης λῃστευομένης, μηδὲ περὶ τειχῶν πολιορκουμένων, μηδὲ περὶ σωμάτων φθειρομένων· σμικρὰ ταῦτα, ἐφήμερα ταῦτα. τμηθήσεται λήϊον, κἂν Πελοποννήσιοι ἀπόσχωνται· λῃστευθήσεται θάλαττα, κἂν Ἀθηναῖοι μὴ ναυμαχῶσιν· καταβαλεῖ τὰ τείχη, καὶ εἰ μὴ Φίλιππος, ἀλλ᾽ ὁ χρόνος· φθαρήσεται τὰ σώματα, κἂν ἀπέλθῃ ὁ λοιμός· ἀνδρὸς δὲ ἀρετὴ

πάλιν ἐλθεῖν οὔτε λεϊστή,
οὔθ᾽ ἑλετή.

περὶ ταύτης ἔρου δή, ὅτε ψυχὴ τέμνεται, λῃστεύεται, πολιορκεῖται, νοσεῖ· χρησμοῦ σοι δεῖ, μαντείας σοι δεῖ, εὖξαι τῷ θεῷ·

κλῦθί μευ, ἀργυρότοξ᾽, ὃς Χρύσην
ἀμφιβέβηκας,

7. The human soul experiences desire, fear, pain, and envy, and is prey to all sorts of different emotions, and within it you can see bitter strife with no truce. Describe for me this kind of war and let the Persian War go; describe this sickness for me and let the plague go. Tell me whom I shall trust to take command and heal me, and let Hippocrates heal bodies and Themistocles command at sea. Tell me who will be a doctor for the soul; tell me who will be its commander. If you cannot find any men, then turn to the gods. Do not, however, inquire about land being laid waste, nor about the sea infested with pirates, nor about walls being besieged, or bodies wasting away. These are insignificant; they come and go. Crops will be cut down, even if the Peloponnesians hold back; the sea will have pirates, even if the Athenians stop their naval warfare. Walls will be torn down, if not by Philip,[24] by time itself; and bodies will waste away, even if the plague goes away. A man's virtue, however,

> cannot return, nor can it be plundered
or won back.[25]

Ask then about virtue, when a soul is being cut down, plundered, besieged, and beset with sickness. Here you need an oracle, you need a prophecy, so pray to the god,

> Hear me, wielder of the silver bow, who rule over
> Chryse.[26]

[24] Philip II of Macedon was notorious for besieging cities.
[25] *Il.* 9.408–9, Achilles speaking of a man's life, not virtue.
[26] *Il.* 1.37, the opening of Chryses' prayer, asking Apollo to shoot his arrows of plague at the Greeks.

21

κλῦθι, ὦ Ἄπολλον καὶ Ζεῦ καὶ εἴ τις ἄλλος θεὸς ἰα-
τικὸς ψυχῆς νοσούσης,

εἴ ποτέ τοι χαρίεντ᾽ ἐπὶ νηὸν ἔρεψα,
ἢ εἰ δή ποτέ τοι κατὰ πίονα μηρί᾽ ἔκηα.

ἀκούσεται ὁ Ἀπόλλων τοιαῦτα εὐχομένου θᾶττον ἢ
τοῦ Χρύσου· οὐ γὰρ ἐπὶ λοιμὸν παρακαλεῖς τὸν θεὸν
οὐδὲ ἐπὶ τοξείαν ὀϊστῶν θανατηφόρων οὐδὲ ἐπὶ φθο-
ρὰν κυνῶν καὶ ἀνδρῶν καὶ ὀρέων· οὐ γὰρ ταῦτα ἔργα
μουσικοῦ θεοῦ καὶ σοφοῦ καὶ μαντικοῦ. Ὅμηρος δὲ
αὐτῷ προσέθηκεν τὴν φήμην, αἰνιττόμενος τὴν ἡλίου
ἀκτῖνα δι᾽ ἀέρος χωροῦσαν ὀϊστοῦ θᾶττον, ἀκρατο-
τέραν τῆς τῶν σωμάτων συμμετρίας. ἐμοὶ δὲ ἀδέτω
εἴτε καὶ Ὅμηρος εἴτε Ἡσίοδος εἴτε τις ἄλλος ποιητὴς
δαιμόνιος θεὸν παιᾶνα ψυχῆς παθημάτων· ἄξια ταῦτα
τοῦ Ἀπόλλωνος, ἄξια τοῦ Διός.

Hear me, Apollo, Zeus, and any other god who can heal a
sick soul,

> if ever I built a temple that pleased you,
> or if ever I burned fat thigh pieces for you.[27]

Apollo will heed you praying for such things sooner than
he heeded Chryses, because you are not calling on the god
to inflict a plague, shoot death-dealing arrows, or kill dogs,
men, and mules,[28] for these are not the actions of a god of
music, wisdom, and prophecy! Homer indeed attributed
that account to him, but he was actually alluding to his
sunbeams flying through the air swifter than any arrow and
purer than perfectly constituted bodies.[29] Let Homer,
Hesiod, or any other inspired poet, sing to me of a god who
heals the sufferings of the soul: those are songs worthy of
Apollo, worthy of Zeus.

[27] *Il.* 1.39–40.

[28] Cf. *Il.* 1.43–52.

[29] The text of the last part of the sentence is uncertain. For
Apollo as the sun, cf. *Orr.* 4.8 and 37.5.

ORATION 23

INTRODUCTION

This first of a pair of rhetorical exercises argues that soldiers are more beneficial to a city than farmers. It opens by identifying virtue (*aretē*) with military prowess, as validated by Homer, who extols Agamemnon's capability as a spearman, but relegates agriculture to the character of old Laertes, who has been driven from his own city. Further proof is Odysseus' famous statement that Ithaca is too rugged for agriculture but is a good nourisher of young men (§1). Since Homer might be considered too biased toward war, evidence is produced from the practices of four states, beginning with Sparta, whose constitution under Lycurgus assigned warfare to the purebred Spartiates, but relegated agriculture to the helots and slaves. Examples of famous Spartan commanders and military exploits follow (§2). The argument turns to the issue of freedom and slavery. The Cretans were free until they became farmers, and the Athenians became free when they shook off the Pisistratid tyranny and defeated the Persians at Marathon and Salamis. Pericles too is praised for allowing the Peloponnesians to ravage Athenian agriculture in order to keep the city free (§3). Foreign examples of enslaved peoples (Egyptians and Assyrians) are contrasted with free ones (Scythians and Persians). Animals too are cited: deer and grackles are slaves; lions and eagles are free (§4). Agriculture was unknown in the reign of Cronus and still today the earth produces crops all on its own. It is desire for certain foreign foods that turns agriculture into the servant of pleasure (§5). An interlocutor objects that the criterion of freedom and servitude should be replaced with that of war and peace. If agriculture is a peaceful activity, as indicated in the argument, then people should display their valor in successful farming. The speaker counters by arguing that in reality wars are everywhere, sparked by human desires (*epithymiai*), so that flourishing farmlands in fact invite armed aggression, as shown by the invasions of Cambyses, Darius, and Xerxes, and by those of the Athenians, Spartans, and Thebans (§6). No fertile land is safe. Not even India was too distant for Alexander to invade it. Farming is truly a good thing, but that very goodness provokes both war and internal strife. As Thucydides pointed out, it was because the soil of Attica was so thin that the Athenians avoided civil strife and were never driven out. The conclusion: leave the land uncultivated to avoid inciting war (§7).

ORATION 23

Τίνες λυσιτελέστεροι πόλει, οἱ προπολεμοῦντες,
ἢ οἱ γεωργοῦντες· ὅτι οἱ προπολεμοῦντες

1. Ἔχεις εἰπεῖν τίνας ὀνομάζει Ὅμηρος ἐν τοῖς ἔπεσιν
διογενεῖς καὶ θεοῖς εἰκέλους καὶ λαῶν ποιμένας, καὶ
ἄλλα ὅσα ποιητὴν εἰκὸς ἀποσεμνύνοντα τοῖς ὀνόμα-
σιν ἀρετὴν ἀνδρός; ἆρα τοὺς ἐπὶ σκαπάνῃ καὶ αὔλακι
πρὸς τῇ γῇ διαπονουμένους, δεινοὺς ἀροῦν, ἀγαθοὺς
φυτεύειν, ἐν ἀμήτῳ δεξιούς, ἐν ὀρχάτῳ φιλοπόνους; ἢ
τούτων μὲν οὐδὲ τὴν ἀρχὴν ἠξίωσεν καταμίξαι τὰ
ἔργα τῇ αὐτοῦ ᾠδῇ, ὅτι μὴ νησιώτῃ γέροντι ἀναθεὶς
αὐτά, ἐκπεπτωκότι τῆς ἀρχῆς ὑπὸ ὑβριστῶν νέων, ἐν
γουνῷ οἰνοπέδου ἀλωῆς ἐπὶ φύλλων χαμαὶ βεβλη-
μένων ὥρᾳ θέρους ἀναπαυομένῳ;

Οἱ δὲ μακάριοι αὐτῷ ἄνδρες, οὓς ἐκεῖνος ἐπαινῶν
χαίρει, ἕτεροί εἰσιν ἐξ ἑτέρων ἐπιτηδευμάτων καὶ
ἔργων, ἢ Ἀχιλλεὺς διώκων ἢ Αἴας μονομαχῶν ἢ
Τεῦκρος τοξεύων ἢ Διομήδης ἀριστεύων, ἤ τις ἄλλος
τῶν δεινῶν τὰ ἀριστευτικά· μεστὰ δὲ αὐτῷ τὰ ἔπη
ἀσπίδων μεγάλων καὶ κορύθων φαεινῶν καὶ δοράτων
μακρῶν καὶ ἁρμάτων καλῶν καὶ ἵππων θεόντων, καὶ

ORATION 23

Which group benefits a city more,
soldiers or farmers? Soldiers

1. Can you tell me which people in his epics Homer calls "Zeus-born," "godlike," and "shepherds of the people," and all the other epithets a poet is likely to use in extolling a man's virtue? Are they laborers on the land with spades and plowshares, who are skilled at tilling, good at planting, adept at reaping, and industrious in orchards? Or did he consider their labors wholly unworthy to include in his poetry, except for attributing them to an old islander,[1] who had been driven from his rule by violent young men and who took his rest in summertime on the slope of his vineyard upon a bed of leaves strewn on the ground?

No, the men he considers blessed and whom he takes delight in praising are others with different pursuits and deeds, such as Achilles on the attack, Ajax fighting man-to-man, Teucer shooting arrows, Diomedes carrying the day, and any others skilled at performing heroic deeds. His verses are full of mighty shields, shining helmets, long spears, beautiful chariots with charging steeds, and brave

[1] Laertes, Odysseus' father. The following description comes from *Od.* 11.192–94.

ἀγαθῶν κτεινόντων καὶ δειλῶν κτεινομένων. τὸν μὲν
γὰρ Ἀγαμέμνονα αὐτὸν τὸν τῶν Πανελλήνων βασιλέα οὐκ ἔσχεν ἑτέρως ἐπαινέσαι ἢ τὸν αἰχμητὴν
προσθεὶς τῷ βασιλεῖ, ὡς μόνον δὴ τοῦτο ἔργων ἀρ-
χικώτατον, καί φησιν ὅτι ἦν ὁ Ἀγαμέμνων ἀμφότερον
βασιλεὺς καὶ αἰχμητὴς ἀγαθός· ἐπεὶ καὶ ὁ Μενέλαος
βασιλεὺς μὲν ἦν οὐχ ἧττον ἢ ὁ Ἀγαμέμνων, μαλθα-
κὸς δὲ αἰχμήν, καὶ διὰ τοῦτο ὀλίγον αὐτῷ μετέδωκε
ποιητικῆς εὐφημίας Ὅμηρος.

Ὅ γε μὴν Ἀγαμέμνων οὗτος τί ἦν ἂν ἐπικλεέστερος
τῶν ἄλλων, εἰ κατὰ τὸ Ἄργος μένων, γῆν ἀγαθὴν
ἔχων, γεωργῶν τὴν γῆν, ἀπέφηνεν αὐτὴν εὐκαρπο-
τέραν τῆς Αἰγυπτίας; τοῦ μὲν γὰρ Ὀδυσσέως ἀκούεις
αὐτοῦ σεμνολογουμένου περὶ τῆς Ἰθάκης·

   τρηχεῖ᾽, ἀλλ᾽ ἀγαθὴ κουροτρόφος,

φησίν. οἶδεν γάρ που ἅτε σοφὸς ὢν ὅσον διαφέρει ὁ
τῆς ἀνδρείας καρπὸς οὗτος πυρῶν καὶ κριθῶν, καὶ εἴ
τις ἄλλη ὑποτροφὴ γῆς.

2. Ὅμηρον ἐῶ· τάχα γὰρ καὶ δυσχεράναις ἂν τῷ
λόγῳ προφερομένῳ σοι μάρτυρα φιλοπόλεμον. βούλει
σοι τὰ δεύτερα ἐπ᾽ ἐκείνῳ λέγω τὰ Λακωνικὰ ἢ τὰ
Ἀττικὰ ἢ τὰ Κρητικὰ ἢ τὰ Περσικά; τὴν Σπάρτην
ἐπαινεῖς ὡς εὐνομωτάτην. ὁ δὲ Λυκοῦργος οὐ σοῦ[1]
δήπου ἐπαινέτου δεήσεται· ὁ γὰρ Ἀπόλλων φθάνει
λέγων πρὸς αὐτὸν

---

[1] οὐ σοῦ Stephanus, Davies[2], Dübner: ὃς οὐ Trapp: ὅσου R

men killing and cowards being killed. So, when it came to Agamemnon himself, king of all the Greeks, he could devise no stronger praise than by adding "spearman" to his title of king, indicating that it alone was the most regal activity, when he says that Agamemnon was "both a king and a good spearman."[2] This is true because Menelaus was no less a king than Agamemnon, but was a "weak spearman,"[3] and for that reason Homer bestowed scant poetic praise on him.

And yet, how could this same Agamemnon have become more famous than the others, had he remained in Argos in possession of his rich land, farming it and making it more productive than Egypt? You can also hear Odysseus himself speaking proudly of Ithaca, when he calls it

rugged, but a good nourisher of young men.[4]

For he no doubt knows, wise as he is, how far superior the crop of bravery is to wheat, barley, or any other nourishment from the earth.

2. But now I shall dismiss Homer, for you might take issue with an argument that presents you with a witness so enamored of war. Will you then allow me to offer you a second kind of evidence in addition to Homer, namely the practices of Sparta, Athens, Crete, or Persia? You praise Sparta as having the very best laws. Surely Lycurgus will not need your praises, for Apollo already said to him,

[2] *Il.* 3.179, slightly adapted.
[3] *Il.* 17.588, slightly adapted.
[4] *Od.* 9.27.

δίζω ἤ σε θεὸν μαντεύσομαι ἢ ἄνθρωπον.

ὁ τοίνυν Λυκοῦργος οὗτος, ὃν ὁ θεὸς εἰκάζει θεῷ, τιθεὶς τῇ Σπάρτῃ νόμους, συμβουλευσάμενος τῷ Ἀπόλλωνι, ποῖόν τι πολιτείας ἦθος κατεστήσατο τοῖς αὑτοῦ θρέμμασιν; ἆρα γεωργικὸν καὶ ταμιευτικόν, ταπεινὸν καὶ γλίσχρον καὶ ἐργαστικὸν τὰ σμικρὰ ταῦτα; ἢ ταῦτα μὲν οἱ εἵλωτες αὐτῷ ἔχουσιν καὶ ὁ ἀνδραποδώδης ὅμιλος καὶ οἱ περίοικοι Λακεδαιμονίων, τὸ δὲ καθαρῶς Σπαρτιατικόν, ἄφετον ἐκ γῆς ὂν καὶ ὄρθιον καὶ πρὸς ἐλευθερίαν τετραμμένον, μαστιγούμενον καὶ τυπτόμενον καὶ ἐν θήραις καὶ ὀρειβασίαις καὶ ἄλλοις παντοδαποῖς πόνοις παιδευόμενον, ἐπειδὰν ἱκανῶς τοῦ καρτερεῖν ἔχῃ, ἐπὶ αἰχμῇ καὶ ἀσπίδι τεταγμένον, ὑπὸ στρατηγῷ τῷ νόμῳ προμαχεῖ τῆς ἐλευθερίας καὶ τὴν Σπάρτην σῴζει καὶ τῷ Λυκούργῳ συναγωνίζεται καὶ πείθεται τῷ θεῷ;

Εἰ δὲ ἐγεώργουν Λακεδαιμόνιοι, τίς ἂν ὑπὲρ αὐτῶν Λεωνίδας ἐν Θερμοπύλαις παρετάξατο; τίς ἂν Ὀθρυάδας ἐν Θυρέᾳ ἠρίστευεν; ἀλλ᾽ οὐδὲ Βρασίδας γεωργὸς ἦν, οὐδ᾽ ὁ Γύλιππος ἐκ ληΐου ὁρμηθεὶς Συρακοσίους ἔσωζεν, οὐδὲ Ἀγησίλαος ἐξ ἀμπέλων ὁρμηθεὶς Τισσαφέρνους ἐκράτει καὶ τὴν βασιλέως γῆν ἔτεμνεν καὶ Ἴωνας καὶ Ἑλλήσποντον ἠλευθέρου· οὐκ ἀπὸ σμι-

---

5 Hdt. 1.65.3, spoken by the priestess when Lycurgus entered Apollo's temple.   6 When three hundred Spartans and three hundred Argives fought over Thyrea (ca. 546 BC), Othryadas, the sole Spartan survivor, claimed victory; cf. Hdt.1.82.

I am uncertain whether to declare you a god or a man.[5]

So when this Lycurgus, whom the god likened to a god, was making laws for Sparta after consulting with Apollo, what was the character of the constitution he established to raise his own progeny? Was it one designed for farming and management, one that was low-class, petty, and engaged in such trivial affairs? Or did he reserve those tasks for the helots, the slave population, and the neighboring peoples controlled by the Lacedaemonians, while the purebred class of Spartiates, exempted from farming, with heads held high and intent on freedom, were subjected to whippings and beatings, and trained in hunting, mountaineering, and all other kinds of strenuous activities, and after being sufficiently hardened, were stationed in the ranks with spear and shield, and fought for their freedom with Law as their commander, as they joined forces with Lycurgus in obedience to the god and preserved the Spartan state?

But if the Spartans had been farmers, what Leonidas would have stood in battle on their behalf at Thermopylae? What Othryadas would have carried the day at Thyrea?[6] Brasidas was no farmer, nor did Gylippus set out from his harvest to go and save the Syracusans, nor did Agesilaus set out from his vineyards to go and defeat Tissaphernes, ravage the Persian king's land, and free the Ionians and the Hellespont,[7] any more than Callicratidas

---

[7] Brasidas the Spartan general died fighting the Athenians in 422 BC; Gylippus helped the Syracusans defeat the Athenians in 413 BC; Agesilaus defeated the Persian satrap Tissaphernes in 395 BC.

MAXIMUS OF TYRE

νύης ὁ Καλλικρατίδας, οὐκ ἀπὸ σκαπάνης ὁ Λύσανδρος, οὐκ ἀπὸ ἀρότρου ὁ Δερκυλλίδας. θητικὰ ταῦτα,
εἰλωτικά· ταῦτα ὑπὸ ἀσπίδων σώζεται, τούτων δόρατα
ὑπερμαχεῖ, ταῦτα δουλεύει τοῖς κρατοῦσιν. αὕτη ἡ ἐν
ὅπλοις ἀρετὴ καὶ τὴν Ἀθηναίων γῆν ἔτεμνεν καὶ τὴν
Ἀργείων ἐδήου καὶ Μεσσηνίους ἐλάμβανεν· ἐπεὶ δ᾽
ἐξέκαμεν αὕτη τοῖς Σπαρτιάταις, τὰ μὲν ὅπλα ἀπέ-
θεντο, ἐγένοντο δὲ ἐξ ἐλευθέρων γεωργοί.

3. Ἐλεύθεροι Κρῆτες πότε; ὅτε ὅπλα εἶχον, ὅτε
ἐτόξευον, ὅτε ἐθήρων· δοῦλοι πότε; ὅτε καὶ γεωργοί.
ἐλεύθεροι Ἀθηναῖοι πότε; ὅτε Καδμείοις ἐπολέμουν,
ὅτε καὶ Ἴωνας ἐξέπεμπον, ὅτε καὶ Ἡρακλείδας ὑπε-
δέχοντο, ὅτε Πελασγοὺς ἐξέβαλλον· δοῦλοι πότε; ὅτε
Πεισιστρατίδαι τὸν δῆμον ἐξοπλίσαντες γεωργεῖν
ἠνάγκαζον. αὖθις δὲ ἐπελθόντος αὐτοῖς στόλου Μηδι-
κοῦ, τῆς μὲν γῆς ἐπελάθοντο, ἐπὶ δὲ τὰ ὅπλα ἔδραμον
καὶ μετ᾽ αὐτῶν τὴν ἐλευθερίαν ἀνελάμβανον. οὐ γεωργῶν Κυναίγειρος τὰς Ἀθήνας ἠλευθέρου, οὐκ ἐν
ἀμήτῳ Καλλίμαχος τοὺς Μήδους ἐξέβαλλεν, οὐκ ἐν
γεωργοῖς ἐστρατήγει Μιλτιάδης· ὁπλιτῶν τὰ ἔργα,
μαχομένων τὸ κράτος, νικώντων ἡ ἐλευθερία.

Ἐπεὶ δὲ καὶ τῆς θαλάττης ἔδει, χαίρειν τῇ γῇ

---

8 Three Spartan commanders during and after the Peloponnesian War.   9 In the invasions of Attica (431 BC), Argos
(546 BC), and Messenia (ca. 700 BC).

10 Legendary Athenian achievements often depicted in tragedies and celebrated in eulogies.

left behind his hoe, Lysander his spade, or Dercyllidas his plow.[8] These are the tools of laborers, of helots; they are protected by shields, they are fought for by spears, and they serve the victors. It was their valor in arms that ravaged Athenian fields, plundered Argive land, and captured Messenia.[9] But once it gave out for the Spartiates, they laid down their weapons and became farmers instead of free men.

3. When were the Cretans free? It was when they carried weapons, when they were archers, when they were hunters. And when were they slaves? When they became farmers. When were the Athenians free? When they fought the Cadmaeans, when they sent out Ionian colonies, when they gave refuge to the Heraclidae, and when they expelled the Pelasgians.[10] When were they slaves? When the Pisistratids[11] disarmed the people and forced them to farm the land. But subsequently, when the Persian expeditionary forces attacked them,[12] they forgot all about the land, ran for their weapons and with them regained their freedom. It was not when farming that Cynegirus freed Athens; it was not when harvesting that Callimachus repulsed the Persians; and it was not among farmers that Miltiades was in command.[13] No, hoplites performed these deeds, fighters won the victory, and victors secured their freedom.

Then, when they had to take to the sea,[14] they bade

[11] The family of tyrants who ruled Athens from 546 to 510 BC.

[12] In 490 BC at Marathon.

[13] Three commanders who led the Athenians at Marathon. Cynegirus and Callimachus are also cited at *Or*. 34.9.

[14] During the invasion of Xerxes in 480 BC.

φράσαντες καὶ παραδόντες πυρὶ τὴν ἐκεῖ ἑστίαν καὶ
μόνα ὑπολειπόμενοι τὰ ὅπλα, εἰς τὰς τριήρεις μετῳκί-
σθησαν· ἔπλεεν πόλις Ἀττικὴ καὶ ἠπειρώτης δῆμος,
καὶ πλέων ὁμοῦ ἐναυμάχει, καὶ ναυμαχῶν ἐκράτει, καὶ
κρατῶν εἶχεν καὶ τὴν γῆν καὶ τὴν θάλατταν. ἐπαινῶ
καὶ Περικλέα τῆς στρατηγίας, ὃς ἀμελήσας τῶν γεωργῶν καὶ ὁρῶν τεμνομένας τὰς Ἀχάρνας, ἐφύλαττεν
τὰς Ἀθήνας ἐλευθέρας· μενούσης γὰρ τῆς ἐλευθερίας,
⟨μένει⟩[2] ἡ γῆ, μένει τὰ φυτά, μένει τὰ λήϊα.

4. Ἔα μοι τὰ Ἑλληνικά, ἴθι ἐπὶ τοὺς βαρβάρους.
γεωργοῦσιν Αἰγύπτιοι, πολεμοῦσιν Σκύθαι· ἀνδρεῖον
τὸ Σκυθικόν, δειλὸν τὸ Αἰγύπτιον· ἐλεύθερον τὸ Σκυθικόν, δοῦλον τὸ Αἰγύπτιον. γεωργοῦσιν Ἀσσύριοι,
πολεμοῦσιν Πέρσαι· δουλεύουσιν Ἀσσύριοι, βασι-
λεύουσιν Πέρσαι. ἐπολέμουν Λυδοὶ πρότερον, ἐγεώργουν αὖθις Λυδοί· ἐλεύθεροι μὲν ὄντες ἐπολέμουν,
δουλεύσαντες δὲ ἐπὶ γεωργίαν ἐτράποντο.

Μέτιθι ἐπὶ τὰ ζῷα· καὶ γὰρ ἐνταῦθα ὄψει ἐλευθερίαν καὶ δουλείαν, καὶ βίον ἐξ ἀρετῆς καὶ ἐκ
γῆς βίον. βοῦς ἀροῖ, ἵππος ἀθλεύει· ἐὰν δὲ μεταθῇς
τὰ ἔργα, παρανομεῖς περὶ τὴν φύσιν. τὰ δειλὰ ποιηφάγα, τὰ ἰσχυρὰ ἀγρευτικά· ἔλαφος ποιηφαγεῖ,
λέων ἀγρεύει· σπερμολογεῖ κολοιός, ἀγρεύουσιν ἀε-
τοί· δοῦλα μὲν τὰ σπερμολόγα καὶ ποιηφάγα, ἐλεύ-
θερα δὲ τὰ ἀγρευτικά.

<hr>

[2] suppl. Meiser, Trapp

ORATION 23

farewell to the land, left behind their homes to be burned, and taking with them only their weapons, they migrated onto their triremes. The city of Athens and its mainland population took to the sea, and by taking to the sea they fought, and by fighting on the sea they were victorious, and by winning they held on to both the land and the sea. I praise Pericles as well for his generalship, because he showed no concern for the farmers and looked on as Acharnae was being ravaged, thereby preserving the freedom of Athens.[15] For as long as freedom remains, so too will the land, the trees, and the crops.

4. Leave, if you will, Greek examples, and move on to the barbarians. The Egyptians are farmers, the Scythians are warriors; the Scythians are brave, the Egyptians are cowardly; the Scythians are free, the Egyptians are slaves. The Assyrians are farmers, the Persians are warriors; the Assyrians are slaves, the Persians are rulers. At first the Lydians were warriors, but they later became farmers. They were free when they were warriors, but once they were enslaved, they turned to farming.

Move on to animals, and here too you will see freedom and slavery, a life of valor and a life of the soil. The ox plows, the horse competes in races; if you interchange their roles, you violate nature's laws. Cowardly animals graze on grass, powerful ones hunt. The deer eat grass, the lion hunts. The grackle gathers seeds, eagles hunt. The seed gatherers and grazers are slaves, whereas the hunters are free.

[15] When the Spartans invaded Attica in 431 BC and were ravaging Acharnae, Pericles prevented the Athenians from leaving the city to fight them (Thuc. 2.20–22 and 59–65).

5. Εἰ δὲ καὶ τοὺς περὶ θεῶν μύθους παραδεκτέον, οὐ γεωργὸς ὁ Ζεὺς οὐδὲ Ἀθηνᾶ οὐδὲ ὁ Ἀπόλλων οὐδὲ ὁ Ἐννάλιος, οἵπερ βασιλεύτατοι τῶν θεῶν· ἀλλ' ὀψὲ μὲν Δημήτηρ γεωργεῖ μετὰ πολλὴν πλάνην, ὀψὲ δὲ Διόνυσος μετὰ τὸν Κάδμον καὶ τὸν Πενθέα, ὀψὲ δὲ Τριπτόλεμος μετὰ τὸν Ἐριχθόνιον καὶ τὸν Κέκροπα. εἰ δὲ καὶ τῆς Κρόνου ἀρχῆς ἐπιλαβοίμεθα, τίς ἂν ἡμῖν γεωργίας λόγος; ἀλλ' οὐδὲ νῦν δεῖ γεωργίας· οὐ γὰρ ἐξέκαμεν ἡ γῆ τοὺς καρποὺς αὐτομάτους φέρουσα· φέρει μὲν τροφήν, φηγοὺς καὶ ὄγχνας· φέρει δὲ ποτὸν αὐτοφυές, Νεῖλον καὶ Ἴστρον καὶ Ἀχελῷον καὶ Μαίανδρον, καὶ ἄλλους κρατῆρας ἀενάους ναμάτων καθαρῶν καὶ νηφαλίων· γεωργεῖ δὲ ταῦτα οὐ πρεσβύτης Ἰκάριος οὐδὲ Βοιώτιος ἀνὴρ ἢ Θετταλικός, ἀλλ' ἥλιος αὐτὸς καὶ σελήνη θάλπουσα καὶ ὄμβροι τρέφοντες καὶ ἄνεμοι διαπνέοντες καὶ ὧραι ἀμείβουσαι καὶ γῆ βλαστάνουσα· οὗτοι γεωργοὶ ἀθάνατοι ἐγκάρπων φυτῶν καὶ δένδρων καὶ μηδὲν ἀνθρωπίνης τέχνης προσδεομένων. ταύτην τὴν γεωργίαν οὐδεὶς παύει, οὐ λοιμός, οὐ λιμός, οὐ πόλεμος.

ἀλλὰ τά γ' ἄσπαρτα καὶ ἀνήροτα πάντα φύονται.

ἐὰν δὲ ἐπιθυμῇς Λιβυκοῦ λωτοῦ καὶ Αἰγυπτίων πυρῶν

---

16 That is, Ares.   17 Demeter is responsible for all crops, Dionysus for grapes, and Triptolemus (Demeter's son) for grain. Cadmus and Pentheus were early Theban kings, Erichthonius and Cecrops were early Athenian kings.

5. If the myths about the gods are also admissible as evidence, then Zeus, Athena, Apollo, and Enyalius,[16] the most regal of the gods, are not farmers, and it is only more recently, after much wandering, that Demeter took up farming, and only more recently that Dionysus did so after the time of Cadmus and Pentheus, and Triptolemus only after the time of Erichthonius and Cecrops.[17] And if we were to take up the reign of Cronus, how could we even consider farming?[18] Not even today do we really need farming, for the land has not given up bearing crops on its own. It produces acorns and pears for food and produces naturally flowing water to drink, including the Nile, Ister, Achelous, Maeander, and other ever-flowing sources of clean and pure streams. No old-time Icarius,[19] or a man from Boeotia,[20] or one from Thessaly is needed to tend these, but instead it is the sun itself and the warming moon, the nourishing rains, the blowing winds, the changing seasons, and the earth that brings them forth. These are the immortal farmers, as it were, of crop-bearing plants and trees, that have no additional need of human artifice. No plague, famine, or war can put a stop to this husbandry,

for all these grow without planting or plowing.[21]

But if you desire Libyan lotus,[22] Egyptian wheat, Attic

---

[18] For the preagricultural time of Cronus, cf. *Orr*. 21.5 and 36.1.   [19] An early king of Athens who took in Dionysus.

[20] Perhaps a reference to Hesiod and his *Works and Days*.

[21] *Od*. 9.109, describing the preagricultural life of the Cyclopes.

[22] An edible berry; cf. Hdt. 4.177.

καὶ ἐλαίας Ἀττικῆς ἢ ἀμπέλου Λεσβίας, μετατίθης
τὴν τέχνην εἰς διακονίαν ἡδονῆς.

6. Τὸ δ᾽ ὅλον, παραβάλλεις πόνους ἐλευθέρους
ἀναγκαίοις πόνοις καὶ ἐλευθέραν ἀρετὴν ἀναγκαίᾳ
γεωργίᾳ· οὐ γὰρ εἰρήνην παραβάλλεις πολέμῳ. εἰ
γὰρ τοιοῦτόν ἐστιν ἡ γεωργία, ἄφελε τοὺς πολέμους,
γεωργῶμεν· πᾶς τις ῥίψας δόρυ ἐπὶ σμινύην ἴτω, ἀρι-
στευέτω ἐν γῇ, κρατείτω ἐν γεωργοῖς· κηρύττωμεν τὸν
ἄνδρα τῆς εὐκαρπίας,

οὗτος ἐν ἀνθρώποις νικηφόρος, οὗτος ἄριστος.

Νῦν δὲ μεστὰ πάντα πολέμου καὶ ἀδικίας· αἱ γὰρ
ἐπιθυμίαι πλανῶνται πανταχοῦ περὶ πᾶσαν γῆν τὰς
πλεονεξίας ἐπεγείρουσαι, καὶ πάντα μεστὰ στρατοπέδων ἐπὶ τὴν ἀλλοτρίαν ἰόντων. κάλλος ᾄδεται γυναικὸς Πελοποννησίας· πλέει βάρβαρος ἀνὴρ ἐπ᾽ αὐτὴν
ἀπὸ τῆς Ἴδης, οὐ γεωργός, ἀλλὰ γεωργοῦ ἡμερώτε-
ρος καὶ σχολαίτερος καὶ εἰρηνικώτερος, ποιμὴν καὶ
βουκόλος. ἐπιθυμεῖ Καμβύσης τῆς Αἰγυπτίων γῆς·
πόλεμον ἡ ἐπιθυμία διανίστησιν. ἐπιθυμεῖ Δαρεῖος
τῆς Σκυθῶν γῆς· πολεμοῦνται Σκύθαι. μεταβαίνει ἡ
ἐπιθυμία ἐπ᾽ Ἐρέτριαν καὶ Ἀθήνας, καὶ μετὰ τῆς ἐπιθυμίας οἱ στόλοι· Ἐρέτρια σαγηνεύεται, ἐπιπλεῖται

---

23 An interlocutor objects that if the contrast is not between
freedom and slavery, but between peace and war, then farming is
to be preferred and war should be rejected. The speaker responds
that war exists everywhere and that in fact farming provokes it.

olives, or Lesbian grape vines, then you turn agriculture into a servant of pleasure.

6. In short, you[23] are comparing free labors with servile labors, and martial virtue that is free with agriculture that is servile; you are not comparing peace with war. For if agriculture is such as you claim,[24] then reject wars and let us become farmers. Let every man throw away his spear and go take up the hoe; let him display his valor working the land, and let him be the victor among farmers. Let us herald him for the fertility of his land:

Here stands the winner among men; he is the best.[25]

But in reality, the world is full of war and injustice, for desires circulate everywhere on earth and incite greedy aggression, and everywhere there are armies marching against other people's lands. The beauty of a Spartan woman is celebrated, and a foreign man[26] sails from Ida to abduct her. He is not a farmer, but someone even milder, more leisured, and more peaceful than a farmer, a herder of sheep and cows. Cambyses desires the land of Egypt, and his desire leads to war.[27] Darius desires the land of Scythia, and the Scythians go to war.[28] His desire moves on to Eretria and Athens, and along with this desire come expeditionary forces. Eretria is swept clean of inhabitants

---

[24] That is, if it is peaceable.
[25] The source of this hexameter is unknown.
[26] Paris/Alexander.
[27] In 525 BC (Hdt. 2.1 and 3.1).
[28] In 513 BC (Hdt. 4.1 and 4.83–142).

Μαραθών. ἐπιθυμεῖ ἡ Ξέρξου γυνὴ θεραπαινίδων Λα-
κωνίδων καὶ Ἀτθίδων καὶ Ἀργειάδων, καὶ δι᾽ ἐπιθυμίαν γυναικὸς ἐξαρτύονται στόλοι διαπόντιοι, ἡ Ἀσία
ἐξοικίζεται, ἡ Εὐρώπη ἀνίσταται. ἐπιθυμοῦσιν Ἀθηναῖοι Σικελίας, ἐπιθυμοῦσιν Λακεδαιμόνιοι Ἰωνίας,
ἐπιθυμοῦσιν Θηβαῖοι ἡγεμονίας.

7. Ὦ ἐρώτων πικροτάτων τῇ Ἑλλάδι. ποῦ τις ἐλθὼν
μετὰ ἀσφαλείας γεωργῇ; ποῦ δὲ εὕρῃ τὸ χρύσεον
εἰρήνης πρόσωπον; ποῖον γῆς μέρος ἐραστὰς οὐκ
ἔχει;

Ἄσκρη χεῖμα κακή, θέρει ἀργαλέη·

ἴωμεν ἐπὶ τὴν Ἄσκρην· ἀλλ᾽ αἰγειροφόρος ἡ Βοιωτία.
Λιβύη πόρρω μέν, ἀλλὰ εὔβοτος. ὑπερόριος ἡ Ἰνδῶν
γῆ, ἀλλὰ καὶ αὕτη ἐξεῦρεν Μακεδόνα ἐραστήν, διὰ
πολλῶν γενῶν καὶ πολέμων βαδίζοντα ἐπ᾽ αὐτήν. ποῖ
τις τράπηται; ποῦ τις εὕρῃ γεωργίαν ἀσφαλῆ; πάντα
μεστὰ πολέμων, πάντα ὅπλων. τοιγαροῦν

εὖ μέν τις δόρυ θηξάσθω, εὖ δ᾽ ἀσπίδα θέσθω,
εὖ δέ τις ἵπποισιν δεῖπνον δότω ὠκυπόδεσσιν.

---

29 In 490 BC by Datis and Artaphrenes (Hdt. 6.101–17); cf.
Or. 33.4 for the same examples.
30 Cf. Hdt. 3.134, where she is the wife of Darius, not Xerxes.
31 In 415 BC (Thuc. 6.1).
32 In 401 BC (Xen. Hell. 3).
33 Under the leadership of Epaminondas (371–362 BC); cf.
Xen. Hell. 6.4.3–7.5.27.

and Marathon is attacked by sea.[29] Xerxes' wife desires handmaids from Sparta, Athens, and Argos,[30] and because of one woman's desire expeditions are equipped to cross the sea, Asia is emptied of men, and Europe is forced to evacuate. The Athenians desire Sicily,[31] the Spartans desire Ionia,[32] the Thebans desire hegemony.[33]

7. O what bitter lusts for Hellas! Where can anyone go to farm in safety? Where will he find "the golden countenance of peace"?[34] What place on earth is free from lovers wanting it? If indeed,

Ascra is bad in winter, harsh in summer,[35]

then let us go to Ascra, but then Boeotia is full of poplars.[36] Libya is indeed far away, but it is rich in flocks. India lies far beyond our borders, but even she found her Macedonian lover,[37] who marched through many peoples and fought many battles to reach her. Where is one to turn? Where can one find safe farming? Wars and weapons are everywhere. Therefore

let each man sharpen his spear; let him ready his
    shield;
let him feed good fodder to his swift-footed horses.[38]

---

[34] A quotation from an unknown lyric poet.

[35] Hes. *Op.* 640. Ascra, Hesiod's hometown, was proverbial for its harsh conditions.

[36] That is, since Ascra is located in poplar-rich Boeotia, not even it is safe from rapacious greed.

[37] Alexander the Great.

[38] *Il.* 2.382–83, Agamemnon rallying his generals.

καλὸν ἡ γεωργία, καλόν, ἐὰν μεῖναι δυνηθῇ, ἐὰν σχολῆς τύχῃ, ἐὰν φυλακὴν ἔχῃ· δέδια δέ τοι μὴ τοῦτο ᾖ τὸ καλὸν τὸ τοὺς πολέμους κινοῦν καὶ τὰς στάσεις. λέγει τις παλαιὸς ἀνήρ·

μάλιστα γὰρ τῆς γῆς,

φησίν,

ἡ ἀρίστη τὰς μεταβολὰς τῶν οἰκητόρων ἐλάμβανεν . . . τὴν γοῦν Ἀττικὴν διὰ τὸ λεπτόγεω εἶναι ἀστασίαστον οὖσαν ἄνθρωποι ᾤκουν οἱ αὐτοὶ ἀεί.

ἀκήκοας πῶς πόλεμος γίνεται; μὴ γεώργει, ἄνθρωπε· ἔα τὴν γῆν ἀκαλλώπιστον, αὐχμῶσαν· στάσιν κινεῖς, πόλεμον κινεῖς.

Farming is a good thing, truly good, if it is able to maintain itself, if it has time to itself, if it has protection, but I fear that its very goodness provokes wars and civil strife. In the words of an ancient authority,

> the best land,

he said,

> was especially subject to changes of inhabitants . . . Attica, however, because it had thin soil, remained without civil strife and was always inhabited by the same people.[39]

Do you hear how war arises? Then don't be a farmer, my man. Leave the land uncultivated and squalid. Otherwise, you are inciting civil strife, you are inciting war.

[39] Thuc. 1.2.3 and 5.

ORATION 24

INTRODUCTION

By coming second, farmers prevail rhetorically over soldiers. To counter all the evidence from Homer in the previous oration, the speaker opens with a quotation from
Aratus' *Phaenomena* that decries the invention of swords
and the eating of plowing oxen (§1). The argument turns
to consider whether war is ever just and concludes that
just men do not wage war, but only unjust men do (§2).
Since justice as a criterion proves unable to distinguish
between farmers and soldiers, the speaker turns to considerations of virtue and vice (§3). Warfare and farming
are first contrasted in terms of vices: when it comes to
desire (*epithymia*), war is insatiable, farming is thrifty;
when it comes to anger, war incites it, whereas farming is
gentle. The two are then compared in terms of the virtues.
Self-restraint (*sōphrosynē*): an armed soldier is reckless,
the farmer is temperate. Justice (*dikaiosynē*): war leads to
unjust attacks on others, farming to a reciprocal relationship with the land and equality with fellow citizens (§4).
Piety (*eusebeia*): soldiers are misfits at religious festivals,
whereas farmers actually founded many agrarian rites, and
their pious offerings to the gods are received more favorably than the dedications from generals like Pausanias and
Lysander (§5). Wisdom (*sophia*): soldiers know how to

44

marshal troops; the farmer knows about the seasons and the movements of the heavens. Bravery (*andreia*): unlike the soldier who toils occasionally, the farmer is conditioned by continuous hard work and performs bravely when called upon, like those famous Athenian farmers at the battle of Marathon (§6). Just as the Persians used to fight bravely to protect their beloved concubines who accompanied them on campaign, farmers fight for their beloved vines, olive trees, and crops. The armies of today are full of hoplites who are poorly trained, mercenary, and arrogant, like the ones defeated in Sicily and the Hellespont. The ancient Persians were successful against the Medes when Cyrus the Great hardened them with field work at Pasargadae, but when they stopped farming, they threw away their virtues along with their farm tools.

ORATION 24

Ὅτι γεωργοὶ τῶν προπολεμούντων
λυσιτελέστεροι

1. Ἐπαμύνωμεν τῷ δήμῳ τῶν γεωργῶν, ἐπείπερ λόγῳ
τὰ νῦν γίγνεται ἡ δίαιτα καὶ οὐχ ὅπλοις· εἰ δὲ καὶ
ὅπλων δέοι, τάχα που φανεῖται καὶ ὁ γεωργὸς οὐδὲν
τοῦ ὁπλίτου ἀσθενέστερος. ἀλλὰ τοῦτο μὲν καὶ αὖθις
σκεψόμεθα· λόγῳ δὲ δὴ τὰ νῦν καὶ οὐχ ὅπλοις κριτέον
τοὺς ἄνδρας, καὶ οὐκ εὐλαβητέον οὔτε Ὅμηρον μαρ-
τυροῦντα οὔτε ὅστις Ὁμήρου εὐφωνότερος. εἰ δέ τοι
καὶ τοῦτο δέοι, καὶ αὐτοὶ ἀναβιβασόμεθα ἐκ τοῦ Ἑλικῶνος ποιητὴν ἄλλον οὐδὲν ἀδοξότερον τοῦ Ὁμήρου,
μεμφόμενον τῷ νῦν γένει,

οἳ πρῶτοι κακοεργὸν ἐτεκτήναντο μάχαιραν,
εἰνοδίην, πρῶτοι δὲ βοῶν ἐπάσαντ' ἀροτήρων.

τὸ γάρ τοι τὰ τοιαῦτα ἐπαινεῖν ἀνδρὸς ἂν εἴη δυσχε-
ρεστέρου τῷ βίῳ τῆς τοῦ πολεμεῖν χρείας· ἧς κἂν
ἀφέλῃς τὸ ἄδικον, ἐλεεινὸν αὐτῆς τὸ ἀναγκαῖον.

---

[1] In §6 below.   [2] That is, Aratus of Soli (ca. 315–240 BC),
the latest poet cited in the *Orations*.   [3] Arat. *Phaen.* 131–32.

46

ORATION 24

That farmers are more useful
than soldiers

1. Let us come to the defense of the population of farmers, since it is with words, not with weapons, that our present investigation is being conducted. But should the need for arms arise, it may well turn out that the farmer is in no way weaker than the hoplite. That topic, however, we shall take up at a later point.[1] But for now we must judge these men with words and not with weapons, and we need not be awed by the testimony of Homer or of anyone more eloquent than he. Yet should that need arise, we shall summon another poet from Helicon as our witness,[2] one no less distinguished than Homer, who disparages the present generation of men,

who first fashioned the evil-working sword for
    bandits,
and who first ate the flesh of plowing oxen.[3]

For anyone who would approve of such things could only be a man more hostile to life than the conduct of war itself, for even if you take away war's injustice, its necessity remains lamentable.

2. Οὑτωσὶ δὲ θεασώμεθα. τῶν ἀνθρώπων οἱ μὲν δίκαιοι, οἱ δὲ ἄδικοί εἰσιν. πολεμοῦσιν δέ, ἆρα οἱ δίκαιοι τοῖς δικαίοις; οὐδαμῶς· ἴσοι γὰρ ταῖς γνώμαις ὄντες, τί ἂν καὶ τοῦ πολεμεῖν δέοιντο; πολεμοῦσιν οὖν οἱ ἄδικοι ἢ τοῖς δικαίοις ἢ τοῖς ὁμοίοις· ἄνισοι γὰρ καὶ πρὸς ἀλλήλους καὶ πρὸς τοὺς δικαίους. πολεμοῦσιν δὲ καὶ ἀσθενεῖς, ὀρεγόμενοι τοῦ ἴσου· οἱ δὲ ἰσχυροί, τοῦ πλέονος.

Εἶεν· τρία ταυτὶ συστήματα ἡμῖν πεφώρακεν ὁ λόγος, ὧν τὸ μὲν ἐκεχειρίαν ἀεὶ πρὸς ἑαυτὸ καὶ σπονδὰς ἄγει, τὸ δίκαιον, τοῖν δὲ ἄλλοιν πολεμεῖ ἑκάτερον, τὸ μὲν αὐτὸ αὑτῷ, τὸ δὲ τῷ δικαίῳ. φαίνεται τοίνυν ὁ πόλεμος τοῖς μὲν δικαίοις ἀναγκαῖος ὤν, τοῖς δὲ ἀδίκοις ἑκούσιος. καὶ περὶ μὲν τῶν ἀδίκων τί χρὴ σκοπεῖν; οὐ γὰρ δέος, μή τις αὐτοῖς προσθῇ ἐπαίνου μοῖραν. ἐπεὶ δὲ οἱ δίκαιοι οὐ βουλήσει πολεμοῦσιν ἀλλὰ ἀνάγκῃ, ⟨ἢ⟩[1] σωφρονίζοντες τὸ ἄδικον πᾶν, ὥσπερ ὁ Ἡρακλῆς, ἢ ἐπιόντας ἀμυνόμενοι, ὡς τοὺς Μήδους οἱ Ἕλληνες, πότερα δέξαιντο ἂν οἱ αὐτοὶ οὗτοι, ἀπηλλαγμένοι τῆς τοῦ πολεμεῖν ἀνάγκης, ἀφῃρῆσθαι καὶ τὴν ἐν ὅπλοις ἀρετήν, ἢ σὺν τῷ ἀβουλήτῳ τῆς χρείας τὸ ἀναγκαῖον τῆς ἀρετῆς ἔχειν; ἐγὼ μὲν οἶμαι θάτερον, τὸ πρότερον· καὶ γὰρ οἱ ἰατροί, εἴπερ δίκαιοι εἶεν καὶ φιλάνθρωποι, εὔξαιντο ἂν ἀπολωλέναι τὴν τέχνην σὺν ταῖς νόσοις.

3. Φέρε καὶ ἐπὶ γεωργίας θεασώμεθα εἰ τοῦτον

[1] suppl. Markland, Dübner, Trapp

2. Let us consider the matter in this way. Some men are just, others unjust. When they go to war, do just men fight against just men? Of course not, for if they are like-minded, why would they need to fight? Therefore unjust men make war either on just men or on men like themselves, since they deal unfairly with each other as well as with just men. Then too, weak men go to war because they desire an equal share, while strong men do so because they desire more.

Fair enough. The following three categories are what reasoned argument has detected for us. The first, the category of just men, maintains a continual peace and cessation of hostilities within itself, whereas each of the other two is at war, one with itself, the other with just men. Therefore it is evident that war is forced upon just men, but is voluntarily chosen by unjust men. Now, as far as unjust men are concerned, why consider them? Certainly there is no fear that anyone would accord them any bit of approval. So, since just men do not wage war voluntarily, but fight only when forced to do so, either to restrain injustice of every sort like Heracles, or to defend themselves against invaders, as the Greeks did against the Persians, would these same men choose to give up their prowess in arms, if they could be freed from the necessity of war, or would they maintain their prowess as a necessity, while wishing not to need it? In my opinion, it would be the former of the two. For example, if doctors are just and humane, they would pray for their medical art to vanish if diseases did as well.

3. Come, let us consider whether the same categories

αὐτοῖς ἔχει τὸν τρόπον ὅνπερ καὶ ἡ ἐν τῷ πολεμεῖν χειρουργία. ἅπτονται ἄνθρωποι γῆς, οἱ μὲν σὺν δίκῃ, οἱ δὲ ἄνευ δίκης· σὺν δίκῃ μὲν κατὰ χρείαν καρποῦ, δίκης δὲ ἄνευ ἐπὶ χρηματισμῷ. εἴη ἂν οὖν κἀνταῦθα ἡ δίαιτα οὐ ξυλλήβδην περὶ πάσης γεωργίας· ἀλλὰ ἐπεὶ καὶ τοῦτο κοινὸν δικαίων καὶ μή, κοινὸν δ' ἦν καὶ τὸ πολεμεῖν ἑκατέρῳ τῷ γένει, δέος μὴ λάθῃ ἐξαπατήσας ὁ λόγος οὗτος, οὐ γεωργικῷ τὸ πολεμικόν, ἀλλὰ τῷ δικαίῳ τὸ ἄδικον παραβαλεῖν ἐθέλων. δικαίους οὖν ἄμφω ὑποθέμενοι, καὶ τὸν πολεμικὸν καὶ τὸν γεωργικόν, τὸν μὲν ὑπ' ἀνάγκης ἐπὶ τὸ πολεμεῖν ἰόντα, τὸν δὲ ὑπὸ χρείας γεωργεῖν ἠναγκασμένον, οὕτως σκοπῶμεν περὶ ἑκατέρου.

Καίτοι τί ταῦτα λέγω; εἰ γὰρ ἐπ' ἀμφοῖν τὸ δίκαιον ἴσον καὶ τὸ καλὸν ἴσον καὶ ὁ ἔπαινος ἴσος, καὶ ἀπίασιν ἡμῖν ἄμφω νικηφόροι. βούλει τοίνυν, ἀφελὼν τὸ δίκαιον ἑκατέρου, τὸ ἄδικον προσθεὶς οὕτω σκοπεῖν; ἀλλὰ κἀνταῦθα ἐπ' ἀμφοῖν ἡ κακία ἐπανισουμένη τὸν ἔπαινον ἐξ ἀμφοῖν ἀφαιρεῖ. τῷ ἂν οὖν τις κρίναι τὸ λεγόμενον; βούλει σοι φράσω; καὶ δὴ λέγω. μαντεύεταί μοι ἡ ψυχὴ κατὰ τοὺς Πλάτωνος λόγους εἶναί τι ἀνθρώπων γένος, μήτε ἀρετῆς κομιδῇ ἐπήβολον, μήτ' εἰς κακίαν ἐσχάτην παντάπασιν ἐκκεκυλισμένον, βι-

---

4 As in the treatment of war above, where the topic of unjust men was dismissed.

apply to those engaged in farming as to those who practice warfare. When men work the soil, some do so justly, others unjustly: justly because they need the produce, unjustly in order to make money. So here too our investigation will not be comprehensive and include every aspect of agriculture.[4] No, since farming is also practiced both by those who are just and by those who are not, and since war was seen to involve both groups, there is a risk of our being inadvertently misled by the argument into wishing to compare justice to injustice rather than warfare to farming. Therefore, let us postulate that both our warrior and our farmer are just—the one compelled by necessity to go to war, the other forced by need to farm—and then examine each one accordingly.

And yet, what do I mean by this? If both professions are equally just, honorable, and praiseworthy, then we shall find that both emerge victorious. Are you then willing to take away justice from each one and substitute injustice, and examine them accordingly? No, for then the evil that is shared equally by both will strip both of their praise. How then is anyone to decide the issue? Do you want me to tell you how? Well then, I will. My soul divines, in accordance with Plato's arguments, that there is a certain class of people who neither wholly possess virtue, nor completely wallow in utter depravity,[5] but who live ac-

[5] This view is attributed to Plato at Alcin. *Didasc.* 30.183.31–32: "It must also be recognized that there is an intermediate disposition which is neither vicious nor virtuous" (trans. Dillon). This is in opposition to the Stoics; cf. Diog. Laert. 7.127 (= *SVF* 1.224): "It is a tenet of theirs that between virtue and vice there is nothing intermediate" (trans. R. D. Hicks).

οτεῦον δὲ ἐν δόξαις ὀρθαῖς, τροφῇ καὶ παιδεύσει ὑπὸ
νόμῳ σώφρονι πολιτευόμενον. τοῦτο τοίνυν τῶν ἀνθρώπων τὸ γένος διελόντες δίχα, τὸ μὲν παραδόντες
τῇ γῇ, τὸ δὲ εἰς τὰ ὅπλα ἀποπέμψαντες, ἅτε ἀμφίβο-
λον ὂν καὶ ἐν μεταιχμίῳ ἀρετῆς καὶ κακίας καθωρ-
μισμένον, θεασώμεθα ἀπὸ τῶν ἐπιτηδευμάτων, ἑκάτερον ὑπὸ ἑκατέρου πότερον ἐφ᾽ ὁπότερον ἄγεται
θᾶττον· θεασώμεθα δὲ οὑτωσί.

4. Μέγιστον ἀνθρώπῳ κακὸν ἐπιθυμία. πότερον
ἐπιθυμίας ἐργαστικώτερον, πόλεμος ἢ γεωργία; καὶ
μὴν τὸ μὲν ἀκόρεστον, τὸ δὲ φειδωλόν· ἀκόρεστον μὲν
ὁ πόλεμος, φειδωλὸν δὲ ἡ γεωργία. καὶ τὸ μὲν παντοδαπὸν ὁ πόλεμος, ⟨τὸ δὲ⟩[2] ἁπλοῦν ἡ γεωργία· καὶ τὸ
μὲν ἄδηλον, τὸ δὲ ὡμολογημένον. τί γὰρ ἂν εἴη ἀδη-
λότερον τῆς ἐν πολέμῳ τύχης; βέβαιος δὲ ὁ ἐν γῇ
πόνος. πόλεμος ὑπ᾽ εὐτυχίας μάλιστα θρασύνεται, ἡ
δὲ γεωργία ὑπ᾽ εὐκαρπίας σωφρονίζεται. εἰ δὲ καὶ ὁ
θυμὸς ἀνθρώπῳ σύνοικος χαλεπὸς καὶ δεόμενος πολλῆς παιδαγωγίας, τί ἂν εἴη θυμοῦ παρασκευαστι-
κώτερον πολέμου καὶ ὅπλων; τί δὲ γεωργίας ἠπιώτε-
ρον;

Πρός γε μὴν τὰς ἀρετὰς αὐτὰς οὕτως ἔχει ἑκάτερον, καὶ πρῶτόν γε πρὸς σωφροσύνην· ὅπλα ἔχων
ἀνήρ, ὁ μὲν ἰσχυρὸς ἰταμώτερος, ὁ δὲ δειλὸς σφα-
λερώτερος· καὶ ὁ μὲν θρασὺς ἰταμώτερος, ὁ δὲ ἀσθενὴς θρασύτερος, ὁ δὲ φιλήδονος ἀκολαστότερος· γε-

[2] suppl. Markland, Trapp

cording to correct opinions[6] and, thanks to their upbringing and education, conduct themselves in a restrained manner. So, let us take this category of men, which is ambivalent and is situated in no man's land between virtue and vice,[7] and divide it in two, assigning one group to the soil and dispatching the other to their weapons, and then consider them in light of their particular pursuits, to determine which is more inclined to virtue and which to vice. So, let us proceed accordingly.

4. The greatest evil for a human being is desire. Which category, then, produces more desire, warfare or farming? Certainly the one is insatiable, the other is thrifty: war is insatiable, farming thrifty. War comes in many forms, farming is simple. War is uncertain, farming is consistent. What could be more uncertain than the fortunes of war? In contrast, work on the land is stable. War becomes most reckless when it meets with success; farming acts with restraint when it has a good harvest. If it is a fact that anger dwelling in a human being is unruly and requires a great deal of disciplining, then what produces more anger than war and weapons? And what could be gentler than farming?

And when it comes to the virtues themselves, here is how each group fares. First is self-restraint. When carrying weapons, the strong man becomes more reckless, the coward more likely to get hurt; the bold man becomes more reckless, the weak man bolder, and the hedonist more unbridled. But when he farms, the strong man har-

---

[6] For correct opinions that fall short of actual knowledge, see Pl. *Meno* 97b–99a and *Symp.* 202a.   [7] At *Or.* 20.4 it is love that is situated in between virtue and vice; at *Or.* 38.6 it is the soul.

ωργῶν ἀνήρ, ὁ μὲν ἰσχυρὸς εὐκαρπότερος, ὁ δὲ
ἀσθενέστερος ὑγιεινότερος, ὁ δὲ δειλὸς ἀσφαλέστε-
ρος, ὁ δὲ φιλήδονος σωφρονέστερος.

Εἰ δὲ καὶ πρὸς δικαιοσύνην ἐξετάζοις, πόλεμος μὲν
διδάσκαλος ἀδικίας, γεωργία δὲ δικαιοσύνης. ὁ μὲν
γὰρ πλεονέκτης τέ ἐστιν καὶ ἐπὶ τὰ ἀλλότρια ἄγει,
καὶ αὐτὸς αὑτοῦ κράτιστα ἔχει ἐπειδὰν τὰ μέγιστα
ἀδικῇ καὶ ἀδικῶν εὐστοχῇ. παρὰ δὲ γεωργίας ἴση μὲν
ἡ ἀντίδοσις, δικαία δὲ ἡ ὁμιλία· θεραπεύεις φυτόν,
τὸ δὲ ἀντιδίδωσιν καρπούς· θεραπεύεις λήιον, τὸ δὲ
εὐτροφεῖ· τημελεῖς ἄμπελον, ἡ δὲ εὐοινεῖ· τημελεῖς
ἐλαίαν, ἡ δὲ εὐανθεῖ.

Φοβερὸς γεωργὸς οὐδενί, πολέμιος οὐδενί, φίλος
πᾶσιν, ἄπειρος αἵματος, ἄπειρος σφαγῆς, ἱερὸς καὶ
παναγὴς θεῶν ἐπικαρπίων καὶ ἐπιληναίων καὶ ἁλώων
καὶ προηροσίων· ἴσος μὲν ἐν δημοκρατίᾳ, ὀλιγαρχίαν
δὲ καὶ τυραννίδα πάντων μάλιστα μισεῖ γεωργία· οὐ
γὰρ ταύτης θρέμματα ὁ Διονύσιος οὐδὲ ὁ Φάλαρις,
ἀλλ᾽ ἑκάτερος ἀπὸ τῶν ὅπλων.

5. Ἑορταῖς γε μὴν καὶ μυστηρίοις καὶ πανηγύρεσιν
ποῖον πλῆθος ἐπιτηδειότερον; οὐχ ὁ μὲν ὁπλίτης ἑορ-
ταστὴς ἄμουσος, ὁ δὲ γεωργὸς ἐμμελέστατος; καὶ ὁ
μὲν μυστηρίοις ἀλλότριος, ὁ δὲ οἰκειότατος, καὶ ὁ μὲν
ἐν πανηγύρει φοβερώτατος, ὁ δὲ εἰρηναιότατος; δο-
κοῦσι δέ μοι μηδὲ τὴν ἀρχὴν συστήσασθαι ἑορτὰς
καὶ τελετὰς θεῶν ἄλλοι τινὲς ἢ γεωργοί, πρῶτοι μὲν
ἐπὶ ληνῷ στησάμενοι Διονύσῳ χορούς, πρῶτοι δὲ ἐπὶ

vests more crops, the weak man becomes healthier, the coward becomes more secure, and the hedonist becomes more self-restrained.

Then too, if you compare them in terms of justice, you find that war teaches injustice, farming teaches justice. For war is covetous and leads to attacks on other people's possessions. Indeed, it is at its strongest when committing the greatest injustice and succeeding at it. Farming, however, involves an equal exchange and a just give and take. If you tend a plant, it returns fruit; if you tend a wheat field, it thrives; if you care for a vine, it furnishes good wine; if you care for an olive tree, it bears fine blossoms.

A farmer frightens no one, is no one's enemy; he is a friend to all, free of bloodshed, free of slaughter; he is holy and sacred to the gods who preside over harvests, vintages, threshing floors, and plowing festivals. In a democracy the farmer is an equal citizen, and farmers in general detest oligarchy and tyranny above all other regimes. Neither Dionysius nor Phalaris was brought up on a farm; both were raised with weapons.[8]

5. Which group is more suited for feasts, mysteries, and festivals? Is not the soldier a discordant celebrant and the farmer perfectly attuned? Is not the soldier a stranger to mysteries and the farmer completely at home? Is not a soldier most threatening at a festival and a farmer most peaceable? It seems to me that it was none others than farmers who established feasts and religious rituals in the first place. They were the first to form choruses in honor of Dionysus by the winepress, the first to establish the rites

---

[8] Dionysius II, tyrant of Syracuse from 367 to 357 BC; Phalaris, tyrant of Acragas ca. 570 to 549 BC.

ἅλῳ Δημητρὶ ὄργια, πρῶτοι δὲ τὴν ἐλαίας γένεσιν τῇ
Ἀθηνᾷ ἐπιφημίσαντες, πρῶτοι δὲ τῶν ἐκ γῆς καρπῶν
τοῖς δεδωκόσιν θεοῖς ἀπαρξάμενοι· οἷς εἰκὸς χαίρειν
τοὺς θεοὺς μᾶλλον ἢ Παυσανίᾳ τὴν δεκάτην ἀποθύ-
οντι ἢ Λυσάνδρῳ τὴν δεκάτην ἀνατιθέντι· ἐκ πολέμων
αἱ ἀπαρχαί, ἐκ συμφορῶν αἱ εὐσέβειαι. γεωργῶν δὲ
φιλάνθρωποι μὲν αἱ εὐχαί, εὔφημοι δὲ αἱ θυσίαι, ἀπ'
οἰκείων πόνων, ἄμοιροι συμφορῶν, ἄμοιροι κακῶν.

6. Εἰ δὲ δὴ καὶ πρὸς σοφίαν ἀντεξεταστέον τοὺς
ἄνδρας, ἐρώμεθα ἑκάτερον. οὐκοῦν ὁ μὲν ἐν πολέμῳ
σοφὸς κοσμῆσαι δεινὸς

ἵππους καὶ ἀνέρας ἀσπιδιώτας,

τὸ ἀκοσμότατον τῶν ἐν ἀνθρώποις πραγμάτων καὶ
σκυθρωπότατον· ὁ δὲ ἐν γεωργίᾳ σοφὸς

Πληϊάδων Ἀτλαγενέων περιτελλομενάων

ἀμήτου ἄρχεται,

ἀρότοιο δυομενάων·

μέλει δὲ αὐτῷ καὶ ἐνιαυτοῦ ὡρῶν καὶ σελήνης δρόμου
καὶ ἄστρων ἐπιτολῆς καὶ ὄμβρου μέτρων καὶ πνευμάτων καιροῦ.

Εἰ δὲ καὶ σωμάτων ἀρετῇ τοὺς ἄνδρας κριτέον καὶ
ἀνδρείᾳ πόνων, ὀλίγοι μὲν τῷ στρατιώτῃ οἱ καιροὶ

---

9 The Spartan general who dedicated a tenth of the spoils
from the Battle of Plataea in 479 BC (Hdt. 9.81).

of Demeter by the threshing floor, the first to celebrate Athena for inventing the olive tree, and the first to make offerings of the fruits of the earth to the gods who had provided them. And it is likely that the gods look more favorably on these celebrants than on Pausanias sacrificing his tenth[9] or Lysander dedicating his.[10] Their first fruits came from wars, their acts of piety derived from disasters. But the prayers of farmers are humane and their sacrifices auspicious, for these come from their very own labors, untainted by disasters or evils.

6. And if we need to compare these men for their wisdom, let us inquire about each group. The one who is wise in war is skilled at marshaling

horses and warriors with their shields,[11]

which is the most disruptive and gruesome of human activities. In contrast, the one who is wise in farming begins his harvesting

when the Pleiades, Daughters of Atlas, are rising,
. . . and his plowing when they are setting.[12]

He is concerned with the seasons of the year, the courses of the moon, the risings of the stars, the levels of rainfall, and the times for winds.

And if we also judge these men on the fitness of their bodies and on their bravery in the face of hard work, we see that occasions for a soldier to toil are few, whereas they

---

[10] The Spartan general who defeated the Athenians at the end of the Peloponnesian War.   [11] *Il.* 2.554.
[12] Hes. *Op.* 383–84. The Pleiades rise in May and set in October/November.

τοῦ πονεῖν, τῷ δὲ γεωργῷ διηνεκεῖς· ὑπαίθριος ἀεί,
ἡλίῳ φίλος, συνήθης νιφετῶν, πεπηγώς, νηλίπους,
αὐτουργός, εὔπνους, ὀξὺς δραμεῖν, ἰσχυρὸς φέρειν· εἰ
δέ που καὶ δεήσαι μάχης, ὄψει στρατιώτην ἠσκημέ-
νον πόνοις ἀληθινοῖς, οἵων ἐπειράθη Δαρεῖος ἐπὶ Μα-
ραθῶνα ἐλθών. ἦν γὰρ τότε Ἀθηναίοις στρατιωτικὸν
οὐχ ὁπλιτικόν, οὐ τοξικόν, οὐ ναυτικόν, οὐχ ἱππικόν,
ἀλλὰ κατὰ δήμους νενεμημένον· οἳ καὶ γεωργοῦντες,
ἐπιπλεύσαντος αὐτοῖς βαρβαρικοῦ στόλου ἐπὶ Μαρα-
θῶνα, ἐκ τῶν ἀγρῶν ἔδραμον στρατιῶται ἐργαζό-
μενοι, ὁ μὲν σμινύην ἔχων, ὁ δὲ ὑννιμάχος, ὁ δὲ θε-
ριστηρίῳ ἀμυνόμενος. ὦ στρατιωτικοῦ καλοῦ καὶ
αὐτουργοῦ καὶ μεστοῦ ἐλευθερίας· ὦ γῆς καὶ γεωργίας καλὰ καὶ γενναῖα θρέμματα, ὡς ὑμῶν ἐπαινῶ
μὲν τὰς ἀρετάς, ἐπαινῶ δὲ καὶ τὰ ὅπλα, οἷς ὑπὲρ τῆς
οἰκείας γῆς ἐμαχέσασθε, ὑπὲρ ἀμπέλων ἃς ἐκάμετε,
ὑπὲρ ἐλαῶν ἃς ἐφυτεύσασθε. ἀπὸ τοιούτων πάλιν ἐπὶ
τὴν γῆν ἤλθετε, ἐκ πολέμων γεωργοί, ἐκ γεωργῶν
ἀριστεῖς. ὦ τῆς καλῆς ἀντιδόσεως.

7. Ἀλλὰ Πέρσαις μὲν αἱ παλλακίδες ἕπονται, ἵνα
μάχωνται καλῶς ὑπὲρ τῶν φιλτάτων· γεωργὸς δὲ
ἀνὴρ οὐκ ἀμυνεῖται καλῶς ὑπὲρ τῶν φιλτάτων, ὑπὲρ
ἀμπέλου τεμνομένης, ὑπὲρ ἐλαίας κοπτομένης, ὑπὲρ
ληΐου δῃουμένου; ἐὰν δὲ παραβάλῃς τῷ στρατιωτικῷ
τούτῳ τὰ ὕστερα, εὑρήσεις μὲν ὁπλίτας, ἀλλ᾽ οὐ νικη-
φόρους· ὁπλίτας, ἀλλὰ μισθοφόρους, ὁπλίτας ἐσκια-

are continuous for a farmer. He is always outdoors, loves the sun, is a friend of snowfalls; he is hardy, barefoot, self-reliant, never short of breath, fast at running, and strong enough to carry heavy loads. If need ever arises for battle, you will see a soldier conditioned by true toils, like the men Darius came to know when he attacked Marathon. At that time, the Athenian army was not made up of hoplites, archers, sailors, or cavalry, but was scattered throughout the demes. These were farmers, and when the barbarian fleet sailed against them at Marathon, they ran from their fields—worker-soldiers—one wielding a hoe, another fighting with a plowshare, another defending himself with a sickle. O what a beautiful army of field hands, and one filled with freedom! O beautiful and noble scions of the land and farms, how I praise your prowess and the weapons with which you fought for your own lands, and for the vines you labored over, and for the olive trees you planted! And after such deeds, you returned to your land—from warriors to farmers, from farmers to heroes. O what a beautiful transformation!

7. Persians on campaign were accompanied by their concubines, so that they would fight bravely for those they loved best.[13] Will not a farmer fight bravely for the things *he* loves best, for his vines when they are being ravaged, for his olive trees being cut down, for his crops being destroyed? If you compare later armies to this one, you will find them full of hoplites, but not of victors—hoplites, yes, but mercenaries, hoplites trained indoors, hoplites that

13 Cf. Hdt. 7.83.2.

τροφημένους, ὁπλίτας ὑβριστάς, ἐν Σικελίᾳ ἡττωμέ-
νους, ἐν Ἑλλησπόντῳ λαμβανομένους.

Τὰ δὲ Περσικὰ εἰ λέγοις, στρατιωτικόν μοι καὶ
τοῦτο λέγεις ἐκ γεωργίας. πότε γάρ, πότε[3] Μῆδοι μὲν
ἡττῶνται, κρατοῦσιν δὲ Πέρσαι; ὅτε Πέρσαι μὲν
ἐγεώργουν ἔτι, Μῆδοι δ' ἐπολέμουν· τότε ἦλθεν αὐτοῖς
ἄγων Κῦρος στρατιωτικὸν ἐν Πασαργάδαις ἐνησκη-
μένον γῇ τραχείᾳ, ἐπ' αὐτουργίᾳ στρατιώτας δια-
πεπονημένους· ἀλλ' ἐπεὶ γεωργοῦντες ἐπαύσαντο οἱ
Πέρσαι καὶ τῆς γῆς ἐπελάθοντο καὶ τῶν ἀρότρων καὶ
τῶν ἀμητηρίων, τότε ἀπέβαλον καὶ τὰς ἀρετὰς ὁμοῦ
τοῖς ὀργάνοις.

3 πότε γάρ, πότε Stephanus, Davies[2], Dübner: πότε γάρ
ποτε R

are arrogant—the ones defeated in Sicily, those taken captive in the Hellespont.[14]

And if you bring up Persian history, you can tell me that their army too was brought up on farming. When, when indeed, were the Medes defeated and the Persians victorious?[15] It was when the Persians were still farmers, and the Medes were making war on them, that Cyrus came to their aid with an army trained in the rough terrain of Pasargadae,[16] soldiers conditioned by field work. But later, when the Persians stopped farming and forgot all about their fields, plows, and sickles, that is when they threw away their virtues along with their farm implements.

[14] Athenian defeats at Syracuse in 413 BC and at Aegospotami in 405 BC; cf. *Or.* 3.8.

[15] Cyrus defeated Astyages the Mede ca. 550 BC.

[16] For Cyrus' training of the Persian farmers at Pasargadae, see Hdt. 1.125–26.

ORATION 25

INTRODUCTION

This oration treats the relationship between words and deeds and examines what constitutes proper discourse with respect to pleasure, beauty, and utility. It overlaps with *Or.* 1 in defining philosophical discourse as multifaceted and essentially ethical.[1] It opens with an anecdote of Anacharsis the Scythian searching for wisdom in Greece and finding it in the upright actions and frugal speech of Myson (§1). Pythagoras too could speak succinctly at times, but his actions were far more extensive. There must be a harmony between words and deeds, in order for deeds to be remembered and not washed over by a flood of words. Pleasure must not be the aim of such words (§2). Just as a lion's roar or eagle's shriek or nightingale's song reveals the *ethos* of the animal, so words must reveal the character of the human soul. These words, however, must not merely find favor with the masses for their superficial verbal flourishes (§3). The heart of the matter is what constitutes beauty in discourse. This beauty cannot simply be described; it must be experienced. The correct approach is that of a farmer observing a plant. Like any passerby, he recognizes its beauty, but he reserves his

---

[1] Lauwers (2012) offers an analysis of this speech.

praise for the usefulness of its fruit (§4). The fruit of discourse must be taken into the soul and tested for its ripeness and its ability to produce more good fruit. Eulogistic speech that seeks merely to please can be licentious and lead to disaster, like the Trojan elder's praise of Helen's beauty (§5). The true orator (*rhētōr alēthēs*) is a philosopher, and his discourse raises the soul above the earthly passions. He is a judicious counselor in assemblies, a just pleader in the law courts, a decorous speaker at panegyric festivals, and a knowledgeable teacher in the classroom. He leads a moral life so that his denunciations of vice ring true (§6). Such discourse indeed includes pleasure, but it is the proper form of pleasure that accompanies virtue and is naturally beautiful, like the pleasure experienced at viewing the heavens and the natural beauties on earth. Achilles was pleasant to behold, but his beauty was illuminated by his virtuous actions. The pleasure that Heracles enjoyed was not sensuous, but was the spontaneous pleasure of a soul conditioned to delight in beautiful deeds, pursuits, and words. And so he went joyfully to the pyre, just as Socrates went joyfully to his death (§7).

ORATION 25

Ὅτι οἱ σύμφωνοι τοῖς ἔργοις λόγοι ἄριστοι

1. Ἦλθεν εἰς Ἕλληνας ἐκ τῆς Σκυθῶν γῆς τῶν ἐκεῖ βαρβάρων ἀνὴρ σοφὸς σοφίαν οὐ πολυρρήμονα οὐδὲ λάλον· ἀλλ᾽ ἦν αὐτῆς τὸ κεφάλαιον βίος ἀκριβὴς καὶ γνώμη ὑγιὴς καὶ λόγος βραχύς, εὔστοχος, ἐοικὼς οὐ πελταστῇ μισθοφόρῳ, ἀπροοράτως θέοντι, ἀλλ᾽ ὁπλίτῃ βάδην ἰόντι καὶ κινουμένῳ ἀσφαλῶς. ἐλθὼν δὲ Ἀθήναζε, ἐντυγχάνει αὐτόθι ὁπλίτῃ μὲν οὐδενί, πελτασταῖς δὲ πολλοῖς. καὶ τὸν μὲν τούτων δρόμον καὶ τὴν πτοίαν τοῦ παντὸς ἐδέησεν ὁ Ἀνάχαρσις ἐπαινέσαι, περιῄει δὲ τὴν Ἑλλάδα ἐν κύκλῳ, ποθῶν ἰδεῖν σοφίαν στάσιμον καὶ ἑδραίαν. καὶ εἰ μέν που καὶ ἄλλοθι ἐξεῦρεν, εἰπεῖν οὐκ ἔχω· εὗρε δ᾽ οὖν ἐν Χηναῖς, σμικρῷ καὶ ἀσθενεῖ πολίσματι, ἄνδρα ἀγαθόν· ὄνομα ἦν αὐτῷ Μύσων. ἀγαθὸς δὲ ἦν ἄρα ὁ Μύσων οἶκον οἰκῆσαι καλῶς καὶ γῆν τημελῆσαι δεξιῶς

---

[1] Anacharsis (early 6th c. BC), named below, famous for his pithy quips. *Or.* 17.4 provides an example.

[2] Peltasts were lightly armed mobile skirmishers, often mer-

ORATION 25

That words conforming to deeds are best

1. A wise man[1] once came to Greece from the land of Scythia. He was one of the barbarians in that country and his kind of wisdom was not long-winded or wordy. Indeed, at its core was a scrupulous life, sound judgment, and succinct speech that went straight to its target, like a hoplite marching steadfastly forward, not like a mercenary peltast rushing forward recklessly.[2] When he came to Athens, he found not a single hoplite there, but instead many peltasts. Since Anacharsis could by no means approve of their capriciousness and cowardice, he made a tour all around Greece, hoping to find wisdom that was stable and firm. Whether he found it anywhere else, I cannot say, but in the small, insignificant town of Chenae,[3] he did discover a good man, whose name was Myson.[4] Now Myson was good at managing his household well, tending his farm-

cenaries, who ran forward and cast their javelins into the opposing forces before retreating. Pl. *Tht*. 165d compares a peltast to a quibbler who ambushes arguments with countless objections.

[3] Of uncertain location, either in Laconia or Crete.

[4] Listed as one of the seven sages at Pl. *Prt*. 343a. Diog. Laert. 1.108 quotes him as saying, "Examine words by actions, not actions by words."

καὶ γάμου προστῆναι σωφρόνως καὶ παῖδα ἐκθρέψαι
γεννικῶς. καὶ ἐξήρκεσεν τῷ Σκύθῃ ξένῳ μηκέτι σοφίαν ζητεῖν λαλιστέραν, παρόντων ἔργων ἃ τότε
ἀκριβῶς ἅπαντα διεσκόπει. ἐπεὶ δὲ ἱκανῶς εἶχεν τῆς
θέας, λέγει πρὸς αὐτὸν ὁ Χηνεὺς Μύσων· "διὰ ταῦτά
τοι, ὦ Ἀνάχαρσι, καὶ σοφοὶ δοκοῦμεν οὐκ οἶδα ὅπως
ἀνθρώποις εἶναι· εἰ δὲ ἐγὼ σοφὸς ταῦτα ἐπιτηδεύων,
ποῖ ποτε οἰχήσεται φερόμενον τὸ μὴ σοφόν;" ἠγάσθη
μάλα τοῦ Ἕλληνος ξένου ὁ Ἀνάχαρσις τὴν ἀφθονίαν
τῶν ἔργων καὶ τὴν φειδὼ τῶν λόγων.

2. Ἦσαν δέ που καὶ οἱ Πυθαγόρου λόγοι ἐοικότες
τοῖς νόμοις, βραχεῖς καὶ ἐπίτομοι· τὰ δὲ ἔργα μακρὰ
καὶ διηνεκῆ, καὶ νύκτωρ καὶ μεθ' ἡμέραν μηδαμοῦ
τὴν ψυχὴν ἀνιέντα μηδὲ εἰς ῥαθυμίαν χαλῶντα.
ὥσπερ γὰρ ἐν ταῖς τῶν μελῶν ἁρμονίαις τὸ παραλει-
φθέν, κἂν σμικρὸν ᾖ, διαλύει τὸν κόσμον τοῦ μέλους,
οὕτω κἂν τῇ τοῦ βίου ἁρμονίᾳ, εἴπερ μὴ ἐκμελὴς ἡμῖν
ἔσται μηδὲ εἰκῇ διαπεραινόμενος, ὁμολογίαν εἶναι δεῖ
ἔργου καὶ λόγου, καὶ μήτε τὰ ἔργα εἰς ἀφάνειαν κομιδῇ ξυνεληλάσθαι, μήτε τοὺς λόγους ὑπὲρ τὰ ἔργα
χωρεῖν, ὥσπερ ἐξ ἀγγείου στενοῦ[1] ἀποχεομένους,
ἀλλ' ἑκάτερα ἑκατέροις συντεταγμένα ἰσομέτρητά τε
καὶ ἰσοχειλῆ εἶναι.

Ὅστις οὖν τῆς ἁρμονίας ταύτης ἐρᾷ καὶ ἐθέλει
ἠχεῖν τὸν τῶν ἔργων φθόγγον, οὗτος ἄν ποτε ἐπ' εὐ-

[1] ἐξ ἀγγείου στενοῦ R· ἐξ ἀγγείου ‹. . .› στενὸν Markland,
Dübner· ἐξ ἀγγείου ‹πλατέος εἰς› στενὸν coni. Koniaris

lands expertly, maintaining a chaste marriage, and raising his son in a noble fashion. His Scythian guest was content to discontinue his search for any wordier wisdom, when presented with these deeds which he was then examining in detail. When he was satisfied with his inspection, Myson of Chenae said to him: "It is because of this, O Anacharsis, that for some reason people consider me wise, but if these practices make me wise, then where will nonwisdom ever end up?" Anacharsis was greatly impressed with his Greek host's abundant deeds and thrifty words.

2. There were also some sayings of Pythagoras that were brief and succinct like laws,[5] but his deeds were extensive and continuous, and they would not allow his soul to relax or lapse into idleness either day or night. For just as any omitted element in the harmonies of songs, no matter how small, destroys the arrangement of the song, so too in the harmony of life, if ours is not to be out of tune and lived out haphazardly, our words and deeds must be in agreement. Deeds must not be reduced to utter oblivion,[6] nor must words wash over our deeds, as if spilling out of a narrow vessel,[7] but the two must be coordinated with each other so as to be of equal volume and measure.

Therefore, would anyone who loves this kind of harmony and wishes the voice of his deeds to resound, ever

[5] The ἀκούσματα, brief prescriptions for proper behavior. Cf. Diog. Laert. 8.34–35 and Iambl. *VP* 82–86 (= Pythagoras D 20 L-M).

[6] That is, with no words to memorialize them.

[7] That is, out of a vessel too narrow to admit the flow of words. The text and precise details of this comparison are uncertain.

γλωττία σεμνύνοιτο; πολλοῦ μοι δοκεῖ δεῖν. οὐδὲ γὰρ
τοὺς ταὼς ἡδίστους ὄντας ὀρνίθων ἰδεῖν μακαρίσαι
ἄν τις τοῦ κάλλους οὐδὲν αὐτοῖς εἰς εὐπτησίαν συντε-
λοῦντος, ἥπερ ἐστὶν ὀρνίθων ῥώμη· καὶ τῶν ἀηδόνων
τῆς ᾠδῆς ὅσα μὲν ἐς ἡδονὴν ἀκοῆς ἀποδεχόμεθα, τὸ
δὲ ἡμῖν τερπνὸν ἀσύμβολον ἐκείναις εἰς σωτηρίαν.

3. Ἀετοῦ κλάγξαντος ἢ λέοντος βρυχησαμένου
γνωρίσαι ἄν τις τῷ λυπηρῷ τῆς ἀκοῆς τὴν ῥώμην τοῦ
φθεγγομένου. εἰ μὴ φαυλότερον ἦχος ἀνδρὸς μηδὲ
ἀσθενέστερον ἐλέγξαι τὸ τοῦ λέγοντος ἦθος βρυχηθ-
μοῦ λέοντος καὶ ἀετῶν κλαγγῆς, ἆρα οὐκ ἄξιον ἐκ-
θηρᾶσθαι τῇ ἀκοῇ πότερον ἀηδὼν τὸ φθεγγόμενον,
γλῶττα δειλὴ καὶ ᾠδὴ ἐφήμερος, ἢ ἀετὸς ἤ τι ἄλλο
ζῷον ἄρρεν καὶ θυμοῦ μεστόν;

Ἀλλ' ὁ μὲν Ζώπυρος ἐκεῖνος δεινὸς ἦν τῇ προσ-
βολῇ τῶν ὀφθαλμῶν, τοῖς τοῦ σώματος τύποις ἐντυγ-
χάνων, γνωρίζειν τὸ ἦθος καὶ καταμαντεύεσθαι τῆς
ψυχῆς διὰ τῶν ὁρωμένων, μαντείαν ἀσαφῆ· τίς γὰρ
ἐπιμιξία πρὸς ὁμοιότητα ψυχῆς καὶ σώματος; εἰ δ'
ἔστι μαντείαν ἐπὶ ψυχῇ θέσθαι οὐ διὰ ἀμυδρῶν οὐδὲ
ἀσθενῶν συμβόλων, τοῖς μὲν ὀφθαλμοῖς παραχωρη-
τέον τὴν χρωμάτων τε καὶ σχημάτων καὶ τῆς ἐν
τούτοις ἡδονῆς καὶ ἀηδίας ὁμιλίαν, τῇ δὲ ἀκοῇ ἐξ-
ιχνευτέον τὸ τῆς ψυχῆς ἦθος, οὐ κατὰ τοὺς τῶν πολ-

pride himself on a mellifluous tongue? Far from it, in my opinion. For example, peacocks are the most pleasant birds to look at, but no one would consider them blessed for a beauty that contributes nothing to their ability to fly, which is the strength that birds possess. Then too we greatly enjoy hearing the song of nightingales, but what we find pleasing contributes nothing to their survival.

3. But when an eagle shrieks or a lion roars, one can recognize from the pain it gives the ear the strength of the animal making it. So, if the sound of a man's voice is no weaker or less able to reveal the speaker's character than the roar of a lion or the shriek of eagles, would it not be worthwhile to use our sense of hearing to ascertain whether a nightingale, whose voice is timorous and song is fleeting, is making the sound, or an eagle, or some other powerful animal full of mettle?

Now famous Zopyrus[8] had the ability, simply by casting his eyes on someone and observing the features of his body, to recognize his character and divine his soul's nature from what he observed. What an imprecise kind of divination! For what is the bond of similarity between soul and body? But if it is possible to divine the nature of a soul without recourse to such faint and tenuous signs, then we should let the eyes deal with colors and shapes and with the pleasant and unpleasant qualities they possess, and use our sense of hearing to seek out the character of the soul. We must not, however, follow the thinking of the masses,

[8] A fifth-century BC physiognomist from Syria, notorious for his incorrect diagnoses of Socrates. Cf. Cic. *Tusc.* 4.80 and esp. *Fat.* 10–11, where Zopyrus was said to declare that Socrates was addicted to women, at which Alcibiades burst out laughing.

λῶν λογισμοὺς οἷς ἀπόχρη πρὸς ἔπαινον λόγου
γλῶττα εὔτροχος ἢ ὀνομάτων δρόμος ἢ ῥήματα Ἀττικὰ ἢ περίοδοι εὐκαμπεῖς ἢ ἁρμονία ὑγρά· τὰ δ'
ἐστὶν πάντα κατὰ τὸν ἐν Διονύσου ποιητήν,

ἐπιφυλλίδες . . . καὶ στωμύλματα,
χελιδόνων μουσεῖα, λωβηταὶ τέχνης.

4. "Ποῖον οὖν ἐστιν τὸ ἐν λόγοις καλόν;" φαίη ἄν
τις. μήπω με, ὦ τάν, ἔρῃ· ὄψει γὰρ αὐτὸς ἐπειδὰν
ἰδεῖν δυνηθῇς. οὐδὲ γὰρ τῷ Κιμμερίῳ διηγήσασθαι
δύναταί τις τὸ τοῦ ἡλίου κάλλος, οὐδὲ τῷ ἠπειρώτῃ
τὴν θάλατταν, οὐδ' Ἐπικούρῳ τὸν θεόν· οὐ γὰρ δι'
ἀγγέλων ἡ ἱστορία ἔρχεται, ἀλλ' ἐπιστήμης πρὸς
ταῦτα δεῖ· μέχρι δὲ ἄπεστι τὸ εἰδέναι, ἀνάγκη πλανᾶ-
σθαι καὶ τὰς κρίσεις.

Καὶ γὰρ τῶν ἐκ γῆς φυομένων παντοδαπὸς μὲν
θεατὴς ὁδοιπόρος, ὁ δὲ γεωργός, ὑγιής· ὁ μὲν ἄνθος
ἐπαινεῖ φυτῷ, ὁ δὲ μέγεθος ἢ σκιάν, ὁ δὲ χρόαν· τῷ
δὲ γεωργῷ ὁ καρπὸς τὸν ἔπαινον μετὰ τῆς χρείας
ἔχει. εἰ μὲν δή τις καθ' ὁδοιπόρον πλησιάζει τῷ λόγῳ,
οὐ νεμεσῶ τῆς ἡδονῆς παρατρέχοντι ἐπαινεῖν· εἰ δὲ
κατὰ τοὺς γεωργοὺς τάττεται, οὐκ ἀνέχομαι τῶν
ἐπαίνων πρὶν ἄν μοι καὶ τὴν χρείαν τῶν ἐπαινουμένων
φράσῃ.

5. Λέγε, τίνας εἶδες καρποὺς ἐν τῷ λόγῳ; τίνας

---

9 Ar. *Ran.* 92–93, Dionysus speaking (trans. Henderson).

whose only requirements for praiseworthy discourse are a
glib tongue, a flood of words, Attic diction, well-rounded
periods, and flowing composition—all of which are, in the
words of the poet in the theater of Dionysus,

> castoffs . . . empty chatter,
> choirs of swallows, wreckers of their art.[9]

4. Someone might ask, "Then what *does* constitute
beauty in discourses?" Do not ask me yet, my friend, for
you will see it for yourself when you are able to see it. No
one is able to describe the beauty of the sun to a Cimme-
rian,[10] or the sea to an inland dweller, or god to Epicurus,
because comprehension of such things does not come
through reports of others, but requires firsthand knowledge. As long as this knowledge is lacking, judgments necessarily go awry.

For example, all kinds of passersby observe plants
growing in a field, but only the farmer's view is sound. One
traveler praises a plant for its blossoms, another for its size
or for the shade it provides, and another for its color, but
for the farmer it is its fruit that wins his praise for its usefulness. Now if anyone approaches discourse like such a
traveler, I do not begrudge him praising it for its pleasantness as he passes by, but if he is one of those farmers, I
will not abide his praise until he also apprises me of the
usefulness of what he is praising.

5. Tell me, what fruits have you seen in this discourse?
Which ones have you plucked and what is their condition?

---

[10] Mythical people living in perpetual darkness described at
Od. 11.14–19.

ἔλαβες; πῶς ἔχοντας; ἐπειράθης, ἐξήτασας, εἰ τελεσι-
ουργοὶ καὶ γόνιμοι ἑτέρων καρπῶν; ἐξέφυσέ τί σοι ἡ
ψυχὴ ἀπ' αὐτῶν χρηστὸν καὶ ἔγκαρπον; ἢ ὄγχνη μὲν
ἐπὶ ὄγχνῃ γηράσκει καὶ ἐπὶ μήλῳ μῆλον, καὶ στα-
φυλὴ σταφυλῇ ἐπιφύεται καὶ σῦκον σύκῳ, λόγου δὲ
ἄρα ἐφήμερος μὲν ἡ γένεσις, ἄσπερμος δὲ ὁ καρπὸς
καὶ οὐ τρόφιμος οὐδὲ ἀνακιρνάμενος τῇ ψυχῇ,

ἀλλά τέ μιν καθύπερθεν ἐπιρρεῖ ἠΰτ' ἔλαιον;

ταύτην μοι διήγησαι τὴν γεωργίαν, τοὺς δὲ ἐπαίνους
ἔα. ἐὰν γὰρ ἀφέλῃς αὐτῶν τὴν χρείαν, ὑποπτεύω τὴν
αἰτίαν, καὶ τὸν ἐπαινέτην ἐλεῶ καὶ τὸν ἔπαινον μέμ-
φομαι. τοῦτον τὸν ἔπαινον φθέγγεται τὰ μέρη τῆς
ψυχῆς τὰ ἀκόλαστα, τὰ κρίνειν ἀσθενῆ, τὰ ἀπατᾶ-
σθαι πεφυκότα·

οὐ νέμεσις Τρῶας καὶ εὐκνήμιδας Ἀχαιοὺς
τοιῇδ' ἀμφὶ γυναικὶ πολὺν χρόνον ἄλγεα
πάσχειν.

ὁρᾷς τοῦ ἐπαίνου τὴν μοχθηρίαν, ἀντικαταλλασσομέ-
νου γύναιον ἓν καὶ τὴν ἀπ' αὐτοῦ ἡδονὴν Ἑλληνικῶν
καὶ Τρωικῶν κακῶν;

Ἔστι κἀνταῦθα ἐπαινέτης τοιοῦτος, ἐπειδάν τις
ἐντυχὼν ἀκολάστῳ λόγῳ, τὸ μὲν ἀπατηλὸν αὐτοῦ μὴ
γνωρίσῃ, τὸ δὲ ἡδὺ στέρξῃ, κατὰ βραχὺ ὑποφερόμε-

---

11 Adapted from *Od.* 7.120–21, describing the perennial
flourishing of Alcinous' gardens, also cited at *Or.* 14.1.

Have you tested and examined them to see if they are ripe and capable of producing more fruit? Has your soul sprouted anything good and fruitful from them? Or when pear grows ripe upon pear, and apple upon apple; and grape is generated upon grape, and fig upon fig,[11] is then the generation of discourse to be short-lived, and its fruit to produce no seed, provide no nourishment, and not mingle with the soul,

> but flow over its surface like olive oil?[12]

Describe for me that kind of farming and forgo your words of praise, for if you exclude usefulness from them, then I find their motivation suspicious, feel sorry for the praiser, and find fault with his praise, because that is the sort of praise given voice by the parts of the soul that are licentious, weak at making sound judgments, and naturally susceptible to being deceived.

> I do not blame the Trojans and well-greaved
>   Achaeans
> for suffering so long over a woman like her.[13]

Do you see the depravity of such praise that takes one woman and the pleasure she provides in exchange for the sufferings of the Greeks and Trojans?

In our own time as well that kind of praiser exists, whenever he comes across licentious speech and does not recognize its deception. He cherishes its sweetness and is

---

[12] *Il.* 2.754, said of Titaressus flowing over Peneius without mixing its waters.

[13] *Il.* 3.156–57, spoken by a Trojan elder about Helen.

νος ταῖς καθ᾽ ἡμέραν ἡδοναῖς ἀψοφητί, ὥσπερ τῶν
πλεόντων οἱ πνευμάτων μὲν ἐξ οὐρίας πρὸς τὸν ἀληθῆ
δρόμον οὐ τυχόντες, ῥεύματι δὲ γαληνῷ δι᾽ ἀκυμάν-
του τῆς θαλάττης εἰς ἠϊόνας ἐρήμους ἢ ῥαχίας δυσ-
χερεῖς ἐκπεπτωκότες· μετὰ τοῦτο προσηνέχθη λαθὼν
ἀμαθίᾳ καὶ μετὰ τοῦτο φιληδονίᾳ, πάσης ἠϊόνος ἐρη-
μοτέροις χωρίοις καὶ πάσης ῥαχίας δυσχερεστέροις,
ἀγαπῶν τὴν πλάνην καὶ χαίρων τῇ ψυχαγωγίᾳ,
ὥσπερ οἱ πυρέττοντες, ἐμπιπλάμενοι ποτοῦ καὶ σιτίων παρὰ τοὺς τῆς τέχνης νόμους· παρατιθέντες γὰρ
κακὸν κακῷ, νόσῳ πόνους, αἱροῦνται ἡδόμενοι νοσεῖν
μᾶλλον ἢ πονοῦντες ὑγιασθῆναι.

Καί τις ἤδη ἰατρὸς εὐμήχανος ἀνεκέρασεν βρα-
χεῖαν ἡδονὴν τῷ ἀλγεινῷ τῆς ἰάσεως· ποριστὴς δὲ
ἡδονῆς καὶ παντοίας ἡδονῆς οὔτε ὁ Ἀσκληπιὸς οὔτε
οἱ Ἀσκληπιάδαι, ἀλλ᾽ ὀψοποιῶν τὸ ἔργον. οὐδὲν δὲ
σεμνότερον ἀκόλαστος λόγος τῶν τῆς γαστρὸς κολα-
κευμάτων· ἐὰν γὰρ τούτου ἀφέλῃς μὲν τὸ ὠφελοῦν,
τερπνὸν δὲ προσθῇς ἰταμὸν καὶ ἄκρατον, ἰσοτιμίαν
καὶ ἰσηγορίαν χειροτονεῖς λόγου πρὸς τὰ αἰσχρὰ
πάντα, ὅσα δι᾽ αἰσθήσεων ἐπὶ ψυχὴν ἔρχεται ὑφ᾽ ἡδονῆς παραπεμπόμενα.

6. Ἀλλὰ τοὺς μὲν ὀψοποιοὺς τούτους τοῖς συμπο-
σίοις ἐῶμεν, καὶ γαστρὸς καὶ ἀκοῆς ὑπηρέτας πονη-
ρούς· ἡμῖν δὲ δεῖ λόγου ὀρθοῦ καὶ διανεστηκότος,
μέγα βοῶντος, καὶ τὰς ψυχὰς αὐτῷ συνεπαίροντος

gradually and silently carried away by its pleasures, day
after day, just like passengers on a ship who fail to secure
favoring winds that lead them on a true course, but instead
are carried on a gentle current over a waveless sea and
washed up on deserted shores and dangerous reefs. But
then, without realizing it, the praiser is borne first by his
ignorance and then by his love of pleasure to places more
desolate than any shore and more dangerous than any reef,
all the while happy to drift and enjoy the entertainment,[14]
just like patients with a fever who stuff themselves with
food and drink against the rules of medicine. By equating
one bad thing with another, namely physical exertion with
sickness, they prefer to have pleasure when sick, rather
than to make an effort to get well.

And many an enterprising doctor eases the pain of his
cure by adding a small amount of pleasure, but providing
pleasure, especially pleasure of all sorts, is not the job of
Asclepius or of the Asclepiadae, but of chefs.[15] And licentious discourse is not one bit more respectable than ap-
petizers for the belly, for if you deprive discourse of its
benefit and add unrestrained and unalloyed pleasure, then
you are granting it the privilege and freedom to advocate
all the shameful things that enter the soul through the
senses, escorted there by pleasure.

6. So let us leave those chefs to their symposia, the
debased servants of the belly and of the ears. What we
need is discourse that stands up straight and tall and
shouts out loud and clear, that raises our souls with it up

[14] Cf. *Or*. 30.3 for the Epicurean pleasure ship that ends in
shipwreck.

[15] For cookery as perverse flattery of medicine, cf. *Or*. 14.8.

ὑπὲρ τὴν γῆν ἄνω καὶ ὅσα περὶ γῆν παθήματα ἡδονῶν καὶ ἐπιθυμημάτων καὶ φιλοτιμιῶν καὶ ἐρώτων καὶ
ὀργῆς καὶ λύπης καὶ μέθης ἐχόμενα· ὧν συμπάντων
κρείττονα χρὴ γενέσθαι τὸν τῷ φιλοσόφῳ λόγῳ συν-
ανιστάμενον ῥήτορα ἀληθῆ, οὐκ ἀργὸν οὐδὲ ἐκλελυμένον οὐδ' ἐπίχριστον κατὰ τὴν τέχνην, οὐδὲ ἐν δικαστηρίῳ μόνον ἐπ' ἀμφιβόλῳ ἐπικουρίᾳ τεταγμένον,
ἀλλὰ πανταχοῦ καὶ ἐν ἅπαντι ἐξεταζόμενον, ἐν μὲν
ἐκκλησίαις σύμβουλον φρόνιμον, ἐν δὲ δικαστηρίοις
ἀγωνιστὴν δίκαιον, ἐν δὲ πανηγύρεσιν ἀγωνιστὴν
σώφρονα, ἐν δὲ παιδείᾳ διδάσκαλον ἐπιστήμονα· οὐ
περὶ Θεμιστοκλέους μόνον τοῦ μηκέτι ὄντος, οὐδ' ἐπ'[2]
Ἀθηναίοις τοῖς τότε, οὐδ' ὑπὲρ ἀριστέως τοῦ μηδαμοῦ, οὐδὲ κατὰ μοιχοῦ λέγοντα μοιχὸν ὄντα, οὐδὲ
κατὰ ὑβριστοῦ ὑβριστὴν ὄντα, ἀλλ' ἀπηλλαγμένον
τῶν παθῶν τούτων, ἵνα γένηται κατήγορος ἀδικη-
μάτων ἀληθής. τοιοῦτος ἐξ ἀγαθῆς παλαίστρας ἀγωνιστὴς γίγνεται, λόγων μεστὸς ἀκολακεύτων καὶ
ἠσκημένων ὑγιῶς καὶ δυναμένων ἄγειν πειθοῖ καὶ βίᾳ
ἐκπληκτικῇ τὸ πλησιάζον πᾶν.

7. Εἰ δὲ καὶ ἡδονῆς πρὸς τὴν ἀγωγὴν ταύτην δεη-
σόμεθα, †καὶ τυράννου†[3] δότω μοί τις ἡδονήν, οἵαν

[2] ἐπ' Markland, Trapp: ἐν R
[3] obel. Trapp: del. Davies: καὶ Τυρταίου Markland, Dübner

above the earth and beyond all the earthly suffering that ensues from pleasure, desire, ambition, lust, anger, grief, and drunkenness. All these the true orator who allies himself with philosophical discourse must rise above. He must not be some lazy, feeble, meretricious practitioner of his art, whose only job is to provide indiscriminate aid in a courtroom.[16] No, he must prove himself everywhere and on every occasion to be a judicious adviser in assemblies, a just contender in law courts, a decorous performer at panegyric festivals,[17] and a knowledgeable teacher in the classroom. He should not speak only of long-dead Themistocles, or about the Athenians of that time,[18] or about some nonexistent hero; he should not denounce an adulterer, being one himself, or denounce an abuser, being one himself, but should be free of all such passions, so that he may become a true denouncer of injustices. That is the kind of competitor who comes from a good palaestra;[19] he is filled with discourses that are free of flattery, made healthy by training, and able to win over every audience within hearing by their persuasion and powerful inspiration.[20]

7. But if we shall also need pleasure to aid in this endeavor, then let me have the kind of pleasure produced by

[16] Cf. *Or.* 22.3 for perverse courtroom discourse that pleads both just and unjust causes.   [17] Panegyric orations were stock-in-trade for rhetoricians from Gorgias and Isocrates to Dio Chrysostom and Aelius Aristides.   [18] Maximus presumably differentiates his own frequent use of such examples from their use in declamatory exercises.   [19] That is, one trained in philosophical discourse.   [20] Cf. *Or.* 1.7–8 for a similar description of ideal philosophical discourse that is adaptable to many situations.

καὶ ἐπὶ σάλπιγγος ἁρμονίᾳ ἐν μέσοις τοῖς ὁπλίταις
τεταγμένης καὶ ἐξορμώσης τὰς ψυχὰς τῷ μέλει· τοιαύτης δέομαι ἡδονῆς λόγου, ἣ φυλάξει μὲν αὐτοῦ τὸ
μέγεθος, οὐ προσθήσει δὲ τὴν αἰσχύνην· τοιαύτης
δέομαι ἡδονῆς, ἣ οὐκ ἀπαξιώσει ἡ ἀρετὴ ὁπαδὸν
αὐτῇ γίνεσθαι. ἀνάγκη γὰρ παντὶ τῷ φύσει καλῷ
συντετάχθαι χάριτας καὶ ὥραν καὶ πόθον καὶ εὐφροσύνην καὶ πάντα δὴ τὰ τερπνὰ ὀνόματα. οὕτω καὶ ὁ
οὐρανὸς οὐ καλὸς μόνον, ἀλλὰ καὶ ἥδιστον θεαμάτων,
καὶ θάλαττα πλεομένη καὶ λήϊα καρποτρόφα καὶ
ὄρη δενδροτρόφα καὶ λειμῶνες ἀνθοῦντες καὶ νάματα
ῥέοντα.

Ἥδιστον ἦν θέαμα ὁ Ἀχιλλεύς (πῶς δὲ οὐκ ἔμελ-
λεν;), ⟨ἀλλ᾽⟩[4] οὐ διὰ τὴν ξάνθην κόμην· καὶ γὰρ ὁ
Εὔφορβος εὐκόμης ἦν, τῷ δὲ Ἀχιλλεῖ τὸ καλὸν ἥδιστον ἦν ὑπὸ τῆς ἀρετῆς ἐξαπτόμενον. ἥδιστον ἐν πο-
ταμοῖς θέαμα ὁ Νεῖλος, ἀλλ᾽ οὐ δι᾽ ἀφθονίαν ὕδατος·
καὶ γὰρ Ἴστρος εὔρους· ἀλλὰ ὁ Ἴστρος οὐ γόνιμος, ὁ δὲ Νεῖλος γόνιμος. ἥδιστον θέαμα ὁ Ζεύς, ἀλλ᾽
οὐ τολμῶ παραπεμψάμενος τὴν ἀρετὴν τοῦ θεοῦ ἡδονὴν αὐτῷ ἐπιφημίσαι. ἐγὼ καὶ τῶν Φειδίου ἀγαλ-
μάτων αἰσθάνομαι μὲν τῆς ἡδονῆς, ἐπαινῶ δὲ τὴν
τέχνην· καὶ τῆς Ὁμήρου ᾠδῆς συνίημι μὲν τῆς ἡδονῆς, ἀλλ᾽ ἐκ τῶν σεμνοτέρων αὐτὴν ἐπαινῶ.

Ἀλλ᾽ οὐδὲ τὸν Ἡρακλέα ἔγωγε ἡγοῦμαι ἄγευστον

---

[4] suppl. Renehan, Trapp

the strains of a trumpet stationed in the midst of the hoplites that rouses their souls with its notes. I need the kind of pleasure in a discourse that will preserve its grandeur, but not add anything shameful. I need the kind of pleasure that Virtue will not deem unworthy to be her companion. For it is necessary that charm, beauty, desire, joy, and indeed everything pleasant you can name, should go together with all that is naturally beautiful. Thus the heavens are not only beautiful, but also the most pleasant of sights, along with a sea full of ships, rich fields of grain, tree-covered mountains, flowering meadows, and flowing streams.

Achilles was a most pleasing sight to behold (how could he not be?), but not because of his golden hair, for Euphorbus too had lovely hair.[21] But in Achilles' case his beauty was at its most pleasing when illuminated by his virtue. Among rivers the Nile is most pleasing to see, but not because of the volume of its water, for the Ister also has an abundant flow; it is because the Nile is fertile, whereas the Ister is not. Zeus is most pleasant to behold, but I do not dare to dismiss the god's virtue when ascribing pleasure to him. I also feel the pleasure that Phidias' statues inspire, but it is their artistry that wins my praise. I understand the pleasure of Homer's poetry, but I praise it for its more venerable qualities.[22]

I do not believe that even Heracles lived his entire life

[21] A Trojan slain by Menelaus; cf. *Il.* 17.52: "his hair, like unto the Graces, was drenched with blood." He is also cited at *Or.* 10.2 as a former soul of Pythagoras.

[22] These qualities are philosophical (*Or.* 4.8), inspirational (*Or.* 17.4), and ethical (*Or.* 26.8–9).

καὶ ἀμέτοχον ἡδονῆς διαβιῶναι—οὐ πείθομαι παντάπασι τῷ Προδίκῳ—ἀλλ᾿ εἰσὶν γὰρ καὶ ἀνδρὸς ἡδοναὶ
παραμυθούμεναι τοὺς δι᾿ ἀρετῆς πόνους, οὐ διὰ σαρκῶν οὐδέ γε δι᾿ αἰσθήσεων ἐπίρρυτοι, ἀλλ᾿ αὐτοφυεῖς
τινες καὶ ἔνδοθεν διανιστάμεναι, ἐθιζομένης τῆς ψυχῆς χαίρειν τοῖς καλοῖς καὶ ἔργοις καὶ ἐπιτηδεύμασιν
καὶ λόγοις. οὕτω καὶ ὁ Ἡρακλῆς ἔχαιρεν ἐπὶ τὸ πῦρ
ἰών, καὶ Σωκράτης ἔχαιρεν ἐν τῷ δεσμωτηρίῳ μένων
καὶ πειθόμενος τῷ νόμῳ. παραβάλλωμεν τὴν Σωκράτους κύλικα ἐκείνην τῇ Ἀλκιβιάδου· πότερος
αὐτῶν ἔπινεν ἀλυπότερον, Ἀλκιβιάδης τὸν οἶνον ἢ τὸ
φάρμακον Σωκράτης;

ORATION 25

without tasting and experiencing pleasure—here I do not
wholly agree with Prodicus[23]—for there are in fact manly
pleasures that can soothe the toils of virtue, not ones that
flow in through the flesh or indeed through the senses, but
instead certain spontaneous ones that spring up within us,
when the soul is conditioned to take delight in beautiful
deeds, pursuits, and words. That is why Heracles was joyful on his way to the pyre, and why Socrates was joyful
when he remained in prison and obeyed the law. Let
us compare Socrates' famous cup to that of Alcibiades.
Which one drank with less distress—Alcibiades his wine
or Socrates his poison?

[23] Prodicus' fable of Heracles rejecting pleasure and choosing
toilsome virtue is narrated at Xen. *Mem.* 2.1.21–34 and refash-
ioned in *Or.* 14.1–2.

ORATION 26

INTRODUCTION

Maximus consistently portrays Homer as a philosopher *avant la lettre*, whose thought is expressed in allegories (*ainigmata*; see *Orr.* 4.3–9 and 17.4). Here he goes a step further and traces Plato's very concepts to Homer. The oration opens with an impressive survey of Homer's wide-ranging subject matter, which is attributed to the flight of his soul through the universe, a frequent trope in the *Orations*. Philosophy is defined as the knowledge of human and divine matters and the source of human virtue and reason (§1). In early times, this philosophy was cloaked in rituals and stories, but with the advent of the sophists, philosophy was exposed as naked doctrines, open to everyone and subject to warring schools; what was noble (*to kalon*) in Homer and Hesiod was disregarded and the Good (*to agathon*) was lost from view (§2). Although Plato banished Homer from his ideal polis, he nonetheless shared Homer's conceptions, and in that regard was more akin to Homer than to Socrates (§3). When Homer took up philosophy, he rendered it in a form of Greek verse that was comprehensible to all Greeks and could be universally enjoyed. Unlike Hesiod, who composed works on separate subjects, he combined all his experience into narratives about Troy and Odysseus, which contain a harmonious

ORATION 26

blending of theology, politics, and ethics (§4). Like the painters Polygnotus and Zeuxis, Homer blended artistry with examples of virtuous behavior. Even Socrates modeled his interactions with his contemporaries on Odysseus' treatment of his fellow soldiers in the *Iliad* (§5). A few examples illustrate Homer's treatment of virtue and vice (§6). A comparison of Homeric passages with Plato's single statement "great Zeus in heaven" shows that they share the same general concept of the gods (§7). Allegorical interpretations reveal philosophical principles in Homer: Athena represents virtue; Aphrodite, love; Hephaestus, craftsmanship; and so on. Even the war between elements is implicit in the battle between Hephaestus (fire) and the river Xanthus (§8). Politics and ethics are on display in the contrast between life in Phaeacia and that in Ithaca. The oration concludes with Odysseus' virtuous qualities that rescue him from desperate situations and render him "like the gods," a state of likeness to god (*homoiōsis theōi*) that Plato believed to constitute human happiness (§9).

ORATION 26

Εἰ ἔστιν καθ᾽ Ὅμηρον αἵρεσις

1. Βούλομαι καθ᾽ Ὅμηρον αὐτὸν παρακαλέσαι ἐπὶ τὸν λόγον—τίνα μέντοι θεῶν; ἢ τὴν αὐτὴν ἐκείνῳ, τὴν Καλλιόπην;

> ἄνδρα μοι ἔννεπε, Μοῦσα, πολύτροπον, ὃς μάλα πολλὰ
> πλάγχθη,

οὐ γῆν ἄξενον ἐπιπορευόμενος, οὐδὲ θάλατταν χαλεπὴν περαιούμενος, οὐδὲ ἀνθρώποις ἀγρίοις συμφερόμενος· ἀλλὰ ταῦτα μὲν αὐτῷ οἱ μῦθοι ἔχουσιν, αὐτὸς δὲ τῇ ψυχῇ, κούφῳ χρήματι καὶ πολυπλανεστέρῳ τῶν σωμάτων, πανταχοῦ περιεφέρετο, πάντα ἐπεσκόπει, ὅσα οὐρανοῦ κινήματα, ὅσα γῆς παθήματα, θεῶν βουλάς, ἀνθρώπων φύσεις, ἡλίου φῶς, ἄστρων χορόν, γενέσεις ζῴων, ἀναχύσεις θαλάττης, ποταμῶν ἐκβολάς, ἀέρων μεταβολάς, τὰ πολιτικά, τὰ οἰκονομικά,

---

[1] Homer never names his Muse, whom Maximus consistently calls Calliope. Pl. *Phdr.* 259d associates Calliope (and Urania) with philosophy.   [2] *Od.* 1.1–2.   [3] That is, Odysseus.

84

ORATION 26

Whether there is a Homeric school of philosophy

1. Like Homer himself, I wish to summon a god to aid me with my discourse, but which god is it to be? Is it the same one he summoned, namely Calliope?[1]

Tell me, Muse, of the man of many ways, who
wandered far and wide,[2]

but I do not mean that man[3] who traveled through foreign lands, and crossed stormy seas, and engaged with savage men. No, that is what Homer's stories contain, but it was by means of his soul, a light thing able to journey far more widely than physical bodies, that he himself traveled everywhere and observed everything[4]—all the movements of the heavens, all the events on earth, the councils of the gods, the various natures of men, the light of the sun, the chorus of stars, the births of animals, the inundations of the sea, the outflows of rivers, changes of climates, politi-

---

[4] The motif of the soul's flight occurs at *Orr.* 9.6 (of the soul becoming a *daimōn* at death), 10.2–3 and 38.3 (of Aristeas' soul), 10.9 (of the soul at death), 11.10 (of the soul's intellect), and 16.6 (of the philosopher's soul). There is also the flight of the soul produced by reading historical narrative at *Or.* 22.5.

τὰ πολεμικά, τὰ εἰρηνικά, τὰ γαμήλια, τὰ γεωργικά,
τὰ ἱππικά, τὰ ναυτικά, τέχνας παντοίας, φωνὰς ποι-
κίλας, ἤθη[1] παντοδαπά, ὀλοφυρομένους, ἡδομένους,
πενθοῦντας, γελῶντας, πολεμοῦντας, ὀργιζομένους,
εὐωχουμένους, πλέοντας· ὥστε ἔγωγε εἰς τὰς Ὁμήρου
φωνὰς ἐμπεσὼν οὐκ ἔχω παρ᾽ ἐμαυτοῦ τὸν ἄνδρα
ἐπαινέσαι, ἀλλὰ κἀνταῦθα δεήσομαι αὐτοῦ ἐπιδοῦναί
μοι τῶν ἐπῶν, ἵνα μὴ διαφθείρω τὸν ἔπαινον ψιλῷ
λόγῳ.

ἔξοχα δή σε βροτῶν, ὦ Ὅμηρ᾽, αἰνίζομ᾽
    ἁπάντων,
ἢ σέ γε Μοῦσα δίδαξε, Διὸς παῖς, ἢ σέ γ᾽
    Ἀπόλλων.

τὰ δὲ Μουσῶν καὶ Ἀπόλλωνος διδάγματα οὐδὲ τὴν
ἀρχὴν θέμις ἄλλο τι ὑπολαβεῖν ἢ ἀφ᾽ ὧν ψυχὴ εἰς
κόσμον καθίσταται· τοῦτο δὲ τί ἂν εἴη ἄλλο ἢ φιλοσοφία; ταύτην δὲ τί ἄλλο ὑποληψόμεθα ἢ ἐπιστήμην
ἀκριβῆ θείων τε πέρι καὶ ἀνθρωπίνων, χορηγὸν ἀρετῆς καὶ λογισμῶν καλῶν καὶ ἁρμονίας βίου καὶ ἐπιτηδευμάτων δεξιῶν;

2. Τῆς δὲ ἐπιστήμης ταύτης τὸ κεφάλαιον τέως μὲν
παντοδαποῖς περιβεβλημένον σχήμασιν μετεχειρί-
ζετο τὰς τῶν ἐντυγχανόντων ψυχὰς διδασκαλίαις
ἀλύποις, τῶν μὲν τελετὰς καὶ ὀργιασμούς τινας ἐπιφημισάντων τοῖς αὑτῶν λόγοις, τῶν δὲ μύθους, τῶν

---

[1] ἤθη Trapp: εἴδη R

cal affairs, household management, war, peace, marriage, farming, horsemanship, navigation, arts and skills of every kind, various languages, customs of every sort, men lamenting, rejoicing, mourning, laughing, fighting, becoming angry, enjoying themselves, and sailing. As a result, whenever I encounter Homer's poems, I am incapable of praising the man all on my own, so once again I shall need him to lend me some of his verses, lest I spoil my praise by speaking in prose:

> O Homer, truly I praise you above all mortals;
> either the Muse, daughter of Zeus, taught you, or
>   Apollo.[5]

It is fundamentally wrong to suppose that the teachings of the Muses and Apollo are anything other than a means to bring order to the soul. And what else could that be but philosophy? And what shall we suppose philosophy to be other than an accurate knowledge of divine and human matters, the source of virtue and noble powers of reason and a harmonious life and refined pursuits?[6]

2. In earlier times the essence of this knowledge clothed itself in all sorts of guises and guided the souls of those encountering it through teachings that were agreeable. Some presented their discourses in the form of rites and rituals, others in myths, others in music, and still

[5] *Od.* 8.487–88, substituting Homer for Demodocus, whom Odysseus was praising.

[6] Trapp translates ἐπιτηδευμάτων δεξιῶν as "sophisticated habits," Heinsius et al. as "moderate behavior" (*mores . . . temperatos*).

δὲ μουσικήν, τῶν δὲ καὶ μαντικήν. καὶ κοινὸν μὲν ἦν
ἅπασιν τὸ ὠφελοῦν, ἴδιον δὲ ⟨ἑκάστῳ⟩² τὸ σχῆμα τοῦ
λόγου. χρόνῳ δὲ ὕστερον ὑπὸ σοφίας οἱ ἄνθρωποι
νεανιευόμενοι, ἀποκαλύψαντες ταυτὶ τὰ τοῦ λόγου
προκαλύμματα, ἀπέφηναν φιλοσοφίαν γυμνὴν καὶ
ἐξωνειδισμένην καὶ πάγκοινον καὶ πρόχειρον εἰς συν-
ουσίαν παντί τῳ, ὄνομα μόνον ἔργου καλοῦ πλανώμε-
νον ἐν δυστήνοις σοφίσμασιν.

Τοιγαροῦν τὰ μὲν Ὁμήρου καὶ Ἡσιόδου ἔπη καὶ
πᾶσα ἡ παλαιὰ μοῦσα ἐκείνη καὶ ἔνθεος μύθου χώραν
ἔχει, καὶ ἀγαπᾶται αὐτῶν ἡ ἱστορία μόνον καὶ τὸ
προσηνὲς τῶν ἐπῶν καὶ τὸ εὐανθὲς τῆς ἁρμονίας, ὡς
αὐλήματα, ὡς κιθαρίσματα, παρορᾶται δὲ τὸ ἐν αὐτοῖς καλὸν καὶ ἀποχειροτονεῖται τῆς ἀρετῆς. καὶ
Ὅμηρος μὲν ἀποκηρύττεται φιλοσοφίας, ὁ ἡγεμὼν
τοῦ γένους· ἀφ' οὗ δὲ τὰ ἐκ Θρᾴκης καὶ Κιλικίας σο-
φίσματα εἰς τὴν Ἑλλάδα παρέδυ καὶ ἡ Ἐπικούρου
ἄτομος καὶ τὸ Ἡρακλείτου πῦρ καὶ τὸ Θαλοῦ ὕδωρ
καὶ τὸ Ἀναξιμένους πνεῦμα καὶ τὸ Ἐμπεδοκλέους
νεῖκος καὶ ὁ Διογένους πίθος, καὶ τὰ πολλὰ τῶν φιλοσόφων στρατόπεδα ἀντιτεταγμένα ἀλλήλοις καὶ
ἀντιπαιωνίζοντα, λόγων μὲν πάντα μεστὰ καὶ ψιθυ-
ρισμάτων, σοφιστῶν σοφισταῖς συμπιπτόντων, ἔργου δὲ ἐρημία δεινή· καὶ τὸ θρυλούμενον τοῦτο τὸ
ἀγαθόν, ὑπὲρ οὗ διέστηκεν καὶ διεστασίασται τὸ Ἑλ-
ληνικόν, οὐδεὶς ὁρᾷ.

² suppl. Trapp: ⟨ἑκάστοις⟩ Reiske

others in prophecy. Common to all of them was the benefit they provided; peculiar to each was the form their discourse took. In later times, however, when men ran wild
with their wisdom, they stripped away these garments that
covered their discourse and exposed philosophy all naked
and contemptible—accessible to all, available for anyone
to consort with, nothing more than the name of a noble
pursuit wandering about in the midst of wretched sophist-
ries.[7]

As a result, the poems of Homer and Hesiod, and all
that divinely inspired poetry of ancient times, are considered mere myths, and are prized only for their storytelling,
the pleasantness of their verses, and the brilliance of their
composition, just like pipe playing or lyre playing, while
what is noble in them is overlooked and deemed irrelevant
to virtue. Even Homer, the leader of this group, is banished from philosophy. For ever since sophistic notions
stole into Greece from Thrace and Cilicia,[8] along with
Epicurus' atoms, Heraclitus' fire, Thales' water, Anax-
imenes' air, Empedocles' strife, and Diogenes' pithos,[9]
and all those armies of philosophers, each arrayed against
the others and claiming victory over them, everything has
become a matter of words and slanders, as sophists attack
sophists, while effective deeds are in terribly short supply.
And that much-touted Good, over which the Hellenic
world has squared off and split into factions, is nowhere to
be seen.

[7] For the gentler form of philosophy expressed in verse before
being stripped bare as naked doctrine, see *Or.* 4.3.
[8] Protagoras and Democritus were from Abdera in Thrace,
and Chrysippus the Stoic was from Soli in Cilicia.　　[9] The large
storage jar serving as a house for Diogenes the Cynic.

3. Τὰ ⟨δὲ⟩[3] παλαιὰ ἐκεῖνα, ἐν οἷς ἔτι ἡ Ὁμήρου ᾠδὴ
ἐδυνάστευε,[4] γενναῖα καὶ ἀληθῆ καὶ γνήσια φιλοσοφίας θρέμματα ἐπαίδευέν τε καὶ ἐξέτρεφεν. ἐκείνης
τῆς ᾠδῆς θρέμμα ἦν Πλάτων· κἂν γὰρ ἐξομόσηται
διδάσκαλον, ὁρῶ τὰ γνωρίσματα καὶ συνίημι τῶν
σπερμάτων·

κείνου τοι τοιοίδε πόδες τοιαίδε τε χεῖρες,
ὀφθαλμῶν τε βολαὶ κεφαλή τ᾽ ἐφύπερθέ τε
χαῖται·

ὥστε καὶ ἐπιτολμήσαιμι ἂν εἰπεῖν ἔγωγε, ἐμφερέστε-
ρον εἶναι Πλάτωνα Ὁμήρῳ μᾶλλον ἢ Σωκράτει, κἂν
τὸν Ὅμηρον φεύγῃ, κἂν διώκῃ τὸν Σωκράτην. μή με
οἰηθῇς τὰς Πλάτωνος φωνὰς εἰκάζειν Ὁμήρῳ καὶ τὰ
ὀνόματα καὶ τὰ ῥήματα (ἔστιν μὲν γὰρ καὶ ταῦτα
ἐκεῖθεν, ἐκείνης τῆς ἁρμονίας ἀπορροή, ὡς ἐξ Ὠκεα-
νοῦ ἡ Μαιῶτις, ὡς ἐκ τῆς Μαιώτιδος ὁ Πόντος, ὡς ἐκ
τοῦ Πόντου ὁ Ἑλλήσποντος, ὡς ἐξ Ἑλλησπόντου ἡ
⟨καθ᾽ ἡμᾶς⟩[5] θάλασσα), ἀλλὰ τὴν γνώμην τῇ γνώμῃ
προσάγω καὶ τὴν συγγένειαν ὁρῶ. καὶ τοῦτο μέν σοι
καὶ αὖθις παρ᾽ ἐμοῦ λελέξεται· ἐπανάγωμεν δὲ τὸν
λόγον ἐπὶ τὴν Ὁμήρου γνώμην, διεξιόντες περὶ αὐτῆς
τὰ εἰκότα.

4. Δοκεῖ μοι Ὅμηρος, φύσει τε κεχρημένος ἐνθεω-
τάτῃ καὶ φρονήσει δεινοτάτῃ καὶ ἐμπειρίᾳ πολυτρο-

---

[3] suppl. Russell, Trapp: ⟨καὶ μὴν⟩ ante τὰ Stephanus, Davies², Dübner   [4] Russell, Trapp: δυναστεύει R
[5] suppl. Markland: lacunam stat. Trapp

3. And yet, as long as Homeric song still exercised authority, those ancient times educated and raised noble, true, and legitimate progeny of philosophy. One such offspring of that poetry was Plato, for even though he renounces his teacher,[10] I can see the traces and recognize the engendering seeds:

> such indeed were that man's feet and hands,
> the look in his eyes, and his head and hair above.[11]

That is why I would boldly assert that Plato bears a greater similarity to Homer than he does to Socrates, even though he shuns Homer and follows Socrates. Do not, however, think that I am comparing Plato's language, his actual vocabulary and phrases, to Homer's, even though it is true that these too have their source in Homer and flow from his harmonious verse, just as the Maeotis[12] flows from the Ocean, the Black Sea from the Maeotis, the Hellespont from the Black Sea, and our sea from the Hellespont. No, it is by comparing concept with concept that I see the common lineage. You will hear my discourse on this topic at a later time,[13] but for now let us return our discussion to Homer's thought, and review the appropriate arguments about it.

4. It seems to me that when Homer, who possessed a most divinely-inspired nature, an extremely sharp intelli-

---

[10] That is, Homer, whom he banned from his ideal republic. The issue is treated in *Or.* 17.

[11] *Od.* 4.149–50, Menelaus remarking on Telemachus' resemblance to his absent father.

[12] The Sea of Azov.

[13] This appears nowhere in the extant works.

πωτάτῃ, φιλοσοφίᾳ ἐπιθέμενος δημοσιεῦσαι ταύτην
τοῖς Ἕλλησιν ἐν ἁρμονίᾳ τῇ τότε εὐδοκίμῳ· αὕτη δ᾽
ἦν ἡ ποιητική· οὔτε δὲ Ἰωνικὴν ταύτην ἐθελῆσαι εἶναι
αὐτῷ, οὔτε ἀκριβῶς Δώριον, οὔτε Ἀττικήν, ἀλλὰ κοινὴν τῆς Ἑλλάδος· ἅτε οὖν ξύμπασι διαλεγόμενος,
ἀθροίσας ἀναμὶξ τὴν Ἑλλάδα φωνὴν καὶ ἀνακερασά-
μενος εἰς σχῆμα ᾠδῆς, †ὦν†[6] τὰ ἔπη εἰργάσατο προσηνῆ τε ἅμα εἶναι καὶ ξυνετὰ πᾶσιν καὶ κεχαρισμένα
ἑκάστοις· ἐνθυμηθεὶς δέ, ὅτι ὀλίγον μὲν τὸ ξυνετὸν ἐν
ἅπαντι, τὸ δὲ πολὺ δημαγωγεῖσθαι φιλεῖ, οὐδετέρῳ
τῷ γένει ἀποκεκριμένην τὴν ποίησιν ἐξειργάσατο,
καθάπερ ὁ Ἡσίοδος χωρὶς μὲν τὰ γένη τῶν ἡρώων,
ἀπὸ γυναικῶν ἀρχόμενος †καταλέγων τὰ γένη†,[7]
ὅστις ἐξ ἧς<τινος>[8] ἔφυ, χωρὶς δὲ αὐτῷ πεποίηνται οἱ
θεῖοι λόγοι,{ἅμα τοῖς λόγοις θεογονία,}[9] χωρὶς δ᾽ αὖ
ὠφελεῖ τὰ εἰς τὸν βίον, ἔργα τε ἃ δραστέον καὶ
ἡμέραι ἐν αἷς δραστέον.

Οὐχ οὕτω τὰ Ὁμήρου ἔχει, οὐδὲ ἀποκέκριται ἕκαστα χωρὶς οὐδ᾽ αὖ φύρεται ἀκρίτως πάντα ἐν πᾶσιν·
ἀλλά γε ἦν τὸ σχῆμα αὐτῷ τοῦ λόγου <οἷον>[10] οἱ
μῦθοι ἔχουσιν, οἱ Τρωϊκοὶ λόγοι καὶ τὰ τοῦ Ὀδυσσέως παθήματα, μέμικται δ᾽ ἐν αὐτοῖς καὶ θεολογία
σαφὴς καὶ πολιτείας ἦθος καὶ ἀρεταὶ ἀνθρώπων καὶ

---

[6] obel. Trapp, Koniaris: om. edd. pr.
[7] obel. Trapp
[8] suppl. Trapp
[9] del. Trapp ut interpolata
[10] suppl. Trapp: <ὁ> Hobein

gence, and very wide-ranging experience,[14] took up philosophy, he chose to popularize it among the Greeks in the
kind of composition that was highly regarded at the time,
namely poetry, but he did not want his verse to be in Ionic,
or in pure Doric, or in Attic, but in one common to all
Hellas. Since, therefore, he was addressing all of them, he
created a mixture of the Greek language, and by casting it
in the form of poetry, he composed verses that were not
only pleasant and intelligible to all, but also enjoyable for
each group. Recognizing, moreover, that few are knowledgeable in every field, and that people in general want to
be guided, he did not compose a separate kind of poetry
for either group, as Hesiod did, who in one work composed his genealogy of heroes, beginning with women, as
he cited which mother bore which hero; separate from
these are his accounts of the gods; [and together with
these his *Theogony*] and still separate from these are his
useful prescriptions for living—what things should be
done and on which days to do them.[15]

But such is not the case with Homer's poetry: each
thing is not treated separately, nor is everything all mixed
together indiscriminately.[16] No, his discourse took the
form of the stories he tells, the narratives about Troy and
the experiences of Odysseus, but mixed in with them is a
lucid theology, forms of governance, human virtues, vices,

---

[14] The adjective πολυτροπωτάτη recalls Odysseus himself as
πολύτροπον at *Od.* 1.1.　　　[15] References are to Hesiod's
Catalogue of Women, *Theogony*, and *Works and Days*. Trapp
rightly deletes the reference to the *Theogony* as an intrusive gloss.

[16] Cf. the criticism of history for mixing everything together
at *Or.* 22.6.

μοχθηρίαι καὶ παθήματα καὶ συμφοραὶ καὶ εὐτυχίαι.
καὶ τούτων ἕκαστον ὑποθέσεις οἰκείας ἔχει· οἷον εἰ
ξυνείης παναρμόνιόν τι ὄργανον παντοδαπὰς ἱὲν φωνάς, πάσας δὲ ἀλλήλαις ὡμολογημένας· μᾶλλον δὲ
οὕτως, εἰ ἤδη που ἐθεάσω ἄθροισμα ὀργάνων, αὐλὸν
ἠχοῦντα καὶ λύραν ψαλλομένην καὶ ᾠδὴν χοροῦ καὶ
σάλπιγγα ἀναμὶξ καὶ σύριγγα, καὶ ἄλλ᾽ ἄττα ὀργάνων εἴδη καὶ ὀνόματα, ὧν ἕκαστον πεποίηται μὲν
κατὰ οἰκείαν τέχνην, συντέτακται δὲ πρὸς τὸ πλησίον
κατὰ κοινὴν μοῦσαν.

5. Συνελόντι δ᾽ εἰπεῖν, ἡ Ὁμήρου ποίησις τοιάδε τίς
ἐστιν, οἷον εἰ καὶ ζωγράφον ἐννοήσαις φιλόσοφον,
Πολύγνωτον ἢ Ζεῦξιν, μὴ γράφοντα εἰκῇ· καὶ γὰρ
τούτῳ ἔσται τὸ χρῆμα διπλοῦν, τὸ μὲν ἐκ τῆς τέχνης,
τὸ δὲ ἐκ τῆς ἀρετῆς· κατὰ μὲν τὴν τέχνην τὰ σχήματα
καὶ τὰ χρώματα[11] εἰς ὁμοιότητα τοῦ ἀληθοῦς διασώ-
ζοντι, κατὰ δὲ τὴν ἀρετὴν εἰς μίμησιν τοῦ κάλλους
τὴν εὐσχημοσύνην τῶν γραμμάτων διατιθέντι. ταύτῃ
μοι καὶ τὰ Ὁμήρου σκόπει, ὡς ἔστι χρῆμα διπλοῦν,
κατὰ μὲν τὴν ποιητικὴν ἐντεταμένον εἰς μύθου σχῆμα,
κατὰ δὲ φιλοσοφίαν εἰς ζῆλον ἀρετῆς καὶ ἀληθείας
γνῶσιν συντεταγμένον.

Αὐτίκα πεποίηται αὐτῷ ἐν τοῖς λόγοις μειράκιον
Θετταλικὸν καὶ ἀνὴρ βασιλικός, Ἀχιλλεὺς καὶ Ἀγα-
μέμνων· ὁ μὲν ὑπ᾽ ὀργῆς εἰς ὕβριν προφερόμενος ὁ
Ἀγαμέμνων, ὁ δὲ Ἀχιλλεὺς προπηλακισθεὶς μηνιῶν·

---

11 χρώματα Markland, Trapp: σώματα R

experiences, disasters, and successes. And each of these topics has its own proper role to play. Imagine, if you will, a musical instrument with a full range of notes producing all kinds of sounds, all in harmony with the others. Or better still, if you have ever seen a collection of instruments—a pipe being played, a lyre being strummed, a choir singing an ode, together with a trumpet and pan-pipes and all other kinds of instruments with different names, each of which has been fashioned for its particular artistry, but is stationed next to its neighbor to produce a common musical sound.

5. To sum up, Homer's poetry may be understood along the following lines. Imagine a painter who is a philosopher, a Polygnotus or Zeuxis,[17] who does not paint haphazardly, because his project will entail two aspects, one of artistry, the other of virtue. By means of artistry, he preserves a likeness to reality in his shapes and colors; by means of virtue, he imitates beauty itself in the decorous arrangement of his lines. I wish you to consider Homer's work in the same way, as having two aspects: in terms of poetry, being cast in the form of a story; in terms of philosophy, being composed toward an emulation of virtue and knowledge of truth.

For instance, his narrative features a young Thessalian, Achilles, and a king, Agamemnon. Agamemnon is carried away by anger to act abusively, and Achilles is enraged at

[17] Both fifth-century BC painters. Polygnotus was renowned for the ethical content of his paintings, Zeuxis for his trompe l'oeil technique.

εἰκόνες παθῶν, νεότητος καὶ ἐξουσίας· ⟨ἀλλ'⟩[12] ἀντίθες τοι ἑκατέρῳ τὸν Νέστορα, παλαιὸν τῷ χρόνῳ,
ἀγαθὸν φρονεῖν, δεινὸν εἰπεῖν. πάλιν αὖ Θερσίτης
πεποίηται αὐτῷ αἰσχρὸς ἰδεῖν, φωνὴν ἐπεσβόλος,
γνώμην ἄτακτος, οἷος εἶναι εἰκὼν ἀκολάστου δήμου·
ἀλλ' ἀντίθες καὶ τούτῳ ἄνδρα ἀγαθόν, ἡγεμόνα
ἀκριβῆ, ἐπιπορευόμενον,

οὕ τινα μὲν βασιλῆα καὶ ἔξοχον ἄνδρα ἐφεύροι,
τόν ῥ' ἀγανοῖς ἐπέεσσιν ἐρητύσασκε παραστάς·
ὃν δ' αὖ δήμου τ' ἄνδρα ἴδοι βοόωντά τ' ἐφεύροι,
τὸν σκήπτρῳ ἐλάσασκεν.

ἆρά σοι οὐ δοκεῖ αὐτὸ τοῦτο ποιεῖν καὶ ὁ Σωκράτης,
τοὺς μὲν βασιλικοὺς καὶ ἐξόχους ἄνδρας ἀγανοῖς λόγοις γεραίρων καὶ ἀποδεχόμενος, Τίμαιόν τινα ἢ
Παρμενίδην ἢ ἄλλον βασιλικὸν ξένον·

ὃν δ' αὖ δήμου τ' ἄνδρα ἴδοι βοόωντά τ' ἐφεύροι,

τοῦτον ἐλαύνων τῷ λόγῳ, Θρασύμαχόν τινα ἢ Πῶλον
ἢ Καλλικλέα, ἤ τινα ἄλλον λωβητῆρα καὶ ἐπεσβόλον;
6. Πάλιν αὖ ἐπανίωμεν ἐπὶ τὸν Ὅμηρον καὶ τοὺς
παρ' αὐτῷ βαρβάρους· καὶ γὰρ ἐνταῦθα ὄψει ἀρετὴν
καὶ κακίαν ἀντιτεταγμένας ἀλλήλαις· ἀκόλαστον μὲν
τὸν Ἀλέξανδρον, σώφρονα δὲ τὸν Ἕκτορα· δειλὸν τὸν
Ἀλέξανδρον, ἀνδρεῖον τὸν Ἕκτορα· κἂν τοὺς γάμους

12 suppl. Renehan, Trapp

being insulted—illustrations of the passions of youth and of authority. To both of them contrast Nestor, advanced in years, a wise thinker and skilled speaker. Then too, Homer includes Thersites, an ugly man with a scurrilous tongue and deranged mind, who serves as the image of an unruly populace. To him contrast a good man,[18] a scrupulous leader, who goes about the camp in this fashion:

> Whenever he encountered a king or a prominent man,
> he would go up to him and restrain him with gentle
> words . . .
> But whenever he saw a common man and found him
> bellowing,
> he would strike him with his scepter.[19]

Do you not agree that Socrates does this very thing, when he pays respect to "kingly and prominent men" and welcomes them "with gentle words," men such as Timaeus, Parmenides, or any other "kingly" visitor?

> But whenever he saw a common man and found him
> bellowing,[20]

he would strike him with his argument—men such as Thrasymachus, Polus, Callicles, or any other "scurrilous loudmouth."[21]

6. But let us return to Homer and to the Trojans in his poem. Here too you will see virtue and vice opposed, with unruly Alexander and sensible Hector, cowardly Alexander and courageous Hector. If you compare their mar-

---

[18] Odysseus. [19] *Il.* 2.188–89 and 198–99, also quoted at *Or.* 15.9, where they describe Diogenes' conduct.
[20] *Il.* 2.198. [21] Words describing Thersites at *Il.* 2.275, whom Odysseus struck with his scepter (not argument).

αὐτῶν ἐξετάζῃς, ὁ μὲν ζηλωτός, ὁ δὲ ἐλεεινός· ὁ μὲν
ἐπάρατος, ὁ δὲ ἐπαινετός· ὁ μὲν μοιχικός, ὁ δὲ νόμι-
μος. θέασαι δὲ καὶ τὰς ἄλλας ἀρετὰς νενεμημένας
κατ' ἄνδρα, τὴν μὲν ἀνδρείαν κατὰ τὸν Αἴαντα, τὴν
δὲ ἀγχίνοιαν κατὰ τὸν Ὀδυσσέα, τὸ δὲ θάρσος κατὰ
τὸν Διομήδην, τὴν δὲ εὐβουλίαν κατὰ τὸν ‹Νέστορα.
τὸν δ'›[13] Ὀδυσσέα αὐτὸν οὕτως ἄρα εἰκόνα ἡμῖν ὑπο-
τίθεται χρηστοῦ βίου καὶ ἀρετῆς ἀκριβοῦς, ὥστε καὶ
ἀπέδωκεν αὐτῷ ἥμισυ μέρος τῶν αὐτοῦ ἔργων, καὶ
ταῦτα μέν, ὡς συλλήβδην εἰπεῖν, ἴχνη βραχέα μακρῶν λόγων.

7. Εἰ δέ τι χρὴ καὶ περὶ θεῶν ὀλίγα ἄττα δείγματα
τῆς Ὁμήρου γνώμης ἐξενέγκασθαι, ἑνὶ τῷ παρὰ
Πλάτωνος ὥσπερ εἰκόνι τὰ λοιπὰ εἰκάζωμεν κατὰ τὸ
ἦθος τοῦ λόγου, τὰ πρεσβύτερα τοῖς νεωτέροις. ἐπείπερ ταύτῃ κριτέον,

ὁ γὰρ δὴ μέγας ἐν οὐρανῷ Ζεύς,

λέγει που καὶ ὁ Πλάτων, καὶ ὀχεῖται αὐτῷ ὁ Ζεὺς ἐπὶ
πτηνοῦ ἅρματος καὶ ἡγεῖται θεῶν· Ὁμήρῳ δὲ ὁ στρατηγός, ὁ Ζεύς, λέγει·

μήτε τις οὖν θήλεια θεὸς τόδε μήτε τις ἄρσην
πειράτω διακέρσαι ἐμὸν ἔπος, ἀλλ' ἅμα πάντες
αἰνεῖτ', ὄφρα τάχιστα τελευτήσω τάδε ἔργα.

13 suppl. Trapp: ‹Νέστορα· Ὀδυσσέα δὴ› Davies[2]

riages, the one is enviable, the other pitiful; the one is
despicable, the other praiseworthy; the one is adulterous,
the other lawful. Consider too how the other virtues
are distributed among individuals, with bravery to Ajax,
quick-wittedness to Odysseus, boldness to Diomedes, and
good counsel to Nestor. And as for Odysseus, Homer presents him to us as such an example of a good life and of
scrupulous virtue, that he devoted half of his own works
to him. In a word, these instances are but brief vestiges of
his extensive narrations.

7. If we need as well to produce a few samples of Homer's conception of the gods, let us compare all the rest
of them to a single statement from Plato that serves as an
example, following the practice of our argument of comparing older passages with newer ones. Since this is how
we must decide the issue, does not Plato also say at one
point,

> for indeed great Zeus in heaven?[22]

His Zeus rides in a winged chariot and leads the gods in
procession, whereas Homer's Zeus is a commander who
says,

> Let no god, neither female nor male, attempt
> to thwart my word, but all together
> assent, so that I may quickly accomplish these
>   deeds,[23]

---

[22] Adapted from Pl. *Phdr.* 246e: "Zeus, the great leader
(*hēgemōn*) in heaven. . . ." The tag, "great Zeus in heaven" is also
cited in Luc. *Pisc.* 22 and *Bis. Accus.* 33. The following description of Zeus is modeled on Pl. *Phdr.* 246e–47a.

[23] *Il.* 8.7–9.

καὶ μετὰ τοῦτο αὐτῷ καὶ τὸ ἅρμα ζεύγνυται καὶ οἱ
ἵπποι θέουσιν

ὠκυπέτα χρυσέῃσιν ἐθείρῃσιν κομόωντε.

ζεύγνυται δὲ καὶ Ποσειδῶνι ἅρμα ἐν θαλάττῃ,

βῆ δ᾽ ἐλάαν ἐπὶ κῦμα, ἄταλλε δὲ κήτε᾽ ὑπ᾽ αὐτοῦ.

ἔχει δὲ καὶ ὁ Ἅιδης αὐτῷ τρίτην ἀρχήν· τριχθὰ δὲ
Ὁμήρῳ δέδασται τὰ πάντα. Ποσειδῶν μὲν ἔλαχεν

πολιὴν ἅλα ναιέμεν αἰεί,
. . . Ἅιδης δ᾽ ἔλαχεν ζόφον ἠερόεντα,
Ζεὺς δὲ . . . οὐρανόν.

ὦ τῆς δικαίας καὶ φιλοσόφου νομῆς.

8. Εὕροις δ᾽ ἂν καὶ ἄλλας παρ᾽ Ὁμήρῳ ἀρχὰς καὶ
γενέσεις παντοδαπῶν ὀνομάτων, ὧν ὁ μὲν ἀνόητος ὡς
μύθων ἀκούει, ὁ δὲ φιλόσοφος ὡς πραγμάτων. ἔστιν
αὐτῷ καὶ ἀρετῆς ἀρχή, ἀλλὰ Ἀθηνᾶ λέγεται καὶ τῷ
ἔχοντι παρίσταται

ἐν πάντεσσι πόνοισιν.

ἔστι καὶ ἔρωτος, ἀλλὰ τὴν αἰτίαν ἡ Ἀφροδίτη ἔχει καὶ
τοῦ κεστοῦ κρατεῖ καὶ μεταδίδωσιν τοῦ πόθου. ἔστιν
καὶ τέχνης, ἀλλ᾽ ὁ Ἥφαιστος τὴν αἰτίαν ἔχει καὶ τοῦ

24 Il. 8.42.
25 Il. 13.27.
26 Il. 15.190–92 (adapted).

100

after which his chariot is yoked for him and his horses gallop off,

> swift in flight with flowing manes of gold.[24]

Poseidon's chariot too is yoked in the sea,

> and he drove over the waves, and the fish frolicked beneath him.[25]

Hades possesses the third realm in his poem, for Homer divided the entire world into three parts. Poseidon was allotted

> the gray sea as his home forever,
> . . . and Hades was allotted the murky darkness,
> and Zeus ⟨was allotted⟩ heaven.[26]

O what a just and philosophical distribution!

8. You can find other principles and origins bearing various names in Homer, which to the simpleminded sound like myths, but to the philosopher are realities. Homer includes the principle of virtue, but it is called Athena and she stands beside the man of virtue,[27]

> in all kinds of toils.[28]

He also includes the principle of love, but Aphrodite is the cause of it, and she possesses the girdle of love and imparts desire.[29] He also includes the principle of craftsmanship, but Hephaestus is the cause of it, and he controls the forge

---

[27] Athena is allegorized as a *daimonion* at *Or.* 8.5–6 and as intelligence (*phronēsis*) at *Or.* 4.8.

[28] *Od.* 13.301, spoken by Athena to Odysseus.

[29] Cf. *Il.* 14.188–224.

πυρὸς κρατεῖ καὶ μεταδίδωσι τῆς τέχνης. ἄρχει δὲ αὐτῷ καὶ Ἀπόλλων χοροῦ καὶ Μοῦσαι ᾠδῆς καὶ Ἄρης πολέμου καὶ Αἴολος πνευμάτων καὶ Ὠκεανὸς ποταμῶν καὶ Δημήτηρ καρπῶν· καὶ οὐδὲν μέρος Ὁμήρῳ ἄθεον οὐδὲ δυνάστου ἄπορον οὐδὲ ἀρχῆς ἔρημον, ἀλλὰ πάντα μεστὰ θείων λόγων καὶ θείων ὀνομάτων καὶ θείας τέχνης.

Κἂν ἐπὶ τὰ στοιχεῖα ἔλθῃς καὶ τὸν τούτων πόλεμον, ὄψει μάχην ἐν τῷ Τρωϊκῷ πεδίῳ, οὐ Τρώων καὶ Ἀχαιῶν καὶ ὀλλύντων καὶ ὀλλυμένων, αἵματι ῥεούσης τῆς γῆς, ἀλλὰ πυρὸς καὶ ποταμοῦ μάχην, τοῦ μὲν οἰδαίνοντος καὶ ἀνισταμένου λάβρῳ καὶ συνεχεῖ τῷ κύματι, τοῦ δὲ ταῖς δίναις ἐμπίπτοντος ἀκμαίᾳ ῥιπῇ, φλέγοντος μὲν τὰς κόμας καὶ τὸ κάλλος τοῦ ποταμοῦ, ἰτέας καὶ μυρίκας καὶ λωτὸν καὶ θρύον, φλέγοντος δὲ αὐτοῦ τὰ φορήματα καὶ τὰ θρέμματα·

τείροντ’ ἐγχέλυές τε καὶ ἰχθύες οἱ κατὰ δίνας,
οἳ κατὰ καλὰ ῥέεθρα κυβίστων ἔνθα καὶ ἔνθα.

ἄπαυστος δ’ ἂν ἦν ὁ πόλεμος οὗτος, ἀλλὰ ἡ Ἥρα σπένδεται καὶ διαλύει τὸν πόλεμον, καὶ τὰ στοιχεῖα συνάγει.

9. Ἔα μοι ταυτὶ τὰ αἰνίγματα· σκόπει τὰ σά, τὰ ἀνθρώπινα. οὗτός σοι πολιτείας τρόπος, οὐκ ἐν Πειραιεῖ πλαττόμενος, οὐδὲ ἐν Κρήτῃ νομοθετούμενος, ἀλλ’ ἐπὶ προφάσει ἡρωϊκῇ ὑπὸ φιλοσόφου δεικνύμε-

and passes on his skills. In Homer Apollo presides over choral dances, the Muses over song, Ares over warfare, Aeolus over the winds, Ocean over rivers, and Demeter over crops. There is nothing in Homer that is devoid of divinity, or without a master, or lacking an original principle; indeed his entire work is full of narratives about the gods, names of gods, and the arts belonging to the gods.

And if you turn your attention to the primal elements and the strife among them, you will see a battle raging on the Trojan plain, but not between Trojans and Achaeans, "with the ones slaying and the others being killed, and the earth running with blood,"[30] but a battle between fire and a river,[31] the one swelling and resisting with its violent and unremitting wave, the other attacking the river's eddies with full force, scorching the river's hair and beauty, his willows, tamarisks, clover, and rushes, and scorching the creatures he supports and sustains:

> the eels and fish in the eddies were tormented,
> and they plunged this way and that in the beautiful
>   streams.[32]

This battle would never have ended, had not Hera called a truce, resolved the conflict, and reconciled the elements.

9. But set aside, if you will, these allegories and consider your own human affairs. Here you have a kind of government that is not devised in the Piraeus, or legislated on Crete,[33] but presented by a philosopher in the form of a

---

[30] Adapted from *Il*. 4.451.   [31] This elemental battle between fire (Hephaestus) and water (Xanthus) is recounted at *Il*. 21.349–82.   [32] *Il*. 21.353–54.   [33] That is, like the ones proposed in Plato's *Republic* and *Laws*.

νος, δι᾽ οἰκονομίας ἡρωϊκῆς. ἄρχοντες αὐτουργοί,
προβουλευόμενοι· ἀριστεῖς ἀγαθοί, προπολεμοῦντες·
γυνὴ σώφρων, ἀντιταττομένη ὑβρισταῖς νεανίαις·
βασιλεὺς δίκαιος, ξενοδοχῶν ἀλήτην ξένον· ἀνὴρ σώφρων, παντοίαις συμφοραῖς ἀντιτεχνώμενος. δείξω δέ
σοι καὶ πολιτείας ἀλλήλαις ἀντιτεταγμένας· δημιουρ-
γεῖ δὲ αὐτὰς Ὅμηρος μὲν λόγῳ, Ἥφαιστος δὲ χρυσῷ·

ἐν τῇ μέν ῥα γάμοι τε

καὶ ᾠδὴ καὶ χοροὶ καὶ δικάζοντες βασιλεῖς καὶ ἑπό-
μενοι λαοί·

τὴν δ᾽ ἑτέρην πόλιν ἀμφὶ δύο στρατοὶ εἴατο
λαῶν.

κἂν ἀπιστῇς τῷ πράγματι, οὐκ ἀπορήσεις λόγων
ἀληθεστέρων. αὐταί σοι νησιωτικαὶ πόλεις, ἡ μὲν
Φαιάκων, ἡ δὲ Ἰθακησίων· τῶν μὲν ἄρχει αἰδώς, τῶν
δὲ ὕβρις· τῶν μὲν βασιλεῖς ἔννομοι, τῶν δὲ ἄδικοι
μνηστῆρες· οἱ μὲν τὸν βασιλέα

ἐρχόμενον . . . θεὸν ὣς εἰσορόωσιν,

οἱ δὲ τοῦ βασιλέως ἐπιβουλεύουσιν τῷ γάμῳ· τέλος
δὲ ἑκατέροις, τοῖς μὲν εὐφροσύνη διηνεκὴς καὶ βίος
ἄλυπος καὶ ὑποδοχὴ ξένων καὶ θαλάττης στόλοι καὶ
γῆς καρποί· τοῖς δὲ ἑτέροις ὄλεθρος ἀθρόος ἐν αὐταῖς

heroic story composed in epic verse. There are sovereign
rulers taking counsel; noble heroes defending their country; a virtuous woman[34] resisting violent young men; a just
king taking in a wandering stranger;[35] a virtuous man[36]
devising schemes in all sorts of desperate situations. I will
also show you cities contrasted with each other, which Homer composes in words, but Hephaestus fashions in gold:

> in the one city were marriages[37]

with singing and dancing, with kings administering justice
and subjects obeying them,

> but around the other city two armies of men were
> encamped.[38]

And even if you have doubts about this example,[39] you will
not lack more realistic accounts, for you have two island
cities, Phaeacia and Ithaca. In the one, due respect rules,
in the other, violence; in the one, law-abiding kings, in the
other, lawless suitors; in the one, they respect their king,
and

> when he approaches . . . they look upon him like a
> god;[40]

in the other, they plot against the king's marriage. Each
has a different outcome. The ones enjoy never-ending festivity, a life free of grief, entertainment of guests, safe
sailing over the sea, and fruitful lands; the others die en

---

[34] Penelope.   [35] That is, Alcinous who took in Odysseus.
[36] Odysseus.   [37] *Il*. 18.491.   [38] *Il*. 18.509.
[39] That is, because the cities fashioned on the shield are fictitious.   [40] *Od*. 8.173.

ταῖς ἡδοναῖς. τοῦτο τέλος μοχθηρίας ὑβριζούσης, τοῦτο τέλος ἀνεπιτιμήτου ἐξουσίας.

Αὐτόν γε μὴν τὸν Ὀδυσσέα οὐχ ὁρᾷς ὡς παντοίαις συμφοραῖς ἀντιτεχνώμενον ἀρετὴ σῴζει καὶ τὸ δι' ἐκείνην θάρσος; τοῦτο αὐτῷ τὸ ἐν Κίρκης μῶλυ, τοῦτο τὸ ἐν θαλάττῃ κρήδεμνον, τοῦτο τῶν Πολυφήμου χειρῶν τὸν ἄνδρα ἐξάγει, τοῦτο ἐξ Ἅιδου ἀνάγει, τοῦτο πήγνυσιν σχεδίαν, τοῦτο πείθει Ἀλκίνουν, τοῦτο ἀνέχεται βαλλόντων μνηστήρων, Ἴρου παλαίοντος, Μελανθίου ὑβρίζοντος· τοῦτο ἐλευθεροῖ τὴν ἑστίαν, τοῦτο τιμωρεῖ τῷ γάμῳ, τοῦτο ἄνδρα ποιεῖ διογενῆ καὶ θεοῖς εἴκελον, οἷον ἀξιοῖ Πλάτων εἶναι τὸν εὐδαίμονα.

masse in the midst of their pleasures. Such is the result of violent depravity; such is the result of unchecked license.

Then too, can you not see how virtue and the confidence it inspires rescues Odysseus, as he devises schemes in all sorts of desperate situations? That is what is meant by the moly on Circe's island and by the veil he is given at sea. That is what rescues the man from the hands of Polyphemus, brings him back from Hades, fashions his raft, wins over Alcinous, endures the suitors' blows, Irus' wrestling,[41] and Melanthius' abuse. It liberates his household, avenges the attacks on his marriage, and finally renders him "Zeus-born"[42] and "like the gods,"[43] just as Plato deems the happy man to be.[44]

[41] Actually boxing.

[42] An epithet used exclusively of Odysseus in the *Odyssey*.

[43] The actual epithet in Homer is *theois epieikelos*, and it always describes Achilles.

[44] For the Platonic concept of "likeness to god" (ὁμοίωσις θεῷ) as the *telos* of life, see Pl. *Tht.* 176a–b and *Resp.* 10.613a–b, Alcin. *Didasc.* 2.153.5–12 and 28.181.19–20, and Diog. Laert. 3.78.

ORATION 27

INTRODUCTION

The oration obliquely approaches the Platonic problem of whether virtue can be taught, by examining whether it is an art (*technē*) and how that art is related to knowledge (*epistēmē*). It opens with an interlocutor arguing that since artisans learn an art to make their products, then a philosopher should also be able to learn the art of virtue (§1). After faint praise, the speaker replies that the goal of art is not to teach the art, but to produce something (§2). As the art of medicine produces health and the art of sculpture produces a shapely statue, the art of virtue must produce a healthy and ordered soul (§3). Art, defined as reason seeking an end, is divided into three kinds: manual arts that produce physical objects; practical arts that aim for success, health, or justice; and intellectual arts like mathematics and geometry. The art of virtue partakes of both the practical and the intellectual kinds (§4). To explain how virtue participates in both theory and practice, the speaker resorts to a twofold division of the soul into reason and emotion, which he attributes to Plato, Aristotle, and Pythagoras. Vice occurs when the emotions flood the rational part and disturb the plantings of reason, causing false opinions to sprout up (§5). The analogy shifts to a political one. The emotions are compared to an unruly populace that takes over the reasonable element, and the examples of Alcibiades and Cleon illustrate what disasters can result (§6). The proper state of virtue is like Sparta's constitution, where the reasonable element rules and the rest obeys. Virtue is not simply knowledge, but the application of that knowledge to command the vast army of emotions down the chain of command (§7). For god, knowledge and virtue are identical, because god does not have a divided soul that must cope with unruly elements. For humans, however, knowledge is a form of virtue, but virtue is not a form of knowledge. If the latter were true, sophists could sell knowledge that would bring virtue to souls (§8). That is not the case, because even if there are clear arguments for virtue, they are blocked by vicious emotions, bad habits, and a wicked upbringing. One must have a good and capable (*chrēstos*) natural disposition for virtue as a foundation, which is then sustained by proper upbringing and good habits that engender an enduring affection in the soul for everything beautiful (*ta kala panta*). What produces a happy soul and a good (*agathos*) man is the guidance of the emotions by reason and a voluntary obedience to the dictates of knowledge (§9).

ORATION 27

Εἰ τέχνη ἡ ἀρετή

1. "Καὶ πῶς ἄν τις τοῦ φιλοσόφου ἀποδέξαιτο, ἄλλο τι τὴν ἀρετὴν λέγοντος εἶναι καὶ μὴ τέχνην; σχολῇ γὰρ ἂν εἴη τέχνη τι ἄλλο, εἴπερ μὴ ἡ ἀρετή· πλὴν εἰ μὴ ἄροτρον μὲν τέχνης ἔργον καὶ ἀσπὶς τέχνης καὶ ναῦς καὶ τειχίον, τὸ δὲ τούτοις χρώμενον καὶ ἐπιστατοῦν καὶ παρέχον τὴν ἑκάστου χρείαν ἅπαντι τῷ ἔχοντι εἰς δέον, καὶ τὴν ἐξ ἁπάντων ὠφέλειαν συντάττον εἰς κοινὸν τέλος, τοῦτο δή που ἀτεχνίαν φήσομεν. δεινόν γε, ὦ θεοί, καὶ δεινοῦ πέρα, εἰ ὁ μὲν κεραμεὺς ἐπὶ τέχνῃ μανθάνει καὶ ὁ σκυτοτόμος καὶ ὁ τέκτων, ὁ δὲ φιλόσοφος μανθάνει μέν, καὶ τὸ τέλος αὐτῷ ἡ ἀρετὴ ἔχει, ἔστι δὲ τοῦτο οὐ τέχνη, ἀλλά τι μάθημα ὑπὸ ἀτεχνίας διδασκόμενον."

2. Καλῶς·[1] ἔχε ἀτρέμας· οὐ γὰρ ἀτόπως ὑφηγῇ οὐδὲ ἀτέχνως, μὰ Δία. ἐγὼ δέ σου τὴν μὲν τέχνην ἐπαινῶ, τὸ δὲ κεφάλαιον αὐτῆς φέρε ἴδω τί καὶ λέγεις. κερα-

---

[1] καλῶς del. Trapp ut interpolatum

110

ORATION 27

Whether virtue is an art

1. "So how could anyone agree with a philosopher who says that virtue is not an art, but something else?[1] For surely nothing else could be an art if virtue is not one. Unless, that is, we are going say that plows, shields, ships, and walls are products of art, but that the very thing which puts them to use, controls them, makes available the use of each to anyone who possesses them when need arises, and coordinates the benefits of them all to a common end—that this is somehow no art at all. Good heavens, strange—indeed beyond strange—if a potter, cobbler, and carpenter each learns in order to acquire an art, but that a philosopher, whose goal is virtue, may indeed learn it, though not as an art, but as some kind of learning taught without the use of art."

2. Well put! But wait. The way you begin is not beside the point nor artlessly expressed, by Zeus! I praise your view of art, but allow me to consider what you claim its

[1] This opening paragraph is spoken by an assumed interlocutor. Art (*technē*) connotes skill, expertise, a set of rules, and a method. Trapp uses the term "science" to stress its intellectual aspect. The related issue of whether virtue can be taught is taken up in Plato's *Protagoras* and *Meno*.

μεύς, φής, κεραμεύειν μανθάνει τέχνη, καὶ σκυτοτόμος σκυτοτομεῖν καὶ τεκταίνειν τέκτων. ἐγὼ δέ σοι
ταυτὶ μὲν δίδωμι, μανθάνειν ἕκαστον τῶν δημιουρ-
γῶν, ἃ μανθάνει δρᾶν, {κἂν}[2] τέχνῃ· τῆς δὲ τέχνης
ἑκάστης οὐκ εἶναι τέλος τὸ μαθεῖν τὴν τέχνην παρ'
ἄλλου ἄλλον. τὴν μὲν γὰρ διαδοχὴν τοῦ εἰδέναι
μάθησις ποιεῖ· ἡ δὲ χρεία τῶν τεχνῶν οὐχ ὑπὸ τέχνης
γενέσθαι τέχνην, ἀλλ' ὑπὸ μὲν κεραμέως ἀμφορέα,
ὑπὸ δὲ αὐλητοῦ αὔλημα, ὑπὸ δὲ στρατηγοῦ νίκην,
τούτων δὲ ἕκαστον ἄλλο τι παρὰ τὴν τέχνην, τέχνης
τέλος καὶ οὐ τέχνη. οὐ γὰρ ὅ τι μὴ τέχνη καὶ ἀτεχνία
εὐθύς. ἀτεχνία μὲν γὰρ ἀφαίρεσις τέχνης, ἔνθα δεῖ
τέχνης· οὐ τέχνη δὲ τὸ ὑπὸ τέχνης μὲν γεγονός, ἕτερον δὲ ὂν παρὰ τὴν τέχνην.

3. Ἆρ' ἡγεῖ με σαφῶς λέγειν, ἢ φραστέον σοι
οὑτωσὶ ἐνδηλότερον; καλεῖς τινα τέχνην ἰατρικὴν καὶ
ἄλλην αὖ ἀγαλματουργικήν; τέλος δὲ ἑκατέρας, οὔτε
ἰατρικῆς ἰατρική, οὔτε ἀγαλματουργικῆς ἀγαλμα-
τουργία, ἀλλὰ ἄγαλμα μὲν ἀγαλματουργίας, ὑγίεια
δὲ ἰατρικῆς; τί οὖν; ἄλλο τι εἶναι ἡγεῖ τὴν ἀρετὴν ἢ
ψυχῆς ὑγίειάν τε καὶ εὐσχημοσύνην; οὑτωσὶ δὲ αὐτὸ
σκέψαι, ψυχῇ καὶ σώματι καὶ λίθῳ, τρισὶ τούτοις,
ἐπινείμας τέχνας τρεῖς, ὧν αἱ μὲν ὗλαι κόσμου ἐνδε-
εῖς, ἡ δὲ τέχνη, προσαγαγοῦσα ἑκάστη ἑκάστῳ τὸ
οἰκεῖον σχῆμα, περιέβαλε[3] τὸν μὲν λίθον ῥυθμοῖς καὶ

[2] del. Dübner, Trapp   [3] περιέβαλε Stephanus, Davies[2],
Dübner, Koniaris: περιέβαλλεν R

essence to be. You say that a potter learns to make pots by means of art, as a cobbler learns to make shoes, and a carpenter to make things of wood. I concede to you that each craftsman learns what he learns to do by means of art. However, the goal of each art is not simply that one person should learn it from another. Learning indeed passes on that knowledge, but the goal of these arts is not for art to produce art, but rather for a potter to produce an amphora, a piper a piece of music, and a general a victory, each of which is something other than the art, namely its product and not the art itself. It is not the case that the lack of art is simply artlessness, for artlessness is the complete absence of art where it is required. The product of art is not art itself, but something distinct from it.

3. Do you think that I am expressing myself clearly, or do I need to give you a clearer explanation, along these lines? Do you not call a particular art medicine and another sculpture? And do you not concede that the goal of each art is not medicine itself in the case of medicine, nor sculpture itself in the case of sculpture, but a statue in the case of sculpture and health in the case of medicine? Well then, do you think that virtue is anything other than the health and decorous arrangement of the soul?[2] Consider the matter in this way, by assigning three different arts to three separate objects—soul, body, and stone. Now in each case these materials lack order, but then each art, by applying a configuration appropriate for each object, furnishes the stone with shapely gestures to produce a visible

[2] A similar analogy between decorous arrangement (in painting) and the soul's virtue is drawn at *Or.* 26.5.

MAXIMUS OF TYRE

σχήμασιν εἰς μορφῆς εἶδος, τὸ δὲ σῶμα ἁρμονίαις
καὶ κράσεσιν εἰς ὑγιείας μέτρον, τὴν δὲ ψυχὴν συμ-
μετρίαις καὶ εὐκινησίαις εἰς ἀρετῆς κόσμον. κἂν
καλῇς τι τούτων τέχνην, τὸ τοῦ δράσαντος ὄνομα τῷ
ποιηθέντι ὑπὸ φιλίας προστιθείς, οὕτω μοι δοκεῖς κα-
λεῖν ὥσπερ ἂν εἰ καὶ ἥλιον καλοίης τὴν ἐξ ἡλίου
αὐγήν, ἑτέραν οὖσαν τοῦ ἡλίου, ποίημα ἡλίου καὶ οὐκ
αὐτὸ ἥλιον.

4. Καὶ μὲν δὴ καὶ ἀμφοτέρωθεν σκόπει τὸ λεγόμενον. ἐξετάζωμεν τί μὲν τέχνη, τί δὲ ἀρετή. τέχνην
τοίνυν ἄλλο τι ἡγεῖ ἢ λόγον ἐπὶ τέλος ἰόντα· τὸν μὲν
διὰ χειρουργίας σῶμά τι ἀπεργαζόμενον, ὃ καλοῦμεν
ποίημα, οἷον οἰκίαν οἰκοδόμου καὶ ναυπηγοῦ ναῦν καὶ
γραφέως εἰκόνα· τὸν δὲ αὖ πράξεώς τινος ἐργαστικόν,
οὐκ ἄνευ σώματος ἀπεργαζόμενον, ἀλλ' ἐν μὲν στρα-
τηγίᾳ νίκην, ἐν δὲ ἰατρικῇ ὑγίειαν, ἐν δὲ πολιτικῇ
δικαιοσύνην· τρίτον δ' αὖ τεχνῶν εἶδος αὐτὸ λόγον
ἄνευ σωμάτων ἐφ' ἑαυτοῦ κρατυνόμενον καὶ περὶ αὐτὸν τὴν πραγματείαν ἔχοντα, ὁποῖαι γεωμετρικαὶ καὶ
ἀριθμητικαὶ καὶ ὅσαις τὸ τέλος διανοητικὸν αὐτὸ
τοῦτο, οὔτε δὴ πρακτικόν, οὐδὲ ποιητικόν.

Εἶεν· τριῶν τούτων τέχνης γενῶν, κατὰ ποῖον αὐτῶν
τὴν ἀρετὴν τάξομεν, εἴπερ τέχνη; κατὰ τὸ ποιητικόν;
οὐδὲ αὐτὸς φήσεις· ἀλλὰ ἀμφισβητήσιμον ἔσται σοι
τὸ τῆς πράξεως πρὸς τὴν θεωρίαν· ἐγὼ δὲ οὐδέτερον
μὲν ἀφαιρῶ τῆς ἀρετῆς, ἀλλ' ἑκάτερον ἑκατέρῳ ἀνα-
κεράσας, ἐπιμετρήσας τι ἐπὶ τούτοις καὶ ἄλλο, τὸ ἐξ
ἁπάντων ξυστὰν ἕτερον εἶναι φημὶ ἑκάστου ἀφ' ὧν

114

form, furnishes the body with harmonious mixtures to produce a healthy balance, and furnishes the soul with well-balanced responses to produce the good order of virtue. But if you call any of these results an art, and apply the name of the agent to what is produced, simply because of their affinity, to me it would be like your calling the sun "sunshine," when it is distinct from the sun, being the product of the sun and not the sun itself.

4. Then too, consider the subject from both sides, and let us examine what art is, and what virtue is. So, do you think that art is anything other than reason aiming for some end? One kind operates through handiwork to produce some kind of physical object, which we call its product, such as the house of a builder, the ship of a shipwright, or the picture of a painter. A second kind entails some activity that it performs in the physical realm, such as victory in the case of generalship, health in the case of medicine, and justice in the case of politics. There is also a third kind of art that consists of pure reason with no physical component, wholly in charge of itself and dealing only with itself, such as the arts of geometry, mathematics, and all the others whose goals are purely intellectual and entail neither physical activity nor a material product.

Well then, given these three categories of art, in which should we place virtue, if indeed it is an art? In the productive? You would never say so yourself. But will you hesitate to choose between the practical and theoretical categories? I myself cannot deny the relevance of either one to virtue. Instead, I would combine the two and add something more to them, and say that the combination of them all is distinct from each of the elements that comprise it.

115

MAXIMUS OF TYRE

συνέστη· οἷον εἴ τις τὸ τοῦ ἀνθρώπου σῶμα πῦρ εἶναι
λέγοι ἢ γῆν ἢ ἀέρα, ἢ νὴ Δία ὕδωρ, εἴποιμι ἂν δήπου
ὡς οὔτε πῦρ ἐστιν τὸ σῶμα οὔτε γῆ οὔτε ἀὴρ οὔτε
ὕδωρ· τὸ γὰρ ἐξ ἁπάντων μιχθὲν οὐκ ἔστιν ἕκαστον
ἐκείνων ἀφ' ὧν ἐμίχθη.

5. Πῶς οὖν ἀρετὴ μετέχουσα θεωρίας καὶ πράξεως
οὐκ ἔστιν τέχνη; ταύτῃ μοι λέγοντι ἐφέπου. λέξω δὲ
οὐκ ἐμαυτοῦ λόγον, ἀλλὰ ἐξ Ἀκαδημίας ὁρμηθέντα
καὶ ἐπιχώριον τῆς Πλάτωνος μούσης τε καὶ ἑστίας·
ἀπεδέξατο δὲ αὐτὸν καὶ Ἀριστοτέλης αὐτός·[4] ἐγὼ δὲ
καὶ πορρωτέρω ἐπανάγω· ὑποπτεύω γὰρ ἐξ Ἰταλίας
Ἀθήναζε ἐλθεῖν τὸν λόγον, Πυθαγορείων τινῶν ἐμ-
πορίαν ταύτην καλὴν στειλαμένων εἰς τὴν ἀρχαίαν
Ἑλλάδα. ὁ δ' οὖν λόγος ταύτῃ ἔχει. ἡ τοῦ ἀνθρώπου
ψυχὴ νενέμηται δίχα κατὰ πρώτην νομήν, καὶ τὸ μὲν
αὐτῆς ἐστιν λόγος, τὸ δὲ πάθος· τούτων δὲ ἑκάτερον
πονηρῶς ἔχον καὶ κινούμενον ἀτάκτως συλλήβδην
καλεῖται ὀνόματι ἑνὶ τῷ αἰσχίστῳ, κακία προσαγο-
ρευόμενον. γίγνονται δὲ αἱ πηγαὶ καὶ αἱ γενέσεις τοῦ
αἰσχροῦ τούτου ἐκ τῆς θατέρου τῶν μορίων πλημ-
μύρας τε καὶ ἐπιρροῆς, ἐπειδὰν τὰ πάθη ζέσαντα ἐπι-
κλύσῃ τὴν ψυχήν, καὶ τὰς τοῦ λόγου βλαστήσεις τε
καὶ ἐκφύσεις ἐπιταράξῃ.

[4] αὐτός Stephanus, Davies², Dübner, Koniaris: αὐτῷ R: αὐτοῦ
Trapp

[3] As Trapp (1997a, 226n7) points out, "The analogy seems a
clumsy one: the body is *composed of* its constituent elements,

116

In the same way, if a person should say that the human body is fire, earth, air, or indeed water, I would certainly reply that the body is neither fire, nor earth, nor air, nor water, because the combination of them all is not the same as any one constituent element.[3]

5. How then can virtue participate in both theory and practice, and yet not be an art? Follow along as I try to explain it this way. It is not my own argument, but it comes from the Academy and is a native of Plato's Muse and hearth, which Aristotle himself also accepted. Yet I can trace it even further back, for I suspect that the argument came from Italy to Athens, when some Pythagoreans[4] journeyed to ancient Greece with that fine merchandise. This is what the argument says. The human soul, as in its initial formation, is divided into two aspects: reason and emotion.[5] When either of these two becomes disordered and thrown into disarray, this condition is given one single, comprehensive name of utmost shame, namely vice. The sources and beginnings of this shameful state stem from a flooding and inundation by one of the elements, when the passions boil up and flood the soul and disturb the sprouts and shoots of reason.

but—as Maximus is at such pains to insist—Virtue is *produced by* the combined operations of theoretical and practical science."

[4] Plato's adoption of Pythagorean doctrines is well known. According to Diog. Laert. 3.6, the Pythagoreans Philolaus and Eurytus directly influenced Plato.

[5] The same division of the soul is ascribed to Plato at *Or*. 20.4. [Plut.] *Plac*. 898e attributes the twofold division of the soul into rational and irrational parts to Pythagoras and Plato. For the tripartite (political) division of the soul, see *Or*. 16.4–5.

Καθάπερ τῶν ποταμῶν οἱ χείμαρροι, ὑπὲρ τὰς νομίμους ὁδοὺς ἀναχεόμενοι ἐπὶ γεωργῶν ἀροτοὺς καὶ φυτουργίας, ἐπεθόλωσαν τὴν σωτηρίαν τῶν ἔργων καὶ τὸν κόσμον, οὕτω καὶ ψυχὴ ὑπὸ ἀμετρίας παθῶν ἐξίσταται τῶν λογισμῶν, καὶ δόξαι τότε αὐτῇ ψευδεῖς καὶ πονηραὶ παρὰ τὴν αὑτῆς φύσιν διανίστανται, αὐτὸ ἐκεῖνο τὸ τῶν μεθυόντων πάθος· ἡ πλησμονὴ ἐπεγείρασα τὰ ἔνδον νοσήματα, ὥσπερ ἐκ φωλεοῦ ἑρπετά, συγχεῖ τὸν νοῦν καὶ φθέγγεσθαι προσαναγκάζει τὰς τῶν ἑρπετῶν τούτων φωνάς.

6. Εἰ δέ σοι καὶ σαφεστέρας εἰκόνος δεῖ, ὀχλοκρατίᾳ τινὶ εἰκαστέον τὴν τῆς ψυχῆς πονηρίαν, ἐπειδὰν πόλεως τὸ μὲν ἐπιεικὲς πᾶν βιασθὲν δουλεύῃ, τὸ δὲ ἀνόητον καὶ παντοδαπὸν ἐπιχειρῇ ἄρχειν, ὑπὸ ἐξουσίας ἀδεοῦς θρασυνόμενον· ἀνάγκη γάρ που τὴν τοιαύτην πόλιν πολύφωνόν τε εἶναι καὶ πολυμερῆ καὶ πολυπαθῆ καὶ μεστὴν παντοδαπῶν ἐπιθυμημάτων, ἀκόλαστον μὲν ἐν ἡδοναῖς, ἀκατάσχετον δὲ ἐν ὀργαῖς, ἄμετρον δὲ ἐν τιμαῖς, ἀστάθμητον δὲ ἐν εὐτυχίαις, δυσανάκλητον δὲ ἐν συμφοραῖς.

Ὅταν Περικλῆς μὲν οἴχηται, φεύγῃ δὲ Ἀριστείδης, ἀποθνήσκῃ δὲ Σωκράτης, ἀνίστηται δὲ Νικίας, ἐπιθυμῇ δὲ Κλέων μὲν Σφακτηρίας, Θράσυλλος δὲ Ἰωνίας, Ἀλκιβιάδης δὲ Σικελίας, καὶ ἄλλος ἄλλης γῆς ἢ θαλάττης, συνεπιθυμῇ δὲ αὐτῷ πλῆθος ἀργὸν

Just as when rivers swollen by winter rains pour over their normal channels onto the fields that farmers have plowed and sown, and the muddy flow threatens the survival and orderliness of their work, just so the soul, under an imbalance of passion, is forced to abandon its powers of reasoning, whereupon false and wicked opinions sprout up in it that are opposed to its very nature, just like what happens to drunks, whose excessive drinking rouses up the diseased elements inside them, like reptiles from their lairs, and throws the mind into confusion and forces it to speak the language of these reptiles.

6. But if you need an even clearer illustration, compare this disorder of the soul to a form of mob rule, when every reasonable element in a city is overpowered and enslaved, and the senseless multitude attempts to govern, emboldened by its power that fears no retribution. I should think that such a city is bound to have a cacophony of voices, many divisions, many passions, and be full of all sorts of desires—unbridled in its pursuit of pleasures, uncontrollable in its fits of rage, inequitable in its distribution of honors, unstable in successful times, and hard to rally during disasters.

When Pericles passes away, Aristides is in exile, and Socrates is dead; when Nicias is forced to depart, and Cleon covets Sphacteria, Thrasyllus covets Ionia, and Alcibiades covets Sicily;[6] and when others covet some other land or sea, and when the lazy, disorderly, mercenary,

---

[6] Nicias was sent off reluctantly to command the disastrous Sicilian Expedition in 415 BC; Cleon captured three hundred Spartans on Sphacteria in 425; Thrasyllus campaigned in Ionia in 410–406; Alcibiades championed invading Sicily in 415.

καὶ ἄτακτον καὶ μισθοφόρον, πανταχοῦ περιφερόμε-
νον, ἀνάγκη τὰς ἐπιθυμίας ταύτας δουλείας γεννᾶν
καὶ συμφορὰς καὶ τυραννίδας καὶ πάντα δὴ τὰ ἔκτοπα
ὀνόματα. εἰσὶν καὶ ἐν ψυχῇ δημαγωγοὶ πονηροὶ καὶ
δῆμος ἀκόλαστος, Ἀλκιβιάδαι πολλοὶ καὶ Κλέωνες,
τὴν δειλαίαν οὐκ ἐῶντες ψυχὴν ἀτρεμεῖν καὶ παραχω-
ρεῖν τῷ ἐν αὐτῇ λόγῳ καὶ νόμῳ. αὕτη τῆς ἐν ἀνθρώπῳ
πολιτείας μοχθηρία.

7. Ἀρετὴ δέ, ἧσπερ εἵνεκεν τοὺς πολλοὺς λόγους
κατεστησάμεθα, ἔμπαλιν ἔχει, αὐτὸ ἐκεῖνο κατὰ τὴν
Λακωνικὴν πολιτείαν, ἧς τὸ τοιοῦτο μὲν πλῆθος ἄρχεται, τὸ δὲ ὀλίγον καὶ ἐπιεικὲς ἄρχει· καὶ τὸ μὲν
σῴζει, τὸ δὲ σῴζεται· καὶ τὸ μὲν προστάττει, τὸ δὲ
πείθεται· τὸ δὲ ἐξ ἀμφοῖν ἔργον ἐλευθερία· ἑκάτερον
δὲ ἑκατέρου ἐνδεές, καὶ τὸ ἄρχον τῶν ἀρχομένων καὶ
τὸ ἀρχόμενον τῶν σωζόντων. καὶ περὶ ψυχὴν τὴν
ἔχουσαν καλῶς τὸν αὐτὸν τρόπον σῴζει μὲν ὁ λόγος,
σῴζεται δὲ τὰ πάθη, καὶ μετρεῖ μὲν ὁ λόγος, μετρεῖται
δὲ τὰ πάθη· τὸ δὲ ἐξ ἀμφοῖν ἔργον εὐδαιμονία.

Τάττε δή μοι πᾶν ὅσον θεωρητικὸν τέχνης εἶδος
κατὰ τὸν λόγον, τὸ δὲ ὑπ' αὐτοῦ κοσμούμενον κατὰ
τὰ πάθη· καὶ τὸ μὲν σοφίαν κάλει, ἐπιστήμην οὖσαν,
τὸ δὲ ἀρετήν, ὑπὸ ἐπιστήμης γινόμενον. ἐὰν δὲ μεταθῇς τὰ ὀνόματα καὶ τὴν ἐπιστήμην ἀρετὴν καλῇς,
ἐρήσομαί σε, ὑπὸ τίνος αὕτη γέγονεν· ἐκεῖνο γὰρ
ἔσται ἡ ἐπιστήμη, οὐ τὸ ὑπ' αὐτῆς γενόμενον. τέχνην

fickle multitude shares their desires, it is inevitable that such cravings should spawn slavery, disasters, tyrannies, and indeed everything abnormal you can name. And in the soul as well there are wicked demagogues and an unruly populace, with many an Alcibiades and Cleon,[7] who will not allow the poor soul to rest and yield to the reason and law within it. Such is the depravity of the constitution within a human being.

7. Virtue, however, which is the subject of our lengthy discussion, is the very opposite and is just like the Spartan constitution, under which a multitude like the one described is subservient, and a small and reasonable element governs. The one party provides security and the other is kept safe; the one gives orders and the other obeys. What is achieved by both parties is freedom. Each needs the other: the rulers need obedient subjects, and they in turn need rulers to keep them safe. And the same holds true for a soul in good condition: reason provides security and the emotions are kept safe; reason provides moderation and the emotions are moderated. What is achieved by both parties is happiness.

If you will, put everything that comprises the theoretical aspect of art in the category of reason, and that which is kept in order by reason in the category of emotion. Call the former wisdom, since it is a kind of knowledge, and the latter virtue, since it is a product of knowledge. If you switch the terms and call knowledge virtue, I shall ask you what has produced it, for this is what knowledge will be, the producer rather than the product. Do you call knowl-

---

[7] Cf. *Or.* 7.4, where Alcibiades and Cleon exemplify the fever of desire that overcame the soul of Athens.

τεχνῶν τὴν ἐπιστήμην καλεῖς; ἀκήκοα· ἐπιστήμην
ἐπιστημῶν; μανθάνω, καὶ ἀποδέξομαι τοῦ λόγου ἐὰν
ἕν τί μοι δῷς μικρὸν πάνυ. τέχνην τεχνῶν τὴν τέχνην
λέγε, ἐπιστήμην ἐπιστημῶν τὴν ἐπιστήμην λέγε·
ἀπαλλάγηθι τοῦ ἑτέρου μέρους, καὶ σπένδομαι τῷ
λόγῳ. εἰ δὲ τὴν ἐπιστήμην φυλάττων καὶ ἐξαίρων τὰ
πάθη τὸ τούτων σχῆμα τῇ ἐπιστήμῃ δίδως, ὅμοιον
δρᾷς ⟨οἷον⟩[5] εἴ τις τὴν Φειδίου φυλάξας τέχνην, τὴν
ὕλην ἀφελὼν προσθείη τῇ τέχνῃ τὸ τῆς ὕλης ὄνομα.

Ἐπιστήμην ἄρχειν βούλει βίου καλοῦ; ἀρχέτω·
λόγον ἄρχειν βούλει; ἔστω κοίρανος οὗτος εἷς,

ᾧ ἔδωκε Κρόνου παῖς ἀγκυλομήτεω.

ἀλλ᾽ ἄρχει τίνων; τίνας αὐτῷ δίδως ὑπηρέτας; τίνας
χειρουργοὺς τῶν πράξεων; τὸ σῶμα; εὐθὺς ὅρα τί
δρᾷς· διαπηδᾷς τὴν τάξιν τῶν ἀρχομένων, ἀπὸ τοῦ
στρατηγοῦ ἐπὶ τοὺς σκευοφόρους. οὐχ ὁρᾷς τὸν κόσμον; ὁ στρατηγός, εἶτα οἱ λοχαγοί, καὶ μετὰ τούτους
οἱ ἐνωμοτάρχαι, εἶτα οἱ ὁπλῖται, οἱ πελτασταί, οἱ

---

5 ⟨οἷον⟩ Trapp: ⟨ὡς⟩ Stephanus, edd.

---

8 Trapp (1997a, 229n17): "Maximus here plays with the definition of philosophy as τέχνη τεχνῶν καὶ ἐπιστήμη ἐπιστημῶν,
known also from, for example, Philo, Spec. Leg. 4.156 . . . . His
quibbling might have had a more obvious point to it had he been
at pains in the rest of the lecture to distinguish clearly between a
τέχνη and an ἐπιστήμη."   9 Trapp (1997a, 229n18): "I.e. it
is as ridiculous to treat knowledge (which is a question of pure

edge the art that deals with forms of art?[8] I hear what you
say. Do you call it knowledge of forms of knowledge? I
understand, and I will accept your definition, if you will
grant me one small concession. Call art the art that deals
with forms of art, and call knowledge the knowledge of
forms of knowledge, but remove one of the two elements
and I will make peace with your definition. But if you keep
knowledge as it is, and take away the emotions from virtue
and transfer their arrangement to knowledge, you are acting just like someone who would keep Phidias' artistry as
it is, while removing his materials and calling his materials
his artistry.[9]

Do you wish knowledge to govern a good life? Then let
it rule. Do you wish reason to rule? Then let it be this "one
leader,"

given authority by the son of crooked-counseling
    Cronus.[10]

But over whom does it rule? What subordinates do you
assign to it? What agents to carry out its commands? Is it
the body? Be careful of what you are doing. You are skip-
ping over the chain of command that runs from the general to the baggage carriers. Can you not see the hierarchi-
cal order? There is the general, then the captains, after
them the platoon leaders, then the hoplites, the peltasts,
and the archers. The chain of command descends by de-

intellect) as identical to Virtue (which is a matter of the proper
organization of the passions) as it would be to speak of an artist's
raw materials as responsible for their own organization into a
work of art."   [10] *Il.* 2.204–5, said of Agamemnon by Odysseus, as he marshals the disorderly army.

τοξόται· καταβαίνει ἠρέμα ἡ ὑπηρεσία {ἀπὸ}[6] τοῦ
ὅλου ἀπὸ τῶν ἀρίστων ἐπὶ τὰ φαυλότατα.

8. Ἀλλ᾽ ὁρῶ τὸ πρόχειρον δὴ τοῦτο. ὁ θεὸς οἰκονο-
μεῖ τὸ πᾶν τοῦτο καλῶς καὶ τεχνικῶς καὶ ἐπιστη-
μόνως· τί δὲ οὐ μέλλει; τί οὖν μᾶλλον ἡ ἐπιστήμη ἢ
ἀρετή; εἰ μὲν γὰρ τὴν ἐπιστήμην τοῦ θεοῦ ἀρετὴν
καλεῖς, οὐ νεμεσῶ τῶν ὀνομάτων· οὐ γάρ ἐστιν θεῷ,
καθάπερ ἀνθρώπῳ, τῆς ψυχῆς τὸ μὲν ἄρχον, τὸ δὲ
ἀρχόμενον· ἀλλ᾽ ἁπλοῦν τὸ θεῖον, αὐτὸ ὅτιπερ νοῦς
καὶ ἐπιστήμη καὶ λόγος. εἰ δὲ ἐν τῇ κράσει τοῦ κρείττονος πρὸς τὸ χεῖρον, τὸ τοῦ ἀρχομένου ὄνομα μετατίθης πρὸς τὸ κρεῖττον, μέχρι μὲν τῆς φωνῆς ἀνέχομαι, τὸ δὲ πρᾶγμα οὐ δίδωμι. ἀρετὴν τὴν ἐπιστήμην,
εἰ βούλει, κάλει, ἀλλ᾽ ἐπιστήμην τὴν ἀρετὴν μὴ
κάλει.

Καὶ γὰρ ψευδὴς ὁ λόγος καὶ ἐπισφαλής, νὴ Δία,
εἴ τις ἔσται τοῖς ἀνθρώποις πίστις ὅτι θεωρημάτων
ἀριθμοὶ καὶ μαθήματα ἄττα ἐπὶ τὴν ψυχὴν ἐλθόντα
τὴν ἀρετὴν αὐτοῖς συνεισάγει. πολλοῦ μέντ᾽ ἂν ἦν
ἄξιον τὸ τῶν σοφιστῶν γένος, τὸ πολυμαθὲς τοῦτο
καὶ πολύλογον καὶ πολλῶν μεστὸν μαθημάτων, κα-
πηλεῦον ταῦτα καὶ ἀπεμπολοῦν τοῖς δεομένοις· ἀγορὰ
πρόκειται ἀρετῆς, ὤνιον τὸ χρῆμα.

9. Εἰ δ᾽ οἱ μὲν λόγοι σαφεῖς καὶ πρόχειροι καὶ
μεστὰ πάντα διδασκάλων καὶ μαθημάτων, ἀντιτυπεῖ
δὲ ἔνδοθεν ταῖς τῶν λόγων ὁδοῖς παθήματα χαλεπὰ

---

[6] del. Acciaiolus, Trapp

grees through the entire army from the most important constituents to the least.[11]

8. I can see, however, this immediate objection. God governs the universe with beauty, artistry, and knowledge—how could he not? And what then is his knowledge if not virtue? If you say that god's knowledge *is* virtue, I do not oppose your equating those terms, because god, unlike man, does not have a soul where one part rules and the other obeys. No, god is a unified whole, being pure intellect, knowledge, and reason. But if, in a case where superior and inferior elements are mixed together, you transfer the name of the subordinate element to the ruling one, I can tolerate the manner of speaking, but I do not concede its validity. Call knowledge a form of virtue, if you will, but do not call virtue a form of knowledge.

This is because the argument will prove to be false and dangerous, by Zeus, if men come to believe that mere theoretical principles and certain doctrines can enter the soul and bring virtue along with them. If that were true, then the tribe of sophists would be of great value—those wordy polymaths full of many doctrines, which they peddle and sell to anyone who requests them. A marketplace of virtue is open, and the sale is on!

9. If, however, there are arguments for virtue that are clear and readily accessible, with teachers and doctrines everywhere to be seen, but yet the access of these argu-

[11] Trapp (1997a, 230n20): "Maximus' point here . . . is that the lower division of the bipartite soul is an essential intermediary between intellect and the body (and thus that Virtue must involve the training of this quasi-rational part of the person as well as the acquisition of purely theoretical knowledge by the rational part)."

καὶ ἄγρια καὶ ἐθισμοὶ φαῦλοι καὶ ἀσκήσεις ἄδικοι
καὶ ἐπιθυμίαι ἀλλόκοτοι καὶ τροφαὶ πονηροί, ἐνθυμη-
τέον ὅτι φύσεως δεῖ πρῶτον χρηστῆς, ὥσπερ κρηπῖ-
δος ἀνισταμένῳ τειχίῳ, καὶ μετὰ τοῦτο τροφῆς καὶ
ἔθους πρὸς σωτηρίαν τῆς φύσεως, ὑφ᾽ ὧν φιλία τῇ
ψυχῇ ἐγγίγνεται πρὸς τὰ καλὰ πάντα, συντρεφομένη
τοῖς χρόνοις καὶ συνθέουσα ταῖς ἡλικίαις· ἐπὶ δὲ
τούτοις προσελθεῖν δεῖ τέχνην ἐπισφραγιζομένην βε-
βαιότητι τὰ τῶν παθῶν μέτρα.

Οὕτω γίγνεται εὐδαίμων ψυχὴ καὶ βίος ὑγιὴς καὶ
δόξαι ὀρθαί, ὑπὸ ἁρμονίας καὶ κράσεως συντατττόμε-
ναι. ταῦτα νομοθετεῖ θεός, ταῦτα ἀποφαίνει ἄνδρα
ἀγαθόν, ἀγωγῇ παθῶν ὑπὸ τοῦ λόγου καὶ πειθαρχίᾳ
πρὸς ἐπιστήμην ἑκούσιος· μοχθηρία δὲ χρῆμα ἀκού-
σιον ὑφ᾽ ἡδονῆς ἑλκόμενον.

ments is blocked from within by harsh and fierce passions, bad habits, unjust practices, strange desires, and a wicked upbringing, then one must conclude that the very first requirement is a good[12] natural disposition that is like the foundation for a wall rising upon it, followed by an upbringing and habits that will preserve that nature. These engender in the soul an affection for all beautiful things, which grows over time and matures as one ages. Finally, in addition to all this, art must be on hand to seal with stability the moderation of the emotions.

This is what produces a happy soul, a healthy life, and correct opinions,[13] put in order by harmonious blending. This is what god ordains and what makes a man good, namely the guidance of the emotions by reason and voluntary obedience to the dictates of knowledge. Depravity is involuntary;[14] it is dragged along by pleasure.

[12] *chrēstos* connotes both ethically good and capable.

[13] For the Platonic concept of correct opinions, see *Or.* 24.3.

[14] For the doctrine that nobody willingly does wrong, cf. Pl. *Prt.* 345d–e and Alcin. *Didasc.* 31.184.42–43: "From the fact that virtue is a voluntary thing, it follows that vice is involuntary" (trans. Dillon). Contrast *Or.* 7.2: "depravity is voluntary, misfortune is involuntary."

ORATION 28

INTRODUCTION

This oration, the shortest in the collection, explores the relationship of soul and body with respect to pain, both physical, denoted by *odynē* and *algos*, and psychological, denoted by *lypē* (often contrasted with pleasure).[1] It is closely related to *Or.* 7 ("Which illnesses are more grave, those of the body or those of the soul?") and arrives at a similar emphasis on the primacy of the soul. It opens with the example of Chiron, the famous educator of heroes such as Jason, Achilles, and Asclepius (cf. Pind. *Nem.* 43–55), who hardened their bodies and sharpened their minds, and taught both medicine and justice. But today's medicine is no longer whole, for it has been divided up into specialties (§1). An analysis of physical pain shows that it can invade the entire body, like a fever, or transfer pain immediately from one part to another, as when one stubs a toe. This happens because the soul pervades the entire body (with the exception of nails and hair). Conversely, when the soul is distressed with sorrow or strong passions, the body suffers physically as well (§2). The task then becomes finding a single art, like that of Chiron,

[1] The word *alypos* (free from pain) in the title implies psychological pain.

which can heal both soul and body (§3). Socrates argued in the *Charmides* that when the whole is well the part will also be well, but when it comes to the relationship between the soul and the body, the solution lies in healing the superior element, the soul. It is implied that philosophy and virtue may bring health to the soul and that even if the body cannot be cured, at least the soul can disdain the body's suffering (§4).[2]

[2] Pherecydes serves as such an example at *Or.* 7.4.

ORATION 28

Πῶς ἄν τις ἄλυπος εἴη

1. Πῶς ἄν τις ἀλυπίαν τῇ ψυχῇ περιποιήσαιτο; ἢ δεῖ κἀνταῦθα ἰατροῦ, καθάπερ ἐν ταῖς τοῦ σώματος ὀδύναις, καὶ πρὸς τῷ ἰατρῷ φαρμάκων τινῶν καὶ διαίτης κεκραμένης πρὸς ὑγίειαν καλῶς; τίς ἂν οὖν ἡμῖν γένοιτο ψυχῆς ἰατρός; καὶ ποῖα τὰ φάρμακα; καὶ τίς ὁ τῆς διαίτης οὗτος τρόπος; ἐγὼ μὲν ὑπὸ φιλίας πρὸς τὰ ἀρχαῖα πάντα οὐ διαιρῶ τὰς τέχνας, πείθομαι δὲ τοῖς ποιηταῖς ὅτι ἦν ἐν Πηλίῳ ἀνὴρ ἰατρικός· Χείρωνα αὐτὸν καλοῦσιν· ἡ δὲ τέχνη τῷ Χείρωνι ἦν τείνουσα ἐφ᾽ ἑκάτερα· καὶ γὰρ τὸ σῶμα ἐξεπόνει τῶν προσιόντων αὐτῷ εἰς τὸ ἀκρότατον τοῦ ὑγιεινοῦ θήραις καὶ ὀρειβασίαις καὶ δρόμοις καὶ εὐναῖς ἐπὶ στιβάδων καὶ σιτίοις ἐξ ἄγρας καὶ πώμασιν ἐκ ναμάτων, καὶ τὴν ψυχὴν ἐπεμελεῖτο μηδὲν ἀπολείπεσθαι τοῦ σώματος εὐκινησίᾳ λογισμῶν καὶ τῷ ἀνδρώδει τῶν παθη-

---

[1] A distinction is maintained throughout the oration between psychological pain, *lypē* (and its negated forms *alypos* and *alypia*), and physical pain, *odynē* and *algos* (and its verbal and adjectival forms *algein* and *algeinos*).

ORATION 28

How someone may be free from pain

1. How might someone secure freedom from pain for his soul? Or do we need a doctor here too, as in the case of physical pains?[1] And, in addition to a doctor, do we need certain drugs and a regimen that is well constituted to promote health? Who then might become such a doctor for our souls? And what drugs might be called for? And what form of regimen would this take? For my part, because of my affection for all ancient matters, I do not make a distinction between these two arts, but believe the poets when they say that there was a man on Pelion who was a physician, whom they called Chiron.[2] Now, Chiron's expertise extended to both body and soul, for he would train the bodies of those who came to him to the peak of health through hunting, mountaineering, running, sleeping on beds of leaves, eating wild game, and drinking from streams; but he also saw to it that their souls were in no way inferior to their bodies with regard to the agility of their powers of reason and the manliness of their emo-

---

[2] Chiron, "the most just of the Centaurs" (*Il.* 11.832), taught medicine to numerous heroes, including Asclepius, with whom he is paired at *Orr.* 36.5 and 40.3.

μάτων· καὶ διὰ τοῦτο ἄρα ἰατρικώτατός τε καὶ δικαι-
ότατος ὁμοῦ ἔδοξεν εἶναι ὁ αὐτός, δύο ὀνόματα τέχνῃ
μιᾷ ἐπιφημισάντων τῶν ποιητῶν.

Εἰ δὲ ἐν τῷ παρόντι διεστασίασται πρὸς ἑαυτὴν ἡ
τέχνη, μήπω σοι τοῦτο θαυμαστὸν φανῇ, πρὶν ἄν μοι
δείξῃς καὶ τὴν ἰατρικὴν μίαν τε οὖσαν καὶ ἠθροι-
σμένην, ἀλλ’ οὐ διαλαχοῦσαν τοῦ σώματος τὰ χωρία
ἄλλην ἄλλο τι, τὴν μὲν ὀφθαλμούς, τὴν δὲ ὦτα, τὴν
δὲ ἄλλο τι μόριον, καὶ κινδυνεύουσαν, κατασμικρυνο-
μένην ἑκάστοτε εἰς λεπτὰ καὶ ἀγεννῆ μόρια, ἀφανι-
σθῆναι παντάπασι, καθάπερ τὴν Μακεδόνων φασὶν
ἀρχήν, ἐμπεσοῦσαν εἰς ἄνδρας πολλοὺς οὐκ ἀξιουμέ-
νους βασιλείας ὅλης μετὰ τὸν Ἀλέξανδρον.

2. Τί δὴ οὖν ὁ Χείρων ἦλθεν ἡμῖν δεῦρο ἐπὶ τὸν
λόγον; φέρε ἴδω μετὰ σοῦ εἰ μὴ ἐν δέοντι. εἴπερ γάρ
μοι καλεῖς τι ὀδύνην σώματος—καλεῖς μέντοι—ταύτης τοίνυν, ἡ μὲν ἐξ ἴσου τὸ σῶμα ὑποδῦσα πᾶν καὶ
ἀνακραθεῖσα ἐπιεικῶς ὅλῳ διετάραξεν αὐτοῦ τὴν
κατὰ φύσιν οὐσίαν, καθάπερ σίδηρον πῦρ—αὐτὸ
τοῦτο ὃ καλοῦμεν πῦρ, ὑποκοριζόμενοι δ’ οἱ ἰατρικοὶ
μετέβαλον τοὔνομα, ὡς ἔλαττον ἡμῖν τὸ δεινὸν φα-
νούμενον εἰ πυρετὸς καλοῖτο, ἀλλὰ μὴ πῦρ.

Ἕτερον δ’ αὖ ἐστιν ὀδύνης γένος, ἐπειδὰν μόριον
μὲν ᾖ τὸ τὴν αἰτίαν ἔχον καὶ τὴν πηγὴν τοῦ νοσή-
ματος, ὁρμηθὲν δὲ ἐντεῦθεν τὸ δεινὸν συνελκύσηται
καὶ συνεπισπάσηται τῇ ὀδύνῃ καὶ τὸ ἄλλο σῶμα πᾶν·
καὶ ἔστιν οὕτω δή τις ὀξύτατος ὁ τοῦ ἀλγεῖν δρόμος

tions. And for this reason he himself came to be regarded as foremost in both medicine and justice, and the poets applied both names to his one art.

But if today this art has been torn by internal strife, do not be surprised, unless you can show me that the art of medicine is a single, unified entity, that has not allocated a different art to different parts of the body, with one treating the eyes, another the ears, and so on, and that it does not run the risk of disappearing altogether by dividing up at every opportunity into small and paltry fragments, as the Macedonian empire is said to have done after Alexander, when it fell into the hands of many men not deemed worthy to rule the whole kingdom.[3]

2. So why is it that Chiron has entered our discussion? Let us consider together whether his presence is relevant. Now, is there something you call physical pain—of course there is. Now such pain takes two forms: one form invades the entire body uniformly, and being mingled with nearly all of it, disrupts its natural state as fire does to iron—although the very thing we call fire, doctors have renamed so as to soften its severity, thinking that the affliction would seem less frightening to us, if it was called fever rather than fire.[4]

There is, moreover, another type of physical pain, when a single part of the body is the cause and source of the malady, and the distress originating from it draws together and involves all the rest of the body in the pain. In such a case, there is a very rapid movement of pain from

---

[3] The breakup of the Macedonian empire after Alexander's death in 323 BC is the latest historical event mentioned in the *Orations*.   [4] That is, *pyretos* rather than *pyr*.

ἐπὶ τὸ ὑγιαῖνον ἀπὸ τοῦ κάμνοντος, ὡς μάθοις ἂν τῷ προσπταίσματι ἄκρῳ τῷ ποδί· ἐκ γὰρ ὀνύχων, φασίν, ἐπὶ τὴν κεφαλὴν τὸ ἀλγεινὸν ἐν ἀκαρεῖ θεῖ.

Τοῦτο δὲ οἴει γίγνεσθαι ἄν, εἰ μὴ ἐτύγχανεν ἡ ψυχὴ διειληφυῖα τὸ σῶμα πᾶν πάντοθεν καὶ ἀνακεκραμένη αὐτῷ καθάπερ τὸ φῶς τῷ ἀέρι; ἢ μᾶλλον οὑτωσὶ λέγωμεν· καθάπερ αἱ τῶν θυμιαμάτων ὀδμαὶ καὶ τοῖς πόρρω οὖσιν προσέβαλον, ἀνακεράσασαι τὸν διὰ μέσου ἀέρα τῇ εὐωδίᾳ, ἢ καθάπερ τὰ χρώματα ἐν ὀφθαλμοῖς πόρρωθεν ἔρχεται ὡς ἐπιγράψαντα καὶ ταῦτα τὸν ἀέρα τῇ αὑτῶν φύσει, ταύτῃ νόμιζε καὶ τὴν ψυχὴν πανταχοῦ διεληλυθέναι καὶ μηδὲν εἶναι ἄψυχον σώματος μέρος· τρίχας δὲ καὶ ὄνυχας ἐξαιρῶ λόγου· καὶ γὰρ τῶν δένδρων τὰ φύλλα· καὶ γὰρ ταῦτά ἐστιν ὅσα ἐν φυτοῖς τὰ ἀναισθητότατα· οὕτω δὴ πρὸς τὸ σῶμα ἡ ψυχὴ ἔχουσα ἀνακέκραται αὐτοῦ ταῖς λύπαις καὶ ταῖς ἡδοναῖς, καὶ τὸ ἀλγεῖν ἐστιν αἰτία μὲν σώματος, ψυχῆς δὲ πάθος.

Μία μὲν δὴ αὕτη χορηγία ὀδύνης τῷ ἀνθρώπῳ. δευτέρα δὲ ἥδε, ἔμπαλιν αὖθις αὖ πρὸς τὴν προτέραν ἔχουσα· ἀπὸ γὰρ τῆς ψυχῆς αὕτη ἔρχεται καὶ τελευτᾷ ἐπὶ τὸ σῶμα. ψυχῆς γοῦν καμούσης λύπῃ συγκάμνει τὸ σῶμα καὶ ὑποτήκεται, τοῦτο μὲν ἐκ τῶν ὀφθαλμῶν ἀπολεῖβον δάκρυα, τοῦτο δὲ πᾶν ὠχραινόμενον καὶ ἰσχναινόμενον, ὁποῖα αἱ ἐξ ἐρώτων λῦπαι ἀπεργάζονται καὶ διὰ πενίαν τρυχώσεις καὶ διὰ πένθη ἀκομιστίαι. ἀποπέμπουσιν δὲ τῷ σώματι ὀδύνας καὶ θυμοὶ

134

the suffering part to the healthy part, as you can learn from stubbing your toe: the pain travels in an instant, as they say, from toenail to head.

Do you think that this could happen if the soul were not distributed everywhere throughout the entire body and mingled with it as light mingles with air? Or rather, let us put it this way. Just as the smell of incense reaches even those who are far away, because it infuses the intervening air with its fragrance, or just as colors enter the eyes from afar, because they inscribe, as it were, their own nature on the air, in just the same way you can reckon that the soul pervades the entire body, and that no portion of the body is inanimate.[5] I exempt from consideration, however, hair and nails, on the analogy of leaves on trees, for these are the most insensible parts of plants. The soul bears that same relationship to the body: it is implicated in the body's distresses and pleasures, and although the body may cause the pain, the soul nonetheless experiences it.

That is one source of pain for humans. The second is this, which bears an inverse relationship to the first, for it comes from the soul and terminates in the body. For example, when the soul is in distress with sorrow, the body is distressed as well and pines away. At times, tears pour from its eyes, and at other times the entire body becomes pale and gaunt, as with the sorrow resulting from love, the exhaustion caused by poverty, and the physical neglect caused by mourning. Conveyers of pains to the body also

[5] Literally, without soul.

καὶ ὀργαὶ καὶ φθόνοι καὶ τῶν τῆς ψυχῆς παρὰ μέλος
κινημάτων οὐδὲν ὅ τι οὔ.

3. Τί δὴ οὖν τούτων ἐπιμέμνημαι; ὅτι τὸ ἀλγεῖν καὶ
ἀπὸ ψυχῆς σώματι ἐπιπεμπόμενον καὶ ἀπὸ σώματος
ἐπὶ ψυχὴν παραγινόμενον, εἰκότως ἄρα δέοιτο ἂν καὶ
ἰατρικῆς μιᾶς πρὸς ἀλυπίαν, καθάπερ ὁ Εὔριπος κυβερνητικῆς μιᾶς πρὸς εὔπλοιαν.

Καὶ τοῦτο μὲν ταύτῃ μοι ἔστω ἀποπεφασμένον· τὴν
δὲ ἰατρικὴν αὐτήν, ἥτις ἀμυνεῖται τὰ δεινὰ ἀμφοτέρωθεν ἐπιόντα, τίς ἡμῖν λέξει; ἐγὼ μὲν γὰρ ἀπορῶ, εἴ
τινα ἐξευρήσω δεινὸν τὴν τέχνην κατὰ τὸν Χείρωνα
ἐκεῖνον, ἵνα μοι διπλᾶ τἀγαθὰ ἔλθῃ· καὶ οὔτε πιστεύω
τῷ τεχνιτεύματι (τὸ γὰρ ἔργον μέγα, τῆς Ὄσσης καὶ
τοῦ Ὀλύμπου ὑψηλότερον) οὔτε ἀπιστῶ κομιδῇ· τί
γὰρ οὐκ ἂν ἐθελήσασα πάντολμος ψυχὴ ἐπιτεχνή-
σαιτο;

4. Διὰ μέσου δὴ ἥκων πίστεως καὶ ἀπιστίας, {καὶ}[1]
πρὸς ἄγνοιαν τοῦ εἰδέναι τῇδέ μοι δοκῶ διαιτήσειν
τὴν στάσιν. ὑποπτεύω τοι μίαν μὲν εἶναι τὴν τέχνην,
μὴ μέντοι δυοῖν, ψυχῆς καὶ σώματος, ἀλλὰ τῇ πραγ-
ματείᾳ τοῦ κρείττονος τὴν τοῦ ἑτέρου ἐλάττωσιν ἐξ-
ιωμένην. ὑπῆλθεν γάρ με λέγοντα ὁμοῦ τὸ τοῦ Σωκράτους πρὸς τὸν Χαρμίδην, οὐκ αὐτὸ ἐκεῖνο ἡ
Θρᾴκιος ἐπῳδή, ἀλλὰ ἀντιστρόφως. ὁ μὲν γάρ φησιν
σὺν τῷ ὅλῳ ἰᾶσθαι καὶ τὸ μέρος, καὶ ἀδύνατον εἶναι

---

[1] del. Markland, Dübner, Trapp

include passion, anger, envy, and all the other discordant agitations of the soul, without exception.

3. So why have I mentioned all this? It is because if pain is conveyed from the soul to the body, and also comes to the soul from the body, then it is reasonable that a single medical art would be needed to relieve the distress, just as the Euripus requires one navigational art to sail safely through.[6]

Let us then consider this matter settled. But who is going to tell us what that medical art is, which will ward off the afflictions coming from both quarters? For I am at a loss as to whether I will find anyone skilled in the art like the aforementioned Chiron, so that I might receive its twofold benefits. And neither do I believe in such an art (for the task is great, indeed loftier than Ossa and Olympus),[7] nor yet do I completely disbelieve in it, for what can the all-daring soul not devise if it but has the will?

4. Finding myself at this point in between belief and disbelief, and faced with my inability to know for certain, I think that I may resolve the issue in the following way. I suspect that there is indeed a single art, but that it does not treat two separate entities, soul and body. Instead, by treating the superior element,[8] the defect of the inferior one is healed. But just as I was saying this, I recalled what Socrates said to Charmides—though not exactly his Thracian incantation—but I take his comments the other way around. Socrates said that when the whole is cured, the part is cured as well, and that it is impossible for relief to

---

[6] For the treacherous ebb and flow in these straits, see *Or.* 5.6.   [7] The attempt of the Aloidae to scale heaven by piling Ossa on Olympus is also cited at *Or.* 12.1.   [8] That is, the soul.

σωτηρίαν παραγίνεσθαι τῷ μορίῳ πρὶν καὶ τῷ παντὶ
ἔλθῃ· ὀρθῶς λέγων, κἀγὼ πείθομαι, ὅσα γε ἐπὶ σώματος, ἐν δὲ τῇ ψυχῆς καὶ σώματος συζυγίᾳ ἀντιστρόφως φημὶ ἔχειν· ᾧ γὰρ ἂν τὸ μέρος καλῶς ἔχῃ, ἀνάγκη ⟨καὶ⟩² τὸ πᾶν τούτῳ ἔχειν καλῶς, οὐχ ὁποτερονοῦν
τοῖν μεροῖν, θάτερον δέ.³ ἢ γὰρ τοῦ χείρονος πρὸς τὸ
κρεῖττον ὁμιλία ἐκ τῆς τοῦ κρείττονος σωτηρίας ἀν-
άπτει τὸ χεῖρον. ἤ σοι δοκεῖ ἄνθρωπος ὑγιαίνων τῇ
ψυχῇ λόγον τινὰ ποιεῖσθαι προσπεσούσης ὀδύνης ἐκ
τραυμάτων ἤ τινος ἄλλης κακουχίας σωμάτων; οὐδαμῶς μὰ Δία.

Ἐκείνην δὴ τὴν ἰατρικὴν μαστευτέον καὶ βασανι-
στέον, καὶ ἐκείνην τὴν ὑγίειαν ποριστέον καὶ ἐκθηρα-
τέον, ᾗ τάχα μὲν καὶ περὶ τουτὶ τὸ σῶμα ῥᾳστώνη
ἕψεται, εἰ δὲ μή, πάντως γε ἡ ὑπεροψία τῶν ἐν αὐτῷ
δεινῶν.

2 suppl. Renehan, Trapp
3 δὲ ⟨οὔ⟩ suppl. Reiske, Trapp

come to a part, before it comes to the whole.[9] He was correct, and I agree, at least with regard to the body, but I maintain that the reverse is true when it comes to the combination of soul and body. For if the one part[10] of a person is functioning well—not whichever of the two parts, but only the one—then it is necessary that whole will do well.[11] For the relationship of the lesser part[12] to the greater makes the wellbeing of the lesser one dependent on the wellbeing of the greater one. Or do you think that a man whose soul is healthy takes any account of pain besetting him from wounds or from any other physical distress? Certainly not, by Zeus![13]

This is the kind of medical art[14] that we must search for and put to the test, and this is the kind of health[15] that we must hunt down and obtain, one which, perhaps, will be followed by relief for the body, but even if not, at least be followed by disdain for the body's afflictions.

---

[9] This discussion about curing Charmides' headaches (including the Thracian incantation) is at Pl. *Chrm*. 155e–57c.

[10] That is, the soul.

[11] Trapp, following Reiske, adds οὖ after δὲ and translates the sentence: "If the one constituent in any person is in good condition, then necessarily the whole must be too; it cannot be that one of the two constituents is, while the other is not."

[12] That is, the body.

[13] This point is argued in *Or*. 7.5.

[14] Presumably, philosophy.

[15] Presumably, virtue.

ORATION 29

INTRODUCTION

This is the first of five orations concerned with the role of philosophy in human life. The series concludes with *Or.* 33, which bears the same title as the present one, "What the ultimate end (*telos*) of philosophy is." The philosopher claims to aim for happiness, but there is no agreement on what that word means: every human enterprise can claim happiness as its end. Examples of misguided desires in pursuit of happiness follow. First are foreign rulers: Sardanapallus, Cambyses, and Xerxes (§1). Second are Greek rulers: Pisistratus, Polycrates, Philip II, and Alexander the Great (§2).[1] Third are ordinary people, divided into those with serious pursuits, such as farmers, sailors, soldiers, and even bandits and thugs, and those with frivolous pursuits, such as flatterers, jesters, and contortionists (§3). Two entertaining examples of foolish attempts at happiness follow: an unnamed Ionian who could land balls of dough from a distance on the point of a needle, and a Libyan named Psaphon who taught birds to sing that he was a god and came to be considered one by his people (§4).

The focus shifts from the desire for happiness to a

[1] Both sets of rulers are in chronological order. The overall list is carefully structured and highly satirical.

search for the Good (*to agathon*). Because men do not know what the Good is, their search for it resembles men trying to find gold and silver in the dark by weight and touch. Since they do not know if they have actually found it or if someone else has it, the result is confusion, quarreling, seizing, and distrust (§5). This state of affairs causes myriad evils, such as wars and tyrannies (§6). Divine oracles may speak of impending events such as wars, earthquakes, and plagues, but what is really needed is an oracle that tells how to avoid wars and not fear plagues. Only philosophy can deliver an oracle that tells how to live securely (*asphalōs*). Unfortunately, philosophy itself is riven by factions. The Good itself is indivisible, but philosophy separates the human herd into philosophical camps led by Pythagoras, Thales, Heraclitus, Socrates, Carneades, Diogenes the Cynic, and Epicurus. Whom should one heed (§7)? In fact, this last faction, Epicurean hedonism, will be the subject of the following four orations.

ORATION 29

Τί τέλος φιλοσοφίας

1. Ὁ μὲν Κροτωνιάτης ἐρᾷ κοτίνου Ὀλυμπικῆς, ὁ δὲ
Ἀθηναῖος νίκης τριηρικῆς, ὁ δὲ Σπαρτιάτης ὁπλιτι-
κῆς, ὁ Κρητικὸς θήρας, ὁ Συβαρίτης χλιδῆς, ὁ Θη-
βαῖος αὐλῶν, ὁ Ἴων χορῶν· καὶ ἔτι δ' αὖ ὁ μὲν χρηματιστὴς χρυσοῦ, ὁ δὲ φίλοινος μέθης, ὁ δὲ μοιχὸς[1]
ἔρωτος, ὁ δὲ φιλῳδὸς μελῶν, ὁ δὲ ῥήτωρ λόγων· τουτὶ
δὲ τὸ θρέμμα ὃν καλοῦσιν οἱ ἄνθρωποι φιλόσοφον,
πότερα ἀνέραστος ἡμῖν ἐστιν πάντων χρημάτων; ἢ
λίθου ἂν εἴη ὁ βίος, μή τί γε ζῴου ὁρῶντος καὶ ἐμπνε-
ομένου καὶ κινουμένου καὶ φρονοῦντος, ἔχοντος ὁρ-
μὰς καὶ αἰσθήσεις καὶ ὀρέξεις. ἀλλὰ ἐφίεται μέν τινος, εἰπεῖν δὲ οὐκ ἔχει ξυλλήβδην ὀνόματι ἑνὶ ὅτου
ἐρᾷ. εὐδαιμονίας, φησί. μακάριος τῆς εὐηθείας, εἰ οἴει
τῶν παιδικῶν ἐκστήσεσθαί σοι ἕνα γέ τινα τῶν ἐκ τοῦ
καταλόγου ἀνδρῶν, ἀλλ' οὐκ ἀποκρινεῖσθαι ἕκαστον
ὡς εὐδαιμονίας εἵνεκα ὁ μὲν ἀθλεῖ, ὁ δὲ πίνει, ὁ δὲ
χρηματίζεται, ὁ δὲ κυνηγετεῖ, ὁ δὲ γεωργεῖ, ὁ δὲ πολεμεῖ, ὁ δὲ ἐρᾷ, ὁ δὲ ᾄδει, ὁ δὲ λέγει.

---

[1] μοιχὸς tent. Trapp: φιλήδονος coni. Meiser: μουσικὸς R

ORATION 29

What the ultimate end of philosophy is

1. The man from Croton longs for Olympic olive,[1] the Athenian for a naval victory, the Spartan for an infantry victory, the Cretan for hunting, the Sybarite for luxury, the Theban for pipes, and the Ionian for choruses. Then too, the moneymaker longs for gold, the drunkard for intoxication, the seducer[2] for sex, the music lover for songs, and the orator for speeches. But are we to find that this creature men call a philosopher longs for nothing at all? If so, that would be the life of a stone, certainly not of a being who sees, breathes, moves, thinks, and has impulses, perceptions, and appetites. No, he aims for something, but he cannot state in one comprehensive word what exactly he longs for. He says it is happiness. You are blessed for your naiveté, if you think that any ordinary individual will abandon his predilections in deference to you, without each one responding that it is for the sake of happiness that one man competes, another drinks, or makes money, or hunts, or farms, or goes to war, or loves, or sings, or makes speeches.

---

[1] Croton was famous for its athletes, including Milo (6th c. BC), mentioned in *Or.* 1.5.   [2] I am accepting Trapp's suggestion of "seducer" for the manuscript's "cultured man."

*Ἦ οἴει ὁ Σαρδανάπαλλος ἐκεῖνος, ὁ τὸ σῶμα ἐκτε-
τριμμένος καὶ τὼ ὀφθαλμὼ ἐκτετηκὼς καὶ τὴν χαίτην
διαπεπλεγμένος, καὶ ἐν πορφυρίσιν κατορωρυγμένος
καὶ ἐν βασιλείοις κατακεκλεισμένος καὶ παλλακίσιν
ἀναμεμιγμένος, ἄλλο τι ἐδίωκεν, οὐκ εὐδαιμονίαν; οὐ
γὰρ δὴ κακοδαίμων ἑκὼν ἦν. τί δὲ ὁ Πέρσης ὁ τὰ
Αἰγυπτίων ἱερὰ ἀφανίζων πυρὶ καὶ λοιδορούμενος τῷ
ποταμῷ καὶ καταθύων τὸν βοῦν τὸν Ἄπιν, ἄλλο τι ἢ
καὶ οὗτος ἐπὶ ταὐτὰ σπεύδων ταῦτα ἔδρα; ὁ μὲν γὰρ
Ξέρξης καὶ ἀμφισβητῆσαι ἄν μοι δοκεῖ πρὸς τὸν Δία
περὶ εὐδαιμονίας—τοσοῦτον αὐτὸν οἶμαι ἐπειλῆφθαι
αὐτῆς—καὶ ὅτι αὐτῷ ἡ Ἀσία πρὸς τὴν Εὐρώπην ξυνε-
δεῖτο θαλαττίαις ὁλκάσιν εἰς γεφύρας σχῆμα, ἐφη-
μέρῳ δεσμῷ. καὶ μὴν Ὁμήρῳ ὁ Ποσειδῶν ἰσοτιμίαν
ἄγει, παρὰ δὲ τούτου, ὡς ᾤετο, καὶ πληγὰς λαμβάνει,
εἰς δεσμωτήριον ἐμβάλλεται.

2. Τί λέγω βασιλεῖς βαρβάρους; οὐχ ὁρᾷς τὸν
Πεισίστρατον τὸν Ἕλληνα, τὸν Ἀθηναῖον, ἐπὶ τὴν
ἀκρόπολιν ἀεὶ θέοντα, ὥσπερ τῆς εὐδαιμονίας αὐτῷ
κατορωρυγμένης ἐκεῖ σὺν τῇ ἐλαίᾳ τῇ παλαιᾷ, κἂν
ἐκπέσῃ, μὴ ἀνεχόμενον καθ' ἡσυχίαν ζῆν; Πολυκράτην μὲν γὰρ οὐδὲ τὸ ἐξ Αἰγύπτου νουθέτημα ἔπεισεν
μὴ φρονεῖν μέγα ἐπὶ εὐδαιμονίᾳ, ὅτι ἐκέκτητο θάλατ-

---

3 Cf. *Or.* 7.7: "The poor wretch puts on cosmetics, removes
his facial hair, and fills his eyes with erotic desire." Maximus frequently mentions him as an example of extreme hedonism. A
longer description of his effeminacy and sensuality is at Diod. Sic.
2.23.

Or do you think that notorious Sardanapallus with his wasted body, melting eyes, and braided hair, who was buried in purple robes, confined to his palace, and surrounded by concubines, was pursuing anything other than happiness?[3] He certainly was not intentionally miserable! And what about the Persian[4] who burned the sacred objects of the Egyptians, insulted their river, and sacrificed the bull god Apis? Wasn't he too in pursuit of the very same thing by doing all that? And Xerxes, it seems to me, could have rivaled even Zeus in terms of happiness, so much of it, I think, he held in his grasp, considering the fact that he united Asia and Europe with transport ships in the form of a bridge—albeit a short-term union. Then too Poseidon, who in Homer claims an equal status with Zeus,[5] received lashes from Xerxes (or so Xerxes imagined) and was thrown into prison.[6]

2. Why mention only foreign kings? Do you not see Pisistratus, the Athenian Greek, forever running up onto the Acropolis,[7] as if his happiness were buried up there with the ancient olive tree, and being unable to tolerate a peaceful life, even when deposed?[8] Not even the warning that came from Egypt could persuade Polycrates to stop priding himself on his happiness, because he possessed

---

[4] Cambyses, who burned the corpse of Amasis (Hdt. 3.16.2) and killed the bull-god Apis (Hdt. 3.29).

[5] Cf. *Il*. 15.187–93, a passage also cited at *Or.* 26.7.

[6] For Xerxes' symbolic whipping and shackling (not imprisonment) of the sea, see Hdt. 7.35.1.

[7] That is, in order to seize power.

[8] For his two failed coups and eventual success in 546 BC, see Hdt. 1.59–64.

ταν Ἰωνικὴν καὶ τριήρεις πολλὰς καὶ σφενδόνην
καλήν, καὶ Ἀνακρέοντα ἑταῖρον καὶ παιδικὰ Σμερ-
δίην.

Ἀλλ᾽ οἶδε μὲν ἐοίκασιν οἱ δυνάσται ἐξηπατημένοις
ὑπὸ ἁβρότητος καὶ ἡδονῆς, εὐπροσώπων κακῶν.
Ὁμήρου δὲ οὐκ ἀκούεις ἐγκωμιάζοντος τοὺς Αἰακίδας,
ὅτι ἦσαν ἄνδρες

πολέμῳ κεχαρηότες ἠΰτε δαιτί;

καὶ τί ἂν εἴη πολέμου ἀχαριστότερον; ἀλλὰ καὶ ὡς τὸ
ἄχαρι δήπου πρᾶγμα ἔτυχεν καὶ τοῦτο οὐ φαύλων
ἐραστῶν· οἷος ἦν καὶ ὁ Φίλιππος αὖθις ποτέ, ὃς κατὰ
Μακεδονίαν ἐξὸν μένειν καὶ ζῆν ἐπὶ τοῖς Ἀμύντου
ἀγαθοῖς καὶ τῇ Περδίκκου εὐδαιμονίᾳ, ἐζήτει ταύτην
περιιὼν ἄλλοθι, ὥσπερ ἐκπεπτωκυῖαν τῆς Μακεδόνων
γῆς. καὶ διὰ τοῦτο, ὡς ἔοικεν, Τριβαλλοῖς ἐπολέμει,
Ἰλλυριοῖς ἐπῄει, ἐπολιόρκει Βυζάντιον, κατέσκαπτεν
Ὄλυνθον, Ἀθηναίους ἐξηπάτα, Θετταλοῖς συνετίθετο,
Θηβαίοις ἐσπένδετο, Ἐλάτειαν ἐλάμβανεν, Φωκέας
ἀνίστη, ἐπιώρκει, ἐψεύδετο, ἐπηροῦτο· οὐδὲν ἦν Φι-
λίππῳ ἀπώμοτον, οὐ ῥῆμα, οὐκ ἔργον, οὐκ αἰσχύνη,
οὐκ ἀδοξία. ἐρώμεθα τὸν Φίλιππον· "τίνος ἀντικαταλ-
λάττῃ πόνους τοσούτους καὶ κινδύνους πραγμάτων
καὶ πηρώσεις ὀμμάτων; κακοδαιμονίας ἐρᾷς;" γελοῖον

---

9 For the warning of the Egyptian king Amasis and Polycrates'
precious ring, see Hdt. 3.39–42. For Polycrates, Anacreon, and
Smerdies, see *Or.* 20.1. For Polycrates' demise, see *Or.* 34.5.

the Ionian Sea, a large fleet of triremes, and a precious ring, as well as having Anacreon as his companion and Smerdies as his boyfriend.[9]

These rulers resemble men deceived by those specious evils, luxury and pleasure. But do you not also hear Homer praising the Aeacidae[10] for being men who

delighted in war and feasting?[11]

What could be more unpleasant than war? Nonetheless, even this clearly unpleasant enterprise has had its share of no ordinary lovers. One such was Philip in his day. He could have remained in Macedon living off the wealth amassed by Amyntas and the happiness achieved by Perdiccas,[12] yet went around seeking it elsewhere, as if happiness had been banished from Macedonian territory. It was apparently for this reason that he made war on the Triballi, attacked the Illyrians, laid siege to Byzantium, razed Olynthus, deceived the Athenians, allied with the Thessalians, made a treaty with the Thebans, captured Elatea, displaced the Phoceans, broke his oath, lied, and lost his eye. Nothing was off limits for Philip—no word, deed, shame, or infamy.[13] So, let us ask Philip, "What do you expect to gain from all your efforts, dangerous exploits, and your damaged eyes? Do you long for unhappiness?" What a ridiculous question! Philip obviously did

[10] Descendants of Aeacus, notably Achilles and Ajax.

[11] Hes. *Cat*. fr. 206 M-W, not from Homer.

[12] Amyntas III was Philip's father; Perdiccas I was the first king of Macedon; cf. Hdt. 8.137–39.

[13] For an indictment of Philip's perfidiousness, cf. Dem. *Olynth*. 2.5–8.

147

τὸ ἐρώτημα. ἀλλ' οὐχ εὗρε δήπου τὸ ζητούμενον ὁ Φίλιππος, ἀλλ' ἐξέστη² αὐτὸν ἡ εὐδαιμονία.

Καὶ διὰ τοῦτο ὁ Ἀλέξανδρος, χαίρειν τῇ Εὐρώπῃ φράσας ὡς ἐρήμῳ ἀγαθῶν εἰς τὴν Ἀσίαν ἐπεραιοῦτο, ὑποπτεύων τὴν εὐδαιμονίαν ἢ ἐν Σάρδεσιν ἐν τῷ χρυσῷ ψήγματι κατορωρύχθαι, ἢ ἐν Καρίᾳ ἐν τοῖς Μαυσωλοῦ θησαυροῖς, ἢ ἐν τοῖς Βαβυλωνίων τείχεσιν, ἢ ἐν τοῖς Φοινίκων λιμέσιν, ἢ ἐν ταῖς Αἰγυπτίων ἠιόσιν, ἢ ἐν ταῖς Ἀμμωνίων ψάμμοις· οὐκ ἐξήρκεσεν δ' αὐτῷ οὐ Δαρεῖος φεύγων, οὐκ Αἴγυπτος ληφθεῖσα, οὐκ Ἄμμων πατήρ, οὐ Βαβυλὼν ἁλοῦσα, ἀλλ' ἐπὶ τὴν Ἰνδῶν γῆν ἔδραμεν αὐτοῖς ὅπλοις. ἐρώμεθα τὸν Ἀλέξανδρον τὴν αἰτίαν τοῦ δρόμου· "τί ποθεῖς; τίνος ἐρᾷς; ἐπὶ τί σπεύδεις;" ἄλλο τί φησιν ἢ εὐδαιμονίαν;

3. Ἔα μοι τοὺς βασιλεῖς καὶ τοὺς δυνάστας. τὰ δημοτικὰ οὐχ ὁρᾷς, ὡς πᾶς ἀνὴρ πανταχόθεν ἐπὶ ταὐτὸ θεῖ, ὁ μὲν γῆς ἁπτόμενος, ὁ δὲ περὶ θάλατταν πραγματευόμενος, ὁ δὲ περὶ πολέμους ἀσχολούμενος, ὁ δὲ περὶ λόγους σχολὴν ἄγων, ὁ δὲ γάμον λαμβάνων, ὁ δὲ παῖδας τρέφων, ὁ δὲ ληστεύων, ὁ δὲ ὑβρίζων, ὁ δὲ δωροδοκῶν, ὁ δὲ μοιχεύων, ὁ δὲ μισθοφορῶν, κινδυνώδεις ὁδοὺς καὶ σφαλερὰς οἱ πολλοὶ ἰόντες ἐπ' αὐτῶν τῶν κρημνῶν καὶ τῶν βαράθρων· οὓς οἰκτείραι ἄν τις· †τοῦτο δὲ οὐκ, ἂν λάθωσιν†.³ καὶ

---

² ἐξέστη coni. Reiske: ἐξανέστησεν coni. Stephanus, Davies², Dübner: ἐξαναισθεν R: obel. Trapp, Koniaris

³ obel. Trapp, Koniaris

not find what he was seeking, because happiness kept eluding him.

Likewise, Alexander bade farewell to Europe, because he considered it devoid of good things, and crossed over to Asia, suspecting that happiness was buried in Sardis in its gold dust, or in the treasury of Mausolus in Caria, or in the walls of Babylon, or in the harbors of Phoenicia, or in the shores of Egypt, or in the sands of the Ammonians. He was not satisfied with putting Darius to flight,[14] conquering Egypt, gaining Ammon as his father,[15] or capturing Babylon, so he hastened with his army to the land of India. Let us then ask Alexander the reason for his expedition. "What do you desire? What do you long for? What are you in pursuit of?" Will his answer be anything other than happiness?

3. Set aside, if you will, these kings and rulers. Do you not see how among ordinary people everyone runs from every quarter after the same thing? One man works the land, another plies his trade on the sea; one is occupied with war, another spends his time on oratory; one man takes a wife, another raises children; others are bandits, thugs, bribe takers, adulterers, or mercenaries—most of them traveling down slippery and dangerous paths along the very edge of cliffs and precipices.[16] One might well pity them [but not if they avoid detection].[17] And yet these are

---

[14] Darius III fled after the battles of Issus (333 BC) and Gaugamela (331 BC).   [15] The Egyptian god Zeus Ammon called Alexander his son; cf. *Or*. 41.1.

[16] For the dangers on "the road of life," cf. *Orr*. 1.3, 19.1, 34.2, and 39.3.

[17] Trapp rightly considers this an interpolated comment.

οὗτοι μὲν σπουδαστικοί τινες τοῖς βίοις· τὸ δὲ ἀργὸν
καὶ ἀλύον τοῦτο πλῆθος, ἆρα καὶ τοῦτο προήκατο τὴν
τοῦ ἀγαθοῦ ἐλπίδα; οὐδαμῶς μὰ Δία. οὐ γὰρ ἂν οὔτε
οἱ κόλακες πράγματα εἶχον τὰς τῶν πλουσίων ἐπιθυμίας θεραπεύοντες, οὔτε οἱ βωμολόχοι τωθασμῶν καὶ
γελώτων ἐκθηρώμενοι γενέσεις τε καὶ ἀγωγάς, οὔτε
οἱ τὰ θαύματα ἐπιδεικνύμενοι, ἐκκλώμενοί τε καὶ
στρεβλούμενοι τὰ σώματα, οὔτε ἄλλος ἄλλο τι ἐπι-
μηχανώμενος σπουδῇ, κἂν μάταιον ᾖ.

4. Ἦλθεν εἰς Βαβυλῶνα ἀνὴρ Ἴων παρὰ τὸν μέγαν
βασιλέα, τέχνην τινὰ ἐπιδεικνύμενος διαφέρουσαν εὐ-
μηχανίᾳ· μάζας στέατος ποιούμενος μικρὰς στρογ-
γύλας, κατὰ βελόνης ὀρθίου πόρρωθεν ἀφιείς, τῆς
βελόνης ἄκρας ἐτύγχανεν, καὶ ᾤετο δήπου μέγα εἶναι
αὐτῷ ἀγαθὸν τὴν εὐστοχίαν τῆς βελόνης, οὐχ ἧττον
ἢ ὁ Ἀχιλλεὺς τὴν τῆς μελίας τῆς ἐκ τοῦ Πηλίου. καὶ
ἐν Λιβύῃ ἀνὴρ Λίβυς, Ψάφων ὄνομα, ἐραστὴς εὐδαιμονίας οὐ ταπεινῆς, μὰ Δία, οὐδὲ τῆς περιθεούσης
ταύτης, ἀλλὰ ἤθελεν γὰρ θεὸς εἶναι δοκεῖν, ξυλλαβὼν
οὖν τῶν ᾠδικῶν ὀρνίθων πολλούς, ἐδίδασκεν ᾄδειν
τοὺς ὄρνιθας "Μέγας θεὸς Ψάφων," καὶ ἠφίει αὖθις
ἐπὶ τὰ ὄρη. οἱ δὲ αὐτοί τε ᾖδον καὶ οἱ ἄλλοι ὄρνιθες
ἐθιζόμενοι τῇ φωνῇ. Λίβυες δὲ θείαν νομίσαντες εἶναι
τὴν φήμην ἔθυον Ψάφωνι καὶ ἦν αὐτοῖς θεὸς ὑπὸ ὀρνίθων κεχειροτονημένος, οὐδὲν οἶμαι τοῦ Περσικοῦ

people who at least lead earnest lives. What about the lazy and idle majority? Have they abandoned their hopes of gaining the Good? Certainly not, by Zeus! Otherwise, flatterers would not take the trouble to pander to the desires of the rich; buffoons to search for material and ways to provoke jeers and laughter; contortionists to display the wonders of their art by bending and twisting their bodies;[18] nor anyone else to take pains to devise some other trick, no matter how pointless.

4. An Ionian once came before the Great King at Babylon and displayed an art of exceptional skill. He would make little balls from bread dough, throw them from a distance at an upright needle, and land them on the tip of the needle. He clearly took no less pride in the accuracy of his aim at the needle than Achilles did in the accuracy of his spear of Pelian ash. There was also a native of Libya whose name was Psaphon, who did not long for happiness that was vulgar or of the commonplace kind, by Zeus! No, he wished to be considered a god. So he gathered a great many songbirds and taught them to sing, "Psaphon is a great god." He then released them back into the mountains, where they sang and were joined by the other birds that had grown accustomed to their song. The Libyans, believing that this was the voice of the gods, began sacrificing to Psaphon, and he became their god by the vote of birds,[19] and in my view he was not a bit shoddier than the

[18] Entertainment by contortionists at a symposium is decried at Xen. *Symp.* 7.3.

[19] A similar story is told of Hanno the Carthaginian at Ael. *VH* 14.30, where his trick fails because the birds revert to their natural songs.

φαυλότερος, ὃν οὐ πρότερον προσεκύνησαν Πέρσαι
πρὶν αὐτὸν ἐχειροτόνησεν ἐπὶ τὴν ἀρχὴν ὑβριστὴς
ἵππος.

5. Οὕτως ἄρα οὐδὲν ἕτερον ἑτέρῳ ὁμολογεῖ τῶν
ἀνθρωπίνων, ἀλλὰ πάντες ἔρωτος κοινωνοῦντες ἑνὸς
τοῦ πρὸς τὸ ἀγαθὸν ἵενται πολλὰς καὶ παντοδαπὰς
ὁδούς, ἄλλος ἄλλης πράξεως νενεμημένος καὶ μοῖραν
καὶ τύχην. καὶ κοινὸς μὲν πᾶσιν ὁ τοῦ ἀγαθοῦ πόθος,
τυγχάνει δὲ τοῦ ζητουμένου οὐδὲν μᾶλλον ἄλλος ἄλ-
λου· ἀλλὰ ὥσπερ οἱ ἐν σκότῳ χρυσὸν καὶ ἄργυρον
μαστεύοντες, ἄποροι ὄντες τοῦ τὸ θηρώμενον ἐλέγξον-
τος φέγγους,[4] βρίθει καὶ ἐπαφῇ ἄπιστον εἰκασίαν
λαβόντες, περιπίπτοντες ἀλλήλοις καὶ διαδάκνοντες,
οὔτε ἀφιέναι τολμῶσιν, μὴ ἄρα ἔχωσιν, οὔτε παύσασθαι πονούμενοι, μὴ ἄρα οὐκ ἔχωσιν· ἔνθα δὴ θόρυ-
βος καὶ στάσεις καὶ παρακελεύσεις, φωναὶ ζητούν-
των, στενόντων, διωκόντων, ὀδυρομένων, ἁρπαζόντων,
ἀφαιρουμένων· καὶ βοῶσιν μὲν πάντες καὶ παιωνίζου-
σιν, ὡς δῆτα ἐντετυχηκότες τῷ ἀγαθῷ, ἔχει δὲ οὐδείς,
ὑπὸ δὲ ἀπιστίας τὰ τοῦ πλησίον ἕκαστος εὑρήματα
διερευνᾶται.

6. Τοῦτο τὸ πάθος ταράττει τὴν γῆν καὶ τὴν θάλατταν, τοῦτο ἀθροίζει τὰς ἐκκλησίας, τοῦτο συνάγει τὰ
δικαστήρια, τοῦτο πληροῖ τὰ δεσμωτήρια, τοῦτο πήγνυσιν ναῦς, τοῦτο τριήρεις καθέλκει, τοῦτο πολέμους

---

[4] φέγγους Heinsius, Trapp: φθόγγου R: φθόγγῳ Davies[2],
Dübner, Koniaris

Persian, whose people did not pay him obeisance until a sexually aroused horse elected him to his reign.[20]

5. So it turns out that no human pursuit agrees with another, but nonetheless all men share a single desire for the Good, although they take many different routes in pursuit of it, with different men having been allotted different occupations by fortune and destiny. And though they all share a desire for the Good, no one has any greater success at finding what he seeks than anyone else. They are just like people searching for gold and silver in the dark. Because they lack any light to verify what they seek, they make uncertain guesses by means of weight and touch. They then collide with one another and fight tooth and nail, afraid to let go in case they actually have what they seek, and yet afraid to stop struggling in case they do not in fact have it. The result is confusion, quarreling, exhortations, and the cries of people searching, groaning, pursuing, lamenting, seizing, and being despoiled. Everyone is shouting and declaring victory, as if really having found the Good, whereas no one actually has it, while each one, driven by mistrust, tries to examine what his neighbor has found.

6. This state of affairs throws the land and sea into turmoil, it convenes assemblies, summons juries, fills the prisons, builds ships, launches triremes, starts wars, puts

[20] Darius' groom used the scent of a mare in heat to elicit a whinny from Darius' horse as an omen to elect him king (Hdt. 3.85–87).

συνάπτει, τοῦτο ἀνεβίβασεν ἐπὶ ἵππους ἱππέας, ἐπὶ
ἅρματα ἡνιόχους, ἐπὶ ἀκρόπολιν τυράννους. διὰ τοῦτο
ξεναγοί, διὰ τοῦτο μισθοφόροι

ἄνδρας μὲν κτείνουσι, πόλιν δέ τε πῦρ ἀμαθύνει,
τέκνα δέ τ᾽ ἄλλοι ἄγουσι βαθυζώνους τε
  γυναῖκας·

καὶ ἄλλων μυρίων κακῶν ἀνέχονται οἱ ἄνθρωποι δι᾽
οὐδὲν ἄλλο ἢ δι᾽ ἐλπίδα ἀγαθοῦ καὶ ἄγνοιαν. ἐνέφυσεν γάρ τι ὁ θεὸς ζώπυρον τῷ τῶν ἀνθρώπων γένει
τῆς προσδοκίας τοῦ ἀγαθοῦ, ἀπέκρυψεν δὲ αὐτοῦ τὴν
εὕρεσιν·

ῥίζῃ μὲν μέλαν ἔσκε, γάλακτι δὲ εἴκελον ἄνθος.

οὐ γὰρ ἐξαπατήσει με Ὅμηρος τῷ ὀνόματι· ὁρῶ τὸ
μῶλυ καὶ συνίημι τοῦ αἰνίγματος καὶ σαφῶς οἶδα ὡς
χαλεπὸν εὑρεῖν τὸ χρῆμα τοῦτο

ἀνδράσι γε θνητοῖσι· θεοὶ δέ τε πάντα ἴσασιν.

7. Νῦν δὲ τοῖς ἀνθρώποις περὶ μὲν ἀτόπου λέβητος
ὁ Ἀπόλλων λέγει ἑψομένου ἐν Λυδοῖς, καὶ τὸ ξύλινον
τεῖχος λέγει καὶ τὸν στέννυρον ἰσθμὸν καὶ σεισμὸν
μέλλοντα καὶ ἐπιόντα πόλεμον καὶ κατιόντα λοιμόν·
τὸν δὲ τούτων πρεσβύτερον χρησμὸν οὐ λέγει, ὅπως

---

21 Il. 9.593–94, Phoenix describing the sack of a city.
22 Cf. Or. 5.8 for the "spark" of philosophy, and Or. 31.4 for
the "spark" of intellect.

cavalrymen on their horses, charioteers on their chariots, and tyrants on the Acropolis. Because of this, generals and their mercenaries

> kill the men and burn down the city, while the others lead away the children and the deep-girded women.[21]

And humans endure myriad other evils, caused by nothing other than their hope of attaining the Good and their ignorance of what it is. That is because god has engendered in the human race an expectation of the Good like a spark,[22] but has hidden where to find the Good.

> It was black at the root, but its flower was white as milk.[23]

Homer's name for this substance will not fool me, for I can see his moly, I understand its allegorical meaning, and I know full well how difficult this thing is to find

> for mortal men, whereas the gods know everything.[24]

7. But as it is, Apollo speaks to humans about some strange kettle boiling in Lydia, he speaks of the wooden wall, the narrow isthmus, an imminent earthquake, an approaching war, and a coming plague.[25] He does not, however, deliver an oracle more important than these, namely one that tells how war may be averted, or how I may not

---

[23] *Od.* 10.304, describing the magical plant moly, given to Odysseus by Hermes to counteract Circe's spells.

[24] *Od.* 10.306.

[25] The boiling kettle (Hdt. 1.47.2), the wooden wall (Hdt. 7.141.3), the earthquake (Hdt. 6.98.3), and the plague (Thuc. 2.47). For the "narrow isthmus" in the time of the Heraclidae, cf. Apollod. 2.8.2. For the folly of such oracles, see *Or.* 13.1–2.

πόλεμος μὴ γένηται, πῶς τείχους μὴ δεηθῶ, πῶς λοιμὸν μὴ φοβηθῶ. ἀλλ᾽ ὁ μὲν Ἀπόλλων ταῦτα ἐκ Δελ-
φῶν οὐ λέγει, οὐδὲ ὁ Ζεὺς ἐκ Δωδώνης λέγει, οὐδὲ ἐξ
ἄλλης γῆς ἄλλος θεός, φιλοσοφία δὲ λέγει. ὦ χρησμοῦ καλοῦ καὶ μαντικῆς πολυωφελεστάτης· πείσο-
μαι τῇ χρησμῳδίᾳ, ἐὰν ὡμολογημένην ταύτην ἴδω.
ἀστασίαστόν μοι χρησμὸν λέγε· τοιαύτης δέομαι
μαντικῆς, ᾗ πεισθεὶς βιώσομαι ἀσφαλῶς. ποῖ πέμ-
πεις τὸ τῶν ἀνθρώπων γένος; τίνας ὁδούς; ἐπὶ ποῖον
τέλος; ἐν τοῦτο ἔστω, κοινὸν ἔστω.

Νῦν δὲ καὶ φιλοσοφίας ὁρῶ πολλὰς ἀποικίας, ἄλλον ἀλλαχοῦ στελλόμενον· ὡς ἐπὶ Βοιωτίαν Κάδμον,
ὡς Ἀρχίαν ἐπὶ Συρακούσας, ὡς Φάλανθον ἐπὶ Τά-
ραντα, ὡς Νηλέα ἐπὶ Μίλητον, ὡς Τληπόλεμον ἐπὶ
Ῥόδον. ἢ τὴν μὲν γῆν ἀνάγκη νενεμῆσθαι τοῖς τό-
ποις, καὶ οἰκεῖν ταύτης ἄλλους ἄλλην μοῖραν· τὸ δὲ
ἀγαθὸν ἕν, ἀνέμητον, ἄφθονον, ἀνενδεές, πολυαρκὲς
πάσῃ φύσει λογικῇ καὶ διανοητικῇ, ὡς ἥλιος εἷς ἀγαθὸν ἐν φύσεως ὁρατικῆς, καὶ μουσικὴ μία ἀγαθὸν ἐν
φύσεως ἀκουστικῆς, καὶ ὑγίεια μία φύσεως σαρκίνης.

Ἀλλὰ τοῖς μὲν ἄλλοις ζῴοις κατ᾽ ἀγέλην ἑκάστην
ἀποκέκριται πρὸς σωτηρίαν ἀγαθὸν ἕν, καὶ κοινωνεῖ
ἴσου βίου καὶ τέλους ἑνὸς τὰ ὅμοια τοῖς ὁμοίοις, ἕκαστα ἑκάστοις, τὰ πετόμενα, τὰ βαδίζοντα, τὰ ἕρ-

---

26 For the superiority of internal peace over external harm,
see *Orr.* 22.7 and 28.4.   27 That is, a philosophical oracle
not subject to rival sects, like those listed below.

need any wall at all, or how I need not fear a plague.[26] No, Apollo does not announce such things from Delphi, nor Zeus from Dodona, nor any other god from any other land—only philosophy does that. Oh, what a beautiful oracle and a most beneficial kind of prophecy! I shall heed this oracle, if only I can see that it has consistency. Give me an oracle that is not riven with factions.[27] I require the kind of prophecy that I may heed and thereby lead a secure life. Where are you sending the human race? By which routes? To what end? Let it be just one end, let it be one common to all.

But as things now stand, I can see many colonies of philosophy, each setting off for a different place, like Cadmus to Boeotia, Archias to Syracuse, Phalanthus to Tarentum, Neleus to Miletus, and Tlepolemus to Rhodes.[28] Now, there is no escaping the fact that the earth is divided into localities, and that different people inhabit different portions of it. But the Good is one single thing, indivisible, abundant, inexhaustible, and of much benefit to every creature with a rational and intelligent nature, just as the sun alone is the single good for all nature that can see, music alone is the single good for all nature that can hear, and health alone is the good for all nature that consists of flesh.

Now when it comes to the other creatures, each species has its own single good to ensure its survival, and those similar members share with one another a similar mode of existence with a single end,[29] whether they fly, walk, or

[28] All founders of colonies.
[29] This *telos* is survival.

πόντα, τὰ τὴν ὑγρὰν δίαιταν ἀσπαζόμενα, τὰ σαρκο-
φάγα, τὰ ποιηφάγα, τὰ καρποφάγα, τὰ ἀγελαστικά,
τὰ ἥμερα, τὰ ἄγρια, τὰ εὔκερω, τὰ ἄκερω· κἂν μεταθῇς τοὺς βίους, παρανομεῖς περὶ τὴν φύσιν.

Τὴν δὲ τῶν ἀνθρώπων ἀγέλην, τὴν σύννομον, τὴν
ἡμερωτάτην, τὴν κοινωνικωτάτην, τὴν λογικωτάτην,
κινδυνεύει διαλύειν καὶ διασπᾶν οὐκ ἐπιθυμία δημώ-
δης μόνον οὐδὲ ὀρέξεις ἄλογοι οὐδὲ ἔρωτες κενοί,
ἀλλὰ καὶ τὸ βεβαιότατον τῶν ὄντων φιλοσοφία. πολλοὺς καὶ αὕτη δήμους ποιεῖ καὶ νομοθέτας μυρίους,
διασπᾷ καὶ διασκίδνησιν τὴν ἀγέλην καὶ πέμπει ἄλλον ἀλλαχοῦ, Πυθαγόραν μὲν ἐπὶ μουσικήν, Θαλῆ δὲ
ἐπὶ ἀστρονομίαν, Ἡράκλειτον δὲ ἐπὶ ἐρημίαν, Σωκράτην δὲ ἐπὶ ἔρωτας, Καρνεάδην δὲ ἐπὶ ἄγνοιαν,
Διογένην ἐπὶ πόνους, Ἐπίκουρον ἐφ' ἡδονήν. ὁρᾷς τὸ
πλῆθος τῶν ἡγεμόνων, ὁρᾷς τὸ πλῆθος τῶν συνθημάτων; ποῖ τις τράπηται; ποῖον αὐτῶν καταδέξωμαι;
τίνι πεισθῶ τῶν παραγγελμάτων;

crawl; whether they prefer to live in water, or eat flesh, grass, or fruit; whether they live in herds, or are tame or wild, or have horns or not. And if you interchange their modes of existence, you violate nature's laws.

Yet our human herd, which congregates together and is the most gentle, sociable and rational herd of all, is in danger of being broken up and torn apart not only by vulgar desires, irrational appetites, and vain lusts, but even by the most stable thing of all, philosophy! It produces many communities and countless legislators; it tears apart the herd and scatters it, sending one member here another there—Pythagoras to music, Thales to astronomy, Heraclitus to solitude, Socrates to love affairs, Carneades to skepticism,[30] Diogenes to toils, and Epicurus to pleasure. Do you see the multitude of leaders? Do you see the multitude of watchwords?[31] Where is anyone to turn? Which of them should I accept? Which of their precepts am I to heed?

[30] Carneades (ca. 214/3–129 BC) was head of the so-called Skeptical Academy.
[31] Various camps of philosophy have their watchwords (e.g., music, astronomy, etc.).

ORATION 30

INTRODUCTION

This and the following two orations take up the challenge put forth in §4 that the speaker will abandon virtue for pleasure on the condition that pleasure is secure (*asphalēs*).[1] Extended nautical analogies enliven the discussion. Whereas horses and dogs can attain excellence (*aretē*) through skillful training, no expertise (*technē*) exists to educate humans to be good. Indeed, when people first take up philosophy, which deals with this issue, they become so confused by its conflicting claims that they give up hope of attaining their proper end (*telos*), and, like inexperienced sailors in a storm, their souls are so shaken that they despair of reasoned argument and of ever anchoring in a stable port (§1). Human opinions and emotions, the very subjects of philosophy, are so complex that they are like a vast sea that requires an expert skipper to navigate. Who will be that helmsman? First is Epicurus, whose philosophical ship is pleasant enough to see from

[1] The need for security and stability (denoted by such adjectives as ἀσφαλής, βέβαιος, ἑδραῖος, ὡμολογημένος, and στάσιμος) that only philosophy can provide in the face of continual flux (here exemplified by the sea) is a frequent theme in the *Orations*.

land but is completely unprepared for storms (§2). A lengthy description of a pleasure barge, based on one outfitted by Antiochus IV, serves as an analogy of Epicurean philosophy, which indulges in so very many pleasures but is unequipped to deal with adversity and founders in a storm (§3). The speaker vows to give up virtue for pleasure, if only pleasure can be shown to be stable and never involve pain (*lypē*).[2] The two are, however, inextricably intertwined, and therefore the soul can never be free from pain, because it, like an inexperienced helmsman, must continually live in fear of troubled waters (§4). The oration concludes with examples of the disasters that follow upon indulging in pleasure: from Homer (the suitors and Paris), and from history (Sardanapallus, Polycrates of Samos, the Sybarites, Syracusans, and Corinthians), at which point the oration breaks off (§5).

[2] For the distinction between psychological pain (*lypē*) and physical pain, see *Or.* 28.1 n. 1.

ORATION 30

Περὶ ἡδονῆς, ὅτι εἰ καὶ ἀγαθόν,
ἀλλ᾽ οὐ βέβαιον. α΄

1. Χαλεπὸν ἐσθλὸν ἔμμεναι,

κατὰ παλαιὸν ᾆσμα. πότερα δὲ ἵππῳ χαλεπὸν ἐσθλὸν
ἔμμεναι τὴν ἵππου ἀρετὴν καὶ κυνὶ τὴν κυνός; ἢ ἵππῳ
μὲν καὶ κυνὶ οὐ χαλεπὸν τὸ οἰκεῖον ἀγαθόν, ἀλλὰ ῥᾳστώνη τούτων ἑκάστῳ ἐπιλαβέσθαι τῆς αὑτοῦ ἀρετῆς, εἰ ὁ μὲν ἵππος ὑπὸ τέχνης πωλευθείη καλῶς, ὁ
δὲ κύων ἐν θήρᾳ σκυλακευθείη δεξιῶς· τῷ δὲ ἀνθρώπῳ
μόνῳ δυσθήρατον τὸ ἀγαθὸν καὶ δύσληπτον καὶ ἀμφισβητήσιμον, καὶ οὐδεμία πω ἐξεύρηται τέχνη, ὑφ᾽
ἧς παιδευθὲν τουτὶ τὸ γένος οὐ παρέξει τοῖς σοφισταῖς προφάσεις λόγων καὶ διαφωνίας καὶ ἔριδος,
οὐδὲ ἀφαιρήσει αὐτοῦ[1] τὴν ἐλπίδα τοῦ τέλους, οὐδὲ
προήσεται τὴν σωτηρίαν διὰ τὸ ἀστάθμητον τῶν λόγων ὑποτετμημένος τὰς προσδοκίας, οὐδὲ ἀμελήσει
τοῦ μανθάνειν, οὐδὲ πείσεται ὅπερ τῶν πλεόντων οἱ

---

[1] αὑτοῦ Heinsius, Markland, Davies[2], Koniaris: αὐτοῦ R

ORATION 30

On pleasure, that even if it is good,
it is not stable. Part I

1. It is difficult to be good,[1]

according to the ancient song. But is it difficult for a horse
to be good by the standards of a horse's excellence, or for
a dog in the case of its? Or is it that a horse or a dog has
no difficulty as regards its own particular good, but rather
that each one finds it easy to attain its own excellence, as
long as the horse is well raised as a colt by an expert, and
the dog is skillfully trained as a puppy to hunt, whereas
only for humans is the Good hard to hunt down, difficult
to catch, and a matter of dispute?[2] And is it that no expertise has yet been discovered, which can educate our human species so that it won't furnish the sophists pretexts
for arguments, disagreements, and rivalry, or lose hope of
attaining its proper end, or abandon its security because
its expectations[3] have been thwarted by its inability to
evaluate the arguments,[4] or forget all about learning, or

---

[1] Simonides, fr. 542.13 PMG, quoted and discussed at length
at Pl. *Prt*. 339a–47a.   [2] This picks up the argument from *Or*.
29.5–7.   [3] That is, expectations of attaining the Good.

[4] That is, claims by the philosophical factions about what constitutes the Good, as outlined in *Or*. 29.7.

δυσέλπιδες² δὴ καὶ θαλάττῃ πρῶτον ἐντετυχηκότες, οὓς ἐὰν καὶ σμικρὸς ὑπολάβῃ κλύδων, ἐκπλαγέντες τῇ ἀηθείᾳ καὶ καταλιπόντες τὴν ναῦν καὶ ἀμελήσαντες τῆς σωζούσης τέχνης, παρέδωκαν αὑτοὺς τῷ κύματι καὶ προαναλώθησαν τῆς νεώς· τοιοῦτόν τι γάρ μοι δοκοῦσιν δρᾶν καὶ ὅσοι φιλοσοφίας ἐπιλαμβανόμενοι, ἐμπεσόντες αὐτῆς ταῖς πολυφωνίαις, οὐχ ὑπομένουσιν τὸν τῆς ψυχῆς σάλον, ἀλλ' ἀπεγνώκασιν τοῦ λόγου, ὡς στησομένου ποτὲ καὶ καθορμιοῦντος αὐτοὺς εἰς ἑδραίους λιμένας.

2. Ἦ ἀγνοεῖς ὅτι ἀνθρώπων δόξαι καὶ παθήματα καὶ αἱ τούτων αἰτίαι καὶ γενέσεις καὶ ἐπανορθώσεις καὶ σωτηρίαι, ὑπὲρ ὧν οἱ φιλόσοφοι ὁσημέραι πραγματεύονται καὶ λέγουσιν, χρῆμα οὐ στενὸν οὐδὲ ἁπλοῦν οὐδὲ ἐοικὸς τοῖς εὐθυπόροις τῶν ποταμῶν, οἷς ἔστιν παραδόντα τὴν ναῦν ἀφεῖναι τῷ ῥεύματι κατάγειν αὐτὴν ὡμολογημένας ὁδούς; ἀλλ' ἔστιν γὰρ κἀνταῦθα πέλαγος πλατὺ καὶ μέγα, παντὸς Σικελικοῦ καὶ Αἰγυπτίου πολυπλανέστερον.

Ἡ δὲ τέχνη οἶδε ⟨μὲν⟩³ τὴν ὁδὸν καὶ πρὸς τὸν οὐρανὸν ἀφορᾷ καὶ τοὺς λιμένας γνωρίζει, πέπονθεν δὲ αὐτὸ ἐκεῖνο ὅπερ καὶ τῶν κυβερνητῶν οἱ πολλοί· ἐφίεται μὲν γὰρ ἕκαστος τοῦ εἰδέναι, ἀπολείπονται δὲ οἱ πολλοὶ τοῦ ὀρθῶς εἰδέναι, καὶ τῶν μὲν λιμένων ἀστοχοῦσιν, ἐκφέρονται δ' οἱ μὲν ἐπὶ ῥαχίας δυσχε-

---

² δυσέλπιδες Reiske, Dübner, Koniaris: δυσάντιδες R: obel. Trapp   ³ suppl. Reiske, Trapp

suffer what happens to despondent sailors when they first
encounter the sea? For if even a gentle swell takes them
by surprise, they are terrified because of their inexperi-
ence and abandon ship; they forget all about the expertise
that could save them, entrust themselves to the waves, and
succumb even before the ship does. It seems to me that
those who first take up philosophy behave in a similar
fashion. When they encounter its many conflicting claims,
they cannot withstand the pitching and tossing of their
souls and come to despair that reasoned argument will
ever steady itself and bring them to anchor in stable harbors.

2. Or are you unaware that human opinions and emotions, along with their causes and origins and the ways to
correct and preserve them—topics that philosophers deal
with and discuss on a daily basis—constitute no narrow or
simple matter, like straight-flowing rivers to which you
may entrust a ship and allow the current to carry it down-
stream on a stable course? No, in this case we have a broad
and vast sea more bewildering than any Sicilian or Egyptian waters.

Now expertise[5] may well know the route, look to the
heavens for direction, and recognize the ports of call, but
what happens to it is precisely what happens to most
helmsmen. Although each one aims for knowledge, most
of them fall short of correct understanding and miss their
harbors. Some are carried to rugged reefs, others to soft

[5] That is, the expertise of true philosophy.

ρεῖς, οἱ δὲ ἐπ᾽ ἠϊόνας μαλθακάς, οἱ δὲ ἐπὶ τὰς Σειρῆ-
νας, οἱ δὲ ἐπὶ τοὺς Λωτοφάγους καὶ ἄλλους ἄνδρας ἢ
διὰ μοχθηρίαν ἀξένους, ἢ δι᾽ ἀμαθίαν ἀθέους, ἢ ὑφ᾽
ἡδονῆς διεφθαρμένους· εἰ δέ πού τίς ἐστιν ἀγαθὸς καὶ
εὔστοχος κυβερνήτης, εὐθὺ τῶν λιμένων χωρεῖ τῶν
ἀσφαλεστάτων,

ἔνθ᾽ οὐ χρεὼ πείσματός ἐστιν,
οὔτ᾽ εὐνὰς βαλέειν οὔτε πρυμνήσι᾽ ἀνάψαι.

Τίς οὖν ἐστιν ὁ κυβερνήτης οὗτος, καὶ τίνι φέροντες ἑαυτοὺς ἐπιτρέψομεν; μήπω με τοῦτο, ὦ τάν, ἔρη,
πρὶν ἂν τοὺς ἄλλους ἴδῃς καὶ ἐξετάσῃς· καὶ πρῶτόν
γε αὐτῶν τὸν ἁβρὸν τοῦτον καὶ ἥδιστον κυβερνήτην
ἡδίστης νεὼς ὥς γ᾽ ἐκ γῆς ἰδεῖν, ἐν δὲ τῷ πλῷ ἀχρει-
οτάτης καὶ πονηρᾶς ἀεί, καὶ δυσέργου ταῖς ὑπηρε-
σίαις καὶ ἐκτετιμημένης τὰ ὄργανα καὶ πρὸς τὰς τοῦ
χειμῶνος ἐμβολὰς ἀσθενεστάτης καὶ ἐνδοσίμου.

3. Ἐπεὶ δὲ ὁ λόγος οὐκ οἶδ᾽ ὅπως εἰκόνος θαλαττίας
ἐπελάβετο, μὴ ἀφῶμεν αὐτὸν ἀπελθεῖν ἡμῖν πρὶν
ἐξεργάσηται σαφῶς τὴν γραφήν, εἰκάζων τὴν Ἐπικούρου φιλοσοφίαν βασιλικῇ ὁλκάδι †Αἰήτου†[4] βασιλέως. λέγω δὲ οὐ μῦθον πλάττων, ἀλλὰ οὐ πολὺς
χρόνος ὅτε ἐξ Αἰγύπτου ἐς Τροίαν ἔπλει βασιλεὺς
τῶν ὑπὲρ Φοινίκης βαρβάρων, ἐκείνων τῶν ἀνδρῶν,

οἳ οὐκ ἴσασι θάλατταν,

4 obel. Trapp, Koniaris: ἀνοήτου coni. Sauppe et Bottermann

166

beaches; some to the Sirens, some to the Lotus-Eaters, and others to men who are inhospitable through wickedness, or godless through ignorance, or corrupted by pleasure. But if there is any good helmsman with a true sense of direction, he heads straight for the most secure harbors,

> where there is no need of moorings,
> neither casting anchors nor securing stern cables.[6]

Who, then, is such a helmsman, and to whom should we turn and entrust ourselves? Do not ask me yet, my friend. Wait until you have seen the others and have examined them. The first of these is that refined and extremely pleasant helmsman,[7] whose ship is most pleasant to behold from land, but under sail is utterly useless and always in a sorry state, unfit for service, lacking proper equipment, and far too weak and lax to cope with the assaults of a storm.

3. Now, since our argument has somehow seized upon a nautical analogy, we should not allow it to leave us until it has filled out the picture in clear detail, by comparing the philosophy of Epicurus to the royal barge of a foolish king.[8] This story is not my own invention. Not so very long ago, there was a king who set sail from Egypt to Troy. He ruled over a foreign population that lived inland from Phoenicia, being people

> who know nothing of the sea,[9]

[6] *Od.* 9.136–37, describing the island across from the Cyclopes.   [7] Epicurus.   [8] I have translated the conjecture of "foolish king" for the manuscript's "King Aeëtes."

[9] *Od.* 11.122, said of an inland people Odysseus was predicted to encounter.

οὐδὲ

     ἀλέγουσι τοῦ Αἰγιόχου Διὸς
οὐδὲ θεῶν μακάρων.

παρεσκευάσατο δὴ μέλλων πλεῖν ὁ ἄθεος οὗτος καὶ
ἀθάλαττος βασιλεὺς μεγάλην καὶ εὐρύχωρον ναῦν,
ἵνα αὐτῷ πᾶσαι αἱ ἡδοναὶ συμπλέωσιν· τὸ μὲν γὰρ
αὐτῆς βασίλεια ἦν, οἷα κάλλισται παστάδες καὶ εὐ-
ναὶ καὶ δρόμοι·

    ἔκτοσθεν δ᾽ αὐλῆς μέγας ὄρχατος ἄγχι θυράων
    τετράγυος,

καὶ δένδρα ἐπεφύκεσαν, ῥοιαὶ καὶ ὄγχναι καὶ μηλέαι
καὶ ἄμπελοι· τὸ δὲ αὐτῆς λουτρὸν ἦν καὶ γυμνάσιον,
τὸ δὲ ὀψοποιοῖς χώρα, τὸ δὲ θάλαμοι παλλακίσιν, τὸ
δὲ συμπόσιον, τὸ δὲ ἄλλο τι μέρος τρυφώσης πόλεως.
περιεβέβλητο δὲ ἡ ναῦς πολλὰς μὲν χρόας ἡδίστας
ἰδεῖν, πολὺν δὲ χρυσὸν καὶ ἄργυρον, καὶ διέφερεν οὐδὲν ἀνδρὸς δειλοῦ κεκοσμημένου ὅπλοις χρυσοῖς.
ἐθαύμαζον οὖν τὸ θέαμα οἱ Αἰγύπτιοι καὶ τὸν ἐπι-
βάτην ἐμακάριζον, καί πού τις εὔξατο ναύτης γενέσθαι ἡδίστης νεώς.

    Ἐπεὶ δὲ ὥρα ἀνάγεσθαι ἦν, ἐξέπλει μὲν ἡ μεγάλη
αὕτη ναῦς καὶ πολυτελής, καὶ ἀπεσάλευεν τῶν λι-

---

10 *Od.* 9.275–76, said of the Cyclopes. It alludes to the "athe-
ism" of Epicurus.

and who

> pay no heed to aegis-bearing Zeus
> nor to the blessed gods.[10]

In preparation for the voyage, this godless king with no experience of sailing had a large and capacious ship outfitted, so that he could have all his pleasures on board with him.[11] One part of the ship consisted of a palace with the most beautiful colonnades, sleeping quarters, and galleries;

> and outside the courtyard near the gate was a great orchard of four acres,[12]

with trees growing there, pomegranates, pears, apples, and grapevines.[13] Another part consisted of baths and a gymnasium, a galley for cooks, chambers for courtesans, a banquet hall, and every other feature of a luxurious city. The ship was decorated with many colors most pleasant to behold and with much gold and silver—not at all unlike a coward sporting golden armor. For their part, the Egyptians were amazed at the sight and considered any passenger on it to be blessed, and no doubt many a man prayed to join the crew on this most delightful ship.

But when the time came for it to put to sea, and this massive, opulent ship began to sail away, it lumbered out

---

[11] The following passage draws on the account by the historian Callixeinus of Rhodes (2nd c. BC) of a gigantic "houseboat" built by Ptolemy IV (r. 221–204 BC), described at Ath. 5.204d–6d.

[12] *Od.* 7.112–13, referring to the orchard outside Alcinous' palace.

[13] The list is adapted from *Od.* 7.114–15.

MAXIMUS OF TYRE

μένων καθάπερ νῆσος πλωτή. ἐξέπλεον δὲ καὶ αἱ ἄλλαι ὁλκάδες αἱ δημοτικαί, εὔζωνοι καὶ πρὸς τὴν χρείαν παρεσκευασμέναι. μέχρι μὲν ἦν τὸ πνεῦμα πρᾶον, ἐκράτει ταῖς ἡδοναῖς ἡ βασιλικὴ ναῦς καὶ κνίσης ἦν πάντα μεστά,

αὐλῶν συρίγγων τ᾽ ἐνοπῆς ὁμάδου τ᾽ ἀνθρώπων.

ἐπεὶ δὲ ἐξ αἰθρίας ἄφνω χειμὼν ἐπετάραξεν τὸν αἰθέρα καὶ πνεῦμα κάτεισι λάβρον σὺν πολλῷ πατάγῳ, ἔγνωσαν τότε τίς μὲν ἡδονῆς χρεία, τίς δὲ τέχνης. αἱ μὲν γὰρ ἄλλαι ὁλκάδες ξυνενεικάμεναι τὰ ἱστία πρὸς τὸν κλύδωνα ἡμιλλῶντο καὶ τὸ πνεῦμα ἔφερον καὶ τὴν ἐμβολὴν τοῦ κακοῦ ἀπεμάχοντο· ἡ δὲ κακοδαίμων ἐκείνη ναῦς περιεφέρετο καθάπερ ἀνδρὸς σῶμα μέγα καρηβαροῦν καὶ ὑπὸ μέθης σφαλλόμενον· καὶ οὔτε ὁ κυβερνήτης ὅ τι χρήσαιτο τῇ τέχνῃ εἶχεν, ὅ τε ἁβρὸς ἐκεῖνος ὄχλος ἔκειτο ἐκπλαγὴς καὶ στένων· κατήρειπεν δὲ ὁ χειμὼν τὰ θαυμαστὰ ἐκεῖνα πάντα,

πολλὰ δ᾽ ὅ γε προθέλυμνα χαμαὶ βάλε δούρατα μακρά·

διελύετο δὲ καὶ τὰ βασίλεια καὶ οἱ θάλαμοι καὶ τὰ λουτρά, καὶ ἐξέπιπτεν εἰς γῆν πόλεως ναυάγια·

οἱ δὲ κορώνῃσιν ἴκελοι περὶ νῆα μέλαιναν κύμασιν ἐμφορέοντο.

170

of the harbor like a floating island. At the same time, other ships were sailing out, ordinary ones well-fitted and properly equipped for their tasks. As long as the breeze was gentle, the royal ship reigned supreme with its pleasures, and the air was filled with the savor of meat being cooked

> and the sound of pipes and pan flutes and the din of
> men.[14]

But when suddenly out of the blue a storm shook the heavens, and a furious wind bore down with a mighty crashing, they came to realize at that point the difference between the usefulness of pleasure and that of expertise. For the other ships had furled their sails and were contending with the swell, riding the wind, and fighting off the attack of the storm; but that miserable barge was being tossed about like a fat man's body tottering and staggering from too much wine. The skipper did not know how to use his expertise, while that decadent crowd of passengers just lay there stunned and moaning. Meanwhile the storm was tearing down all those marvelous furnishings:

> it uprooted many tall trees and threw them to the
> ground.[15]

The palace, chambers, and baths were being broken apart, and the wreckage of a city was washing up on land,

> while around the black ship they, like sea crows,
> were being carried on the waves.[16]

[14] *Il.* 10.13, describing festivities in the Trojan camp, also cited at *Or.* 22.2.   [15] *Il.* 9.541, Phoenix describing the damage done to the orchard of Oeneus by the Calydonian boar.
[16] *Od.* 12.418–19, describing Odysseus' shipwrecked crew.

τοῦτο τέλος ἀνοήτου ἐπιβάτου καὶ ἀχρήστου νεὼς καὶ
ἀκαίρου τρυφῆς.

4. Ἐπανάγωμεν δὲ αὖθις ἐπὶ τὸν λόγον ᾧ τὴν
εἰκόνα ταύτην παρελάβομεν. ἔοικεν γὰρ ἀμέλει καὶ
οὗτος, οὐ πλοῦν βραχὺν οὐδὲ ἡμερῶν ὀλίγων ἡμῖν
δρόμον διαγωνιουμένοις ἀλλὰ τὸν τοῦ ζῆν ξύμπαντα
χρόνον, νομοθετεῖν ἡδονὰς οὐδὲν τῶν θαλαττίων ἐκείνων ἀσφαλεστέρας· μήπω γάρ τις ἡμᾶς πειθέτω λόγος, ὡς οὐκ ἀγαθὸν ἡδονή, ἀλλὰ ἀγωνιζέσθω ἐὰν
πεῖσαι δυνηθῇ <ὡς ἀμετάβλητος>·[5] εἰ δὲ μεταβάλλειν
μὴ δυνηθῇ,[6] ἀνέξομαι ἡδόμενος τὸν πάντα χρόνον καὶ
ἀμελήσω τῆς ἀρετῆς, ἐάν μοι δείξῃς ἡδονὴν ἀσφαλῆ
καὶ λύπης ἀμιγῆ, ἡδονὴν ἀμετάγνωστον, ἡδονὴν
ἐπαινουμένην.

Δείξεις δὲ πῶς; οὐ μᾶλλον ἢ λύπην· οὐδὲν γὰρ
ὑγιὲς οὐδὲ εἰλικρινὲς τούτων κατεστήσατο τοῖς ἀνθρώποις ἡ φύσις, ἀλλὰ ἀναμέμικται πανταχοῦ τὰ
λυπηρὰ τοῖς ἡδέσιν, ἑκάτερον ἐν ἑκατέρῳ φυρόμενον·
ἀνάγκη δὲ αἱρούμενον θάτερον καὶ τοῦ ἄλλου μετ-
έχειν εὐθύς· ἅτε γὰρ ἀλλήλοις συμπεφυκότα, τὸ ἕτερον τῷ ἑτέρῳ ἐπιρρεῖ καὶ ἀντικαταλλάττεται τὰς γενέσεις καὶ ἀμείβει τὰς συνουσίας. ὑπὸ δὲ τῆς παλιρροίας
ταύτης ψυχὴ κυκωμένη, πῶς ἄν ποτε ἐπιλάβοιτο ἀλυ-

---

[5] suppl. Trapp: <ὡς ἀσφαλής> Hobein: obel. Koniaris
[6] εἰ δὲ μεταβάλλειν μὴ δυνηθῇ locus conclamatus: obel
Trapp, Koniaris

Such was the end of a foolish passenger, a useless ship, and inappropriate luxury.

4. But let us return to the topic[17] that our analogy was employed to illustrate. For it certainly seems to prescribe pleasures for us in no way more stable than those seagoing ones we described, although we ourselves will be undergoing no brief voyage, nor a journey of a few days, but one lasting our whole lives. For we should not yet allow any argument to persuade us that pleasure is *not* a good, but should let it to try its best to persuade us ⟨that it is immutable⟩.[18] And if it is not capable of change,[19] then I shall be content to indulge in pleasure all life long and forget about virtue—if, that is, you can show me any pleasure that is secure and that has no admixture of pain, any pleasure that is not subsequently regretted, any pleasure that is praiseworthy.

But how will you show me this? Certainly no more than you will in the case of pain, because nature has allotted no whole and pure form of either one to humans. No, everywhere pains are mixed with pleasures, the one being entangled with the other. Choosing one inevitably involves the other right away, for since they are united by nature, one flows into the other, one produces the other, and they keep alternating their presence. So how could the soul, confounded by this fluctuation, ever achieve freedom

17 That is, the philosophy of Epicurus broached in §3.

18 The supplement is Trapp's.

19 The text is corrupt and no satisfactory emendation has been proposed, but the sense seems clear.

πίας, συνοῦσα ἀγαθοῖς ⟨βεβαιότητος⟩[7] ἐστερημέ
νοις;[8]

Ἐγὼ καὶ θαλάττῃ διὰ τοῦτο ἀπιστῶ, κἂν νήνεμος
ᾖ, κἂν γαλήνην ἔχῃ· ὑποπτεύω γὰρ αὐτῆς τὴν ἡσυ
χίαν· εἰ δέ με βούλει πιστεῦσαι γαλήνῃ, ἄγε λαβὼν
εἰς πέλαγος ἀσφαλές,

ἔνθ᾽ οὐκ ἔστ᾽ οὔτ᾽ ἂρ χειμὼν πολὺς οὔτε ποτ᾽
      ὄμβρῳ

δεύεται,

                              ἀλλὰ μάλ᾽ αἴθρη
πέπταται ἀννέφελος, λευκὴ δ᾽ ἐπιδέδρομεν αἴγλη.

συγκεκλήρωται δὲ καὶ ἡ ψυχὴ τοιούτῳ πάθει· καὶ μέ
χρις ἂν αὐτῇ ἀπῇ μὲν ὁ κυβερνήτης, ἀπῇ δὲ καὶ ἡ
τέχνη, κἂν γαλήνην ἴδῃ χειμῶνα δέδιεν, κἂν χειμῶνι
ἐντύχῃ γαλήνην ποθεῖ. ἀνδρὸς γὰρ βίος πρὸς ἡδονὴν
νενευκότος καὶ λύπην ἐπτοημένου, κοῦφος καὶ ψοφο
δεὴς καὶ ἄπιστος καὶ θαλάττης πάσης ἀδηλότερος.

5. Οὐχ ὁρᾷς τοὺς μνηστῆρας νεανικαῖς ἡδοναῖς
συγγιγνομένους, πίονας αἶγας κατέδοντας καὶ σια
λῶν ⟨σύων⟩[9] ἐμπιμπλαμένους, καὶ ἀοιδοῦ ἀκούοντας[10]
καὶ οἶνον ἀπομισγομένους, καὶ δίσκοις τερπομένους

---

[7] suppl. Davies[2]
[8] ἐστερημένοις obel. Trapp, Koniaris
[9] suppl. Koniaris, Trapp
[10] ἀοιδοῦ ἀκούοντας Trapp: οιακούοντας R: αὐλῶν ἀκούον
τας R[2]

from pain, when it deals with "goods" deprived <of stability>?[20]

This is why I distrust the sea, even when it is windless and calm, for I am suspicious of its tranquility. If you wish me to trust its calmness, then take me into a sea that is safe,

> where there are no heavy storms and rainfall never drenches it,
>
> but cloudless skies
> spread all around, flooded with bright radiance.[21]

The soul too has been allotted a similar experience. As long as it lacks its helmsman and his expertise, it fears a storm even when it sees calm waters, and when it does encounter a storm, all it can do is long for calm. For the life of a man who assents to pleasure and is terrified of pain, is flighty, anxious, mistrustful, and more unpredictable than any sea.[22]

5. Do you not see those suitors indulging in their youthful pleasures, devouring plump goats, gorging themselves on fattened pigs, listening to a singer, mixing themselves wine, and having fun throwing discuses and javelins? Who

---

[20] The text is corrupt. I have accepted the supplement of Davies. The interrelationship of pain and pleasure is famously treated at Pl. *Phd*. 60b–c.

[21] An adaptation of *Od*. 4.566 (describing the Elysian Field) and 6.43–45 (describing Olympus), also quoted at *Or*. 11.10, where it depicts the tranquil realm of truth accessible to the intellect.

[22] The hedonist's constant state of fear and pain is taken up in *Or*. 33.4–6.

καὶ αἰγανέας ἱέντας; τίς οὐκ ἂν αὐτοὺς τῆς ἡδονῆς
ταύτης ἐμακάρισεν; ἀλλὰ ὁ μαντικὸς καὶ γνωριστικὸς
τοῦ μέλλοντος λέγει·

  ἆ δειλοί, τί κακὸν τόδε πάσχετε; νυκτὶ μὲν ὑμῶν
  εἰλύαται κεφαλαί,

παρὰ πόδας τὸ κακὸν καὶ ἐγγύς. παρὰ πόδας τὸ κακὸν ἦν καὶ Ἀλεξάνδρῳ τῷ τὴν θαυμαστὴν ἐκείνην
ἡδονὴν ἐκ Πελοποννήσου ἐκκλέψαντι· ταχὺ γὰρ ἐπ᾽
αὐτῇ στόλος ἐξηρτύθη Ἑλληνικός, μυρίας μὲν ὀδύνας
αὐτῷ τῷ τῆς ἡδονῆς ἐραστῇ ἄγων, μυρίας δὲ τῇ ξυμ-
πάσῃ πόλει.
  Τὰς δὲ Ἀσσυρίους ἡδονὰς οὐ λέγω, ἃς κατέλαβεν
εὐθὺ πῦρ αὐτῷ χρυσῷ καὶ αὐταῖς παλλακίσιν. οὐδὲ
τὰς Πολυκράτους τὰς Ἰωνικὰς οὐ λέγω, ἃς κατέλαβεν
οὐδὲ εὐσχήμων θάνατος. πλήρης ἦν Σύβαρις ἡδονῶν,
ἀλλὰ ἀπώλοντο μετὰ τῶν χρησαμένων αἱ ἡδοναί. εὐ-
δοκίμουν καὶ παρὰ Συρακοσίοις ἡδοναί, ἀλλὰ ἐσω-
φρόνισαν αὐτοὺς μετ᾽ ἐκείνας αἱ συμφοραί. ἀλλ᾽ οὐδὲ
Κορινθίοις ‹. . .›

would not have considered them blessed for this pleasure
of theirs? However, the seer with knowledge of the future
says to them:

> You wretched men! What is this evil you are suf-
>   fering?
> Your heads are shrouded in night,[23]

and evil is near at hand. Near at hand was evil for Alexander too,[24] when he stole that marvelous pleasure from the
Peloponnesus, for right away a Greek fleet was made
ready to retrieve her, bringing countless pains to this pleasure lover himself, and countless others to his entire city.

I shall pass over the Assyrian's pleasures,[25] which fire
quickly overtook, along with his gold and concubines, and
I shall pass over the Ionian pleasures of Polycrates, which
not even a decent death overtook.[26] Sybaris was full of
pleasures, but those pleasures perished along with those
who indulged in them.[27] Pleasures were highly esteemed
by the Syracusans, but they were chastened by the disasters that followed those pleasures.[28] But not even for the
Corinthians . . .[29]

---

[23] *Od*. 20.351–52, spoken by Theoclymenus to the suitors
shortly before their demise.   [24] That is, Paris.

[25] That is, of Sardanapallus, who perished on a pyre; cf. *Or.*
7.7.   [26] He was tortured and crucified ca. 522 BC by the
Persian satrap Oroetes (Hdt. 3.125).   [27] Sybaris, notorious
for its luxury, was destroyed by Croton in 510 BC.

[28] Trapp suggests that the disasters refer to the reign of Dionysius II; cf. *Orr.* 5.5 and 7.2.   [29] The rest is missing and it
is unclear what example followed. Most likely it was the tyranny
of Periander in the sixth century BC; cf. *Or.* 5.5.

ORATION 31

INTRODUCTION

This oration picks up the question of whether pleasure is a good, which was raised in *Or.* 30.4, but left open: "We should not yet allow any argument to persuade us that pleasure is *not* a good." The speaker now rejects the sophistic argument that simply assumes pleasure to be a good and considers only whether or not it possesses security (*to asphales*). But to be a good, it must be stable (*bebaion*) (§1). Since the Good (*to agathon*) is not always pleasurable (but always stable), and pleasure is not always good (but always unstable),[1] then pleasure is chosen as a good only because it *appears* to be good. It resembles counterfeit currency that is accepted only because it seems to be genuine (§2). How then shall humans assess true good from fake? The speaker appeals to nature, where each animal has natural endowments that enable it to perform properly and survive (§3). In sum, the good for each creature depends on its actions (*erga*) to accomplish its needs, and its actions depend on its instruments (*organa*).[2] In contrast to all other animals, humans have rea-

---

[1] *Or.* 30.4 argued that pleasure is unstable because it is inseparable from pain.

[2] Instruments refer to natural endowments.

son (*logos*) to distinguish between what is true and what is false. Nature has also implanted in us a spark called intellect (*nous*) that safeguards our existence in the face of all the advantages enjoyed by the other creatures (§4).[3] Our human good can be found in the instruments given us by nature that ensure the survival of our species. Is it pleasure that assures our survival? It cannot be, because pleasure is shared by all other creatures. Furthermore, what are its instruments? The eyes and the ears are respectable enough, but as you go further down the paths of pleasure, you arrive at the genitals. These hardly constitute the instrument of good that ensures survival, or indeed that leads to happiness (§5).

[3] The special endowments given to humans for their survival are the subject of Protagoras' myth at Pl. *Prt*. 320d–22d.

ORATION 31

Περὶ ἡδονῆς, ὅτι εἰ καὶ ἀγαθόν,
ἀλλ᾽ οὐ βέβαιον. β΄

1. Ἐπεχείρει ἐχθρὸς λόγος τις παρελθὼν πείθειν
ἡμᾶς ὡς αἱρετέον ἡδονήν, ἐὰν προσγένηται αὐτῇ τὸ
ἀσφαλές· σοφιστὴς λόγος καὶ ἀπατεὼν δεινῶς, ὃς
ἐξὸν σκοπεῖν τὴν ἡδονῆς φύσιν, καθόσον ἡδονὴ ποῦ
τάττεται, ἐν ἀγαθοῖς ἢ κακοῖς, ἐν ποτέρῳ χορῷ παρεὶς
τὸ σκέμμα, ὡς ἀγαθοῦ τῆς ἡδονῆς οὔσης, ἐσκοπεῖτο
εἰ βέβαιον τὸ ἀγαθὸν τοῦτο.

Καὶ ποῖον ἄν τις ἐπινοήσαι ἀγαθὸν σαλεῦον καὶ
κραδαινόμενον; ὥσπερ γὰρ οἶμαι καὶ τῆς ὅλης[1] γῆς
εἰ ἀφέλοι τις τῷ λόγῳ τὴν ἕδραν καὶ τὴν μονήν, συναφεῖλεν αὐτῆς καὶ τὸ εἶναι· καὶ τοῦ ἡλίου εἰ ἀφέλοι
τις τὴν κίνησιν καὶ τὸν δρόμον, συναφεῖλεν αὐτοῦ
τὴν οὐσίαν· οὕτως καὶ τοῦ ἀγαθοῦ εἴ τις ἀφέλοι τὴν

---

[1] ὅλης U: ἄλλης R

---

[1] That is, chosen as a good, referring back to *Or.* 30.4, where
the question remained open as to whether or not pleasure was a
good. This sophistic argument amounts to a *petitio principii*.

ORATION 31

On pleasure, that even if it is good,
it is not stable. Part II

1. A hostile argument came forward and tried to persuade us that pleasure had to be chosen,[1] if it had the additional attribute of security. It was a sophistic and cleverly deceptive argument, for when it needed to examine the nature of pleasure and determine where pleasure itself falls, either in the category of good things or bad things, it simply avoided an investigation into which class it fell, and assumed that pleasure was a good, and then went on to consider whether this supposed good was stable.

Yet what kind of good could anyone imagine that pitches and shakes?[2] For I believe that if someone should hypothetically deprive the earth as a whole of its fixedness and permanence, he would also take away its very being; and, conversely, if someone should deprive the sun of its movement and orbit, he would also deprive it of its very essence; in precisely the same way, if someone should deprive the Good of its exactitude and immobility, he would

[2] That is, like a ship at sea, continuing the nautical analogy of the previous oration. For the various terms denoting stability, see the Introduction to *Or.* 30.

ἀκρίβειαν καὶ τὴν στάσιν, συναφεῖλεν αὐτοῦ καὶ τὴν
φύσιν· οὐ γὰρ χρόνῳ τὸ ἀγαθὸν ἀνθεῖ, ὡς ὥρα σώματος.

Πῶς ἂν οὖν τις περὶ ἡδονῆς σκοποῖ, τὸ μὲν ἀγαθὸν
αὐτῇ προσθείς, ἀφελὼν δὲ τὸ βέβαιον; εἰ γὰρ ἀνάγκη
ἀγαθὸν ὂν βέβαιον εἶναι, τῇ τοῦ βεβαίου ἀπουσίᾳ
καὶ τὸ ἀγαθὸν τῆς ἡδονῆς συναπέρχεται. καὶ πότερος
τούτων τῷ πιθανῷ πλησιαίτερος, ὁ λέγων τὴν ἡδονὴν
ἀγαθὸν εἶναι, κἂν μὴ βέβαιον ᾖ, ἢ ὁ ἀγαθὸν λέγων
μὴ εἶναι, ἂν μὴ καὶ βέβαιον ᾖ; ἐγὼ μὲν οἶμαι θάτε-
ρον· κρεῖττον γὰρ ἀφελεῖν ἡδονὴν ἀγαθοῦ, προσθέν-
τας τὸ βέβαιον αὐτῷ, ἢ προσθεῖναι ἡδονῇ τἀγαθόν,
ἀφελόντας αὐτῆς τὸ ἀσφαλές.

2. Ἐπεὶ τοίνυν τὸ μὲν ἀγαθὸν οὐχ ἡδὺ πάντως,
βέβαιον δὲ πάντως, τὸ δὲ ἡδὺ οὐ πάντως ἀγαθόν,
ἀβέβαιον δὲ πάντως, λείπεται δυοῖν θάτερον, ἢ τὴν
ἡδονὴν διώκοντας ἀμελεῖν τἀγαθοῦ, ἢ τὸ ἀγαθὸν αἱ-
ρουμένους μὴ διώκειν ἡδονήν. οὐθὲν δὲ οἶμαι διωκτὸν
ὅ τι μὴ ἀγαθόν, ἀλλ' ἀγαθοῦ φαντασίᾳ τὸ μὴ ἀγαθὸν
διώκεται ἐν χώρᾳ ἀγαθοῦ, καθάπερ ὑπὸ τῶν χρημα-
τιστῶν τὰ κίβδηλα τῶν νομισμάτων, οὐ διότι κίβδηλα αἱρετὰ ὄντα, ἀλλὰ τῇ πρὸς τὸ ἀληθὲς ὁμοιότητι
τὴν τοῦ κιβδήλου φύσιν ἐπικρυπτόμενα. ἀλλ' ἐνταῦθα
μὲν οἱ ἀργυρογνώμονες τῇ τέχνῃ διέκριναν τοῦ ἀληθοῦς τὸ μὴ δόκιμον, ἐν δὲ τῇ τῶν ἀγαθῶν νομῇ δια-
κρινεῖ ὁ λόγος ἀπὸ τῶν ὄντων ἀγαθῶν τὰ φαινόμενα
μέν, οὐκ ὄντα δέ· ἀλλὰ λησόμεθα ὥσπερ οἱ μοχθηροὶ

also deprive it of its very nature, because the Good does not come into bloom over time, as physical beauty does.

How then could anyone conduct a proper examination of pleasure, if he adds goodness to it, but takes away its stability? For if a good must be stable, then in the absence of stability the goodness of pleasure must also disappear. Which one of these comes closer to being persuasive, the person who claims that pleasure is a good even if it lacks stability, or the person who claims that it is not a good unless it is also stable? I believe that it is the latter position, for it is better to deprive pleasure of goodness, while attributing stability to the Good, than to attribute goodness to pleasure, while depriving pleasure of its security.

2. Moreover, since the Good is not pleasurable in all cases, but in all cases is stable; and since pleasure is not good in all cases, but in all cases is unstable; we are left with one of two options, either to pursue pleasure and disregard the Good, or to choose the Good and not pursue pleasure. I do not think that anything is worth pursuing unless it is a good. Even so, that which is not good is pursued in place of the Good because it *appears* to be good, just as counterfeit coins are accepted by merchants, not *because* they are counterfeit, but because they hide their counterfeit nature through their similarity to what is true. In this case, silver assayers use their expertise to distinguish the fake from the genuine, whereas in the distribution of good things, it is reason that distinguishes which things are actually good from those that appear to be good but really are not. So shall we then, like in-

χρηματισταὶ θησαυροὺς ταμιευόμενοι κιβδήλων ἀγαθῶν;

3. Τίς ἂν οὖν καὶ γένοιτο ἡ σκέψις ἡμῖν; καὶ τίς ὁ τῆς δοκιμασίας οὗτος τρόπος; φέρε, εἴ τις ἐπεχείρει τὸν βοῦν ὑπολύσας τῶν ἀρότρων καὶ τὸν ἵππον τῶν ἁρμάτων, ὑπαλλάξας ἑκατέρου τὴν ἐργασίαν, ὑπαγαγεῖν τὸν μὲν βοῦν τῷ ἅρματι, τὸν δὲ ἵππον τῷ ἀρότρῳ, ἆρ᾽ οὐκ ἂν ἦν πρὸς μὲν τὴν φύσιν παράνομος, πρὸς δὲ τὰ ζῷα αὐτὰ ὑβριστής, πρὸς δὲ τὰς τέχνας ἀμαθής, πρὸς δὲ τὴν χρείαν ἀκερδής, πρὸς δὲ τὴν ὑπηρεσίαν καταγέλαστος; τί δὲ τὰ τούτων ἔτι ἀτοπώτερα, εἰ τῶν μὲν ὀρνίθων ἀφελὼν τὰ πτερὰ βαδιστικὰ ἐκ πτηνῶν εἶναί σοι θέλῃς, τὸν δὲ ἄνθρωπον πτερώσας παραδῷς τῷ αἰθέρι φέρεσθαι δι᾽ αὐτοῦ ὄρνιθος δίκην; οὐκ ἔσῃ καταγέλαστος τῆς ἀλλαγῆς, ὁπότε μηδὲ ὁ μῦθος τὸν Δαίδαλον ἠνέσχετο ἀτόπους οὕτω τέχνας πραγματευόμενον, ἀλλὰ ἀπέρριψεν αὐτῷ τὸν παῖδα τοῦ αἰθέρος εἰς γῆν κάτω αὐτοῖς πτεροῖς;

Φασὶν δὲ καὶ Καρχηδόνιον νεανίαν ἀγρεῦσαι λέοντα ἄρτι ἐκ γάλακτος καὶ ἡμερῶσαι τοῦτον παρανόμῳ τροφῇ καὶ τὸν θυμὸν αὐτοῦ ἐξελεῖν διαίτῃ νόθῳ, ὥστε ἐπιθεὶς αὐτῷ φορτίον ἤλαυνεν δι᾽ ἄστεος ὄνου δίκην· ἀλλὰ ἀπέκτεινάν γε αὐτὸν Καρχηδόνιοι μισήσαντες τῆς παρανομίας, ὡς τύραννον μὲν τῇ φύσει, ἰδιώτην δὲ τῇ δυστυχίᾳ.

4. Ὥσπερ οὖν τῷ ἵππων γένει συγκεκλήρωται πρὸς

---

3 Other versions tell of Hanno the Carthaginian general. Plut.

competent merchants, unwittingly store up treasures of counterfeit goods?

3. What then is to become of our inquiry? And what form shall this assay of ours take? Tell me, if someone tried unyoking an ox from its plow and a horse from its chariot and interchanged their tasks by yoking the ox to the chariot and the horse to the plow, would he not violate the laws of nature, mistreat the animals themselves, prove ignorant of the two arts, gain nothing from their use, and be ridiculous for the service they provide? And even more absurd than this, what if you were to remove wings from birds and wish them to walk rather than fly, and put wings on men and send them off to fly through the air like birds? Would you not be ridiculous for making this exchange, when not even myth allowed Daedalus to succeed with such unnatural arts, but hurled his son from the air to the ground below, wings and all?

People also tell how a young Carthaginian once captured a lion cub that was just weaned and tamed it with an unnatural diet and took away its ferociousness with an abnormal regimen, to the point where he could put a load on it and drive it through the town like a donkey. The Carthaginians, however, put the man to death in disgust at his transgression, judging him to be a tyrant by nature, although he was a lowly citizen.[3]

4. Just as horses as a species have been allotted swift

Praec. 799e reports that he was banished (not executed) "on the charge of aspiring to be tyrant, because he used a lion on his campaigns to carry his luggage" (trans. H. N. Fowler). Plin. *HN* 8.21.55 reports that the Carthaginians impeached him because they were unwilling to entrust their freedom to someone who could subdue such ferocity.

σωτηρίαν δρόμος καὶ τῷ βοῶν πόνοι καὶ ὄρνισι
πτερὰ καὶ λέουσιν ἀλκὴ καὶ ἄλλοις ἄλλο τι, οὕτως
ἀμέλει καὶ ἀνθρώπῳ ὑπάρχει δύναμις ξυμφυὴς δια-
σωστικὴ τοῦ γένους· ταύτην δὲ ἑτέραν εἶναι δεῖ παρ'
ἕκαστον τῶν ἄλλων, εἰ μέλλει ἄνθρωπος ὢν μὴ ὑπὸ
ἀλκῆς σωθήσεσθαι ὥσπερ οἱ λέοντες, μηδὲ ὑπὸ δρόμου ὥσπερ οἱ ἵπποι, μηδὲ ἀχθοφορεῖν ὄνου δίκην,
μηδὲ ἀροῦν βοὸς δίκην, μηδὲ πέτασθαι κατὰ ὄρνιθας,
μηδὲ νήχεσθαι κατὰ ἰχθύας, ἀλλ' ἔστι τι καὶ τούτῳ
ἔργον ἴδιον, διασωστικὸν τοῦ βίου. εἶεν· νενέμηται τὰ
ζῷα τὰς δυνάμεις, ἑκάστην ἕκαστον κατὰ τὴν χρείαν
τοῦ βίου, καὶ τὰ ἔργα κατὰ τὰς δυνάμεις, καὶ τὰ ὄργανα κατὰ τὰ ἔργα †καὶ τἀγαθά†.[2]

Καὶ ξυνελόντι εἰπεῖν, τὸ ἑκάστου ἀγαθὸν ἐν τῷ
ἐπιχωρίῳ τῶν ἔργων μένει, τὰ δὲ ἔργα ἐν τῷ τῆς
χρείας ἀναγκαίῳ, ἡ δὲ χρεία ἐν τῷ τῆς δυνάμεως εὐ-
πόρῳ, ἡ δὲ δύναμις ἐν τῷ τῶν ὀργάνων εὐμηχάνῳ, τὰ
δὲ ὄργανα ἐν τῷ τῆς φύσεως ποικίλῳ. παντοδαπὴ γὰρ
ἡ φύσις, καὶ διὰ τοῦτο περιέβαλεν καὶ διεκόσμησεν
τὰ ζῷα ἕκαστα ἐπὶ σωτηρίᾳ τοῦ βίου ἄλλα ἄλλοις
ὅπλοις, τὰ μὲν ὀνύχων ἀκμαῖς, τὰ δὲ ὀδόντων ὀξύτητι,
τὰ δὲ κεράτων ῥώμῃ, τὰ δὲ ποδῶν τάχει, τὰ δὲ θυμῷ,
τὰ δὲ ἰῷ· τὸν δὲ ἄνθρωπον ἀποδύσασα τουτωνὶ τῶν
περιβλημάτων ἀπέφηνεν γυμνὸν καὶ ἀσθενῆ καὶ
ἄτριχον, {καὶ ῥώμην ἀσθενῆ}[3] καὶ θεῖν βράδιστον καὶ
ἀνίπτασθαι ἀμήχανον καὶ νήχεσθαι ἀμβλύτατον·
ἐνέφυσεν δέ τι αὐτῷ ζώπυρον ἀφανὲς πρὸς σωτηρίαν

[2] obel. Trapp   [3] del. Koniaris, Trapp

speed for their survival, and oxen the capacity for hard work, and birds wings, lions strength, and so on, in exactly the same way humans too have an innate ability to preserve their species. This must, however, be something different from all the rest, if a human being is going to survive, not by means of strength like lions, or by running like horses, or by carrying loads like donkeys, plowing like oxen, flying like birds, or swimming like fish. No, man too possesses his own particular action that can preserve his life. So then, various abilities have been distributed to living creatures to match the needs of each one's existence; their actions match their abilities, their instruments[4] match their actions, and their goods . . .[5]

To sum up, the good for each creature resides in the scope of its particular actions, its actions in the necessity of its needs, its needs in the use of its ability, its ability in the capacity of its instruments, and its instruments in the variety of nature. That is because nature assumes many different forms, and for this reason has attired and adorned each living creature with its own weapons for survival, some with strong claws, others with sharp teeth, others with powerful horns, and still others with swift feet, ferocity, or poison. But nature has stripped man of these very accoutrements and has presented him naked, weak, and hairless; slowest to run, unable to fly, and a very poor swimmer. But yet, nature has engendered in him a certain invisible spark to safeguard his life, a spark men call intel-

---

[4] That is, their natural endowments.

[5] The sentence breaks down. Trapp suggests "and their individual goods [match] ⟨their characteristic tools.⟩"

βίου, ὃ καλοῦσιν οἱ ἄνθρωποι νοῦν, ᾧ διατελεῖ σωζό-
μενος, καὶ τὰς ἀπορίας ἐξιώμενος τοῦ βίου, καὶ θερα-
πεύων τὴν ἔνδειαν τῶν σωμάτων, καὶ ἀντιτεχνώμενος
ταῖς τῶν ἄλλων ζῴων πλεονεξίαις, καὶ πάντων κρατῶν καὶ ὑπάγων τῷ τοῦδε νόμῳ καὶ λόγῳ.

5. Ἔρου δή με καὶ περὶ τοῦ ἀνθρώπου· σκεπτέον
τὸ τούτου ἀγαθόν, ποῦ καὶ τίνα τρόπον. ἀποκρινοῦμαί
σοι ὡς περὶ τοῦ λέοντος, ὡς περὶ τοῦ ὄρνιθος, ὡς περὶ
τῶν ἄλλων ἁπάντων ἀπεκρινάμην. ἐνταῦθα ζήτει τὸ
ἀνθρώπου ἀγαθόν, ὅπου τὸ ἀνθρώπου ἔργον· ποῦ δὲ
εὕρω τὸ ἔργον; ὅπου τὸ ὄργανον· ποῦ δὲ εὕρω τὸ ὄργανον; ὅπου τὸ σῶζον. ἐντεῦθεν ἄρξαι· τί ἀνθρώπου
διασωστικόν; ἡδονή; πρᾶγμά μοι κοινὸν λέγεις ἐπὶ
πάσας φύσεις ἐξικνούμενον, καὶ διὰ τοῦτο αὐτοῦ τὴν
προτιμίαν οὐκ ἀνέχομαι· ἥδεται καὶ βοῦς, ἥδεται καὶ
ὄνος καὶ σῦς καὶ πίθηκος. ὅρα ποῦ τάττεις τῶν ἀνθρώπων τὸ γένος, τίνας αὐτῷ κοινωνοὺς τῶν ἀγαθῶν
δίδως.

Εἰ δὲ ἡδονὴ τὸ σῶζον, ζήτει μετὰ τοῦτο τί ἡδονῆς
ὄργανον· ἐντεύξῃ δὲ πολλοῖς καὶ παντοδαποῖς· καὶ
μέχρι μὲν ὀφθαλμῶν καὶ ὤτων τίμια τὰ ὄργανα, ἐὰν
δὲ προέλθῃς περαιτέρω ἐπὶ τὰς ἡδονῆς ὁδούς, ὅρα
τίσιν ὀργάνοις ἀνατίθης τὴν σωτηρίαν. εὗρες τὰ ὄργανα, ζήτει τὰ ἔργα· λιχνευέτω ἡ γλῶττα, τηκέσθω-
σαν οἱ ὀφθαλμοί, ἐκλυέσθω ἡ ἀκοή, πληρούσθω ἡ
γαστήρ, ὑβριζέτω τὰ ὑβρίζειν πεφυκότα. εὗρες τὰ
ἔργα, ἐντετύχηκας τῷ ἀγαθῷ. τοῦτο ἡ σωτηρία; τοῦτο
ἡ εὐδαιμονία;

lect, by means of which he constantly protects himself, remedies the deficiencies of his life, sees to his bodily needs, devises schemes to counter the advantages of the other animals, and conquers them all and subjects them to the law and reason of his intellect.

5. Ask me then about man as well, for we must investigate his good, to determine where it lies and what its nature is. I shall give you the same answer I gave in the case of lions, birds, and all the other creatures: seek the good of man where his proper action lies. Where shall I find this action? Where his instruments lie. Where shall I find his instruments? Where his survival lies. Begin from there with this question: what safeguards a human's life? Pleasure, you say? You cite a common attribute that belongs to all species, and for that very reason I cannot allow its privileged status. The ox feels pleasure, as do donkeys, pigs, and apes. See, then, where you are placing the human race; see what partners you are giving it to share in those goods!

But if pleasure really is what insures his survival, then next seek what instrument pleasure employs, and you will find that they are many and various. Instruments up to and including the eyes and ears are respectable enough, but if you go further down the paths of pleasure, consider to which instruments you are entrusting human survival. Now that you have found the instruments, seek their actions. Let the tongue gourmandize, the eyes melt with lust, the ears indulge themselves, the belly be stuffed, and the naturally wanton organs be wanton. You have now found your actions; you have encountered your good. But is this survival? Is this happiness?

ORATION 32

INTRODUCTION

This oration presents the Epicurean response to the criticisms of pleasure in the foregoing *Orr.* 30 and 31. It opens with a fable of a shepherd telling a lion that he had not seen a fleeing doe, while pointing to where she was hiding (§1). Epicurus could use this fable to illustrate how those who disavow pleasure are actually pointing to it, because our affection (*philia*) for it is innate and predates knowledge, reason, intellect, and expertise. In fact, it provides the foundation for the survival of our species (§2). Sophists unfairly criticize pleasure by citing the extravagant luxuriousness of Sardanapallus and others, but such luxuries are not the product of pleasure but of human ingenuity. In fact, they actually violate pleasure's laws, for when reason and pleasure properly combine, reason moderates pleasure, and pleasure enhances reason's appeal (§3). The speaker responds to the criticism raised in the previous oration (*Or.* 31.5) that pleasure is not a specifically human good, because all sentient creatures need it to preserve their species. But pleasure is no less a good for being shared: so too are all necessities, such as sunlight, air, water, and food (§4).

The speaker turns to the relationship between virtue and pleasure. These too, like reason and pleasure, go together, for no good (*kalon*) thing is chosen without the attraction of pleasure, either immediate or anticipated. The Good (*to kalon*) cannot be good without being pleasurable (§5). In fact, pleasure is more worthy of being chosen than virtue, because it actually provides the motivation for virtuous labors. Thus, affection for virtue implies the presence of pleasure (§6). Even if you follow the Stoics and call pleasure joy (*chara*), you will find that Heracles found joy in all his labors (§7). As for historical examples, Socrates took pleasure in all his loves, for it is possible to enjoy physical pleasure in chaste love (§8). Diogenes too found pleasure in his simple, austere life, which in fact was superior to the lives of such famous exemplars as Xerxes, Sardanapallus, Alexander, and Croesus, because their pleasures were mixed with great pains, all of which Diogenes avoided by his freedom from care (§9). As for governments, Sparta trades its painful upbringing for the great pleasure of keeping the city safe from attack and fear, as illustrated by the noble deaths of its heroes. Then too, Athens finds pleasure in its recurring festivals and even finds enjoyment during wartime (§10).

ORATION 32

Περὶ ἡδονῆς, ὅτι εἰ καὶ ἀγαθόν,
ἀλλ' οὐ βέβαιον. γ΄

1. Αἰσώπῳ τῷ Φρυγὶ πεποίηνται διάλογοί τε θηρίων
καὶ ξυνουσίαι, διαλέγεται δὲ αὐτῷ καὶ τὰ δένδρα καὶ
οἱ ἰχθύες, ἄλλο ἄλλῳ καὶ ἀνθρώποις ἀναμίξ· κατα-
μέμικται δὲ ἐν τοῖς λόγοις τούτοις νοῦς βραχὺς αἰνιτ-
τόμενός τι τῶν ἀληθῶν. ᾄδεται δή τις αὐτῷ καὶ
τοιοῦτος μῦθος. ἔλαφον διώκει λέων. ἡ δὲ φεύγουσα
ὑπεξάγει καὶ καταδύεται εἰς δρυμὸν βαθύν. ὁ δὲ λέων
(ὅσα γὰρ ἀλκῇ προὔχει, τάχει λείπεται) ἐπιστὰς τῷ
δρυμῷ ἐρωτᾷ ποιμένα εἴ που εἶδεν πτήξασαν τὴν ἔλαφον. ὁ δὲ ποιμὴν οὐκ ἔφη ἰδεῖν, καὶ ὁμοῦ λέγων τὴν
χεῖρα ἀποτείνας ἔδειξε τὸ χωρίον. ᾤχετο ὁ λέων ἐπὶ
τὴν δειλαίαν ἔλαφον. ἡ δὲ ἀλώπηξ (σοφὴ γάρ τις
αὕτη τῷ Αἰσώπῳ ἐστίν) πρὸς τὸν ποιμένα λέγει· "ὡς
δειλὸς ἄρα καὶ πονηρὸς ἦσθα· δειλὸς μὲν πρὸς λέοντας, πονηρὸς δὲ ἐς ἐλάφους."

2. Δοκεῖ μοι δὴ χρήσασθαι ἂν καὶ ὁ Ἐπίκουρος τῷ

ORATION 32

On pleasure, that even if it is good,
it is not stable. Part III

1. Aesop the Phrygian composed dialogues and conversations between animals, and even his trees and fish could talk to one another, as well as to men, all mingled together. Included in these stories is a concise message that hints at a some truth. One such fable he tells is the following. A lion was pursuing a doe. She eluded him by fleeing and jumped into a deep thicket. The lion, her superior in power as much as her inferior in speed, stopped at the edge of the thicket and asked a shepherd if he had seen the doe hiding anywhere. The shepherd said that he had not seen her, but as he was speaking he extended his hand and pointed to the place. The lion then rushed upon the poor doe, whereupon a fox, the clever character in Aesop, said to the shepherd, "How cowardly and wicked you have proven to be—cowardly toward lions and wicked toward deer!"[1]

2. I really do think that Epicurus could use this Phry-

---

[1] Versions of this fable are Babrius 50 (fox and hunter) and Phaedrus, Perotti's Index 28 (rabbit and hunter), but they differ in outcomes and messages. The other fables at *Orr.* 15.5, 19.2, and 36.1 are explicitly inventions of Maximus.

Φρυγίῳ τούτῳ αἰνίγματι πρὸς τὸν τῆς ἡδονῆς κατ-
ήγορον, τῇ μὲν φωνῇ ἀνδριζόμενον, τῇ δὲ γνώμῃ,
καθάπερ τῇ χειρί, ἐκτεινόμενον ἐφ' ἡδονήν. τίς γὰρ
οὕτω πολεμῆσαι αὐτὸς αὑτῷ ὥστε τὸ μόνον δὴ πραγμάτων τῇ αὑτοῦ φύσει ἐπαγωγότατον ἀποσείσασθαι
ἑκών; τὰ μὲν γὰρ ἄλλα ἃ ὑπ' ἀνθρώπων διώκεται
ἢ πείρᾳ γνωρισθέντα παρεδέχθη, ἢ τέχνῃ δοκιμα-
σθέντα ἐτιμήθη, ἢ λόγῳ ἐξετασθέντα ἐπιστεύθη, ἢ
χρόνῳ βασανισθέντα ἠγαπήθη· ἡδονὴ δέ, καὶ λόγου
ἀδεὴς καὶ τέχνης πρεσβυτέρα, καὶ τὴν πεῖραν φθάνει
καὶ οὐκ ἀναμένει χρόνον, ἀλλὰ συμφυὴς[1] ἡ πρὸς
αὑτὴν φιλία καὶ ἡλικιῶτις τῶν σωμάτων ὥσπερ κρη-
πὶς τῇ σωτηρίᾳ τοῦ ζῴου ὑποβέβληται· ἣν εἴ τις
ἀφέλοι, τὸ γενόμενον εὐθὺς οἴχεσθαι δεῖ. ἐπιστήμην
μὲν γὰρ καὶ λόγον καὶ τοῦτο δὴ τὸ θρυλούμενον, τὸν
νοῦν αὐτόν, προϊὼν τῷ χρόνῳ ὁ ἄνθρωπος, τῇ κατὰ
βραχὺ ἐντεύξει τῶν αἰσθήσεων διὰ τῆς πείρας ξυν-
ενεγκάμενος, ἤθροισεν ἐφ' ἑαυτῷ· ἡδονὴν δὲ αὐτοδίδακτος παρὰ τῆς φύσεως λαβὼν ἔχει ἐξ ἀρχῆς εὐθύς.
καὶ ταύτην μὲν ἀγαπᾷ, πολεμεῖ δὲ τῷ ἀλγεινῷ, καὶ
ὑπὸ μὲν ταύτης σώζεται, ὑπὸ δὲ τοῦ ἀλγεῖν φθείρεται.

3. Φαῦλόν τι χρῆμα ἡδονή; οὐκ ἂν ἦν ξύμφυτον,
οὐδὲ τῶν σωζόντων ἡμᾶς τὸ πρεσβύτατον. τὰ δὲ ὑπὸ
τῶν σοφιστῶν θρυλούμενα ἐς αὐτήν, ἡ Σαρδαναπάλ-
λου τρυφὴ καὶ ἡ Μηδικὴ χλιδὴ καὶ ἡ Ἰωνικὴ ἁβρότης

[1] συμφυὴς Markland, Trapp: ὑπερφυὴς R

gian allegory against someone condemning pleasure, whose talk is bold, but whose mind, like the shepherd's hand, is actually pointing to pleasure. For who is so at odds with himself that he is willing to shake off the single thing that is most appealing to his very nature? All the other things pursued by humans have either been accepted because they were discovered by experience, or valued because they were tested by expertise, or trusted because they were examined by reason, or welcomed because they stood the test of time. But pleasure needs no assistance from reason, is more ancient and venerable[2] than any expertise, predates experience, and does not wait for time to pass, because the affection for pleasure is innate and coexistent with the body, like a foundation laid down to support the creature's survival; and if anyone should remove it, what has come into being is bound to perish right away. For it is only over the course of time that humans have accumulated for themselves knowledge, reason, and that much-touted attribute, the intellect itself, having built them up through experience by the gradual encounters of their senses.[3] But from the very beginning, man naturally seizes and holds on to pleasure without needing any instruction. He welcomes it and fights off physical pain; pleasure preserves his life, whereas pain destroys it.

3. Is pleasure, then, some paltry thing? No, for then it would not be innate, nor be the oldest and most venerable means of assuring our survival. But those hackneyed criticisms leveled against it by the sophists, who cite the luxuriousness of Sardanapallus, the lavishness of the Medes,

---

[2] The adjective πρεσβύτερος connotes both older and more venerable.   [3] This process is elaborated in *Or.* 6.2.

καὶ τράπεζαι Σικελικαὶ καὶ ὀρχήσεις Συβαριτικαὶ καὶ
ἑταῖραι Κορίνθιαι, ταῦτα ἀθρόα καὶ ὅσα τούτων ποι-
κιλώτερα οὐχ ἡδονῆς ἔργα ἀλλὰ τέχνης καὶ λόγου,
παρανομησάντων τῶν ἀνθρώπων εἰς ἡδονὰς δι᾽ εὐπορίαν τῶν τεχνῶν ὀψὲ τοῦ χρόνου.

Ὥσπερ οὖν οὐδεὶς λοιδορεῖται λόγῳ ὡς οὐκ ἔστιν
καλὸν τῇ φύσει, κἂν ἀπάγῃ τις αὐτοῦ τὴν χρείαν ἐπὶ
τὸ μὴ φύσει καλόν, οὕτως οὐδὲ τῇ ἡδονῇ λοιδορητέον,
ἀλλὰ τοῖς χρωμένοις ἡδονῇ κακῶς. δύο δὲ ὄντων
τούτων ἐν ἀνθρώπου ψυχῇ, ἡδονῆς καὶ λόγου, λόγῳ
μὲν ἡδονὴ κραθεῖσα, μηδὲν ἀφελοῦσα τοῦ ἀναγκαίου,
προσέθηκεν αὐτῷ τὸ ἀγωγότερον· λόγος δὲ ἡδοναῖς
προσγενόμενος, αὐξήσας αὐτῶν δι᾽ εὐπορίας τὸ μέ-
τριον, ἀφεῖλεν τοῦ φύσει τερπνοῦ τὸ ἀναγκαῖον.

4. "Ἀλλ᾽ οὐκ ἴδιον ἀνθρώπου ἡδονή, κοινὸν δὲ καὶ
τῶν ἄλλων ζῴων." τοῦτο λέγεις τὸ ἐχεγγυώτατον ἡδονῆς πρὸς σωτηρίαν, τὸ παντὸς τοῦ πεφυκότος ζῆν
διασωστικόν. ἢ διὰ τὴν κοινότητά σε ἐνοχλεῖ; ὦ τῆς
πλεονεξίας. σύ μοι δοκεῖς οὐδὲ τοῦ ἡλίου ἀγαπᾶν τὸ
φῶς, ὅτι ἐστὶν κοινὸν ὀφθαλμῶν πάντων, ἀλλὰ ἔδει
γὰρ τὸν ἄνθρωπον μόνον ὁρᾶν, καὶ διὰ τοῦτο οὐκ
ἀγαθὸν ἀνθρώπῳ τὸ φῶς· οὐδέ γε ὁ ἀήρ, εἰσπνεό-
μενός τε καὶ οἰκονομῶν τὰ σώματα ταῖς αὐτοῦ ὁδοῖς,

---

4 For the Epicurean insistence on simple fare and avoidance
of extravagance, cf. Diog. Laert. 10.130–31 and 141 (KD 8): "No
pleasure is in itself evil, but the things which produce certain
pleasures entail annoyances many times greater than the pleasures themselves" (trans. R. D. Hicks).

the decadence of the Ionians, Sicilian gastronomy, Sybaritic dances, and Corinthian prostitutes—all these examples and others even more extravagant, are not the products of pleasure, but of artifice and cleverness, when men have violated the laws of pleasure through the resources provided by recently acquired skills.[4]

Just as no one rails against reason and claims that it is not naturally good, even though someone diverts its use for what is not naturally good, so we should not rail against pleasure itself, but rather against those who put pleasure to bad use. Within the human soul there are two elements, pleasure and reason. When pleasure combines with reason without diminishing reason's constraining power, it adds to reason's appeal. And when reason joins with pleasures and increases their moderation through its resourcefulness, it takes away the constraining power from what is naturally pleasant.[5]

4. "Yet pleasure is not only possessed by humans, but is shared by all other creatures."[6] However, in saying that pleasure serves to preserve the life of every creature that is born, you are offering the surest proof of pleasure's role in human survival as well. Or are you bothered by the fact that it is shared? How selfish of you! To me you seem not to welcome the light of the sun, because it is shared by all eyes, whereas only man ought to see it, and for this reason light is not a good for humans, any more than the air that is breathed in and regulates bodies with its intake, or riv-

---

[5] The text is in doubt, but the argument is Epicurean.
[6] This picks up the criticism of pleasure at *Or.* 31.5.

οὐ ποταμῶν νάματα, οὐ γῆς καρποί· μέχρι γὰρ τῶν
ἀναγκαίων ἐὰν προέλθῃς, πάντα κοινά, ἴδιον δὲ οὐδὲν
οὐδενός. ἐνταῦθά μοι τάττε καὶ τὴν ἡδονήν, ἐν κοι-
νότητι ἀγαθοῦ σώζοντος πᾶσαν αἰσθητικὴν φύσιν.

5. Ἐπεὶ δὲ ἀρετῆς πρὸς ἡδονὴν ἡ ἐξέτασις γίγνεται, οὐ λοιδορήσομαι μὲν τῇ ἀρετῇ (οὐ γὰρ πικρὸς
οὐδὲ βλάσφημος ὁ καθ᾽ ἡδονὴν λόγος) τοσοῦτον δὲ
λέγω, ὡς εἰ τῆς ἀρετῆς ἀφαιρήσει τις τὸ ἡδύ, καὶ τὸ
δυνατὸν αὐτῆς προσαφήρηκεν· οὐδὲν γὰρ τῶν καλῶν
αἱρετὸν ἀπογενομένης ἡδονῆς· καὶ γὰρ ὁ κατ᾽ ἀρετὴν
πονῶν ἑκὼν φιλίᾳ ἡδονῆς πονεῖ παρούσης ἢ προσ-
δοκωμένης.

Ὥσπερ γὰρ ἐν τοῖς χρηματισμοῖς οὐθεὶς ἑκὼν
ἀντικαταλλάττεται δραχμὴν ταλάντου οὐδὲ χρυσοῦ
χαλκόν, ᾧ μὴ

φρένας ἐξέλετο Ζεύς,

ἀλλὰ δεῖ τὰς ἀμοιβάς, κἂν ἰσοστάσιοι ὦσιν, λυσιτε-
λεῖν τῷ ἀλλαττομένῳ κατὰ τὴν χρείαν τοῦ λαβόντος,
οὕτως ἀμέλει κἂν ταῖς τῶν πόνων ὁμιλίαις οὐδεὶς πονεῖ πόνου ἔρωτι (τί γὰρ ἂν εἴη δυσεραστότερον;) ἀλ-
λάττεται δὲ τοὺς παρόντας πόνους, ὡς μὲν εἴποι ἄν
τις τῶν ἀστειοτέρων[2] τοῦ καλοῦ, ὡς δέ τις τῶν ἀλη-

---

[2] ἀστειοτέρων Reiske, Trapp: ἀγροικοτέρων R

---

[7] Cf. Diog. Laert. 10.138 (Epicurus): "And we choose the
virtues too on account of pleasure and not for their own sake, as

ers' streams, or the fruits of the earth. For if you consider necessities alone, they are all shared, and none is the sole possession of any one species. I ask you to place pleasure as well in this category, as a shared good that safeguards the survival of all sentient nature.

5. But since our inquiry now turns to virtue's relationship to pleasure, I shall not rail against virtue (since pleasure's arguments are not harsh or slanderous), but I will say this much. If someone strips virtue of its pleasantness, he also deprives it of its efficacy, because no good thing is chosen in the absence of pleasure, and the man who undertakes virtuous labors does so willingly out of affection for pleasure that is either present or anticipated.[7]

Now when it comes to business dealings, no one willingly exchanges a talent for a drachma or gold for bronze, unless

Zeus has taken away his wits,[8]

and even if exchanges are of equal monetary value, they must benefit the giver consistent with the needs of the receiver. In just the same way, when it comes to undertaking labors, no one toils for the mere love of toil (what love could be more unfortunate?), but he exchanges the present labors for what a more sophisticated[9] person would call the Good, but what a more truthful one would call

we take medicine for the sake of health" (trans. R. D. Hicks). The example of Heracles will illustrate this point in §7 below.

[8] *Il.* 6.234, said of Glaucus when exchanging his gold armor for the bronze armor of Diomedes. This incident is also discussed at *Orr.* 35.3, 39.1, and 40.1.   [9] Accepting the emendation of Reiske and Trapp of ἀστειοτέρων over the manuscript's ἀγροικοτέρων (less sophisticated).

θεστέρων, ἡδονῆς. κἂν γὰρ τὸ καλὸν εἴπῃς, ἡδονὴν
λέγεις· σχολῇ γὰρ ἂν εἴη τὸ κάλλος κάλλος, εἰ μὴ
ἥδιστον εἴη.

6. Ἐγὼ δὲ οἶμαι καὶ αὐτὸ τοὐναντίον, διὰ τούτων
ἀποφαίνεσθαι τὴν ἡδονὴν πάντων χρημάτων αἱρετω-
τέραν, ἧς εἵνεκα ἄν τις καὶ θάνατον ἀλλάξαιτο καὶ
τραύματα καὶ πόνους καὶ ἄλλα μυρία δυσχερῆ. κἂν
γὰρ ἄλλο ἄλλῳ ἐπιτιθῇς ὄνομα τῆς τούτων αἰτίας,[3]
Ἀχιλλεῖ μὲν ἀποθνῄσκοντι ἑκόντι καὶ τιμωροῦντι
ἀποθανόντι τῷ Πατρόκλῳ φιλίαν, Ἀγαμέμνονι δὲ
ἀγρυπνοῦντι καὶ προβουλευομένῳ καὶ προπολεμοῦντι
βασιλείαν, τῷ δὲ Ἕκτορι ἐξηγουμένῳ καὶ προμα-
χομένῳ καὶ ἀριστεύοντι σωτηρίαν πατρίδος, πάντα
ταῦτα ἐρεῖς ἡδονῶν ὀνόματα.

Ὥσπερ γὰρ ἐν ταῖς σωμάτων νόσοις ἀγαπᾷ ὁ
κάμνων τεμνόμενος καὶ ἐμπιμπράμενος καὶ διψῶν καὶ
λιμώττων καὶ τὰ δυσχερῆ τῇ φύσει προσιέμενος
ἑκών, ἀντικαταλλαττόμενος ταῦτα τῆς προσδοκίας
τοῦ ὑγιεινοῦ, εἰ δὲ ἀφέλοις τὴν ἐλπίδα τοῦ μέλλοντος
ἀγαθοῦ, ἀφαιρήσεις τὴν αἵρεσιν τῶν παρόντων κα-
κῶν· οὕτω κἂν ταῖς πράξεσιν ἀντίδοσις γίγνεται πρὸς
ἡδονὰς πόνων, ἣν σὺ μὲν ἀρετὴν καλεῖς, ἐγὼ δὲ τὴν
μὲν ἀρετὴν δίδωμι, ἐρήσομαι δέ σε, εἰ ἄνευ τῆς πρὸς
αὐτὴν φιλίας τὴν ἀρετὴν ἡ ψυχὴ εἵλετο; ἐὰν γὰρ τὴν
φιλίαν δῷς, ἡδονὴν δίδως.

[3] αἰτίας I, Davies[2], Dübner, Koniaris: ἀξίας U[pc], Hobein:
ἀ. .ιας R

pleasure. For even if you call it the Good,[10] you really mean pleasure, for scarcely could the good be good without also being supremely pleasurable.

6. But I believe the very opposite, that these considerations reveal pleasure to be more worthy of choice[11] than all other things, because for its sake people may accept death, wounds, labors, and countless other distressing things. For even if you assign different names to the various causes of each, such as friendship in Achilles' willingness to die and avenge the death of Patroclus; kingship in Agamemnon's staying awake, planning, and fighting for his army; and defense of the homeland in Hector's leading his troops, fighting at the forefront, and being their champion—in all these instances you will speak of pleasures.

For just as in cases of physical disease a patient welcomes surgery, cautery, thirst, and hunger, and willingly accepts these naturally distressing things, while trading them for the health he expects to gain, but if you take away his hope for that future good, you will take away his acceptance of the present suffering; just so, when it comes to ethical actions, there is an exchange of toils for pleasures. You call this exchange virtue, and while I concede the presence of virtue, I shall ask you if the soul would have chosen virtue without an affection for it, because if you grant the affection, you also grant the pleasure.

[10] When virtue is at issue, both here and in the following oration, the Good translates *to kalon* (implying noble or ethical goodness), as opposed to *to agathon*, which is more general.

[11] That is, chosen as the ultimate good.

7. Κἂν ὑπαλλάξῃς τὸ ὄνομα καὶ χαρὰν τὴν ἡδονὴν καλῇς, οὐ νεμεσῶ τῆς ἀφθονίας τῶν ὀνομάτων, τὸ δὲ πρᾶγμα ὁρῶ, καὶ τὴν ἡδονὴν γνωρίζω. ἢ οἴει⁴ τὸν Ἡρακλέα ἐκεῖνον, τὸν τῶν πολλῶν καὶ θαυμαστῶν πόνων ὁμιλητὴν καὶ ἀγωνιστὴν καὶ ἐθάδα, τὸν πρὸς τὰ θηρία παραβαλλόμενον, τὸν τοῖς πανταχοῦ δυνάσταις προσφερόμενον, τὸν πρὸς τοὺς ἀγρίους φιλονεικοῦντα, τὸν ἡμερωτὴν τῆς γῆς, τὸν καθαρτήν, τὸν ἐπὶ τὴν Οἴτην ἰόντα, τὸν ἐπὶ πῦρ παραγιγνόμενον, ἄλλο τι ἢ μεγάλαις καὶ θαυμασταῖς καὶ ἀκράτοις ἡδοναῖς χειραγωγούμενον, ταῖς μὲν παρούσαις ὁμοῦ τοῖς πόνοις, ταῖς δὲ μελλούσαις μετὰ τοὺς πόνους, ἐπὶ ταῦτα ἰέναι ἑκόντα; ἀλλὰ σὺ μὲν τοὺς πόνους ὁρᾷς, τὰς δὲ Ἡρακλέους ἡδονὰς οὐχ ὁρᾷς αἷς ἔχαιρεν. ἔχαιρεν καὶ ὁ Ἡρακλῆς ταῦτα δρῶν, καὶ διὰ τοῦτο ἔδρα· καὶ οὐκ ἂν ἔδρα, εἰ μὴ δρῶν ἔχαιρεν. αἱ μὲν γὰρ Διονύσου ἡδοναὶ καὶ τελετῆς χώραν ἔχουσιν, κῶμοι ἐκεῖνοι καὶ θίασοι καὶ χοροὶ καὶ αὐλοὶ καὶ ᾄσματα· πάντα ταῦτα Διονύσου ἡδονῶν σχήματα ἐν μυστηρίοις ὀργιαζόμενα.

8. Τί λέγω Διόνυσον καὶ Ἡρακλέα; μῦθοι ταῦτα, ἡρωϊκὰ ταῦτα. τὸν Σωκράτην λέγω. ἐρᾷς, ὦ Σώκρατες, Ἀλκιβιάδου καὶ μετὰ τοῦτον Φαίδρου καὶ μετ᾿ ἐκεῖνον Χαρμίδου· ἐρᾷς, ὦ Σώκρατες, καί σε οὐ λαν-

---

⁴ ἢ οἴει Davies², Dübner, Trapp: ἢ ποιεῖ R, Hobein, Koniaris

7. And even if you change the name and call pleasure "joy,"[12] I do not begrudge your abundant use of terms, because I can see the thing for what it is and recognize the pleasure. Or do you think that famous Heracles—the habitual contender engaged in those many astounding labors, who matched himself against wild beasts, who confronted despots everywhere, who contended with savages, who tamed the world and cleansed it, who went to Oeta and presented himself to the fire—did not willingly embark on these, being led on by pleasures that were great, wondrous, and unalloyed, some being simultaneous with his labors, others to come after them?[13] You, however, only see the labors, but do not see the pleasures in which Heracles found joy. He rejoiced when doing them, and for that reason he did them. He would not have performed them had he not rejoiced in doing them. Dionysus' pleasures take the form of rituals—those revels, sacred bands, choruses, pipes, and songs: all are forms of Dionysus' pleasures celebrated in his mysteries.[14]

8. But why bring up Dionysus and Heracles, those subjects of myths and heroic tales? I shall speak of Socrates. You, Socrates, are in love with Alcibiades, and then with Phaedrus, and after him with Charmides. You are in love,

---

[12] That is, *chara*, a Stoic term. Cf. Diog. Laert. 7.115–16: "[The Stoics] say that there are three emotional states which are good, namely, joy, caution, and wishing. Joy, the counterpart of pleasure, is rational elation" (trans. R. D. Hicks).   [13] He ultimately went up to Olympus, where he married Hebe (Youth) and lived in peace (Pind. *Nem.* 1.69–72).   [14] Dionysus, who wandered far and wide and faced much opposition in spreading his ecstatic rituals, is also paired with Heracles at *Or.* 38.7.

θάνει κάλλος Ἀττικόν· ἀλλ' ὁμολόγησον αὐτοῦ τὴν
αἰτίαν καὶ μὴ φοβηθῇς τὴν ἀδοξίαν· ἔξεστιν καὶ μεθ'
ἡδονῆς σωφρόνως ἐρᾶν, ὡς ἔξεστιν καὶ μετὰ λύπης
ἀκολάστως ἐρᾶν. εἰ δὲ καὶ χωρὶς ἡδονῆς ἐρᾷς καὶ
ψυχῆς μόνης καὶ σώματος οὐκ ἐρᾷς, ἐράσθητι Θεαι-
τήτου· ἀλλ' οὐκ ἐρᾷς, σιμὸς γὰρ ἦν· ἐράσθητι Χαιρε-
φῶντος· ἀλλ' οὐκ ἐρᾷς, ὠχρὸς γὰρ ἦν· ἐράσθητι Ἀρι-
στοδήμου· ἀλλ' οὐκ ἐρᾷς, αἰσχρὸς γὰρ ἦν.

Ἀλλὰ τίνων ἐρᾷς; εἴ πού τις εὐκόμης, εἴ πού τις
ὡραῖος, εἴ που ἁβρός, εἴ που καλός. καὶ πιστεύω μὲν
τῇ ἀρετῇ, ὅτι δικαίως ἐρᾷς, οὐκ ἀπιστῶ δὲ τῇ ψυχῇ,
ὅτι δι' ἡδονὴν ἐρᾷς· οὐδὲ γὰρ σώματι ἀπιστῶ ὑπὸ
πυρὸς θερμαινομένῳ, οὐδὲ ὀφθαλμοῖς ὑπὸ ἡλίῳ φωτι-
ζομένοις, οὐδὲ ἀκοαῖς ὑπὸ αὐλῶν γανυμέναις, οὐδὲ
Ἡσιόδῳ ὑπὸ Μουσῶν διδασκομένῳ, οὐδὲ Ὁμήρῳ ὑπὸ
Καλλιόπης λιγαινομένῳ, οὐ⟨δὲ⟩[5] Πλάτωνι ὑπὸ Ὁμήρου μεγαλυνομένῳ· πάντα ταῦτα ὑφ' ἡδονῆς ἕλκεται,
καὶ ὀφθαλμοὶ καὶ ἀκοαὶ καὶ σώματα καὶ λόγοι.

9. Ἀλλὰ καὶ τὸν Διογένην ἐκεῖνον εἰς τὸν πίθον
ἡδονὴ εἰσάγει· εἰ δὲ καὶ ἡ ἀρετὴ αὐτῷ συνεισέβαλ-
λεν, τί τὴν ἡδονὴν ἐξοικίζεις τῷ λόγῳ; ἥδετο ὁ Διογένης τῷ πίθῳ ὡς Βαβυλῶνι Ξέρξης, ἥδετο τῇ μάζῃ
ὁ Διογένης ὡς ὁ Σμινδυρίδης τῇ καρύκῃ, ἥδετο ταῖς

[5] suppl. Trapp

204

and no beauty in all of Attica escapes your notice. Well then, admit the reason for it, and don't fear any disgrace, for it is quite possible to love chastely and feel pleasure, just as it is possible to love licentiously and feel pain. But if your love involves no pleasure at all, and if you love the soul alone and not the body, then you should fall in love with Theaetetus. But you don't, because he had a flat nose.[15] Then you should fall in love with Chaerephon, but you don't, because he was pale.[16] Then you should fall in love with Aristodemus, but you don't, because he was ugly.[17]

With whom, then, do you fall in love? Anyone with beautiful hair, or anyone who is youthful, delicate, or handsome. I trust your virtue, because your love is just, and, conversely, I do not distrust your soul just because your love is pleasurable, any more than I distrust a body being warmed by a fire, eyes being illuminated with sunlight, ears gladdened with the music of pipes, Hesiod being taught by the Muses, Homer being made melodious by Calliope, or Plato being made majestic by Homer. Eyes, ears, bodies, and words—all these are drawn along by pleasure.

9. It was also pleasure that led famous Diogenes to his pithos. And even if virtue was a contributing factor for him, why exclude pleasure from consideration? Diogenes delighted in his pithos just as Xerxes did in Babylon; he delighted in his plain bread just as Smindyrides did in his

---

[15] Cf. Pl. *Tht.* 209c.

[16] Cf. Ar. *Nub.* 103–4.

[17] He was little (Pl. *Symp.* 173b) and his nickname was "Tiny" (Xen. *Mem.* 1.4.2).

κρήναις ταῖς πανταχοῦ ὡς ὁ Καμβύσης Χοάσπῃ
μόνῳ· ἥδετο τῷ ἡλίῳ ὡς Σαρδανάπαλλος ταῖς πορφυρίσιν, ἥδετο τῇ βακτηρίᾳ ὡς Ἀλέξανδρος τῷ δόρατι,
ἥδετο τῷ θυλάκῳ ὡς ὁ Κροῖσος τοῖς θησαυροῖς. κἂν
παραβάλῃς ἡδονὰς ἡδοναῖς, τὰ Διογένους κρατεῖ· τὰ
γὰρ ἐκείνων μεστὰ μὲν ἡδονῆς, ἀλλὰ ἀναμέμικται
λύπῃ πανταχοῦ· ὀδύρεται Ξέρξης ἡττώμενος, στένει
Καμβύσης τιτρωσκόμενος, οἰμώζει Σαρδανάπαλλος
ἐμπιμπράμενος, ἀνιᾶται Σμινδυρίδης ἀπελαυνόμενος,
δακρύει Κροῖσος λαμβανόμενος, λυπεῖται Ἀλέξανδρος μὴ μαχόμενος· αἱ δὲ Διογένους ἡδοναὶ οἰμωγῆς
ἄπειροι, ἄστονοι, ἀδάκρυτοι, ἄλυποι.

Σὺ δὲ τὰς ἡδονὰς αὐτοῦ πόνους καλεῖς· μετρεῖς γὰρ
τὰ Διογένους τῇ σαυτοῦ φύσει, πονηρῷ μέτρῳ· σὺ
μὲν γὰρ ἀλγήσεις ταῦτα δρῶν, Διογένης δὲ ἥδετο.
ἐπιτολμήσαιμι δ' ἂν ἔγωγε εἰπεῖν ὡς οὐδεὶς ἡδονῆς
Διογένους ἦν ἐραστὴς ἀκριβέστερος· οὐχ ἑστίαν ἔνε-
μεν, ἐπίλυπον γὰρ οἰκονομία· οὐ πολιτείας ἐφήψατο,
ἀνιαρὸν γὰρ τὸ χρῆμα· οὐκ ἐπειράθη γάμου, ἤκουεν
γὰρ τὴν Ξανθίππην· οὐκ ἐπειράθη παιδοτροφίας,
ἑώρα γὰρ τὰ δεινά· ἀλλὰ ἄφετος παντὸς τοῦ δεινοῦ,

---

[18] For Smindyrides the Sybarite, see *Or.* 14.2.

[19] Herodotus (1.188) describes how water from the Choaspes
was brought along when the Persian king traveled, and only he
was allowed to drink it. This custom is also mentioned at *Orr.* 33.4
and 34.6.

[20] That is, Alexander the Great.

Lydian sauce;[18] he delighted in spring waters available everywhere just as Cambyses did in the Choaspes alone;[19] he delighted in the sun just as Sardanapallus did in his purple robes; he delighted in his staff just as Alexander[20] did in his spear; he delighted in his rucksack just as Croesus did in his treasuries. And if you compare his pleasures with those of the others, Diogenes' prove superior, for although the lives of the others are full of pleasure, it is everywhere mixed with pain. Xerxes laments when defeated, Cambyses groans when stabbed,[21] Sardanapallus wails as he burns, Smindyrides grieves when sent off empty-handed,[22] Croesus weeps when captured, and Alexander lives in pain when not fighting. In contrast, Diogenes' pleasures were free of wailing, groans, tears, and pains.

You call his pleasures toilsome, because you are measuring Diogenes' actions by your own nature—a poor standard, for you would feel physical pain if you were doing those things, whereas Diogenes took delight in them. In fact, I would venture to maintain that no one was a more fastidious lover of pleasure than Diogenes. He did not live in a home, because managing a household is distressing work. He did not engage in civic life, because it is a grievous affair. He never tried marriage, because he kept hearing about Xanthippe.[23] He never tried to raise children, because he could see the risks involved. No, liber-

---

[21] Cf. Hdt. 3.64.3.

[22] He failed to win the hand of Agariste, the daughter of Cleisthenes of Sicyon (Hdt. 6.127–30).

[23] Socrates' wife, the most difficult woman of all time, according to Xen. *Symp.* 2.10.

ἐλεύθερος, ἄφροντις, ἀδεής, ἄλυπος ἐνέμετο τὴν πᾶσαν γῆν ὡς οἶκον ἕνα, μόνος ἀνθρώπων ἡδοναῖς
συνὼν ἀφρουρήτοις καὶ ἀταμιεύτοις καὶ ἀφθόνοις.

10. Τὸν Διογένην ἐῶμεν καὶ μετίωμεν τοὺς νομοθέτας καὶ πολιτείας σκεψώμεθα. μή με οἰηθῇς ἐπὶ
Σύβαριν ἥξειν, μηδὲ Συρακοσίων μνησθήσεσθαι τῶν
ἁβροτάτων, μηδὲ Κορινθίων τῶν φιληδόνων, μηδὲ
Χίων τῶν πλουσίων, μηδὲ Λεσβίων τῶν εὐοινοτάτων,
μηδὲ Μιλησίων τῶν εὐειμονεστάτων· ἀλλ᾽ ἐπὶ τοὺς
ἡγεμόνας ἔρχομαι, ἐπὶ Ἀθηναίους ἔρχομαι, καὶ τὰ
Λακεδαιμονίων ἐξετάζω. μάστιγες αὗται καὶ πληγαὶ
Λακωνικαὶ καὶ θῆραι καὶ δρόμοι καὶ δεῖπνα λιτὰ καὶ
στιβάδες εὐτελεῖς· ἀλλ᾽ ὁρῶ καὶ τούτων τὰ τερπνά. εὖ
γε, ὦ Λυκοῦργε, σμικρῶν πόνων μεγάλας ἡδονὰς
ἀντεισάγεις· ὀλίγα δούς, μεγάλα ἔλαβες· ἐφημέρους
δοὺς πόνους, ἡδονὰς διηνεκεῖς ἀντέλαβες. τίνες, λέ-
ξεις, Σπαρτιατικαὶ ἡδοναί; πόλις ἀτείχιστος, ἄφοβος,
ἄπειρος πυρός, ἀθέατος πολεμίων, ἀθέατος ξενικῶν
ἀσπίδων, ἀνήκοος στόνων, ἀνήκοος ἀπειλῆς.

Τί δ᾽ ἂν εἴη φόβου λυπηρότερον, τί δὲ δουλείας
ἀνιαρότερον, τί δὲ ἀνάγκης ἐπιπονώτερον; ὅταν δὲ
ταῦτα ἀπαλλάξῃς πόλεως, πολλὰς αὐτοῖς ἡδονὰς
ἀντεισάγεις. ἐκείνης τῆς ἡδονῆς θρέμμα ἦν ὁ Λεωνίδας, ἐκείνης ὁ Ὀθρυάδας, ἐκείνης ὁ Καλλικρατίδας.

ated from every form of trouble, he lived as a free man, without care, fear, or distress, and inhabited the entire world as his single home, the only human being living with pleasures in abundance, ones that needed no one to guard or administer them.

10. Let us leave Diogenes and turn to lawmakers and consider their governments. Do not think that I shall visit Sybaris, or bring up those effete Syracusans, or hedonistic Corinthians, or wealthy Chians, or Lesbians with their excellent wines, or Milesians with their exquisite clothing. No, I shall go to the foremost states. I shall go to Athens, and I shall examine the ways of the Lacedaemonians. Here you find whips, Spartan flagellations, hunting, running, simple meals, and rough bedding. Nevertheless, I can also see the pleasures in these. Well done, Lycurgus! In return for small toils you usher in great pleasures. For small expenditures, you have reaped great profits. In return for short-term toils, you have gained lasting pleasures. What, you will ask, *are* the pleasures that the Spartiates[24] enjoy? A city that needs no walls, that lives without fear, that has never been touched by fire, has never beheld enemies or foreign shields, has never heard lamentation or threats.

And what could be more distressing than fear, more grievous than slavery, more burdensome than oppression? When you banish these from a city, you bring its people many pleasures in return. A student of that pleasure was Leonidas, as was Othryadas, and also Callicratidas.[25] But,

[24] The male Spartans with full citizenship.

[25] Spartan commanders. Leonidas died in 480 BC (cf. *Or.* 3.8, etc.), Othryadas died ca. 546 BC, and Callicratidas died in 406 BC; all three are cited at *Or.* 23.2.

ἀλλ' ἀπέθνησκον οὗτοι. ἀπέθνησκον καλῶς. ὑπὲρ
ποίων ἡδονῶν; καὶ γὰρ τῶν σωμάτων ἐκκόπτεται
μέρη ὑπὲρ ῥαστώνης τοῦ ὅλου· μέρος ἦν ὁ Λεωνίδας
{καὶ}⁶ τῆς Σπάρτης, ἀλλὰ ἀπέθνησκεν ὑπὲρ τῆς Σπάρτης, μέρος ὁ Ὀθρυάδας, Καλλικρατίδας μέρος· τοιγαροῦν ἀφαιρουμένων σμικρῶν μερῶν, ἐσώζοντο αἱ
οἴκοι ἡδοναί.

Τὰ δὲ Ἀθηναίων τί χρὴ λέγειν; πάντα μεστὰ ἑορ-
τῆς τὰ Ἀττικά, πάντα θυμηδίας, καὶ διέλαχον αὐτοῖς
⟨αἱ⟩⁷ ὧραι τὰς ἡδονάς, ἦρος Διονύσια, μετοπώρου
μυστήρια, καὶ ἄλλην ὥραν ἔχει ἄλλος θεός, Παναθήναια, Σκειροφόρια, Ἁλῶα, Ἀπατούρια. ναυμαχοῦσιν
ἐν θαλάττῃ, οἱ δὲ οἴκοι ἑορτάζουσιν· πολεμοῦσιν ἐν
γῇ, οἱ δὲ ἐν Διονύσου γελῶσιν. ἀλλ' οὐδὲ οἱ πόλεμοι,
τὸ σκυθρωπότατον, ἡδονῶν ἔρημοι, ἀλλὰ συντάττεται
τούτοις ἢ Τυρρηνὴ σάλπιγξ ἢ αὐλὸς τριηρικὸς ἢ ᾠδὴ
ἐμβατήριος. ὁρᾷς τὴν ἀφθονίαν τῶν ἡδονῶν;

⁶ del. Trapp
⁷ suppl. Reiske, Trapp

you say, they died. Yes, but they died nobly. For the sake of what pleasures? you ask. Parts of bodies are amputated to provide relief to the whole person. Leonidas was a part of Sparta, but it was for Sparta's sake that he died, as did Othryadas and Callicratidas. So, when these small parts were removed, the pleasures at home were preserved.

What need is there to speak of the ways of the Athenians? Attica is everywhere full of festivity and good cheer, for they have distributed their pleasures throughout the seasons, with the Dionysia in the spring and the mysteries in the fall, while various gods preside in various seasons at the Panathenaea, Scirophoria, Haloa, and Apaturia.[26] While some fight on the sea, the others are feasting at home; while some battle on land, the others are laughing in the theater of Dionysus. And not even their wars, the grimmest of ordeals, are devoid of pleasures, for they are accompanied either by Etruscan trumpets, trireme pipes,[27] or marching songs. Can you not see the abundance of pleasures here?

[26] Panathenaea (August, Athena), Scirophoria (June, Athena and others), Haloa (December, Demeter and others), and Apaturia (October/November, Zeus and Athena). Athenian orators frequently praised the city for its many festivals; cf. Thuc. 2.38, Isoc. *Paneg*. 43–46, and Aristid. *Panath*. 341, 373–75.

[27] Pipes (*auloi*) played tunes to synchronize the rowers.

ORATION 33

INTRODUCTION

This oration concludes the series of five lectures on the *telos* of philosophy, which have mostly concentrated on the issue of pleasure and Epicureanism. It opens with the difficulty of determining an argument that is true, because philosophy has become so contentious (§1).[1] This is true of the present inquiry concerning the relationship of virtue and pleasure, where Epicureanism has used virtue's one ally, reasoned argument (*logos*), to malign virtue and promote pleasure (§2). The Epicurean withdrawal from the active life leads to indolence, and by putting pleasure in charge of virtue it installs a tyrant over the soul that observes no limits in its appetites (§3). Darius exemplifies such excess in his inability to be satisfied with all that he possesses, by constantly seeking new territories. The allegory of Tantalus depicts the desperate thirst of the hedonist, for whom pleasure constantly approaches but then recedes, leaving him in a state of fear and distress (§4). Law and reason secure freedom for the soul, keeping it from grasping for every form of pleasure, like an octopus extending its tentacles (§5). Imagine a person enjoying all

[1] The breakdown of philosophy into competing schools is treated at *Orr.* 26.2 and 29.7.

the pleasures of the senses all at once. His "happiness" will disappear with the passage of time, first because pleasure taken away brings pain (*lypē*), as illustrated by the myth of Tantalus, and second because continual pleasure with no respite brings pain.[2] Such is the sorry state of man (§6). Humans share the pleasures of the flesh with beasts, but the gods furnished their immortal component with intellect (*nous*) and reason (*logos*). The Good (*to agathon*) for humans is to be found in their function, instruments, and survival. Their survival depends on their soul, whose instrument is intellect[3] and whose function is practical intelligence.[4] Herein lies the Good for humans (§7). In contrast, the mythological race of the unruly Centaurs exemplifies bondage to beastly pleasures (§8).

[2] For the interrelationship of pleasure and pain, see *Or.* 30.4.
[3] This point is argued at *Or.* 31.4.
[4] The function of *phronēsis* is treated at *Or.* 6.4–5.

ORATION 33

Τί τέλος φιλοσοφίας

1. Χαλεπὸν εὑρεῖν λόγον ἀληθῆ· κινδυνεύει γὰρ ἡ τοῦ ἀνθρώπου ψυχὴ δι᾽ εὐπορίαν τοῦ φρονεῖν τοῦ κρίνειν ἀπορεῖν. καὶ αἱ μὲν ἄλλαι τέχναι πρόσω ἰοῦσαι κατὰ τὴν εὕρεσιν εὐστοχώτεραι γίγνονται, ἑκάστη περὶ τὰ αὑτῆς ἔργα· φιλοσοφία δὲ ἐπειδὰν αὑτῆς εὐπορώτατα ἔχῃ, τότε μάλιστα ἐμπίμπλαται λόγων ἀντιστασίων καὶ ἰσορρόπων· καὶ ἔοικεν γεωργῷ, ἐπειδὰν ἐν περιουσίᾳ γένηται ὀργάνων πολλῶν, ἀκαρποτέρᾳ τῇ γῇ χρωμένῳ. τὰς μὲν οὖν πολιτικὰς διαδικασίας εὐθύνει ψῆφος καὶ ἀριθμὸς δικαστῶν καὶ γνώμη ῥήτορος καὶ δήμου χεῖρες· ἐνταῦθα δὲ τίς ἡμῖν παρέσται δικαστὴς καὶ τίνι ψήφῳ τἀληθὲς κρινοῦμεν; λόγῳ; ἀλλ᾽ οὐκ ἂν ἔχοις εἰπεῖν λόγον ὅτῳ οὐκ ἂν ἐξεύροις τὸν ἐναντίον. πάθει; ἀλλ᾽ ἄπιστος ὁ δικαστής. πλήθει; ἀλλὰ πλείους οἱ ἀμαθέστεροι. δόξῃ; ἀλλὰ τὰ χείρω ἐνδοξότερα.

2. Αὐτίκα ἐν τῷ παρόντι τούτῳ σκέμματι, ἡδονῆς ἀρετῇ ἁμιλλωμένης καὶ ἀντεξεταζομένης, οὐ παρω-

---

1 Examples are the skeptical arguments of the *Dissoi Logoi*.

ORATION 33

What the ultimate end of philosophy is

1. It is difficult to find an argument that is true, because the human soul, with its great capacity for thinking, runs the risk of being unable to render a judgment. As the other arts progress with new discoveries, they become more effective, each in its own sphere of activity, but it is precisely when philosophy is at its greatest capacity that it is most rife with antithetical arguments that carry equal weight.[1] Indeed, it comes to resemble a farmer with far too many implements working a field that is less and less productive. Now, whereas public disputes are settled by a vote, by a certain number of jurors, by the opinion of an orator, and by a show of hands of the people, in the case of philosophy, who will serve as juror for us, and by what kind of vote shall we determine the truth? By reasoned argument? No, because you could not put forth an argument without coming up with its counterargument. By emotional appeal? No, because that juror is untrustworthy. By the multitude? No, because the majority are too ignorant. By popular esteem? No, because inferior things enjoy the greater esteem.

2. For instance, in this present inquiry, where pleasure is contending with virtue and being compared with it, does

σαμένη τὴν ἀρετὴν ἡδονὴ καὶ δόξῃ κρατεῖ καὶ πλήθει
μαρτύρων ὑπερβάλλεται καὶ κατὰ πάθος δυναστεύει;
ὃ δὲ μόνον ὑπόλοιπον ἦν τῇ ἀρετῇ συμμαχικόν, ὁ
λόγος, καὶ τοῦτο σχίζεται καὶ διαιρεῖται, καὶ ἐξεύρη-
ταί τις καὶ παρ᾽ αὐτοῦ ἐπικουρία ἡδοναῖς, καὶ λέγει
τις καλῶς ὑπὲρ ἡδονῆς λέγων, καὶ τὴν ἀρετὴν φαυλί-
ζει, καὶ μετατίθησιν τὴν ἀρχὴν ἀπὸ τῆς ἀνδρωνίτιδος
ἐπὶ τὴν γυναικωνῖτιν· καὶ τὸ μὲν σχῆμα τοῦ φιλοσόφου μετεκδύεται,[1] τοῦ δὲ ὀνόματος ἀξιοῖ κρατεῖν.

Ἄφες, ἄνθρωπε, καὶ τοὔνομα μετὰ τοῦ λόγου.
παρανομεῖς περὶ τοὺς θεμένους[2] οὐδὲν σοφίᾳ καὶ
ἡδονῇ κοινόν· ἄλλος μὲν ὁ φιλήδονος, ἄλλος δὲ ὁ
φιλόσοφος· διακέκριται τὰ ὀνόματα, διακέκριται τὰ
ἔργα, διῄρηται τὰ γένη, ὡς τὰ Λακωνικὰ τῶν Ἀττι-
κῶν, ὡς τὰ βαρβαρικὰ τῶν Ἑλληνικῶν. ἐὰν δὲ Σπαρτιάτης εἶναι λέγων καὶ Ἕλλην καὶ Δωριεὺς καὶ Ἡρακλείδης θαυμάζῃς τιάραν Μηδικὴν καὶ τράπεζαν
βαρβαρικὴν καὶ ἁρμάμαξαν Περσικήν, περσίζεις,
βαρβαρίζεις, ἀπολώλεκας τὸν Παυσανίαν· Μῆδος εἶ,
Μαρδόνιος εἶ· ἀπόθου τοὔνομα μετὰ τοῦ γένους.

---

[1] μετεκδύεται Davies[2], Trapp: μετενδύεται R: obel. Koniaris
[2] θεμένους R: θεμελίους Acciaiolus, Trapp

---

[2] A play on "support" (*epicuria*) and the name of Epicurus,
which means helper or ally. The wordplay continues in §3 below.
[3] That is, an Epicurean, or Epicurus himself.   [4] A play on
the association of virtue with masculinity and pleasure with effeminacy. Cf. the quip of Diogenes the Cynic contrasting masculine Sparta with effeminate Athens at Diog. Laert. 6.59.

not pleasure push aside virtue and prevail in popular opinion, prove superior with its multitude of witnesses, and predominate with its emotional appeal? And as for virtue's one remaining ally, namely reasoned argument, it too is split and divided, and support[2] for pleasure has been found even in it, when a speaker[3] speaks eloquently on behalf of pleasure, disparages virtue, and transfers authority from the men's quarters to the women's.[4] He forsakes the manner of a philosopher, yet thinks fit to retain the title.

Give up, man, your title along with your arguments. You are wronging those who have established that wisdom and pleasure have nothing in common.[5] A hedonist is one thing, a philosopher another.[6] Their names are different, their endeavors are different, and they belong to races as distinct as Spartans and Athenians, as barbarians and Greeks. If, while claiming to be a Spartiate, a Greek, a Dorian, and a descendant of Heracles,[7] you are in awe of Median tiaras, barbarian feasts, and Persian carriages, then you are a Persian, you are a barbarian, you have lost your Pausanias.[8] You are now a Mede, you are now a Mardonius. Give up your name along with your race.

---

[5] The text is in doubt. Trapp accepts θεμελίους (foundations) and translates the sentence: "You are in error about the very foundations of the matter. Wisdom and Pleasure have nothing at all in common."

[6] Maximus plays on the names φιλ-ήδονος (lover of pleasure) and φιλό-σοφος (lover of wisdom).

[7] All four are Spartan attributes.

[8] Pausanias was the Spartan general who defeated the Persian Mardonius at the battle of Plataea in 479 BC but who was afterward seduced by Persian luxury and colluded with Xerxes. Cf. Thuc. 1.128–35.

3. Τοὺς μὲν οὖν πολλοὺς ἡδονὴν ὑμνοῦντας φέρω·
βάναυσος γὰρ ψυχὴ καὶ ἀπεληλαμένη λόγου, ἐλεεινὴ
μὲν τοῦ πάθους, σύγγνωστος δὲ τῆς ἀγνοίας· Ἐπίκουρον δὲ διὰ τοὔνομα οὐ φέρω, οὐδὲ ἀνέχομαι φιλοσοφίας ὑβριζούσης. οὐδὲ γὰρ στρατηγοῦ ἀνέχομαι τὴν
τάξιν ἀπολείποντος καὶ ἐξηγουμένου τῆς φυγῆς, οὐδὲ
γεωργοῦ ἀνέχομαι ἐμπιμπράντος τὰ λήϊα, οὐδὲ κυβερνήτου ἀνέχομαι ἀποδειλιῶντος πρὸς τὴν θάλατ-
ταν· πλεῖν σε δεῖ, στρατηγεῖν σε δεῖ, γεωργεῖν σε δεῖ·
πόνων ταῦτα μεστά, ἀλλ' οὐδὲν καλὸν ὑπὸ ῥᾳστώνης
γίγνεται. εἰ δὲ ἔπεται ἡδονὴ τοῖς καλοῖς, δίδωμι
τοῦτο· ἐπέσθω, ἀλλ' ἡγείσθω τὸ καλὸν πανταχοῦ·

εἷς κοίρανος ἔστω,

εἷς βασιλεύς, ᾧ ἔδωκεν

ἄρχειν ὁ Ζεύς. ἐὰν δὲ μεταθῇς τὴν τάξιν, καὶ ἄρχῃ
μὲν ἡδονή, ἔπηται δὲ λόγος, δίδως τῇ ψυχῇ τύραννον
πικρὸν καὶ ἀπαραίτητον, ᾧ δουλεύειν ἀνάγκη καὶ
ὑπηρετεῖν ὑπηρεσίας ἀνεπικρίτους καὶ παντοδαπάς,
κἂν αἰσχρὰ προστάττῃ, κἂν ἄδικα προστάττῃ.

Τί γὰρ ἂν εἴη μέτρον ἡδονῆς ἐπιλαβομένης ἐξουσίας ἐπιθυμημάτων; ἀκόρεστος γὰρ ὁ τύραννος οὗτος,
καὶ τῶν παρόντων ὑπεροπτικὸς καὶ τῶν μὴ παρόντων
ὀρεκτικός, καὶ διὰ περιουσίαν ἐξαπτόμενος καὶ ὑπὸ

---

9 That is, both his title of philosopher and his name of
"Helper"; cf. epicuria in §2.

3. Now I can tolerate the majority singing the praises of pleasure, for a vulgar soul divorced from reason deserves pity for what it suffers and forgiveness for its ignorance. But I cannot tolerate Epicurus because of his name,[9] or put up with philosophy that behaves wantonly, any more than I can put up with a general who abandons his post and leads a retreat, a farmer who burns his own crops, or a skipper who is afraid of the sea. You must sail, you must lead armies, you must work the land. All these tasks are full of toil, but nothing good comes about through indolence.[10] If pleasure follows upon the performance of good deeds, I certainly grant it, but let pleasure follow, and let the Good[11] take the lead in every instance:

> let there be one leader,
one king, to whom[12]

Zeus has granted command. But if you reverse their order with pleasure in command and reason following, you are placing over the soul a cruel and implacable tyrant, to which it must submit and perform services of all sorts that cannot be challenged, even when it orders shameful and unjust acts.

For what limitation would pleasure have, if it derives its authority from desires? This is an insatiable tyrant that disdains what is present and craves what is absent, that is inflamed by desire for more and more, lifted up by hopes

[10] An allusion to Epicurean withdrawal from the active life.

[11] As in the previous oration, the Good (*to kalon*) here implies noble or ethical goodness. In §7 below, the overall Good (*to agathon*) for man is at issue.   [12] *Il.* 2.204–5, Odysseus referring to Agamemnon as he rallies the troops.

ἐλπίδος κουφιζόμενος καὶ δι᾽ εὐπορίαν ἐξυβρίζων.
οὗτος ὁ τύραννος ἐπανέστησεν τὰ αἰσχρὰ τοῖς καλοῖς, οὗτος ἐφώπλισεν ἀδικίαν δικαιοσύνῃ, οὗτος
μέτρῳ ἀμετρίαν. ὡς ἥ γε χρεία τῶν σωμάτων τὰς
αὑτῆς ὀρέξεις οὐ χαλεπῶς ἀναπίμπλησιν. διψῇ τις;
κρῆναι πανταχοῦ· πεινῇ τις; φηγοὶ πανταχοῦ· ἥλιος
οὗτος, χλανίδων ἀλεεινότατος· λειμῶνες οὗτοι, θεαμάτων τὰ ποικιλώτατα· ἄνθη ταῦτα, εὐωδίαι φυσικαί.
καὶ μέχρι μὲν τούτων ἔστιν λαβεῖν ὅρους ἡδονῶν τὴν
χρείαν αὐτήν· ἐὰν δὲ ταῦτα ὑπερβῇς καὶ προέλθῃς
περαιτέρω, δίδως ταῖς ἡδοναῖς δρόμον ἄπαυστον καὶ
τὰς ἀρετὰς ἀποτειχίζεις.

4. Τοῦτο γεννᾷ τὰς πλεονεξίας, τοῦτο ποιεῖ τὰς
τυραννίδας. οὐ γὰρ ἱκανὸν βασιλεῖ τῷ Περσῶν χωρίον Πασαργάδαι καὶ τὸ Κύρου κάρδαμον, ἀλλ᾽ ἡ
Ἀσία ἅπασα διέλαχεν χορηγεῖν ἡδοναῖς ἀνδρὸς ἑνός.
τρέφει μὲν αὐτῷ Μηδία Νισαῖον ἵππον, πέμπει δὲ
Ἰωνία παλλακίδας Ἑλληνικάς, τρέφει δὲ Βαβυλὼν
εὐνούχους βαρβάρους, πέμπει δὲ Αἴγυπτος παντοδαπὰς τέχνας, ἐλέφαντα Ἰνδοί, Ἄραβες εὐωδίαν· χορη-
γοῦσιν δὲ καὶ οἱ ποταμοὶ ταῖς βασιλέως ἡδοναῖς,
Πακτωλὸς χρυσόν, Νεῖλος πυρόν, Χοάσπης ὕδωρ· τῷ

---

13 Acorns were the proverbial food of primitive man; cf. Orr.
21.5 and 23.5.

14 That is, move on to pleasures concocted by art; cf. Or. 32.3.

15 In fact, this criticism cannot be leveled against the Epicu-
reans, who limited pleasure to simple, natural needs, guided by
practical reason (phronēsis); cf. Diog. Laert. 10.130–32.

of success, and made wanton by an abundance of resources. This is a tyrant that makes what is shameful rise
up against what is good, that arms injustice against justice,
and excess against limitation. Now when it comes to basic
needs, the body's appetites are satisfied without difficulty.
Is someone thirsty? Springs are everywhere. Is someone
hungry? Oak trees are everywhere.[13] Look around! Here
is the sun, the warmest of cloaks; here are meadows with
the most exquisite sights; here are flowers with their natural fragrances. Up to this point, need itself sets the boundaries of pleasures, but if you go beyond this and proceed
any further,[14] you set pleasures on an unstoppable course,
and you shut out the virtues.[15]

4. This is what begets greed; this creates tyrannies. The
king of Persia[16] was not satisfied with the district of Pasargadae[17] and the watercress of Cyrus,[18] so it fell to all of
Asia to minister to the pleasures of a single man. Media
raises Nisaean horses for him, Ionia sends him Greek
courtesans, Babylon raises barbarian eunuchs for him,
Egypt sends him arts of all kinds, Indians send ivory, and
Arabs send perfumes. Even rivers minister to the king's
pleasures: the Pactolus supplies gold, the Nile wheat, and
the Choaspes water.[19] Yet even these prove insufficient for

[16] Here, Darius.   [17] The rugged district where Cyrus
trained his army (*Or.* 24.7) became the Achaemenid capital, until
Darius moved it to Persepolis.

[18] That is, the simple fare that young Cyrus ate; cf. Xen. *Cyr.*
1.2.8 and 11.

[19] Water from the Choaspes was brought along when the Persian king traveled, and only he was allowed to drink it; cf. *Orr.*
32.9 and 34.6.

δὲ οὐδὲ ταῦτα ἱκανά, ἀλλ᾽ ἐπιθυμεῖ ξένης ἡδονῆς, καὶ
διὰ τοῦτο ἐπὶ τὴν Εὐρώπην ἔρχεται, διώκει Σκύθας,
ἀνίστησιν Παίονας, Ἐρετρίαν λαμβάνει, Μαραθῶνι
ἐπιπλεῖ, καὶ πλανᾶται πανταχοῦ. ὦ τῆς πενίας δυστυ-
χέστατος. τί γὰρ ἂν εἴη πενέστερον ἀνδρὸς ἐπιθυμοῦν-
τος διηνεκῶς;

Ἐπειδὰν γὰρ ἅπαξ ψυχὴ γεύσηται ἡδονῶν ὑπὲρ
τὴν αὑτῆς χρείαν, κόρος αὐτὴν τῶν πρότερον ἔχει καὶ
ἑτέρων ἐρᾷ. καὶ τὸ τοῦ Ταντάλου αἴνιγμα τοῦτο ἦν
ἄρα, δίψα διηνεκὴς ἀνδρὸς φιληδόνου καὶ ἡδονῆς
νάματα προσιόντα καὶ ἀπιόντα αὖθις, καὶ παλίρροια
ἐπιθυμιῶν καὶ λῦπαι πικραὶ ταύταις ἀνακεκραμέναι,
καὶ ταραχαὶ καὶ φόβοι. φοβερὸν μὲν γὰρ παροῦσα
ἡδονὴ μὴ ἀπέλθῃ, ἀνιαρὸν δὲ μὴ παροῦσα μὴ οὐκ
ἔλθῃ· ὥστε ἀνάγκη τὸν διώκοντα ἡδονὴν λυπούμενον
μὲν μὴ παύσασθαι, ἡδόμενον δὲ μὴ αἰσθάνεσθαι,
ἀλλὰ συγκεχυμένον ζῆν ἐν ἀσαφείᾳ πολλῇ.

5. Ὅρα τίνα καὶ ποῖον τύραννον τῇ ψυχῇ δίδως· ὡς
Ἀθηναίοις Κριτίαν, παρωσάμενος τὸν Σόλωνα· ὡς
Λακεδαιμονίοις Παυσανίαν, παρωσάμενος τὸν Λυ-
κοῦργον. ἐγὼ δὲ ἐλευθερίαν ποθῶν νόμου δέομαι, λόγου δέομαι. οὗτός μοι φυλάξει τὴν εὐδαιμονίαν ὀρθὴν
καὶ ἄσειστον καὶ ἀδεῆ καὶ αὐτάρκη, οὐ ταπεινὴν
⟨οὐ⟩δὲ[3] ὑποβεβλημένην ἀνδραπόδων τέχναις, ὑφ᾽ ὧν

---

3 suppl. Reiske, Trapp, Koniaris

him: he desires foreign pleasures, and for these he marches against Europe, invades Scythia, drives out the Paeonians, seizes Eretria, sails against Marathon,[20] and roams everywhere. O how utterly wretched he is in his poverty! For what could be poorer than a man in a constant state of desire?

For once the soul has tasted pleasures beyond its basic needs, it tires of the ones it used to enjoy and longs for new ones. This turns out to be what the allegory of Tantalus depicts: the incessant thirst of a hedonist, and the streams of pleasure that approach and then recede, the ebb and flow of desires and the bitter pains that contaminate them, together with confusion and fear—fear that the present pleasure may go away, and distress that the absent pleasure may not return. As a result, he who pursues pleasure can never stop feeling pain, nor ever have the sensation of pleasure, but must live a muddled life of great uncertainty.

5. Consider, then, the nature of the tyrant you are placing over the soul. It would be like rejecting Solon and installing Critias over the Athenians, like rejecting Lycurgus and installing Pausanias over the Spartans.[21] But in my desire for freedom I need law, I need reason. These two will keep my happiness on a straight path, unshaken, unafraid, and self-sufficient, rather than contemptible and dependent on servile arts, by which I might gather up and

---

[20] The Scythians in 513 BC (Hdt. 4.1–142). Paeonians in 512 BC (Hdt. 5.12–15), and Eretria and Marathon in 490 BC (Hdt. 6.100–114).   [21] Solon and Lycurgus were the ideal lawgivers of moderation. Critias was one of the "Thirty Tyrants," killed in 403 BC; for Pausanias' seduction by luxury, see §2 above.

ἐρανιζόμενος ἀθροίσω τὸ μέγα τοῦτο ὄφελος, ἡδονήν,
αἰτίζων οὐκ ἀκόλους, μὰ Δία, κατὰ τὸν Ὁμήρου πτω-
χεύοντα, οὐδὲ ἄορας καὶ λέβητας μόνον, ἀλλὰ τὰ τούτων ἔτι ἀτοπώτερα· παρὰ μὲν Μιθαίκου ὄψον, παρὰ
δὲ Σαράμβου οἶνον, παρὰ δὲ Κόννου ᾠδήν,[4] παρὰ δὲ
Μελησίου ἑταίραν.[5] καὶ τί τούτων ἔσται μέτρον; τίς
τῆς ἐξ ἡδονῶν εὐδαιμονίας ὅρος; ποῖ στησόμεθα; τίνι
δῶμεν τὰ νικητήρια φέροντες; τίς ὁ μακάριος ἀνὴρ
οὗτος καὶ ἄγρυπνος καὶ ἐπίπονος, ὃν οὐκ ἔλαθεν οὐδὲ
ἐξέφυγεν οὐδεμία ἡδονή, οὐ νύκτωρ, οὐ μεθ' ἡμέραν,
ἀλλὰ ἀποτείνασα αὐτῷ ἡ ψυχὴ τὰς αἰσθήσεις πάσας,
καθάπερ ὁ θαλάττιος πολύπους τοὺς πλοκάμους, διὰ
τούτων πάντοθεν τὰς ἡδονὰς ἐπάξεται πάσας ὁμοῦ;

6. Πλάττωμεν, εἰ δυνατόν, τοιαύτην εἰκόνα, ἄνδρα
εὐδαίμονα τὴν ἐξ ἡδονῶν εὐδαιμονίαν, ὁρῶντα μὲν τὰ
ἥδιστα τῶν χρωμάτων, ἀκούοντα δὲ ἡδίστων ψόφων,
ὀσφραινόμενον ὀδμῶν τερπνοτάτων, γευόμενον χυ-
μῶν ποικιλωτάτων, χλιαινόμενον, ἀφροδισιάζοντα
ὁμοῦ· ἐὰν γὰρ δῷς χρόνον καὶ διαστήσῃς τὰς ἡδονὰς
καὶ τὰς αἰσθήσεις διέλῃς, κολούσεις τὴν εὐδαιμονίαν·
πᾶν γὰρ ὃ παρὸν εὐφραίνει, ἀφαιρεθὲν λυπεῖ. καὶ τίς
⟨ἂν⟩[6] ἀνάσχοιτο ψυχὴ ἡδονῶν τοσούτων ὄχλον ἐπιρ-
ρέοντα αὐτῇ καὶ ἐπιφερόμενον καὶ μηδεμίαν ἀνακω-
χὴν μηδὲ ἀναψυχὴν παρεχόμενον, ἀλλ' οὐκ ἀθλιώτατα
εἰκὸς διάγειν καὶ ἐπιθυμεῖν μεταβολῆς καὶ ἀναπαύλης

---

[4] ᾠδήν Koniaris, Trapp: ἑταίραν R   [5] ἑταίραν Koniaris,
Trapp: ᾠδήν R   [6] suppl. Hahn, Trapp

accumulate that so-called great benefit, pleasure—not by
asking for morsels, by Zeus, like the beggar in Homer, nor
only for swords and cauldrons,[22] but for things even more
outlandish than these: a savory dish from Mithaecus, wine
from Sarambus, a tune from Connus, or a prostitute from
Melesias.[23] And what will be the due measure of all these?
What will be the limit of this "happiness" that derives from
pleasures? Where shall we stop? To whom are we to give
the palm of victory? Who then is this blessed, ever vigilant,
hardworking man, whom no pleasure can elude or escape,
neither at night nor during the day, whose soul extends all
its senses, like a sea octopus extending its tentacles, to haul
in all the pleasures together from everywhere?

6. Let us picture, if even possible, a scene like the following, one of a man whose happiness derives from pleasures, who sees the most pleasant colors, hears the most
pleasant sounds, smells the most delightful fragrances,
tastes the most exquisite flavors, who warms himself and
makes love all the while. But if you allow for the passage
of time and separate the pleasures and interrupt the sensations, you will curtail his happiness, because everything
that brings gladness when present brings pain when taken
away. And what soul could bear the mob of so many pleasures streaming into it and bearing down on it, never al-

[22] At *Od.* 17.222, Melanthius sneers at beggars who beg for
mere morsels rather than for aristocratic items like swords and
cauldrons.

[23] Mithaecus the gastronome and Sarambus the vintner are
cited at Pl. *Grg.* 518b; Connus was a lyre player who taught Socrates (Pl. *Euthd.* 272c); Melesias is unknown, and the text is uncertain.

ἐρᾶν; χρονίζουσα γὰρ ἡδονὴ λύπην γεννᾷ. τί ἂν οὖν
γένοιτο ἀπιστότερον εὐδαιμονίας ἐλεουμένης; ὦ Ζεῦ
καὶ θεοί, πατέρες καὶ ποιηταὶ γῆς καὶ θαλάττης καὶ
ὅσα γῆς καὶ θαλάττης θρέμματα, οἷον τοῦτο ζῷον τῷ
δεῦρο τόπῳ καὶ βίῳ ἐγκατεστήσατε· ὡς θρασὺ καὶ
ἰταμὸν καὶ λάβρον,⁷ ἀγαθοῦ ἄπορον, ἔργου ἔρημον,
ἡδοναῖς βοσκόμενον καὶ δημαγωγούμενον.

   αἴθ' ὄφελεν ἄγονόν τ' ἔμεναι, ἄγαμόν τ'
      ἀπολέσθαι

τὸ γένος τοῦτο πᾶν, εἰ μηδὲν ἕξει παρ' ὑμῶν ἡδονῆς
κρεῖττον.

   7. Καὶ πῶς οὐκ ἔχει; ἀποκρινώμεθα γὰρ καθ' Ὅμηρον ὑπὲρ τοῦ Διός. ἔχει μὲν γάρ, ἔχει νοῦν καὶ λόγον·
συγκέκραται δὲ αὐτῷ ὁ βίος ἐξ ἀθανάτων καὶ θνητῶν
πραγμάτων, ὡς ζῴω τινὶ ἐν μεθορίῳ τεταγμένῳ καὶ
παρὰ μὲν θνητῆς πλημμελείας τὸ σῶμα ἔχοντι, ἐκ δὲ
τῆς ἀθανάτου ἀπορροῆς τὸν νοῦν λαμβάνοντι. ἴδιον
δὲ σαρκῶν μὲν ἡδοναί, νοῦ δὲ λόγος· καὶ κοινὸν μὲν
αὐτῷ αἱ σάρκες πρὸς τὰ θηρία, ἴδιον δὲ νοῦς. ἐνταῦθα
τοίνυν ζήτει τὸ ἀνθρώπου ἀγαθόν, ὅπου τὸ ἔργον·
‹ἐνταῦθα τὸ ἔργον, ὅπου τὸ ὄργανον·›⁸ ἐνταῦθα τὸ
ὄργανον, ὅπου τὸ σῷζον. ἀπὸ τοῦ σῴζοντος ἄρξαι.
πότερον ποτέρου διασωστικόν, σῶμα ψυχῆς, ἢ ψυχὴ

---

⁷ λάβρον Heinsius, Trapp: λάλον R
⁸ suppl. U, edd.

lowing it any cessation or respite? Is it not likely that it
would lead a most miserable existence, and desire change
and long for rest? After all, continuous pleasure generates
pain. What then could be less trustworthy than a happiness that evokes pity? O Zeus and you gods, you fathers
and creators of land and sea, and all you creatures of land
and sea, what an extraordinary animal you have placed
here on earth to live this life! How bold and reckless and
voracious, how lacking in goodness, bereft of function, in
thrall to the pleasures that nourish it. Would that this entire race

> had never been born and had perished unmarried,[24]

if it is going to receive nothing greater than pleasure from
you gods!

7. But of course it does. Let us respond on Zeus' behalf
as Homer regularly does. What in fact it receives is intellect and reason, but its life is composed of mortal and
immortal elements, as befits an animal that occupies an
intermediate position, having a body derived from mortal
discord, and receiving an intellect from an immortal ema-
nation. Specific to the flesh are pleasures; specific to the
intellect is reason. Man shares his fleshly nature with the
beasts, but intellect is his alone. Therefore you should
seek the human good where the human function lies, ‹and
its function where its instrument lies,› and its instrument
where its survival lies.[25] Begin then with survival. Which
sustains the other one more, the body the soul, or the soul

---

[24] *Il*. 3.40 (adapted), addressed by Hector to Paris.
[25] Another version of this argument is at *Or*. 31.5. "Instrument" refers to a natural endowment.

σώματος; ⟨ψυχὴ σώματος·⟩⁹ εὗρες τὸ σῶζον. ⟨ζήτει
τὸ ὄργανον.⟩¹⁰ τί ψυχῆς ὄργανον; νοῦς. ζήτει τὸ ἔργον. τί νοῦ ἔργον; φρόνησις· εὗρες τὸ ἀγαθόν. εἰ δέ
τις τοῦ ἀνθρώπου τὴν μοῖραν ταύτην τὴν φρονοῦσαν
καὶ θεοφιλῆ ἀτιμάσας, τὸ ἄτιμον ἐκεῖνο μόνον
θρέμμα, τὰς σάρκας λέγω, τὸ ἀκόλαστον, τὸ ἀδηφά-
γον, τὸ ἡδοναῖς φίλον, εὐωχεῖν ἐθέλοι, τίνι ἂν εἰκά-
σαιμι τὴν τοιαύτην τροφὴν ἢ τῷ μύθῳ νὴ Δία;

8. Γενέσθαι φασὶν οἱ ποιηταὶ ἄνδρας ἐν Πηλίῳ,
Θετταλικὸν γένος, ἀτόπους τὰ σώματα, ἐξ ὀμφαλοῦ
ἐπισυρομένους ἵππου φύσιν. ἐν δὲ τῇ τοιαύτης ξυνου-
σίας ἀμουσίᾳ πᾶσά που ἀνάγκη βόσκειν ὁμοῦ ⟨τῇ
ἀνθρωπίνῃ⟩¹¹ τὴν θηριώδη φύσιν· φθέγγεσθαι μὲν ὡς
ἄνθρωπον, σιτεῖσθαι δὲ ὡς θηρίον· ὁρᾶν¹² ὡς ἄνθρωπον, ὀχεύειν δὲ ὡς θηρίον. εὖ γε, ὦ ποιηταὶ καὶ ποιητῶν παῖδες, πατέρες παλαιᾶς καὶ γενναίας μούσης,
ὡς ἐναργῶς ἄρα ἡμῖν τὸν πρὸς τὰς ἡδονὰς δεσμὸν
ἠνίξασθε. ἐπειδὰν ψυχῆς θηριώδεις κρατήσωσιν ἐπιθυμίαι, φυλάττουσαι τὴν ἀνθρωπίνην ἐπιφάνειαν, τῇ
τῶν ἔργων ὑπηρεσίᾳ ἀπέφηναν τὸν χρώμενον ἐξ ἀνθρώπου θηρίον. τοῦτο οἱ Κένταυροι, τοῦτο αἱ Γοργό-
νες, τοῦτο αἱ Χίμαιραι, ὁ Γηρυόνης, ὁ Κέκροψ. ἄφελε
τὴν γαστρὸς ἐπιθυμίαν, καὶ ἀφεῖλες τοῦ ἀνθρώπου τὸ

⁹ suppl. Markland, Trapp
¹⁰ suppl. Reiske, Trapp
¹¹ suppl. Markland, Trapp
¹² ὁρᾶν R, Davies², Hobein, Trapp: ἐρᾶν Markland, Dübner,
Koniaris

the body? ‹The soul the body.› You have found what preserves it. ‹Then seek the instrument.› What is the instrument of the soul? Intellect. Now seek its function. What
is the function of the intellect? Practical intelligence. You
have now found the Good. So, if anyone should disdain
this part of man, the part that exercises intelligence and is
beloved by the gods, and should wish to indulge that despicable creature alone (that is, the flesh), which is intemperate, gluttonous, and beloved by pleasures, what could
I use to illustrate such a way of life, other than the following myth, by Zeus?

8. Poets tell that a Thessalian race of men once lived
on Pelion with outlandish bodies, having the form of
horses from the navel down. Such a discordant combination made it absolutely necessary for them to nourish their
bestial nature along with their human one, so as to talk like
a man, but feed like a beast; see[26] like a man, but copulate
like a beast. Well done, you poets and you successors of
the poets, forefathers of an ancient and noble poetry! How
clearly indeed you have allegorized for us the bondage to
pleasures.[27] When the bestial desires dominate the soul,
they preserve the outward appearance of the man, but
through the actions he performs in their service they reveal not a man but a beast. This is what the Centaurs,
Gorgons, Chimeras, Geryon, and Cecrops all represent.
Take away the desire of the belly, and you take away the

[26] Or, reading $\dot{\epsilon}\rho\hat{\alpha}\nu$, "love" like a man.

[27] The race of the unruly Centaurs (like those depicted on the
metopes of the Parthenon) must be distinguished from Chiron
the noble Centaur, son of Cronus, who educated heroes and
taught the art of medicine, cited at *Orr.* 28.1–3, 36.5, and 40.3.

229

θηρίον· ἄφελε τὴν αἰδοίων ἐπιθυμίαν, καὶ διέκοψας τὸ θηρίον. μέχρι δὲ ταῦτά τῳ συζῇ καὶ συντρέφεται καὶ πρὸς αὐτὰ τῇ θεραπείᾳ νένευκεν, ἀνάγκη τὰς ἐκείνων ὀρέξεις κρατεῖν καὶ βοᾶν τὴν ψυχὴν τὰς ἐκείνων φωνάς.

bestial part of man. Take away the desire of the sexual organs, and you cut off the beast. But as long as these parts share life with a man and are given nourishment, and he assents to serve them, their appetites necessarily take over, and his soul is compelled to give voice to their cries.

ORATION 34

INTRODUCTION

This oration argues that evils (*kaka*) and hardships (*dyscherē*) are not only an essential aspect of human existence but even make the exercise of virtue possible, for virtue is inseparable from toil. It opens with an interlocutor complaining that humans foolishly mix together good and evil in their pursuit of the good life, whereas they should keep them completely separate like night and day. The speaker responds to the analogy by stating that humans cannot live exclusively in either night or day (§1). The soul desires the Good (*to agathon*) and fights against evil, but it cannot attain pure good. The virtuous soul does not enjoy a smooth flow of life (as the Stoics claim) or continual good fortune, but must traverse a difficult road of life full of obstacles and pitfalls (§2).[1] Homer claims that good and evil stream to humans from two pithoi in Zeus' palace, one containing unmitigated evil, the other a mixture of good and evil (§3). The speaker acknowledges the aptness of the image but disagrees that streams of both

[1] For the hard road of virtue, see *Or.* 14.1; for fortune as virtue's adversary, see *Or.* 8.7.

good and evil could come from Zeus.[2] Instead, the well-springs of virtue and depravity flow in the human soul: depravity floods the good parts of the soul and renders them unproductive, whereas virtue supplies nourishing waters. Adversity is inextricably implicated in human action and is necessary for men such as helmsmen and generals to gain prudence, because continuous good fortune is dangerous (§4). The long string of good fortunes enjoyed by Croesus and Polycrates ended badly. Bright colors need dark foil to set them off, just as facing hardships fosters a better appreciation of virtue and understanding of good fortune (§5). Humans need thirst to enjoy a drink, hunger to enjoy food, and night to enjoy sunshine. Pampered Artoxerxes II first truly experienced the pleasure of a drink when he was stranded on a bare hilltop and was glad to drink foul water (§6). Can people have too much pleasure, but never too much good fortune? Indeed, in the latter case, they can. Achilles, Nestor, and Odysseus rejected a comfortable life at home to exercise their virtue (§7). Take away Heracles' labors and you take away his virtue. As athletes must have opponents to win victories, so hardship is the opponent of good men in the contest of life (§8). Socrates, Plato, Xenophon, and Diogenes were champions of virtue over various opponents. The Athenians endured casualties in their victory at Marathon, and the Spartans remained free by inculcating pain in their training for virtue (§9).

[2] According to Plato and Maximus, only good comes from the gods. The source of evil in the physical world is taken up in *Or.* 41.

ORATION 34

Ὅτι ἔστιν καὶ ἐκ τῶν περιστάσεων
ὠφελεῖσθαι

1. "Δεινόν γε εἰ οἱ μὲν θεοὶ διέκριναν τοῖς ἀνθρώποις
τἀγαθὰ ἐκ τῆς τῶν κακῶν ὁμιλίας, ἀνεπίμικτον ἑκάτερον ἑκατέρῳ εἶναι θέμενοι καὶ διαστήσαντες αὐτῶν
τὰς φύσεις, καθάπερ ἡμέρας πρὸς νύκτα καὶ φωτὸς
πρὸς ζόφον καὶ πρὸς ὕδωρ πυρός, ὧν ἕκαστον εἰ
ἐθελήσαις πρὸς τοὐναντίον ἀγαγεῖν καὶ ἀνακεράσαι
αὐτῶν τὴν διαφορὰν εἰς κοινὴν φύσιν, διαφθερεῖς τὸ
ἑκατέρου ἴδιον· οἱ δὲ ἄνθρωποι αὐτοὶ ἑκόντες, εὐδαίμονα διώκοντες βίον, καταμιγνύασιν <. . .>¹ αὐτῷ
ζῆν δι᾽ ἡμέρας ἐν φωτὶ λαμπρῷ καὶ διηνεκεῖ, ἀΰπνῳ
καὶ ἀδεεῖ τῆς ἐν νυκτὶ ἀναπαύλης, ἄχθοιτο τῷ ἡλίῳ
μηδέποτε ἐξισταμένῳ μηδὲ εἰς τὸ παλίσκιον παραχω-
ροῦντι."

Ἔχε δὴ αὐτόθι. μὴ ἀποκρινούμεθα †σου πηλίκον†²
ὡς εἰ μέν πού τίς ἐστιν ἀνθρώπου ὄψις <οἵα>³ ἀνέχε-

---

¹ lacunam stat. Trapp
² obel. Trapp: locus conclamatus
³ suppl. Schott, Trapp

234

ORATION 34

That it is possible to benefit from adverse
circumstances

1. "This is a terrible thing![1] To benefit humans the gods separated what is good from any association with what is evil, by decreeing that each must have nothing to do with the other, and by distinguishing their very natures, just like day and night, light and dark, and fire and water, so that if you should wish to bring any one of these over to its opposite number and combine their differences into one common nature, you will destroy what is distinctive of each. And yet humans are willing of their own accord, in pursuit of a happy life, to mix together ‹good and evil in their lives. This is perverse. For who but a fool, were we to allow›[2] him to live in bright and continuous daylight without any sleep or need for rest at night, would be vexed with the sun for never departing or withdrawing into the darkness?"

Hold on here. Perhaps we can provide an answer . . .[3] to the effect that if somehow there exists some human

---

[1] A fictitious interlocutor is speaking.

[2] The text is hopelessly corrupt. I have slightly adapted Trapp's suggested supplement.

[3] The text is unintelligible here.

σθαι φωτὸς διηνεκοῦς, καὶ εἴπερ τις μηχανὴ στῆσαι
τὸν ἥλιον τοῦ κύκλῳ δρόμου, ὥστε ἀνέχειν ὑπὲρ γῆς
αἰεί, καθάπερ πυρσὸν ἐκ κορυφῆς ὑψηλῆς ἐκπέμ-
ποντα ἐφ᾽ ἡμᾶς τὸ παρ᾽ ἑαυτοῦ φῶς, εἰ ταῦτα ὑπάρχοι
καὶ σταίη μὲν ὁ ἥλιος, ἀνέχοιντο δὲ οἱ ὀφθαλμοὶ
πρὸς αὐτὸν διηνεκῶς δεδορκότες, τίς οὕτως ἀνόητος
καὶ ἐπιμανὴς καὶ κακοδαίμων τοῦ ἔρωτος, ὥστε ποθῆ-
σαι νύκτα καὶ σκότος καὶ ὀφθαλμῶν ἀργίαν καὶ
σώματος ῥῖψιν ἐγγύτατα νεκροῦ; εἰ δὲ θᾶττον μὲν
⟨ἂν⟩[4] ἀνάσχοιντο οἱ ὀφθαλμοὶ ἀϋπνίας ἢ σταίη ὁ
ἥλιος, θᾶττον δ᾽ ἂν σταίη ὁ ἥλιος ἢ ἀνάσχοιντο οἱ
ὀφθαλμοὶ ἀϋπνίας, οὐκ εὐχῆς ἔργον ἡ πρὸς τὸ φῶς
φιλία, ἀλλὰ ἀνάγκης ἡ πρὸς νύκτα συνουσία.

2. Ταύτῃ τοι καὶ ὁ πρὸς τὸ ἀγαθὸν ἔρως ἔχει. ἐφίεται μὲν γὰρ αὐτοῦ ἡ ψυχή (τί δὲ οὐ μέλλει;) καὶ
πολεμεῖ τῷ κακῷ (τί δὲ οὐ μέλλει;), ἀλλ᾽ οὐκ ἔστιν
αὐτῇ οὔτε ὧν ἐφίεται καθαρῶς τυχεῖν, οὔθ᾽ οἷς πολεμεῖ μὴ περιπεσεῖν ἐξ ἀνάγκης. οὔπω λέγω τὴν μο-
χθηρὰν ψυχήν—αὕτη μὲν γὰρ πάγκακός τις καὶ ἀγαθῶν ἄμοιρος καὶ ἐν ἐλπίσιν ἄπιστος καὶ ἐν εὐτυχίᾳ
ἀκροσφαλής—ἀλλὰ τὴν ἐπιεικῆ καὶ φρονήσεως ἐπήβολον.

Φέρε ἴδω πότερα καὶ ταύτην φῶμεν ἐπιλαβομένην
τῆς ἀρετῆς εὐροίᾳ τινὶ βίου καὶ εὐτυχημάτων ἀκμῇ
συγγίγνεσθαι ἀεί, ἢ τοῦτο μὲν ἀμήχανον ἐν ἀνθρω-
πίνῃ φύσει· πολλὰ γὰρ τὰ ἐν ποσίν, καθάπερ ἀνδρὶ

4 suppl. Trapp

236

sight capable of enduring continuous light, and if there is some way to make the sun cease its circular orbit so as to remain permanently above the earth, as it sends forth its light to us like a beacon from a high peak—if this could happen, and if the sun could stand still, and if our eyes could bear to gaze continuously at it, who would be so senseless, insane, and unfortunate in his desires, as to long for night and shade, for his eyes to be idle, and for his body to lie prostrate almost like a corpse? But if sooner could our eyes endure sleeplessness than the sun could stand still, and sooner could the sun stand still than our eyes endure sleeplessness, then the point is not that our affection for light is something to be wished for, but that our affinity for darkness is a matter of necessity.

2. The same applies to love for the Good. The soul desires it (how could it not?), and fights against evil (how could it not?), but it is unable either to obtain what it desires in a pure form, or to avoid necessary encounters with what it fights against. I am not considering here a depraved soul—one that is entirely evil, bereft of good qualities, mistrustful in hopeful times, and insecure in successful times—no, I mean a reasonable soul in possession of practical intelligence.

So let us consider whether we can say that such a soul, when it has laid hold of virtue, enjoys a smooth flow of life[4] and supreme good fortune without cease, or whether this is impossible, given human nature, because there are many obstacles in our path, like ditches, cliffs, pits, and

[4] The smooth flow of life (εὔροια βίου) is a Stoic description of living in accordance with nature and virtue; cf. SVF 1.184 (Zeno), etc.

κούφως θέοντι ὀρύγματα καὶ κρημνοὶ καὶ βάραθρα
καὶ τειχία, ἐν οἷς ὁ μὲν ἀμαθὴς τῆς ὁδοῦ καὶ μαλθα-
κὸς θεῖν καὶ διαπηδᾶν ἀσθενὴς καὶ παραθεῖν ἀκρο-
σφαλὴς πταίει καὶ σφάλλεται καὶ ἀποδειλιᾷ, ὁ δὲ
ἀγαθὸς καὶ δρομικὸς ἀνὴρ καὶ ἐπιστήμων τῆς ὁδοῦ,
κατὰ μὲν τὴν ῥώμην ὀξέως θεῖ, κατὰ δὲ τὴν ἐμπειρίαν
ἀπλανῶς, κατὰ δὲ τὴν τέχνην ἀσφαλῶς· οἶδε μὴν τίς
μὲν τῆς ὁδοῦ ἡ λεία καὶ ἄπταιστος, τίς δὲ ἡ διεσκαμ-
μένη, καὶ ἀναγκαία μὲν διελθεῖν, ἀπροαίρετος δὲ τῷ
θέοντι.

3. Τοῦτό τοι καὶ περὶ τῶν βίων Ὅμηρος ᾐνίξατο·

δοιοὶ γάρ τε πίθοι κατακείαται ἐν Διὸς οὔδει,

φησίν, ὁ μὲν πλήρης κακῶν, ἀγαθῶν ἀνεπίμικτος, ὁ
δὲ ἐξ ἀμφοῖν κεκραμένος· τρίτον γὰρ πίθον οὐδαμοῦ
ἐν Διὸς εἶναι λέγει, ἀγαθῶν ἀκεράτων. νέμει δὲ Ζεὺς
τῷ τῶν ἀνθρώπων γένει, κατὰ τὴν Ὁμήρου ᾠδήν, ἐκ
τοῖν πίθοιν τούτοιν ἀρυτόμενος· ἐκ μὲν τοῦ, κακῶν
ἀενάων ῥεῦμα ἰσχυρὸν καὶ βίαιον, μεστὸν ἐρίδων καὶ
ἐρινύων καὶ πτοίας καὶ φόβου καὶ ἄλλων μυρίων δυσ-
αντήτων τε καὶ ἀκράτων κακῶν· ἐκ δὲ τοῦ νέμει, ὡς
μὲν ἂν Ὅμηρος εἴποι, ῥεῦμα μικτὸν ἀγαθῶν καὶ κακῶν, ἐγὼ δὲ ὁρῶ μὲν τὴν μῖξιν καὶ πείθομαι τῷ λόγῳ,

5 For life as a treacherous course to be traveled, cf. *Orr.* 1.3,
8.7, 19.1, 39.3, and 40.4.
6 *Il.* 24.527, spoken by Achilles to Priam.

low walls for a man running swiftly along,[5] such that any person who is unfamiliar with the road, feeble at running, weak at jumping, and unsteady at swerving, stumbles, trips, and gives up in fear. In contrast, the capable and well-trained runner who knows the road uses his strength to run fast, his experience to run on a straight course, and his skill to run without tripping. He knows full well which part of the road is smooth and gives good footing, and which part is dug up and necessary to traverse, though not what the runner would prefer.

3. Homer indeed alluded to this in his allegory about human lives, when he says,

for two pithoi stand on the doorsill of Zeus,[6]

one full of evils with no goods mixed in, the other containing a mixture of both. For nowhere does he mention a third pithos in Zeus' palace containing only good things.[7] Thus, according to these verses of Homer, Zeus distributes to the human race what he draws from these two pithoi. From the one flows a strong and powerful stream of incessant evils, full of strife and vengeance, terror and fear, and countless other unmitigated evils that are hard to bear. But from the other pithos, as Homer would say, Zeus distributes a stream containing a mixture of good and evil. For my part, I can see this mixture and find his ac-

---

[7] In interpreting *Il*. 24.527–33, Maximus sides with Plato (*Resp*. 2.379d) that Homer speaks of only two jars, from one of which Zeus draws lots, whereas Pindar (*Pyth*. 3.80–82) alludes to three jars (two of evils, one of goods) from two of which he draws, thus giving either all evils or a mixture of good and evil.

εὐφημότερον δὲ ὀνομάζειν θέλω τὴν βελτίω παρὰ
Διὸς νομήν· ἔχει γὰρ δὴ ὧδε.

4. Ἀρετὴ ψυχῆς καὶ μοχθηρία, αὗται πηγαὶ τῶν
Διὸς πίθων· ὧν ἡ μὲν μοχθηρία λάβρον καὶ ἔμπληκτον ὀχετὸν ἐξιεῖσα συγχεῖ τὸν βίον καὶ ταράττει,
καθάπερ ἐμβολὴ χειμερίου νάματος ἐπὶ λήϊα καὶ φυτουργίας ὁρμηθεῖσα, ἐχθρὰ μὲν γεωργοῖς, ἐχθρὰ δὲ
καὶ ποιμέσιν, ἐχθρὰ καὶ ὁδοιπόροις, ἄκαρπος, ἄγο-
νος, ἀνόνητος, ἐπισφαλής· αἱ δὲ ἀρετῆς πηγαί, ὅτῳ
ἂν ἐν ψυχῇ διαφανῶσιν, πάντα τούτῳ ποιοῦσιν τὸν
βίον ἔγκαρπον καὶ ἀρόσιμον καὶ τελεσφόρον.

Ἀλλὰ ἱδρῶτος δεῖ τῷ γεωργῷ καὶ πόνου δεῖ καὶ
ταλαιπωρίας δεῖ· οὐδὲ γὰρ ὁ Αἰγύπτιος τῷ Νείλῳ
θαρρεῖ μόνῳ, οὐδὲ παραδίδωσιν αὐτῷ τὰ σπέρματα
πρὶν ἢ τἀρότρῳ ζεύξῃ βοῦν, πρὶν τέμῃ αὔλακα, πρὶν
πονήσῃ μακρά· καὶ μετὰ τοῦτο ἤδη καλεῖ τὸν πο-
ταμὸν ἐπὶ τὰ αὐτοῦ ἔργα. αὕτη μῖξις ποταμοῦ πρὸς
γεωργίαν, καὶ ἐλπίδων πρὸς πόνους καὶ καρπῶν πρὸς
ταλαιπωρίαν· οὕτως ἀγαθοῖς κακὰ κεραννυτέον. εἰ
βούλει, ἄφελε μὲν τὴν δυσφημίαν, ἴσθι δὲ αὐτῶν τὴν
οὐσίαν οὐκ ἀφαιρετέαν οὖσαν τοῖς πονοῦσιν.

Κἂν ἐπὶ τοὺς λιμένας ἔλθῃς, κυβερνήτην λήψῃ οὐ
τὸν ἄπειρον χειμῶνος, οὐδὲ ὅστις ἀθέατος κλύδωνος,
ἀλλ᾽ ἐκ πολλῶν σφαλμάτων ἀθροίσαντα τὴν τέχνην,
ἐκ πείρας κακῶν. ἐγὼ καὶ στρατηγῷ διαπιστῶ πάντα

count persuasive, but I wish to give a more pious name to Zeus' better distribution.[8] Here is how.

4. Virtue and depravity in the soul—these are the wellsprings that fill Zeus' pithoi. One of them, depravity, emits a violent, erratic stream and confounds human life and throws it into confusion, like the onslaught of a winter torrent rushing over wheat fields and plantings, that is abhorrent to farmers, shepherds, and travelers alike. It is unproductive, infertile, unprofitable, and dangerous. But whenever the wellsprings of virtue flow in a man's soul, they render his entire life fruitful, arable, and productive.

Nonetheless, a farmer still needs sweat, toil, and hard work, for not even an Egyptian relies on the Nile alone, nor entrusts his seeds to it, until he has yoked his ox to a plow, cut a furrow, and toiled long and hard. Only then does he summon the river onto his fields. Such is the combination of river and farmwork, hopes and toil, and fruits and hard work. So it is that evils must be mixed in with goods. If you wish, take away the pejorative term "evils," but recognize that their essence is inseparable from men's toils.

If you go down to a harbor, you will not choose a helmsman who has never experienced a storm, or who has never seen rough waters, but one who has accumulated his expertise from many failures and from his experience of evils. I also distrust a general who has always been suc-

[8] That is, the one dispensing a mixture of good and evil. The speaker accordingly transfers the sources of good and evil from Zeus to the human soul. For the Platonic principle that only good comes from the gods, cf. Pl. *Resp.* 2.379c–80b and *Orr.* 38.6 and 41.4.

εὐτυχήσαντι, <. . .>⁵ οἷος ἂν ἦν Ἀθηναίοις στρατηγὸς
Νικίας, σωθεὶς ἐκ Σικελίας, ἢ οἷος ἂν ἦν σωφρο-
νέστερος⁶ δημαγωγὸς Κλέων, ἐπανελθὼν ἐξ Ἀμφι-
πόλεως. ὅταν δὲ ἴδω πάντα εὐτυχοῦντα καὶ κυβερνήτην καὶ στρατηγὸν καὶ ἰδιώτην καὶ ἄρχοντα καὶ
ἄνδρα καὶ πόλιν, διαπιστῶ ταῖς εὐτυχίαις, ὡς Σόλων
Κροίσῳ, ὡς Ἄμασις Πολυκράτει.

5. Κροῖσος μὲν γὰρ εἶχεν εὔιππον γῆν, Πολυκράτης
δὲ εὔνεω θάλατταν· ἀλλ' οὐδὲν τούτων βέβαιον, οὐχ
ἡ γῆ Κροίσῳ, οὐχ ἡ θάλαττα Πολυκράτει, ἀλλ' ἐλάμβανεν Ὀρόντης μὲν Πολυκράτην, Κροῖσον δὲ Κῦρος,
καὶ διαδοχὴ μετ' εὐτυχίαν μακρὰν ἀθρόων κακῶν. διὰ
τοῦτο Σόλων οὐκ εὐδαιμόνισε Κροῖσον, σοφὸς γὰρ
ἦν· διὰ τοῦτο Ἄμασις ἀπείπατο Πολυκράτην, ἀσφα-
λὴς γὰρ ἦν· διὰ τοῦτ' ἐγὼ ἐπαινῶ βίον γευόμενον
κακῶν, ἀλλὰ γευόμενον μόνον—

χείλεα μέν τ' ἐδίην', ὑπερῴην δ' οὐκ ἐδίηνεν—

ἔχοντα μὲν τὴν ἀρετήν, χρώμενον δὲ αὐτῇ καὶ πρὸς
ἀκουσίους τύχας. καὶ γὰρ ὀφθαλμοῖς φίλον μὲν χρωμάτων τὸ λαμπρότατον, ἀλλ' ἐὰν μὴ παραθῇς τὸ

⁵ lacunam stat. Trapp
⁶ σωφρονέστερος del. Meiser, Trapp

⁹ I am adopting Trapp's suggestion for filling the lacuna.
¹⁰ Both had experienced a string of successes. Nicias was
killed retreating from Syracuse in 413 BC; Cleon, the brash demagogue, was killed at Amphipolis in 422 BC.

cessful, ⟨but would put more trust in one who has experienced failure,⟩[9] such as the general Nicias would have become for the Athenians, had he returned alive from Sicily, or as the more sober demagogue Cleon would have become, had he returned from Amphipolis.[10] But whenever I see a helmsman, general, citizen, ruler, man, or city being successful in everything, I distrust their good fortune, as Solon did with Croesus, and Amasis with Polycrates.[11]

5. For Croesus ruled a land of fine horses, and Polycrates ruled a sea[12] with a powerful navy, but none of this was secure, neither the land for Croesus nor the sea for Polycrates. Orontes[13] captured Polycrates and Cyrus captured Croesus, and what followed their long good fortune was a heap of evils all at once. This is why Solon, because he was wise, refused to call Croesus happy; this is why Amasis, because he was prudent, renounced his friendship with Polycrates. And this is why I approve a life that has tasted evils, but only just tasted them—

he wets his lips, but not his palate—[14]

a life that not only possesses virtue, but also exercises it when faced with unwelcome circumstances. For example, the eyes are fond of the color that is brightest, but if you

---

[11] Solon and Croesus (Hdt. 1.32), Amasis and Polycrates (Hdt. 3.40–43).

[12] The Ionian Sea; cf. *Or.* 29.2.

[13] According to Herodotus (3.120–25), it was Oroetes, not Orontes, who captured Polycrates and crucified him.

[14] *Il.* 22.495, spoken by Andromache describing the life of a fatherless orphan who never experiences full acceptance.

φαιόν, ἐλύπησας αὐτοῦ τὴν ἡδονήν· ἐὰν δὲ μίξῃς ταῖς
εὐτυχίαις τὰ δυσχερῆ, μᾶλλον αἰσθήσῃ τῆς ἀρετῆς
καὶ συνήσεις τῆς εὐτυχίας.

6. Ἡ δίψα μὲν σώματι παρασκευάζει ἡδονὴν ποτοῦ, καὶ λιμὸς σώματι παρασκευάζει ἡδονὴν βρωτοῦ,
καὶ νὺξ ὀφθαλμοῖς παρασκευάζει ἡδονὴν ἡλίου, ποθεῖ
<δ'>⁷ ἄνθρωπος καὶ νύκτα μεθ' ἥλιον καὶ λιμὸν μετὰ
κόρον καὶ δίψαν μετὰ μέθην· κἂν ἀφέλῃς αὐτοῦ τὴν
μεταβολήν, λύπην τὴν ἡδονὴν ποιεῖς. οὕτω λέγεται
καὶ Ἀρτοξέρξης ὁ Περσῶν βασιλεὺς τέως μὲν ὑπ'
εἰρήνης μακρᾶς καὶ ἡδονῆς διηνεκοῦς μὴ συνιέναι
τῆς εὐτυχίας· ᾧ παρεσκεύαζε μὲν ἡ Ἀσία τὸ δεῖπνον,
ἔπεμπον δὲ πῶμα ποταμῶν οἱ κάλλιστοι, ἐμηχανῶντο
δὲ αὐτῷ τὴν δίαιταν τέχναι μυρίαι· ἀλλ' ἐπεὶ πόλεμος
αὐτῷ ἐκ θαλάττης ἦλθεν καὶ Ἕλληνες μύριοι καὶ
στρατηγοὶ δεινοί, ἡττηθεὶς ἔφευγεν ἐπὶ ψιλὸν λόφον,
ὅπου τῆς νυκτὸς ἀναπαυόμενος ἐδίψησεν ὁ δύστηνος
πρῶτον τότε, ἔνθα ἦν οὐ Χοάσπης, οὐ Τίγρις, οὐ
Νεῖλος, οὐκ ἐκπώματα, οὐκ οἰνοχόοι, καὶ ἠγάπησεν
παρὰ ἀνδρὸς Μάρδου λαβὼν ἐν ἀσκῷ ὁδῳδὸς ὕδωρ·
καὶ τότε ἄρα ὁ δείλαιος ἔγνω, τίς μὲν δίψης χρεία, τίς
δὲ ἡδονὴ ποτοῦ.

7. Εἶτα ἡδονῆς μὲν ἔσται κόρος, εὐτυχημάτων δὲ
οὐκ ἔσται κόρος; ἐγὼ μὲν οἶμαι, σιτίων καὶ μέθης
ἀνιαρότερος. οὐ γὰρ ἀνασχετὸν εἶναι οὔτε τῷ Ἀχιλλεῖ

⁷ suppl. Trapp

do not set dark foil next to it, you diminish the pleasure it provides. Likewise, if you mix hardships with good fortune, you will gain a better sense of virtue and a greater understanding of good fortune.

6. It is in fact thirst that prepares the body for the pleasure of a drink, and hunger for the pleasure of food, and night prepares the eyes for the pleasure of sunshine. And yet humans also desire night after sunshine, hunger after satiety, and thirst after intoxication, and if you deprive them of this alternation, you turn their pleasure to pain. Thus it is said that Artoxerxes,[15] the king of the Persians, failed to understand his good fortune as long as he enjoyed many years of peace and continuous pleasure, when Asia supplied his dinner, the loveliest rivers furnished his drink, and countless arts devised a comfortable life for him. But once war came to him from across the sea with ten thousand Greeks and their skilled generals, he fled in defeat to a bare hilltop, where, as he rested during the night, the wretched man experienced thirst for the very first time. In that place without the Choaspes, Tigris, or Nile, without cups or cupbearers, he was happy to accept foul water in a leather flask from a Mardian man.[16] Then it was that the unfortunate man came to realize the function of thirst and the pleasure of a drink.

7. So then, can one grow weary of pleasure, but not of good fortune? I believe that indeed one can, and I consider its surfeit more distressing than any caused by food

[15] The anecdote of Artoxerxes II (variant of Artaxerxes) is told at Plut. *Artax.* 12.3–4. It occurred when Cyrus the Younger and the ten thousand Greek mercenaries routed his army in 401 BC.

[16] Mardians were an undistinguished Persian tribe.

τὴν σχολὴν οὔτε τῷ Νέστορι τὴν σιωπὴν οὔτε τῷ
Ὀδυσσεῖ τὴν ἀσφάλειαν· ἐξῆν γάρ που καὶ τῷ Ἀχιλλεῖ <ἐν εἰρήνῃ>[8] ζῆν καὶ βασιλεύειν Μυρμιδόνων καὶ
γεωργεῖν τὴν Θετταλῶν γῆν καὶ γηροκομεῖν τὸν Πη-
λέα· καὶ τῷ Νέστορι ἐν Πύλῳ ἐν εἰρήνῃ ἄρχειν καὶ
γηράσκειν καθ' ἡσυχίαν· καὶ τῷ Ὀδυσσεῖ οἴκοι μένειν περὶ τὸ Νήριτον τὸ εὔφυλλον ἐν τῇ γῇ τῇ κουρο-
τρόφῳ, ἢ τὸ τελευταῖον παρὰ Καλυψοῖ {οὖν}[9] ἐν ἄντρῳ
καταρρύτῳ καὶ κατασκίῳ, ὑπὸ Νυμφῶν θεραπευο-
μένῳ, ἀγήρῳ ὄντι καὶ ἀθανάτῳ· ἀλλ' οὐχ εἵλετο ἀθάνατος εἶναι ἀργὸς ὢν καὶ μηδὲν χρώμενος τῇ ἀρετῇ.
ἀνάγκῃ δὲ τὸν ταύτην μεταχειριζόμενον, ἀνθρωπίνοις
συμπτώμασιν παραβαλλόμενον, πολλάκις βοᾶν,

τέτλαθι δὴ κραδίη· καὶ κύντερον ἄλλο ποτ' ἔτλης.

8. Τίς δ' ἂν ἦν μνήμη τοῦ Ὀδυσσέως, ἐὰν ἀφέλῃς
αὐτοῦ τὰ δυσχερῆ; τίς δὲ τοῦ Ἀχιλλέως, ἐὰν ἀφέλῃς
αὐτοῦ τὸν Ἕκτορα καὶ τὸν Σκάμανδρον καὶ τὰς

δώδεκα μὲν σὺν νηυσὶ πόλεις,

ἔνδεκα δὲ ἠπειρώτιδας; τὸν μὲν γὰρ Ἡρακλέα οὐδὲ
ἄλλοθεν οἱ ἄνθρωποι προσέθεσαν[10] φέροντες τῷ Διὶ ἢ
ἐκ τῆς πρὸς τὰ κακὰ ὁμιλίας, ἀνταγωνισάμενον αὐτοῖς ἀρετῇ.[11] ἐὰν ἀφέλῃς αὐτοῦ τὰ θηρία καὶ τοὺς δυ-

---

[8] suppl. Heinsius, Trapp   [9] del. Trapp   [10] ἂν post
προσέθεσαν suppl. Hobein, Trapp   [11] ἀνταγωνισάμενον
αὐτοῖς ἀρετῇ Trapp: ἀνταγωνισαμένης αὐτοῖς τῆς R: alia alii

246

and wine. For Achilles could not tolerate leisure, nor
Nestor quiet, nor Odysseus safety. No doubt Achilles
could have lived in peace, ruled over the Myrmidons,
farmed his Thessalian lands, and tended to aged Peleus.
Nestor could have ruled in peace in Pylos and grown old
in tranquility. Odysseus could have stayed at home by
wooded Neritus in the land good for raising children,[17] or
in the end could have remained with Calypso in her shady
and well-watered cave, attended by Nymphs, and be age-
less and immortal.[18] But he rejected immortality when it
meant being idle and not exercising his virtue. For when
someone practices virtue, and exposes himself to human
misfortunes, he is bound to cry out again and again,

> Bear up, my heart! You have endured worse before
> now.[19]

8. What memory would there be of Odysseus, if you
deprive him of his hardships? Or of Achilles, if you deprive
him of Hector, Scamander,[20] and those

> twelve cities taken by ships[21]

and eleven on land? Then too, men took Heracles and
elevated him as Zeus' son, for no other reason than his
association with evils, which he fought against with his
virtue. If you deprive him of those wild beasts and tyrants,

---

[17] Adapted from Odysseus' description of Ithaca to Alcinous
at *Od.* 9.21–27. [18] Adapted from *Od.* 5.136, Calypso speaking of what she would do for Odysseus. [19] *Od.* 20.18, spoken
by Odysseus before facing the suitors. [20] Achilles' fight
with the river Scamander is told at *Il.* 21.211–382.

[21] *Il.* 9.328, spoken by Achilles of his previous exploits.

νάστας καὶ τὰς ἄνω καὶ κάτω ὁδοὺς καὶ τὰ δεινὰ
ἐκεῖνα πάντα, ἠκρωτηρίασας τὴν ἀρετὴν τοῦ Ἡρακλέους. ἢ Ὀλυμπίασιν μὲν καὶ Πυθοῖ οὐκ ἔνεστιν
κότινον λαβεῖν οὐδὲ μήλων τυχεῖν αὐτὸν ἐφ᾽ ἑαυτοῦ
κονισάμενον, ἀλλὰ ἀνταγωνιστῶν δεῖ τῷ κηρύγματι·
ἐν δὲ τῷ τοῦ βίου σταδίῳ καὶ τῇ δεῦρο ἀγωνίᾳ τίς ἂν
γένοιτο ἀνταγωνιστὴς ἀνδρὶ ἀγαθῷ, πλὴν τῆς πείρας
τῶν δυσχερῶν;

9. Φέρε τοὺς ἀγωνιστὰς παρακαλῶμεν ἐπὶ τὸ στά-
διον. ἡκέτω ἐκ[12] μὲν Ἀθηνῶν Σωκράτης, ἀγωνιούμενος
πρὸς Μέλητον καὶ πρὸς τὰ δεσμὰ καὶ τὸ φάρμακον,
ἐκ δὲ Ἀκαδημίας Πλάτων, ἀγωνιούμενος πρὸς τυράν-
νου ὀργὴν καὶ θάλατταν πολλὴν καὶ κινδύνους με-
γάλους· ἡκέτω καὶ ἄλλος ἀγωνιστὴς Ἀττικός, ἀγωνιούμενος πρὸς Τισσαφέρνην ἐπιορκοῦντα καὶ Ἀριαῖον
ἐπιβουλεύοντα καὶ Μένωνα προδιδόντα καὶ βασιλέα
ἐπιτιθέμενον. κάλει μοι καὶ τὸν ἐκ τοῦ Πόντου ἀθλη-
τήν· ἀγωνιζέσθω καὶ οὗτος ἀγῶνα ἰσχυρὸν πρὸς
ἀνταγωνιστὰς πικρούς, πενίαν καὶ ἀδοξίαν καὶ λιμὸν
καὶ κρύος· ἐγὼ δὲ αὐτοῦ καὶ τὰ γυμνάσια ἐπαινῶ·

αὐτόν μιν πληγῇσιν ἀεικελίῃσι δαμάσσας,
σπεῖρα κακ᾽ ἀμφ᾽ ὤμοισι βαλών,

οὐ χαλεπῶς διὰ τοῦτο ἐκράτει.

---

[12] ἡκέτω ἐκ Markland, Trapp: ἔχε· τίνες R

his journeys far and wide, and all those terrors he faced, then you strip Heracles of his virtue. In the Olympic and Pythian games it is impossible to obtain the olive or win the apples by competing all alone, for one must have opponents in order to receive the proclamation of victory. So, in the stadium of life and the contests there, who might be the opponent of a good man other than his experience of hardships?

9. So, let us summon the contestants to the stadium. Let Socrates come from Athens to contend with Meletus, the prison, and the poison; let Plato come from the Academy to contend with a tyrant's wrath, a long sea voyage, and great dangers.[22] And let another Athenian competitor[23] come to contend with Tissaphernes when he breaks his oath, Ariaeus when he plots against him, Meno when he betrays him, and the Persian king when he attacks him.[24] Summon for me as well an athlete from Pontus,[25] and let him engage in a difficult contest against those bitter opponents: poverty, contempt, hunger, and cold. I praise as well his physical training:

> subjecting himself to degrading blows
> and throwing a shabby garment about his shoulders;[26]

for by that means he won easy victories.

[22] For Plato's fraught relationship with Dionysius II of Syracuse, see Pl. *Ep*. 7. This example of Plato and the forthcoming ones of Xenophon and Diogenes are also cited at *Or*. 15.9.
[23] Xenophon.   [24] Episodes from Books 1, 2, and 3 of Xenophon's *Anabasis*.   [25] Diogenes the Cynic, from Sinope on the Black Sea (Pontus).
[26] *Od*. 4.244–45, said by Helen describing Odysseus' disguised entry into Troy, also quoted at *Or*. 15.9.

Τοιγαροῦν στεφανῶ τοὺς ἄνδρας καὶ ἀνακηρύττω
νικηφόρους τῆς ἀρετῆς· ἐὰν δὲ ἀφέλῃς αὐτῶν τὴν
πρὸς τὰ κακὰ ἀγωνίαν, ἀποστεφανοῖς τοὺς ἄνδρας
καὶ ἀποκηρύττεις. ἄφελε Ἀθηναίων τὸν ἐπὶ Μαρα-
θῶνα δρόμον καὶ τὸν ἐκεῖ θάνατον καὶ τὴν Κυναι-
γείρου χεῖρα καὶ τὴν Πολυζήλου συμφορὰν καὶ τὰ
Καλλιμάχου τραύματα, καὶ οὐδὲν Ἀθηναίοις καταλεί-
πεις σεμνόν, πλὴν τοῦ Ἐριχθονίου καὶ τοῦ Κέκροπος,
μύθων ἀπιστουμένων. διὰ τοῦτο ἡ Σπάρτη ἐπὶ πλεῖ-
στον ἐλευθέρα, ὅτι ἐν οὐδὲ εἰρήνῃ σχολὴν ἄγει· μάστιγες αὗται καὶ πληγαὶ Λακωνικαὶ καὶ ἔθη κακῶν
ταῖς ἀρεταῖς ἀναμιγνύμενα.

Therefore I crown these men and declare them victors of virtue. But if you deprive them of their contest against evils, you strip the crowns from their heads and banish them from the contest. Deprive the Athenians of their rush to Marathon, and the deaths there, and the hand of Cynaegirus, and the calamity of Polyzelus, and the wounds of Callimachus,[27] then you leave the Athenians with nothing impressive except their unbelievable myths of Erichthonius and Cecrops. The reason why Sparta remained free for the longest time, was because it did not relax even in peacetime: witness those whips and Spartan floggings and habituation to evils implicated in their virtues.[28]

[27] Cf. Hdt. 6.112–17. Cynaegirus' hand was chopped off when he tried to hold back a Persian ship, Polyzelus (Epizelus) was struck blind, and Callimachus died from his wounds.

[28] Spartan conditioning is also praised at *Orr.* 19.5, 23.2, and 32.10.

ORATION 35

INTRODUCTION

This treatment of friendship complements that of *Oration* 14, which distinguishes a friend from a flatterer. It lays out the ethical basis of friendship that is dependent on virtue and ultimately derives from Zeus' care for humankind. So, when Homer calls Zeus "father of gods and men," he does not mean actual paternity, but rather his paternal qualities of salvation and friendship (§1). Divine virtue is called right (*themis*) and justice (*dikē*), whereas human virtue is called friendship (*philia*) and goodwill (*charis*). Humans, however, who must procure physical necessities, extend their friendship to very few individuals. Ideally, the exchange of goods would be from the one with a surplus to the other one in need (§2). The exchange of arms between Glaucus and Diomedes illustrates a fair trade based on friendship, but such reciprocal, open, and generous friendships are rare because of greed, distrust, and desire for pleasure (§3). In contrast to all the fighting in the *Iliad*, the singular friendship of Achilles and Patroclus stands out as the example most conducive to virtue. In Athens the friendship of Harmodius and Aristogeiton marked a high point, after which friendship ceased to exist in Attica and everything degenerated into anger, greed, and ambition (§4). The rest of Greece is also plagued by war and widespread internal strife with the disappearance of friendship (§5). What preparation is required to engage in friendship? A disdain of wealth, pleasure, ambition, and an embrace of toil in order to win the most valuable prize, friendship based on virtue (§6). It is scarce, while its counterfeit is ubiquitous in the hordes of flatterers. But if individuals and states had embraced the reciprocal exchange of friendship, wars and pretexts for wars would have ceased, in the manner of Zeus' armistice for religious festivals. Yet even if a public truce were achieved, the war in the soul would still fill it with envy, wrath, and all kinds of evils (§7). No truce or festival is of value unless the participants are actually friends. A true armistice from Zeus must enter the soul, and philosophy must aid in attaining it (§8).

ORATION 35

Πῶς ἄν τις πρὸς φίλον παρασκευάσαιτο

1. Ἔχεις εἰπεῖν τίνας ποτὲ Ὅμηρος ὀνομάζων χαίρει θεοῖς εἰκέλους καὶ δίους καὶ μῆτιν ἀταλάντους Διί; τίνας γὰρ ἀλλ' ἢ τοὺς ἀρίστους, Ἀγαμέμνονά τε καὶ Ἀχιλλέα καὶ Ὀδυσσέα, καὶ ὅστις ἄλλος συνετέλει αὐτῷ εἰς ἐπαίνου μοῖραν; τί δέ; εἰ μὴ τῷ Διὶ εἴκαζεν αὐτούς, ἀλλ' ἢ Μαχάωνι τῷ ἰατρῷ ἢ Κάλχαντι τῷ μαντικῷ ἢ Νέστορι τῷ ἱππικῷ ἢ Μενεσθεῖ τῷ τακτικῷ ἢ Ἐπειῷ τῷ τέκτονι ἢ Νιρεῖ τῷ καλῷ, ἆρ' οὐκ ἂν εἶχες ἀποκρίνασθαί μοι τῆς εἰκόνος τὴν αἰτίαν; ἢ ἐκεῖ μὲν γνωρίζεις τὴν ὁμοιότητα, ἐνταῦθα δὲ ὅτι μὲν ὅμοιοι τῷ Διὶ οἶσθα, καὶ ἐπαινεῖς τὸν εἰκάσαντα τῆς γνωρίσεως, τὸ δὲ γνώρισμα αὐτὸ ἀγνοεῖς; φέρε οὖν, ἐγώ σοι ὑπὲρ τοῦ Ὁμήρου διηγήσομαι †ωστωσινηρεναιποτ†[1] λέγων·

οὐ γὰρ εἰμι ποιητικός.

---

[1] obel. Trapp, Koniaris: πεζῶς ἄνευ μέτρου tent. Davies[2]: οὑτωσὶ ἠρέμα πω tent. Markland, Dübner

ORATION 35

How to prepare oneself for friendship

1. Can you tell me which men Homer delights in calling "like the gods," "godlike," and "equal to Zeus in counsel"?[1] Who else but the heroes, Agamemnon, Achilles, Odysseus, and anyone else who furnished him an occasion for praise? But what if he compared them not to Zeus, but instead to Machaon the doctor, Calchas the seer, Nestor the horseman, Menestheus the strategist, Epeius the carpenter, or Nireus the handsome soldier? Could you not then tell me the reason for the comparison, if I asked? Or is it that you discern the similarity in these latter cases, but in the former ones, although you understand that these heroes are like Zeus and you praise the poet who made the comparison for his discernment, you nonetheless fail to recognize the actual basis for the comparison? Come then, I shall give you an explanation, speaking on Homer's behalf ‹in prose›,[2]

for I am not a poet.[3]

---

[1] For example, *Il.* 1.131 ($\theta\epsilon o\epsilon i\kappa\epsilon\lambda$ ᾿Αχιλλεῦ), 1.7 ($\delta\hat{\imath}os$ ᾿Αχιλλεύς), 1.145 ($\delta\hat{\imath}os$ ᾿Οδυσσεύς), 2.221 (᾿Αγαμέμνονι δίῳ), 2.169 (᾿Οδυσῆα, Διὶ μῆτιν ἀτάλαντον).   [2] A conjecture for the unreadable text.   [3] Pl. *Resp.* 3.393d, spoken by Socrates.

πατέρα γάρ που θεῶν καὶ ἀνθρώπων εἶναι λέγει τὸν
Δία, οὔτι που διότι ὑπεκδὺς τοῦ οὐρανοῦ, νῦν μὲν ὄρ-
νιθι εἰκασθείς, νῦν δὲ χρυσῷ, καὶ ἄλλοτε ἄλλῳ, γυ-
ναιξὶ θνηταῖς ἐπλησίαζεν,

σπερμαίνων τὰ πρῶτα γένος κυδρῶν βασιλήων·

οὕτω γὰρ ἂν εἴη ὁ Ζεὺς ὀλιγοτεκνότατος· ἀλλὰ τὴν
αἰτίαν ἀναθεὶς αὐτῷ τοῦ εἶναι τὰ γένη ταῦτα καὶ σώζεσθαι προσεῖπεν πατέρα, τῶν ἐν φιλίᾳ ὀνομάτων τὸ
πρεσβύτατον.

2. Εἶεν· οὕτω σοι τὰ τοῦ Διὸς ἔχει. τὰ δὲ τῶν ὁμοίων
τῷ Διὶ ἆρ' ἡγεῖ ἄλλη πῃ ἔχειν; ἢ οὐχ ὁρᾷς ὡς οὐδὲ
τὸν Σαλμωνέα εἴκασαν οἱ ποιηταὶ αὐτῷ, καίτοι κεραυ-
νοὺς ἀφιέντα, ὡς ᾤετο, καὶ μιμούμενον τὸν βροντῶν
κτύπον καὶ τὸ ἀστραπῆς φῶς; ἀλλὰ ταῦτά γε ὁ Σαλ-
μωνεὺς δρῶν ὅμοιος ἦν Θερσίτῃ μιμουμένῳ τὸν Νέστορα. πῶς οὖν γένοιντ' ἂν ὅμοιοι ἄνθρωποι Διί; μιμούμενοι αὐτοῦ τὸ σωστικὸν καὶ φιλητικὸν καὶ
πατρικὸν δὴ τοῦτο. αὕτη θνητῆς πρὸς θείαν ἀρετὴν
ὁμοιότης, ἣ παρὰ μὲν θεοῖς καλεῖται θέμις καὶ δίκη
καὶ ἄλλ' ἄττα μυστικὰ καὶ θεοπρεπῆ ὀνόματα, παρὰ
δὲ ἀνθρώποις φιλία καὶ χάρις καὶ ἄλλ' ἄττα προσηνῆ
καὶ ἀνθρωπικὰ ὀνόματα.

---

4 *Il.* 1.544, etc.   5 Hes. *Cat.* fr. 1.6 Most.

6 That is, the races of gods and men. The word "salvation"
(σώζεσθαι) alludes to Zeus' title of Savior (Σωτήρ), echoed in §2
(σωστικόν) and §7 (σώζειν).

7 A legendary king of Elis who pretended to be Zeus. Cf.

When he calls Zeus "father of gods and men,"[4] I do not think that it is because Zeus descended from the sky and mated with mortal women, at one time as a bird, at another as gold, and so on,

> when he first begot the race of glorious kings,[5]

for in that case Zeus would have fathered very few children indeed. No, it was because Homer considered him responsible for the existence and salvation of these races[6] that he called him "father," the most venerable of the names denoting friendship.

2. So, you see how things stand with Zeus himself. Do you then think that the situation is any different for those who are like Zeus? Or don't you see how not even Salmoneus was compared to Zeus by the poets, although he hurled thunderbolts (or so he imagined) and imitated the crash of thunder and the flash of lightning?[7] For by acting this way, Salmoneus actually resembled Thersites imitating Nestor.[8] In what way, then, might humans come to resemble Zeus? By imitating his very attributes of salvation, friendship, and paternity. Here lies the resemblance between human and divine virtue, which among the gods is called right, justice, and various other mystical, divine names, and which among men is called friendship, goodwill, and various other endearing, human names.

Apollod. 1.9.7: "By dragging dried hides, with bronze kettles, at his chariot, he said that he thundered, and by flinging lighted torches at the sky he said that he lightened. But Zeus struck him with a thunderbolt" (trans. J. G. Frazer).

[8] For Thersites' scurrilous speech in contrast to Nestor's judicious rhetoric, compare the description of Thersites at *Il*. 2.212–42 with that of Nestor at *Il*. 1.247–53.

MAXIMUS OF TYRE

Ἐνδεέστερον δὲ δὴ τὸ ἀνθρώπειον τῆς θείας ἀρετῆς
τά τε ἄλλα καὶ κατὰ φιλίας ἔκτασιν· οὐ γὰρ ἐξ-
ικνεῖται ἡ θνητὴ φύσις ἐπὶ τὸ ὅμοιον πᾶν, ἀλλ' ὥσπερ
αἱ τῶν βοσκημάτων ἀγέλαι οἰκειοῦνται τῷ ξυννόμῳ
μόνον· ἀγαπητὸν δὲ εἰ καὶ τούτῳ παντί. νῦν δὲ ἴδοις
ἂν ἐν ἀγέλῃ μιᾷ ὑπὸ ποιμένι ἑνὶ στάσεις πολλὰς καὶ
διαφωνίας κυριττόντων ἀλλήλους καὶ διαδακνόντων,
μόγις ⟨δὲ⟩² ὄντα που ζώπυρα εἰς βραχὺν ἀριθμὸν φιλίας σαφοῦς ξυνελημαλένα.

Σιτία μὲν καὶ ποτὰ καὶ ἀμπεχόνας, καὶ ὅση ἄλλη
χρεία σωμάτων, πορίζονται οἱ ἄνθρωποι ἀμοιβῇ καὶ
ἀντιδόσει {ἐκ}³ χαλκοῦ καὶ σιδήρου, καὶ τὰ σεμνὰ δὴ
ταῦτα, χρυσοῦ καὶ ἀργύρου, ἐξὸν χαίρειν τῇ τῶν με-
ταλλέων φράσαντας τέχνῃ λαμβάνειν παρ' ἀλλήλων
ταῦτα ἀπονητί, μετρουμένους μέτρῳ τῷ πάντων ἰσαι-
τάτῳ, τὸν μὲν ἐνδεᾶ τὴν χρείαν λαβόντα παρὰ τοῦ
ἔχοντος, τὸν δὲ ἐν περιουσίᾳ ἀφεῖναι κτησάμενον
παρὰ τοῦ λαβόντος, ὧν ἡ ἀντίδοσις οὐχ ἕξει αἰτίαν.

3. Τῷ μὲν Λυκίῳ Γλαύκῳ χρυσὸν δόντι καὶ λαβόντι
χαλκὸν καὶ

ἑκατόμβοι' ἐννεαβοίων

ἀλλαξαμένῳ ὀνειδίζει Ὅμηρος· εἰ δὲ παρωσάμενοι
τὴν τούτων ἀξίαν τῇ γνώμῃ τὰς ἀντιδόσεις διεμε-

² suppl. Russell, Trapp, Koniaris
³ del. Heinsius, Trapp

The human kind of virtue is indeed inferior to divine virtue in many ways, but especially in the reach of its friendship, for our mortal nature does not extend its affection to every fellow being, but just like herds of cattle, it is only friendly with its own group—and welcome it would be if it even befriended every member in it! But in fact, you can see in one flock under a single shepherd many conflicts and disagreements as they butt and bite one another, with scarcely any sparks combining to kindle even a small number of clear friendships.

Humans procure food, drink, clothing, and other physical necessities by bartering and by exchanging bronze and iron for them, as well as those precious metals, gold and silver. And yet they could dispense entirely with the skills of miners and receive these goods from one another without all the effort, if they calculate the exchange by the fairest standard of all, whereby the one in need receives what he needs from the one who has it, while the other who has a surplus to give away gains from the recipient in an exchange that no one will fault.[9]

3. Homer, however, criticizes Lycian Glaucus for giving gold and accepting bronze, and for trading what is worth

a hundred oxen for the worth of nine;[10]

but if they[11] had set aside the material value of these goods and were evaluating the exchange on the basis of sound

[9] What the giver receives is goodwill and friendship. For the equal reciprocity of friends, see *Or.* 14.6.
[10] *Il.* 6.236. At 6.234 Homer says that "Zeus took away Glaucus' wits" in making this unequal exchange.
[11] That is, Glaucus and Diomedes.

τροῦντο, ἦν ἂν δήπου τὸ χρῆμα ἰσόρροπον. νῦν δὲ
καπηλείας πάντα μεστὰ καὶ ἐμπορίας καὶ συμβο-
λαίων πικρῶν, ἀγοραίων τε καὶ θαλαττίων καὶ ἠπει-
ρωτικῶν, ξενικῶν τε καὶ ἀστικῶν καὶ ἐπιχωρίων καὶ
διαποντίων, ἄνω καὶ κάτω στρεφομένης τῆς γῆς καὶ
τῆς θαλάττης, τὰ ἀθήρατα ἐκθηρωμένων καὶ τὰ
ἀφανῆ μεταλλευόντων καὶ τὰ πόρρω διωκόντων καὶ
τὰ σπάνια ποριζομένων, καὶ θησαυροὺς κατορυττόν-
των καὶ κατώρυχας ἐμπιμπλάντων καὶ ταμεῖα σωρευ-
όντων.

Τὸ δὲ τούτων αἴτιον ἀπιστία φιλίας καὶ πλεονεξίας
ἔρως καὶ ἀπορίας δέος καὶ μοχθηρίας ἔθος καὶ ἡδονῆς πόθος· ὑφ' ὧν τὸ φιλεῖν ἐλαυνόμενον καὶ κατορυτ-
τόμενον καὶ βαπτιζόμενον μόγις που σώζει ἀμαυρὰ
ἴχνη καὶ ἀσθενῆ· καὶ τὸ κοινότατον καὶ ἀταμίευτον
καὶ ἀφθονώτατον, διὰ τὴν τῶν χρωμένων σπάνιν, εἴ
που καὶ γένοιτο τῆς Ἑλλάδος ἢ τῆς βαρβάρου γῆς,
ᾄδεται τοῦτο καὶ μύθου σχῆμα ἔχει καὶ ἀπιστεῖται
αὐτοῦ ἡ ἀκρίβεια· καὶ μάλα εἰκότως.

4. Ἦλθεν ἐπὶ τὴν Ἀσίαν Ἑλληνικὸς στόλος νεῶν
χιλίων, πλῆθος ἀνδρῶν τὸ καλλιστεῦον τῆς Ἑλλάδος,
ὁμόσκηνον καὶ ὁμοδίαιτον, δεκαετεῖ χρόνῳ ἀντικαθη-
μένων αὐτοῖς ἐχθρῶν βαρβάρων. ἡ δὲ φήμη τῶν ἔργων τούτων, ἐμπεσοῦσα εἰς τὴν Ὁμήρου ᾠδήν, οὐκ
ἔσχεν ἡμῖν ἑταιρείαν εἰπεῖν ἀκριβῆ ἐν τοσούτῳ στόλῳ
καὶ χρόνῳ πλὴν μιᾶς, Θετταλικοῦ μειρακίου πρὸς Λο-
κρὸν ἄνδρα, ἧς οὐδὲν Ὅμηρος διηγήσατο οὔτε πρὸς

judgment, surely the trade would have been a fair one.[12] But today the world is full of commerce, trade, and acrimonious dealings, in marketplaces and at sea and on land, abroad and in town, locally and overseas, while the land and sea are turned upside down, as men hunt for what has never been caught, mine for what has never been seen, chase after what is far away, procure what is scarce, and bury their treasures, fill their vaults, and heap up their storerooms.

The cause of all this is a distrust of friendship, a lust for gain, a fear of scarcity, an habituation to depravity, and a desire for pleasure, by all of which friendship is driven out, buried, and sunk, and scarcely preserves any faint and weak traces of itself anywhere. And because so few practice it, if ever this most sharing, open-handed, and generous relationship happens to appear anywhere in Greek or barbarian lands, it is celebrated and acquires the status of a legend, whose veracity is doubted, and quite reasonably so.

4. A Greek fleet of a thousand ships came to Asia bringing a multitude of the finest men in Hellas, who shared tents and meals together, while for ten years enemy barbarians were pitted against them. And yet the report of their deeds that appeared in Homer's poem could not tell us of any true comradeship in such a large army over so long a time—except for one, that of a Thessalian youth with a man from Locri.[13] There is nothing in Homer's nar-

---

[12] Their exchange of armor was based on guest-friendship (*xenia*), and they parted as friends. This famous incident is also discussed at *Orr.* 32.5, 39.1, and 40.1.

[13] That is, Achilles and Patroclus. Maximus follows Plato in making Achilles the younger of the two; see Pl. *Symp.* 180a–b.

ἡδονὴν τερπνότερον οὔτε πρὸς ἀρετὴν ἀγωγότερον
οὔτε πρὸς μνήμην ἐπικυδέστερον· τὰ δὲ ἄλλα τοῦ
Ὁμήρου εἰ σκοποίης, πόλεμοι πάντα καὶ θυμοὶ καὶ
ἀπειλαὶ καὶ μῆνις καὶ τὰ τούτων τέλη, οἰμωγαὶ καὶ
στόνοι καὶ θάνατοι καὶ φθοραὶ καὶ ὄλεθροι.

Ἄιδεταί που καὶ διήγημα Ἀττικὸν ὑπὸ φιλίας
σεμνυνόμενον ἐν πολλοῖς τοῖς Ἀθηναίων λόγοις, ἐν
τοῦτο ἄξιον τῆς Ἀθηνᾶς, ἄξιον τοῦ Θησέως, φιλία
καλὴ καὶ δικαία ἀγαθῶν ἀνδρῶν, ἣ παρέδωκεν ἀμφοτέροις ἐπὶ τυράννῳ κοινὸν ξίφος καὶ σύνθημα κοινὸν
καὶ κοινὸν θάνατον· μεθ' ἣν οὐκέτι φιλία Ἀττικὴ ἦν,
ἀλλὰ πάντα ὕπουλα καὶ σαθρὰ καὶ ἄπιστα καὶ δια-
βεβρωμένα, μεστὰ φθόνου καὶ ὀργῆς καὶ ἀπειρο-
καλίας καὶ φιλοχρηματίας καὶ φιλοδοξίας.

5. Κἂν τὴν λοιπὴν Ἑλλάδα ἐπίῃς, ἀφθονίαν ὄψει
σκυθρωπῶν διηγημάτων, ἄνδρα ἀνδρὶ συμπεπτωκότα
καὶ πόλιν πόλει καὶ γένος γένει· οὐ τὸ Δωρικὸν τῷ
Ἰωνικῷ μόνον, οὐδὲ τὸ Βοιώτιον τῷ Ἀττικῷ, ἀλλὰ καὶ
Ἴωνας Ἴωσιν καὶ Δωριέας Δωριεῦσιν καὶ Βοιωτοὺς
Βοιωτοῖς συμπίπτοντας καὶ Ἀθηναίους Ἀθηναίοις καὶ
Θηβαίους Θηβαίοις καὶ Κορινθίους Κορινθίοις, συγ-
γενεῖς καὶ συνεστίους πολεμίους, πάντας πᾶσιν ἐπι-
τιθεμένους, τοὺς ὑπὸ τὸν αὐτὸν ἥλιον καὶ τὸν αὐτὸν
αἰθέρα καὶ τὸν αὐτὸν νόμον, καὶ τὴν αὐτὴν φωνὴν
ἱέντας καὶ τὴν αὐτὴν γῆν νεμομένους καὶ καρποὺς

rative that is more enjoyable to hear, more conducive to
virtue, or more glorious to be remembered than this
friendship. And if you survey the rest of Homer,[14] it is full
of warfare, anger, threats, wrath, and their consequences,
wailing, groaning, death, destruction, and ruin.

There is also a story in Attica, revered for the friendship it recounts and celebrated in many Athenian writings,
the one story worthy of Athena and of Theseus,[15] that tells
of a beautiful and just friendship between two good men,[16]
a friendship that gave the two of them a shared sword
against a tyrant, a shared watchword,[17] and a shared death.
But thereafter friendship ceased to exist in Attica, for everything became diseased, rotten, treacherous, and corrupt, full of envy, anger, vulgarity, avarice, and ambition.

5. And if you turn to the rest of Hellas, you will find
a plethora of dreary stories of man pitted against man,
city against city, and race against race, not only Dorians
pitted against Ionians and Boeotians against Athenians,
but even Ionians against Ionians, Dorians against Dorians,
Boeotians against Boeotians, Athenians against Athenians,
Thebans against Thebans, and Corinthians against Corinthians—kinsmen and family members at war with one
another, everyone attacking everyone else, although living
under the same sun, same skies, and same laws, speaking
the same language, living on the same land, eating the

---

[14] Specifically the *Iliad*.   [15] A reference to Athena's friendship for Odysseus and to Theseus' for Pirithous.

[16] Harmodius and Aristogeiton, cited as exemplars of just love
at *Or.* 18.2. Thuc. 6.54–57 provides an account of their assassina-
tion of Hipparchus and their subsequent deaths in 514 BC.

[17] That is, the signal to attack.

τοὺς αὐτοὺς σιτουμένους καὶ μυστήρια τὰ αὐτὰ τε-
λουμένους, οὓς περιβάλλει τεῖχος ἓν καὶ πόλις μία,
πολεμοῦντας σπενδομένους, ὀμνύντας ἐπιορκοῦντας,
συντιθεμένους μετατιθεμένους, καὶ προφάσεις μικρὰς
⟨ἀρχὰς ποιουμένους⟩[4] μεγίστων κακῶν· οἷς γὰρ ἂν τὸ
φιλεῖν τῆς γνώμης ἐκπέσῃ, πάντα ἤδη ἀξιόχρεα κι-
νεῖν ὀργὴν καὶ ταράττειν, καθάπερ κοίλην ναῦν ἀφαι-
ρεθεῖσαν τοῦ ἕρματος βραχεῖαι ῥοπαὶ σαλεύουσίν τε
καὶ περιτρέπουσιν.

6. Τίς ἂν οὖν παρασκευὴ γένοιτο ἀνδρὶ φιλίας
ἐραστῇ πρὸς τὸ κτῆμα τοῦτο; χαλεπὸν μὲν εἰπεῖν, ῥητέον δὲ ὅμως·

ὡς οὐκ ἔστι λέουσι καὶ ἀνδράσιν ὅρκια πιστά,
οὐδὲ λύκοι τε καὶ ἄρνες ὁμόφρονα θυμὸν
    ἔχουσιν,

⟨οὕτως⟩[5] οὐκ ἔστιν οὐδὲ ἀνδρὶ πρὸς ἄνδρα φιλίας
ὁλκή, μέχρις ἂν αὐτῷ οἱ ὀφθαλμοὶ φαντάζωνται χρυσὸν καὶ ἄργυρον. κἂν τούτων ἀπαγάγῃς τὴν ὄψιν, οὐκ
ἀπόχρη πρὸς φιλίαν ἡ καρτερία, ἀλλ᾽ ἐνοχλεῖ αὖθις
ἡ παιδίσκων ὥρα ἢ γυναικὸς κάλλος· κἂν καταμύσῃς
πρὸς ταῦτα,

εὐπρόσωπος ὁ τοῦ μεγαλήτορος Ἐρεχθέως δῆμος

καὶ τὰ ἐν ἐκκλησίαις κηρύγματα καὶ ἡ ἀπ᾽ αὐτῶν
δόξα, κοῦφον χρῆμα καὶ πᾶσαν γῆν ὀξέως ὑπεριπτά-

---

[4] suppl. Trapp   [5] suppl. Markland, Trapp

264

same produce, initiated into the same mysteries, living in a single city protected by one wall, waging wars and signing treaties, swearing oaths and breaking them, making agreements and changing them, and contriving small pretexts that lead to the greatest disasters. For once friendship is excluded from consideration, then anything is immediately capable of provoking anger and causing mayhem, just as small shoves can rock an empty ship without any ballast and capsize it.

6. What preparation, then, might enable a man who desires friendship to acquire it? It is difficult to say, but I shall speak out nonetheless.

> As lions and men share no trustworthy oaths,
> nor do wolves and lambs have hearts that agree,[18]

so too the attraction of friendship does not exist between one man and another, as long as his eyes set their sights on gold and silver. And even if you turn away your gaze from these, this forbearance does not suffice to produce friendship, for the charming looks of a boy or the beauty of a woman can once again provoke you. And even if you close your eyes to these,

> attractive are the people of greathearted
>   Erechtheus,[19]

and so too are the proclamations in assemblies and the fame they bring, that airy thing that swiftly flits over the

18 *Il.* 22.262–63, Achilles' bitter words to Hector before attacking him.
19 That is, the Athenians. The quotation is from [Pl.] 1 *Alc.* 132a, itself an adaptation of *Il.* 2.547.

μενον· κἂν ὑπερίδῃς ταύτης, οὐχ ὑπερόψει δικαστη-
ρίου· κἂν ὑπερίδῃς τούτου, οὐχ ὑπερόψει δεσμωτη-
ρίου· κἂν ἐνέγκῃς δεσμά, οὐχ ὑπερόψει προσιόντος
τοῦ θανάτου.

Πολλάς σε δεῖ ἡδονὰς παραδραμεῖν καὶ πολλοῖς
πόνοις ἀντιβλέψαι, ἵνα κτήσῃ κτῆμα ἡδοναῖς πάσαις
ἰσοστάσιον καὶ πόνοις πᾶσιν ἀντίρροπον, κτῆμα
χρυσοῦ τιμιώτερον, κτῆμα ὥρας βεβαιότερον, κτῆμα
δόξης ἀσφαλέστερον, κτῆμα τιμῆς ἀληθέστερον,
κτῆμα αὐθαίρετον, αὐτεπάγγελτον, κτῆμα ἀδεκάστως
ἐπαινούμενον, κτῆμα κἂν λύπην, κἂν πρᾶξιν φέρῃ,
εὐφραῖνον τὸν δρῶντα κατὰ τὴν μνήμην τῆς αἰτίας.

7. Σπάνιον δὲ τὸ κτῆμα τοῦτο· τὸ δὲ εἴδωλον αὐτοῦ
πρόχειρον καὶ παντοδαπόν, κολάκων ἑσμοὶ καὶ θίασοι σεσηρότων καὶ σαινόντων καὶ ἐπ᾽ ἄκρα τῇ γλώττῃ
τὸ φιλεῖν ἐχόντων, οὐχ ὑπ᾽ εὐνοίας ἀγομένων ἀλλ᾽
ὑπὸ τῆς χρείας ἠναγκασμένων, καὶ μισθοφόρων ἀλλὰ
οὐ φίλων. καὶ οὐκ ἔστιν ἀπαλλαγὴ τοῦ κακοῦ, μέχρις
ἂν †ω† <. . .>[6] τὸ φιλεῖν νομίζωσιν· τὸ δὲ ἔστιν μέν,
ἀλλ᾽ οὐχ ὁρῶσιν οἱ πολλοὶ τὴν ἀντίδοσιν, οὔτε ἰδίᾳ
οὔτε κατὰ πόλιν· ἢ γὰρ ἂν αὐτοὺς ἐξοπλίσαντες καὶ
χαίρειν φράσαντες στρατηγῶν τέχναις καὶ ὁπλο-
ποιῶν δημιουργίαις καὶ μισθοφόρων ἀθροισμῷ καὶ
συνθημάτων παραδόσει καὶ φρουρίων ἐπιτειχίσει καὶ
στρατοπέδων <τάξεσιν>,[7] πάλαι[8] ἐδέξαντο ἂν τὰς

---

[6] obel. et lacunam stat. Trapp: †ἂν ωτ† obel. Koniaris: alia alii
[7] suppl. Koniaris
[8] πάλαι Markland, Trapp: πάλιν R

whole world. And even if you disdain that, you will not be able to disdain the law court; and even if you disdain that, you will not be able to disdain prison. And even if you can tolerate shackles, you will not be able to disdain death as it approaches.[20]

You must forgo many pleasures and face many toils in order to acquire a possession that is of equal worth to all pleasures and compensates for all toils, a possession more valuable than gold, more lasting than youthful beauty, more secure than fame, and more real than honor, a possession that is freely chosen, freely bestowed, and impartially praised, a possession that even when bringing pain and trouble gladdens the sufferer by reminding him of its cause.[21]

7. This possession is indeed scarce, but its counterfeit is readily available and comes in many forms, with swarms and bands of flatterers, who grin and fawn and speak of friendship on the tips of their tongues, who are not motivated by kindness, but are compelled by need, and are mercenaries, not friends. There is no relief from this evil, until they consider friendship . . .[22] Such is the case, but most people fail to recognize the reciprocal exchange, be they individuals or states. For if they had, they would long since have disarmed themselves, bade farewell to the skills of generals, the handiwork of armorers, the mustering of mercenaries, the distribution of watchwords, the building of forts, the setting up of army camps, and would gladly

[20] This passage draws on Socrates' experiences.

[21] That cause is virtue.

[22] The text is defective, and no satisfactory emendation has been proposed. Trapp suggests filling the lacuna with something like "<to be something that necessarily involves *mutual* benefit>."

σπονδὰς ἑκόντες παρ' αὐτοῦ τοῦ Διός, οὐκ ἐν Ὀλυμ-
πίᾳ οὐδὲ ἀπὸ τοῦ Ἰσθμοῦ τὴν ἐκεχειρίαν κηρύττον-
τος, ἀλλ' ἐξ οὐρανοῦ μέγα βοῶντος·

"σχέσθε, φίλοι, καί μ' οἷον ἐάσατε κηδόμενόν
περ

σώζειν ὑμᾶς καὶ μὴ περιορᾶν ὑπ' ἀλλήλων κακουμέ-
νους."

Νῦν δὲ ἐφημέρους σπονδὰς σπενδόμενοι, τριακον-
τούτιδας, ἀνάπαυλαν κακῶν ἐπορίζοντο⁹ ἀμυδρὰν καὶ
οὐ πάντη ἀσφαλῆ, μέχρις ἂν ἄλλη πρόφασις ἐπιπε-
σοῦσα πάντα ἄνω καὶ κάτω ἐπιταράξῃ αὖθις. ἀλλὰ
κἂν τὰ ὅπλα ἀποδύσωνται, κἂν εἰρήνην ἄγωσιν, ἄλλος αὖ πόλεμος ἐμπεσὼν τῇ ψυχῇ, οὐ δημόσιος ἀλλ'
ἰδιωτικός, οὐ σιδηροφορῶν οὐδὲ πυρφορῶν, οὐδὲ
νηΐτην ἄγων στρατὸν οὐδὲ ἱππικόν, ἀλλὰ γυμνὸς
ὅπλων, ἀσίδηρος, ἄπυρος, λυμαίνεται τῇ ψυχῇ καὶ
πολιορκεῖ αὐτήν, ἐμπιμπλὰς φθόνου καὶ ὀργῆς καὶ
θυμοῦ καὶ προπηλακισμοῦ καὶ ἄλλων μυρίων κακῶν.

8. Ποῖ τις τράπηται; τίνα εὕρῃ ἐκεχειρίαν, ποίαν
Ὀλυμπίαν, τίνα Νεμέαν; καλὰ μὲν τὰ Ἀθήνησιν Διονύσια καὶ Παναθήναια, ἀλλὰ ἑορτάζουσιν μισοῦντες
καὶ μισούμενοι· πόλεμόν μοι λέγεις, οὐχ ἑορτήν.
καλαὶ καὶ ἐν Λακεδαίμονι αἱ Γυμνοπαιδίαι καὶ τὰ
Ὑακίνθια καὶ οἱ χοροί· ἀλλὰ Ἀγησίλαος Λυσάνδρῳ

⁹ πορίζονται fors. Koniaris

have accepted the peace treaty from Zeus himself, who does not proclaim his armistice at Olympia or from the Isthmus,[23] but who shouts from heaven:

"Hold off, my friends, and allow me alone, caring as I do,[24]

to save you and never look the other way when you harm one another."

But as it is, they make short-term treaties of thirty years[25] and procure a weak and completely unstable respite from evils, until some other pretext intervenes to throw everything into utter chaos once again. And even if they do lay down their arms and live in peace, another war breaks out in the soul, not a public but a private war, not bearing iron and fire, nor leading a navy or cavalry, but stripped of weapons, without iron or fire, it ravages and besieges the soul, filling it with envy, anger, wrath, contempt, and countless other evils.

8. Where can one turn? What armistice can one find? What kind of Olympian or Nemean truce? Yes, the Athenian Dionysia and Panathenaea are lovely festivals, but they are celebrated by people who hate one another—that is a war, not a festival, you are telling me of. Lovely too are the Gymnopaediae, Hyacinthia, and choruses at Sparta, but Agesilaus envies Lysander,[26] and Agesipolis hates

---

[23] That is, the truces that allowed safe passage to the Panhellenic festivals. [24] *Il.* 22.416, spoken by Priam, asking the Trojans to let him go alone to the Greek camp.

[25] Athens and Sparta concluded a thirty-year truce in 446 BC that only lasted until the outbreak of the Peloponnesian War in 431. [26] Cf. Xen. *Hell.* 3.4.7–9.

φθονεῖ καὶ Ἀγησίπολις Ἆγιν μισεῖ, καὶ Κινάδων τοῖς
βασιλεῦσιν ἐπιβουλεύει καὶ Φάλανθος τοῖς ἐφόροις
καὶ Παρθενίαι Σπαρτιάταις· οὐ πιστεύω τῇ ἑορτῇ
πρὶν τοὺς ἑορταστὰς ἴδω φίλους.

Οὗτος ἀληθινῆς ἐκεχειρίας νόμος καὶ τρόπος, ὑπὸ
νομοθέτῃ τῷ θεῷ τεταγμένος, ὃν οὐκ ἔστιν μὴ κτησάμενον φιλίαν ἰδεῖν, οὐδ' ἂν πολλάκις τις σπείσηται,
οὐδ' ἂν πολλάκις ἀναγράψηται τὰ Ὀλυμπίασιν καὶ
Ἰσθμοῖ καὶ Νεμέᾳ. εἴσω δεῖ ἐπὶ τὴν ψυχὴν τὸ κήρυγμα
ἐλθεῖν, εἴσω τὴν ἐκεχειρίαν· ἕως δὲ ἄσπονδος καὶ
ἀκήρυκτος ὁ ἐν ψυχῇ πόλεμος, ἄφιλος ἡ ψυχὴ μένει,
ἐχθρά, σκυθρωπή. ταῦτα αἱ Ποιναί, ταῦτα αἱ Ἐρι-
νύες, τὰ δράματα, αἱ τραγῳδίαι. διώκωμεν τὴν ἐκεχειρίαν, παρακαλῶμεν φιλοσοφίαν· ἡκέτω, σπενδέσθω,
κηρυττέτω.

Agis.[27] Cinadon plots against the kings,[28] Phalanthus against the Ephors,[29] and the Partheniae against the Spartiates.[30] I put no trust in any festival until I can see that the celebrants are friends.

This is the manner and form of a true armistice, one that is established by god as its lawmaker, and unless that is achieved, friendship will never be seen, no matter how often treaties are made, or how often the edicts are recorded at Olympia, the Isthmus, and Nemea. No, the edict and the armistice must enter into the soul. For as long as the war in the soul is without a treaty and without a truce, the soul will remain friendless, hateful, and sullen. This is the domain of Poenae and of Erinyes,[31] of dramas and of tragedies. Let us pursue this armistice; let us summon philosophy to our aid. Let it come to us, let it make peace, let it proclaim the armistice.

[27] There is no other record of this rivalry.
[28] Cf. Xen. *Hell*. 3.3.4–11.
[29] Also mentioned at *Or*. 29.7.
[30] Cf. Arist. *Pol*. 5.6.1306b30–32.
[31] Spirits of punishment and vengeance.

ORATION 36

INTRODUCTION

Diogenes the Cynic, whom Plato reportedly called "Socrates gone mad,"[1] provided an extreme example of freedom from external constraints by living according to nature's simplest needs.[2] The oration has numerous points of contact with Dio Chrysostom's Sixth *Oration* ("Diogenes or On Tyranny"), many of which are indicated in the notes.[3] Dio's oration contrasts Diogenes' carefree life with the fearful life of tyrants; here the contrast is between life in a golden age of freedom and life in the present iron age of imprisonment. The oration opens with the fashioning of man by Prometheus and the freedom of the original humans who lived in peace off nature, which easily satisfied all their basic needs (§1). A lengthy catalogue detailing the degeneracy that has followed the golden age, beginning with humans dividing up the land and ending with their disrespect for the gods, is a rhetorical tour de force

[1] Ael. *VH* 14.33.

[2] *Or.* 34 argued that external constraints ($\pi\epsilon\rho\iota\sigma\tau\acute{\alpha}\sigma\epsilon\iota\varsigma$) are an essential feature of exercising virtue; here they represent restrictions on a life of freedom.

[3] The many common elements, including examples and even vocabulary, suggest that Maximus is drawing on Dio's account.

(§2). A representative of each life is asked to present himself before the judgment of reason to determine if he can be persuaded to adopt the other life (§3). The representative of the life of freedom is presented with an analogy of the life of pleasure and pain that is exposed to external circumstances. It is compared to a prison where the shackled inmates try to eke out some pleasures but can never get their fill. In contrast, the other life is one of freedom in the fresh air and sunlight, wherein modest, natural needs are satisfied (§4). The speaker dismisses the previous fables and analogies and chooses an actual exemplar of simple life, Diogenes, who divested himself of all external circumstances, such as those that constrain citizens, fathers, farmers, soldiers, and merchants, and led a healthful and long-lived existence outdoors. He did not show up other men with sophistic arguments, but with his own example (§5). All the pursuits listed above aim at ends that are subject to external circumstances. Even Socrates, Plato, and Xenophon had to contend with external circumstances, and for that reason Diogenes was more free than Socrates, superior to the lawmakers Solon and Lycurgus, and even superior to Alexander the Great (§6).

ORATION 36

Εἰ προηγούμενος ὁ τοῦ κυνικοῦ βίος

1. Βούλομαί σοι κατὰ τὴν τοῦ Λυδοῦ σοφίαν ποιῆσαι μῦθον· διαλέξονται δέ μοι ἐν τῷ μύθῳ οὐχ ὁ λέων οὐδὲ ὁ ἀετὸς οὐδὲ τὰ τούτων ἔτι ἀφωνότερα, αἱ δρύες, ἀλλ᾽ ὡδί μοι λελέξεται. Ζεὺς ἦν καὶ οὐρανὸς καὶ γῆ. οὐρανῷ μὲν πολῖται θεοί, τὰ δὲ γῆς θρέμματα, οἱ ἄνθρωποι, οὔπω τότε ἐν φωτὶ ἦσαν. καλεῖ δὴ Ζεὺς Προμηθέα καὶ αὐτῷ προστάττει κατανεῖμαι τῇ γῇ ἀποικίαν, ζῷον διπλοῦν, "κατὰ μὲν τὴν γνώμην ἐγγύτατα ἡμῖν τοῖς θεοῖς, τὸ δὲ σῶμα αὐτῷ ἔστω λεπτὸν καὶ ὄρθιον καὶ σύμμετρον, καὶ ἰδεῖν ἥμερον καὶ χειρουργεῖν εὔκολον καὶ βαδίζειν ἀσφαλές." πείθεται ὁ Προμηθεὺς Διὶ καὶ ποιεῖ ἀνθρώπους καὶ οἰκίζει τὴν γῆν.

Οἱ δὲ ἐπεὶ γενέσεως ἐπελάβοντο οὐ χαλεπῶς διέζων· καὶ γὰρ τροφὴν αὐτοῖς ἀποχρῶσαν γῆ παρείχετο, λειμῶνας δασεῖς καὶ ὄρη κομῶντα καὶ καρπῶν χορηγίαν ὅσα γῆ φέρειν φιλεῖ μηδὲν ὑπὸ γεωργῶν ἐνοχλουμένη· παρείχοντο δὲ καὶ αἱ νύμφαι κρήνας

ORATION 36

Whether the life of the Cynic is to be preferred

1. I wish to compose a fable for you like one by the Lydian sage.[1] However, the speakers in my fable will not be the lion or the eagle, or even more mute things like oak trees, but it will be told as follows. There was a time when just Zeus, sky, and earth existed. The gods were denizens of the sky, but humans, creatures of the earth, had not yet come to light. So Zeus summoned Prometheus and ordered him to colonize the earth with a creature of dual nature. "Let it be almost like us gods in intelligence, and let it have a body that is slender, upright, and well-proportioned, with a gentle countenance, dexterous hands, and a steady gait." Prometheus obeyed Zeus, created humans, and populated the earth with them.

Once humans came into existence, they lived without any difficulty, because the earth furnished all the food they needed, with its lush meadows, wooded mountains,[2] and abundance of all the fruits which the earth naturally produces when left undisturbed by farmers. The Nymphs also

---

[1] Aesop. Maximus elsewhere calls him Phrygian (*Orr.* 15.5, 19.2, and 32.1), but Callimachus, *Ia*. 2.15–6, says that he was from Lydian Sardis.

[2] The trees furnished acorns; cf. *Orr.* 21.5 and 23.5.

καθαρὰς καὶ ποταμοὺς διειδεῖς καὶ ἄλλων ναμάτων
εὐπόρους τε καὶ δαψιλεῖς πηγάς· πρὸς δὲ καὶ θάλπος
μὲν ἐξ ἡλίου τοῖς σώμασιν περιχεόμενον συμμέτρως
αὐτὰ παρεμυθεῖτο, αὖραι δὲ ἐκ ποταμῶν ὥρα θέρους
ἐπιπνέουσαι ἀνέψυχον αὐτοῖς τὰ σώματα· περιμάχη-
τον δ᾽ ἦν τούτων οὐδὲν ἐν ἀφθόνῳ τῇ τῶν αὐτομάτων
χορηγίᾳ διαιτωμένοις. δοκοῦσιν δέ μοι καὶ οἱ ποιηταὶ
ἐγγύτατα εἶναι τῷ ἡμετέρῳ τούτῳ μύθῳ, ὑπὸ Κρόνῳ
θεῶν βασιλεῖ τοιοῦτόν τινα αἰνιττόμενοι βίον, ἀπόλε-
μον, ἀσίδηρον, ἀφύλακτον, εἰρηνικόν, ἀπεριμάχητον,
ὑγιεινόν, ἀνενδεᾶ· καὶ χρυσοῦν τὸ γένος τοῦτο, ὡς
ἔοικεν, ὁ Ἡσίοδος καλεῖ νεανιευόμενος πρὸς ἡμᾶς.

2. Ἐμοὶ δὲ ὁ μῦθος, ἀπελθὼν ἐκποδὼν καὶ γενόμενος ἐκ μύθου αὐτὸ τοῦτο λόγος, προϊὼν παραβαλλέτω
βίον βίῳ, τῷ προτέρῳ τὸν δεύτερον, εἴτε σιδηροῦν τις
αὐτὸν εἴτε καὶ ἄλλη πη ὀνομάζων χαίρει, ἡνίκα ἤδη
κληρουχήσαντες οἱ ἄνθρωποι τὴν γῆν ἀπετέμοντο
αὐτῆς ἄλλος ἄλλην μοῖραν, περιβάλλοντες αὑτοῖς
ἕρκη καὶ τειχία, καὶ τὰ σώματα σπαργάνοις μαλθα-
κοῖς καθειλίξαντες, καὶ τὼ πόδε σκύτεσιν χαρακώσαν-
τες, καὶ χρυσὸν οἱ μὲν τοῖς αὐχέσιν, οἱ δὲ ταῖς κεφα-
λαῖς, οἱ δὲ τοῖς δακτύλοις περιαρτήσαντες, εὔφημόν
τινα καὶ εὐπρόσωπον δεσμόν, καὶ στέγας οἰκοδομη-
σάμενοι καὶ κλισιάδας καὶ αὐλείους καὶ προπύλαια
ἄττα ἐπιστήσαντες· καὶ παρέχοντες τῇ γῇ πράγματα,

---

3 Hesiod describes the primitive golden race at *Op.* 109–26,
in contrast to the present degenerate race of iron at *Op.* 174–201.

furnished pure springs, clear rivers, and other plentiful and copious sources of flowing water. In addition, the warmth of the sun enveloped their bodies with its moderate heat and comforted them, while the summertime breezes blew in from the rivers and cooled them down. They had no need to fight over any of these things, for they lived in the midst of an unstinting supply of natural resources. It seems to me that the poets come closest to this fable of ours, when they suggest that some such life existed when Cronus was king of the gods, a life without wars, iron, or garrisons, one that was peaceful, with nothing to fight over, a healthy existence free from want. This, it seems, is the race that Hesiod called "golden," while disparaging our present one.[3]

2. But now let me dismiss my fable and convert it from fiction into a straightforward argument, and let it go on to compare the two lives, this earlier one with the later one (whether one prefers to call it "iron" or something else), when, as soon as humans took possession of the land, they set about dividing it up into separate portions among themselves and surrounded themselves with fences and walls. They swaddled their bodies in soft clothing and fortified their feet with strips of leather. Some attached gold around their necks, others around their heads, still others around their fingers, as a kind of auspicious and attractive bond.[4] They built shelters and added inner and outer doors and porches. They harried the earth by mining, hoe-

---

[4] The word "bond" (δεσμόν) looks forward to the "shackles" (δεσμά) and to the "prison" (δεσμωτήριον) in the forthcoming analogy in §§4–5.

μεταλλεύοντες αὐτὴν καὶ σκάπτοντες καὶ ὀρύττοντες·
καὶ μηδὲ τὴν θάλατταν κατὰ χώραν ἐῶντες, ἀλλὰ
ἐπιτειχίσαντες καὶ ταύτῃ σκάφη πολεμιστήρια καὶ
πορευτικὰ καὶ ἐμπορευτικά· καὶ μηδὲ τοῦ ἀέρος ἀπεχόμενοι, ἀλλὰ καὶ τοῦτον ληϊζόμενοι, τὰς ὀρνίθων
ἀγέλας ἰξῷ καὶ ἕρκεσιν καὶ παντοδαπαῖς μηχαναῖς
σαγηνεύοντες· ἀποσχόμενοι δὲ μήτε τῶν ἡμέρων
ζῴων δι᾽ ἀσθένειαν, μήτε τῶν ἀγρίων διὰ δέος, ἀλλὰ
αἵματι καὶ φόνῳ καὶ λύθρῳ παντοδαπῷ γαστριζόμε-
νοι· καὶ ἀεί τι ταῖς ἡδοναῖς εὑρίσκοντες νέον καὶ τῶν
ἑώλων ὑπερορῶντες, καὶ διώκοντες μὲν τὰ τερπνά,
περιπίπτοντες δὲ τοῖς λυπηροῖς· πλούτου μὲν ὀρεγόμενοι, ἀεὶ δὲ τὸ παρὸν ἐνδεέστερον ἡγούμενοι τοῦ
ἀπόντος καὶ τὸ κτηθὲν ἔλαττον τοῦ προσδοκωμένου·
δεδιότες μὲν ἔνδειαν, πληρωθῆναι δὲ μὴ δυνάμενοι·
φοβούμενοι μὲν θάνατον, μὴ φροντίζοντες δὲ τοῦ ζῆν·
εὐλαβούμενοι ⟨μὲν⟩[1] νόσους, τῶν δὲ νοσερῶν οὐκ
ἀπεχόμενοι· ὑποπτεύοντες μὲν ἄλλους, ἐπιβουλεύον-
τες δὲ τοῖς πλείστοις· δεινοὶ μὲν πρὸς τοὺς ἀνόπλους,
δειλοὶ δὲ πρὸς τοὺς ὡπλισμένους· μισοῦντες μὲν τυραννίδα, τυραννεῖν δὲ αὐτοὶ ἐπιθυμοῦντες· ψέγοντες
μὲν τὰ αἰσχρά, τῶν δὲ αἰσχρῶν οὐκ ἀπεχόμενοι· τὰς
εὐτυχίας θαυμάζοντες, τὰς ἀρετὰς μὴ θαυμάζοντες·
τὰς δυστυχίας ἐλεοῦντες, οὐκ ἀπεχόμενοι τῶν μοχθη-
ρῶν· ἐν μὲν ταῖς εὐπραγίαις τολμηταί, ἐν δὲ ταῖς δυσ-
πραγίαις δυσανάκλητοι· μακαρίζοντες μὲν τοὺς τε-
θνηκότας, γλιχόμενοι δὲ τοῦ ζῆν· μισοῦντες μὲν τὸ
ζῆν, φοβούμενοι δὲ ἀποθανεῖν· προβεβλημένοι μὲν

ing, and excavating it; nor did they leave the sea alone, but assaulted it with ships built for war, transport, and commerce; nor did they spare the air, but plundered it too, as they captured flocks of birds with lime, nets, and devices of all sorts. And abstaining neither from tame animals because they were defenseless, nor from wild ones out of fear, they gorged themselves on blood, guts, and gore of all sorts. They constantly invented new forms of pleasure and despised stale ones; they pursued pleasant experiences, but landed in painful ones; they yearned to have wealth, but always believed that what was at hand was inferior to what was far away, and what was in their possession less than what they expected to have. They feared want, but were unable to get their fill; they feared death, but were careless with life; they were wary of diseases, but would not abstain from the things that made them sick; they were suspicious of others, but plotted against most everyone; they were ferocious to those who were unarmed, but cowards before those who bore arms; they loathed tyranny, but longed to be tyrants themselves; they censured immoral acts, but would not refrain from them; they venerated good luck, but not the virtues; they pitied misfortune, but would not refrain from wicked deeds. They were daring in successful times, but dejected in difficult ones; they considered the dead blessed, but clung to life; they hated their lives, but were afraid to die; they

---

[1] suppl. Markland, Dübner, Trapp

τοὺς πολέμους, εἰρήνην δὲ ἄγειν μὴ δυνάμενοι· ἐν μὲν
δουλείᾳ ταπεινοί, ἐν δὲ ἐλευθερίᾳ θρασεῖς· ἐν μὲν δημοκρατίᾳ ἀκατάσχετοι, ἐν δὲ τυραννίδι ἐπτηχότες·
παίδων μὲν ἐπιθυμοῦντες, γενομένων δὲ ὀλιγωροῦν-
τες· εὐχόμενοι μὲν τοῖς θεοῖς ὡς δυναμένοις ἐπαρ-
κεῖν, καταφρονοῦντες δὲ ὡς οὐ δυναμένων τιμωρεῖν·
καὶ δεδιότες μὲν ὡς κολάζοντας, ἐπιορκοῦντες δὲ ὡς
οὐδὲν ὄντας.

3. Τοιαύτης τοίνυν στάσεως καὶ διαφωνίας τὸν
δεύτερον τοῦτον κατεχούσης βίον, τίνι δῶμεν τὰ νικητήρια φέροντες; τίνα, ποῖον αὐτῶν φῶμεν ἁπλοῦν
εἶναι βίον καὶ ἀπερίστατον καὶ ἐλευθερίας ἐπήβολον;
καὶ ποῖον οὐχ ἁπλοῦν, ἀλλὰ ἀναγκαῖον καὶ ἐλεεινὸν
καὶ περιστάσεων γέμοντα; φέρε ἐξ ἑκατέρων ἡκέτω
τις ἡμῖν ἀνὴρ ἐπὶ διαιτητὴν τὸν λόγον· ὁ δὲ αὐτῶν
ἐρέσθω ἑκάτερον, καὶ πρῶτόν γε τὸν πρότερον, τὸν
γυμνὸν ἐκεῖνον καὶ ἄοικον καὶ ἄτεχνον, τὸν πάσης
τῆς γῆς πολίτην καὶ ἐφέστιον· ἐρέσθω δὲ ἀντιτιθεὶς
αὐτῷ τὸν τοῦ δευτέρου βίον καὶ τρόπον, πότερα
αἱρεῖται μένειν ἐν τῇ πρόσθεν τροφῇ καὶ ἐλευθερίᾳ, ἢ
τὰς τοῦ δευτέρου ἡδονὰς λαβὼν σὺν ταύταις καὶ τὰ
λυπηρὰ ἔχειν. ἴτω δὴ μετὰ τοῦτον ὁ ἕτερος· ἀντιτι-
θέτω δὲ αὐτῷ ὁ δικαστὴς τὴν τοῦ προτέρου δίαιταν
καὶ ἐλευθερίαν· καὶ ἐρέσθω πότερα αἱρεῖται τὰ αὐτοῦ

---

⁵ *Peristaseis* designate external factors that are not in our
control.   ⁶ An allusion to Diogenes' claim to be a citizen of
the world (*kosmopolitēs*); cf. Diog. Laert. 6.63.

were averse to war, but unable to live in peace; they were
abject when enslaved, but reckless when free; they were
unrestrained under democracy, but craven under tyranny;
they longed to have children, but neglected them once
they had them; they prayed to the gods in the belief that
they were able to help them, but scorned them in the
belief that they were unable to punish them; they feared
the gods as avengers, but broke their oaths as if they did
not exist at all.

3. So, if such is the dissention and discord that prevails
in this second kind of life, to which one should we turn
and award the crown? Which of them should we say is a
life that is simple, not subject to external circumstance,[5]
and in possession of freedom? And which one is not simple, but restricted, pitiful, and fraught with external constraints? So then, let us have a representative from each
side come before the judgment of reason, and let this
judge question both parties, beginning with the former
representative, the one that is naked, homeless, and un-
skilled, the citizen and inhabitant of the whole world.[6] Let
the judge confront him with the second life and its ways,
and ask whether he prefers to remain with his former way
of life and its freedom, or accept the pleasures of the
second and suffer the distresses[7] that they entail. Then
after him, let the other come forward, and let the judge
confront him with the former style of life and its freedom,
and ask him whether he prefers to stay with what he has,

---

[7] τὰ λυπηρά, psychological pains, as opposed to physical
pains (ὀδύναι). For the distinction, see *Or.* 28.

MAXIMUS OF TYRE

ἔχειν, ἢ μετατίθεται καὶ μετοικίζεται ἐπὶ τὸν εἰρη-
ναῖον ἐκεῖνον βίον καὶ ἄφετον καὶ ἀδεῆ καὶ ἄλυπον.
τίς τῶν ἀνδρῶν αὐτομολεῖ; τίς μετοικεῖ; τίς ἑκὼν ἀλ-
λάττεται βίον βίου;

4. Τίς οὕτως ἀνόητος καὶ δύσερως καὶ κακοδαίμων
ἀνήρ, ὥστε διὰ φιλίαν μικρῶν καὶ ἐφημέρων ἡδονῶν
καὶ ἀγαθῶν ἀμφισβητησίμων καὶ ἀδήλων ἐλπίδων
καὶ ἀμφιβόλων εὐτυχημάτων μὴ ἀνασκευάσασθαι
μηδὲ ἀνοικίσαι αὐτὸν εἰς ὡμολογημένην εὐδαιμονίαν;
καὶ ταῦτα εἰδὼς ὅτι ἀπαλλάξεται πολλαπλασίων κακῶν, ἃ τῷ δευτέρῳ τρόπῳ καὶ βίῳ ἀναπεφυρμένα, πῶς
οὐ περιστατικὴν ποιεῖ κακοδαίμονά τε τὴν διαγωγὴν
τοῦ βίου καὶ σφόδρα ἀτυχῆ;

Ὥστε εἰκάσαιμ' ἂν ἔγωγε ἑκάτερον τῶν βίων, τὸν
μὲν γενναῖον τοῦτον καὶ παντοδαπὸν δεσμωτηρίῳ χα-
λεπῷ κακοδαιμόνων ἀνδρῶν καθειργμένων ἐν ἀφεγγεῖ
μυχῷ, πολὺν μὲν τοῖς ποσὶν σίδηρον περιβεβλη-
μένων, βαρὺν δὲ κλοιὸν περὶ τῷ αὐχένι, κἀκ ταῖν
χεροῖν ἐξηρτημένων δεσμὰ δυσχερῆ, ῥυπώντων καὶ
ἀγχομένων καὶ ῥηττομένων καὶ στενόντων· ὑπὸ δὲ
χρόνου καὶ ἔθους εὐημερίας τινὰς ἑαυτοῖς ἔνδον καὶ
εὐθυμίας μηχανωμένων, μεθυσκομένων ἐνίοτε ἐν τῷ
δεσμωτηρίῳ καὶ ᾀδόντων ἀναμὶξ καὶ γαστριζομένων
καὶ ἀφροδισιαζόντων, καὶ μηδὲ ἠρέμα ἑκάστου ἐμπιμ-
πλαμένων διὰ δέος καὶ ἀπιστίαν καὶ μνήμην τῶν
παρόντων κακῶν· ὥστε ἀκοῦσαι ἄν τις παραστὰς τῷ
δεσμωτηρίῳ οἰμωγῆς ὁμοῦ καὶ ᾠδῆς καὶ στόνου καὶ
παιᾶνος.

or change his ways and migrate to this other life that is peaceful, free from care, free from want,[8] and free from distress. Which of these men, then, abandons his way of life? Which one changes sides? Which one is willing to exchange his life for the other one?

4. What man is so senseless, so misguided in his desires, and so miserable, that for love of petty, ephemeral pleasures, goods of debatable worth, uncertain hopes, and dubious good fortune, he does not decamp and emigrate to indisputable happiness—and especially knowing that he will be free from many times as many evils that are implicated in the second way of life, and which unquestionably expose the conduct of its life to adverse circumstances, and make it miserable and exceedingly unhappy?

In view of this, I wish to depict each of these lives through an analogy, and first compare that so-called noble and complex life to a harsh prison, where miserable men are confined in a sunless cell, with large iron fetters around their ankles, heavy rings around their necks, and chafing shackles attached to their wrists, all filthy, choked, lacerated, and groaning. Through habituation over time, they have managed to contrive some forms of diversion and enjoyment for themselves in there, by occasionally getting drunk in their prison, singing random songs, gorging themselves, and engaging in sex, but with no one even slightly getting his fill because of fear, mistrust, and awareness of the ever-present ills, so that anyone visiting the prison would simultaneously hear wailing and singing, groaning and exultation.

8 Or, "free from fear": ἀδεής has both meanings in Maximus.

Τὸν δὲ ἕτερον αὖ βίον εἰκάζω ἀνδρὶ ἐν καθαρῷ
φωτὶ διαιτωμένῳ, λελυμένῳ τὼ πόδε καὶ τὼ χεῖρε καὶ
τὸν αὐχένα πανταχοῦ περιστρέφοντι, καὶ τὰς ὄψεις
πρὸς τὸν ἥλιον ἀνατείνοντι καὶ τοὺς ἀστέρας ὁρῶντι
καὶ διακρίνοντι νύκτα καὶ ἡμέραν, καὶ τὰς ὥρας τοῦ
ἔτους ἀναμένοντι καὶ τῶν ἀνέμων αἰσθανομένῳ καὶ
ἀέρα σπῶντι καθαρὸν καὶ ἐλεύθερον, ἀπεστερημένῳ
δὲ τῶν ἔνδον ἐκείνων ἡδονῶν ὁμοῦ τοῖς δεσμοῖς, μὴ
μεθυσκομένῳ, μηδὲ ἀφροδισιάζοντι, μὴ γαστριζο-
μένῳ, μὴ στένοντι, μὴ παιωνίζοντι, μὴ ᾄδοντι, μὴ
οἰμώζοντι, μὴ ἐμπιμπλαμένῳ, ἀλλ' ὅσον ἀποζῆν λε-
πτῷ καὶ διερρινημένῳ τὴν γαστέρα.

Τίνα τῶν εἰκόνων μακαρίσωμεν; τίνα οἰκτείρωμεν
τῶν βίων; τίνα ἑλώμεθα; τὸν ἐν τῷ δεσμωτηρίῳ, τὸν
μικτὸν ἐκεῖνον, τὸν ἀσαφῆ, πικραῖς καὶ ἐλεειναῖς ἡδοναῖς δελεασθέντα,

ἔνθα δ' ἄρ' οἰμωγή τε καὶ εὐχωλὴ πέλεν ἀνδρῶν,

ἡδομένων ὁμοῦ καὶ στενόντων;

5. Μὴ σύ γε, ὦ δειλαία ψυχή· ἀπολείπουσά μοι
ταυτασὶ τὰς εἰκόνας αὐτοῖς μύθοις, ἴθι ἐπ' ἄνδρα οὐ
κατὰ τὴν Κρόνου ἐκείνην ἀρχὴν βιοτεύσαντα, ἀλλ' ἐν
μέσῳ τῷ σιδηρῷ τούτῳ γένει, ἐλευθερωθέντα ὑπὸ τοῦ
Διὸς καὶ τοῦ Ἀπόλλωνος. ἦν δὲ οὗτος οὐκ Ἀττικὸς
οὐδὲ Δωριεύς, οὐκ ἐκ τῆς Σόλωνος τροφῆς οὐδ' ἐκ τῆς
Λυκούργου παιδαγωγίας (οὐ γὰρ χειροτονοῦσιν τὰς
ἀρετὰς οἱ τόποι οὐδὲ οἱ νόμοι), ἀλλὰ ἦν μὲν Σινωπεὺς
ἐκ τοῦ Πόντου· συμβουλευσάμενος δὲ τῷ Ἀπόλλωνι

But that other life I compare to a man living in clear daylight, with his feet and hands unbound, who can turn his neck in all directions, raise his eyes to the sun and see the stars, distinguish night from day, look forward to the seasons of the year, feel the breezes, and breathe in the clean air of freedom, having divested himself of those pleasures inside the prison along with their shackles, not getting drunk, nor having sex, nor gorging himself, nor groaning, nor exulting, nor singing, nor wailing, nor filling himself with any more than what he needs to live on with his slight and modest appetite.[9]

Which of these depictions are we to call happy? Which of these lives are we to pity? Which should we choose? Should it be the one in the prison, the life of confusion and darkness, ensnared in bitter and pitiful pleasures,

where arose wailing and men's shouts of triumph,[10]

simultaneously rejoicing and mourning?

5. Not you, my poor soul! You must leave behind these analogies and fables and turn to a man who did not live during the reign of Cronus but in the midst of this present race of iron, a man set free by Zeus and Apollo. He was neither an Athenian formed by Solon's upbringing nor a Dorian trained by Lycurgus' education (for neither places nor laws can legislate the virtues), but he hailed from Sinope on the Black Sea. After consulting with Apollo,[11] he

[9] For Diogenes' contentment with simple, natural fare, see Dio Chrys. *Or.* 6.12–14.

[10] *Il.* 4.450 (= 8.64), describing the sounds of battle.

[11] Apollo advised him "to alter the currency" ($\pi\alpha\rho\alpha\chi\alpha\rho\acute{\alpha}\xi\alpha\iota$ $\tau\grave{o}$ $\nu\acute{o}\mu\iota\sigma\mu\alpha$); see Diog. Laert. 6.20–21. For a full account of Diogenes' flaunting of societal norms, see Diog. Laert. 6.20–80.

τὰς περιστάσεις πάσας ἀπεδύσατο καὶ τῶν δεσμῶν
ἐξέλυσεν αὑτὸν καὶ περιῄει τὴν γῆν ἄφετος, ὄρνιθος
δίκην νοῦν ἔχοντος, οὐ τύραννον δεδιώς, οὐχ ὑπὸ
νόμου κατηναγκασμένος, οὐχ ὑπὸ πολιτείας ἀσχολούμενος, οὐχ ὑπὸ παιδοτροφίας ἀγχόμενος, οὐχ ὑπὸ
γάμου καθειργμένος, οὐχ ὑπὸ γεωργίας κατεχόμενος,
οὐχ ὑπὸ στρατείας ἐνοχλούμενος, οὐχ ὑπὸ ἐμπορίας
περιφερόμενος· ἀλλὰ τούτων ἁπάντων τῶν ἀνδρῶν
καὶ τῶν ἐπιτηδευμάτων κατεγέλα, ὥσπερ ἡμεῖς τῶν
σμικρῶν παίδων, ἐπειδὰν ὁρῶμεν αὐτοὺς περὶ ἀστρα-
γάλους σπουδάζοντας, τύπτοντας καὶ τυπτομένους,
ἀφαιροῦντας καὶ ἀφαιρουμένους· αὐτὸς δὲ βασιλέως
ἀφόβου καὶ ἐλευθέρου δίαιταν διαιτώμενος, οὐκ ἐπι-
τρίβων ἐν χειμῶνι Βαβυλωνίους οὐδὲ Μήδοις ἐνο-
χλῶν ὥρᾳ θέρους, ἀλλ' ἐκ τῆς Ἀττικῆς ἐπὶ τὸν
Ἰσθμὸν καὶ ἀπὸ τοῦ Ἰσθμοῦ ἐπὶ τὴν Ἀττικὴν αὖθις
ὁμοῦ ταῖς ὥραις μετανιστάμενος.

Βασίλεια δ' ἦν αὐτῷ τά τε ἱερὰ καὶ τὰ γυμνάσια
καὶ τὰ ἄλση, πλοῦτος δὲ ἀφθονώτατος καὶ ἀσφαλέ-
στατος καὶ ἀνεπιβούλευτος, γῆ τε πᾶσα καὶ οἱ ἐν
αὐτῇ καρποὶ καὶ κρῆναι γῆς ἔγγονοι, παντὸς Λεσβίου
καὶ Χίου πώματος δαψιλέστεραι· καὶ φίλος ἦν καὶ
συνήθης τῷ ἀέρι, ὥσπερ οἱ λέοντες, καὶ οὐκ ἀπεδί-
δρασκεν τὰς ὥρας τοῦ Διὸς οὐδὲ ἀντεμηχανᾶτο αὐτῷ,

---

[12] At *Or.* 32.9 Diogenes is said to have avoided marriage because he had heard about Socrates' difficult wife.

divested himself of all external circumstances, released himself from their shackles, and went carefree about the world like a bird endowed with intellect, unafraid of any tyrant, unconstrained by any law, untroubled by any government, unimpeded by raising children, unconfined by marriage,[12] unburdened by farming, undisturbed by military service, and not driven hither and yon on business. No, he laughed at all these men and their pursuits, as we would laugh at young children when we see them taking knucklebones seriously, punching each other and grabbing the pieces from one another. He lived the life of a king who was fearless and free, not spending winters in Babylon or burdening the Medes in summertime, but going back and forth between Attica and the Isthmus in keeping with the seasons.[13]

His palaces were the temples, gymnasia, and groves.[14] His wealth was the most abundant, most secure, and least subject to scheming, for it consisted of the whole earth and its fruits, together with the springs issuing from the earth in greater abundance than all the drink from Lesbos and Chios.[15] Just like the lions, he was a friend and companion of the open air, and never shunned the seasons of Zeus or

[13] Dio Chrys. *Or.* 6.1–6 provides a detailed contrast between the Persian king's long seasonal travels to escape harsh weather and Diogenes' short ones from Attica to the Isthmus of Corinth.

[14] Dio Chrys. *Or.* 6.14: "[Diogenes] also said that the most beautiful and healthful houses were open to him in every city: to wit, the temples and the gymnasia" (trans. J. W. Cohoon).

[15] Diogenes' preference for freely available water over hard-to-get wines from Lesbos and Chios is mentioned at Dio Chrys. *Or.* 6.13.

τοῦ μὲν χειμῶνος τεχνιτεύων θάλπος, τοῦ δὲ θέρους
ἀναψύχεσθαι ποθῶν· ἀλλ' οὕτως ἄρα ἐθὰς ἦν τῇ τοῦ
παντὸς φύσει, ὥστε ἐκ τοιαύτης διαίτης ὑγιεινός τε
ἦν καὶ ἰσχυρὸς καὶ κατεγήρα εἰς τὸ ἀκρότατον μηδὲν
φαρμάκων δεηθείς, μὴ σιδήρου, μὴ πυρός, μὴ Χείρω-
νος, μὴ Ἀσκληπιοῦ, μὴ Ἀσκληπιαδῶν, μὴ μάντεων
μαντευομένων, μὴ ἱερέων καθαιρόντων, μὴ γοήτων
ἐπᾳδόντων. πολεμουμένης δὲ τῆς Ἑλλάδος καὶ πάντων πᾶσιν ἐπιτιθεμένων,

οἳ πρὶν ἐπ' ἀλλήλοισι φέρον πολύδακρυν Ἄρηα,

ἐκεχειρίαν ἦγεν μόνος, ἐν ὡπλισμένοις ἄοπλος, ἐν
μαχομένοις ἔνσπονδος πᾶσιν. ἀπείχοντο δὲ αὐτοῦ καὶ
οἱ ἄδικοι καὶ οἱ τύραννοι καὶ οἱ συκοφάνται· ἤλεγχε
μὲν γὰρ τοὺς πονηρούς, ἀλλ' οὐ λόγων σοφίσμασιν,
ὅσπερ ἐλέγχων ἀνιαρότατος, ἀλλὰ ⟨ἔργα⟩[2] ἔργοις
παρατιθεὶς ἑκάστοτε, ὅσπερ ἐλέγχων ἀνυσιμώτατος
καὶ εἰρηνικώτατος· καὶ διὰ τοῦτο οὔτε Μέλητός τις ἐπὶ
Διογένην ἀνέστη οὔτε Ἀριστοφάνης, οὐκ Ἄνυτος, οὐ
Λύκων.

6. Πῶς οὖν οὐ προηγούμενος τῷ Διογένει ὁ βίος
οὗτος, ὃν ἑκὼν εἵλετο, ὃν Ἀπόλλων ἔδωκεν, ὃν ὁ Ζεὺς
ἐπῄνεσεν, ὃν οἱ νοῦν ἔχοντες θαυμάζουσιν; ἢ ἄλλο τι

[2] suppl. Stephanus, Dübner, Trapp, Koniaris

288

tried to outmaneuver the god by contriving warmth in winter, or by desiring to cool off in summer.[16] But in fact he was so attuned to universal nature, that his manner of living made him healthy, robust, extremely long-lived,[17] never in need of medications, surgery, cautery, or of Chiron, Asclepius, and the sons of Asclepius, or of the prophecies of prophets, the purifications of priests, or the incantations of enchanters.[18] And when Hellas was at war and everyone was attacking everyone else,

> who just now were waging tearful war against each
> other,[19]

he alone maintained an armistice, remaining unarmed in the midst of armed soldiers and enjoying a truce with all the fighters. And evildoers, tyrants, and informers stayed clear of him, for he did not refute wicked men by means of sophistic arguments, which is the most painful kind of refutation to endure, but he did so by contrasting his deeds with theirs on every occasion, which is the most effective and diplomatic kind of refutation, and is the reason why no Meletus, Aristophanes, Anytus, or Lycon ever rose up against Diogenes.

6. How then could this life of Diogenes, the one he willingly chose, which Apollo granted him, which Zeus approved, and which intelligent men admire, not be pre-

[16] Dio Chrys. *Or.* 6.8–11 describes Diogenes' life outdoors and his refusal to mitigate the effects of the seasons.

[17] He died at age ninety, according to Diog. Laert. 6.76.

[18] Dio Chrys. *Or.* 6.23–25 provides an almost identical list of cures.   [19] *Il.* 3.132, Iris disguised as Laodice to Helen about the Trojan and Greek armies.

ἡγούμεθα εἶναι τὴν περίστασιν ἢ χρῆσιν πράξεως
οὐκ αὐθαίρετον τῷ ἔχοντι; ἔρου δὴ τὸν γεγαμηκότα,
τίνος εἵνεκεν γαμεῖς; παίδων, φησίν· τὸν παιδοτρο-
φοῦντα, τίνος εἵνεκα ἐτεκνώσατο; διαδοχῆς ἐρᾷ· τὸν
στρατευόμενον, πλεονεξίας ἐρᾷ· τὸν γεωργοῦντα,
καρπῶν ἐρᾷ· τὸν χρηματιζόμενον, εὐπορίας ἐρᾷ· τὸν
πολιτευόμενον, τιμῆς ἐρᾷ.

Τῶν δὲ ἐρώτων τούτων οἱ πολλοὶ ἀμβλισκάνουσιν,
καὶ εἰς τοὐναντίον περιΐστανται, καὶ εὐχῆς ἔργον ἡ
ἐπιτυχία, οὐ γνώμης οὐδὲ τέχνης. ἕκαστος δὴ τῶν
ταῦτα αἱρουμένων περίστασίν τινα διαπεραίνεται τοῦ
βίου καὶ ταλαιπωρίας ἀνέχεται οὐχ ἑκουσίου οὐδὲ δι'
ἄγνοιαν τῶν αὐθαιρέτων ἀγαθῶν.

Τίνα γὰρ ἄν τις καὶ φαίη τούτων ἐλεύθερον; τὸν
δημαγωγόν; δοῦλον λέγεις πολλῶν δεσποτῶν· τὸν
ῥήτορα; δοῦλον λέγεις πικρῶν δικαστῶν· τὸν τύραννον; δοῦλον λέγεις ἀκολάστων ἡδονῶν· τὸν στρατηγόν; δοῦλον λέγεις ἀδήλου τύχης· τὸν πλέοντα; δοῦλον ἀσταθμήτου τέχνης· τὸν φιλόσοφον; ποῖον λέγεις;
ἐπαινῶ μὲν γὰρ καὶ Σωκράτην, ἀλλ' ἀκούω λέγοντος·
"πείθομαι τῷ νόμῳ καὶ ἑκὼν ἐπὶ τὸ δεσμωτήριον
ἄπειμι καὶ λαμβάνω τὸ φάρμακον ἑκών." ὦ Σώκρατες,
ὁρᾷς τί φῄς; ἑκών, ἢ πρὸς ἀκουσίους τύχας εὐπρεπῶς
ἵστασαι; πειθόμενος νόμῳ τίνι; εἰ μὲν γὰρ τῷ τοῦ

---

[20] As the following examples show, we aim for ends that are
subject to external circumstances, not ends chosen for themselves
and under our control.

ferred? Or are we to think that "external circumstance" is anything other than the performance of an action not freely chosen by the agent?[20] Then ask a husband, "Why do you get married?" "To have children," he replies. Ask someone raising children why he gave birth to them; he wants heirs. Ask the soldier; he desires profit. Ask the farmer; he desires crops. Ask the moneymaker; he desires prosperity. Ask the politician; he desires prestige.

Yet most of these desires end in miscarriages and result in the opposite of what was intended, since good luck depends on prayer, not on intelligence or expertise. Indeed, everyone who chooses these things goes through life exposed to some form of external circumstance and endures hardship that is not voluntary, nor caused by ignorance of goods that are freely chosen.[21]

So, which of these men might one say is free? You say the demagogue? He is the slave of many masters. The orator? He is the slave of harsh jurors. The tyrant? He is the slave of unbridled pleasures. The general? He is the slave of uncertain fortune. The sailor? He is the slave of an unreliable skill. The philosopher? Which one do you mean? I ask because I admire Socrates in particular, but I hear him saying, "I am obeying the law, and go willingly to prison, and willingly drink the poison." O Socrates, do you realize what you are saying? Are you really doing this willingly, or are you just behaving with dignity in the face of circumstances you would not have chosen? And what law are you obeying? If it is Zeus', then I approve its lawmaker,

[21] That is, goods that exist independently of circumstances.

Διός, ἐπαινῶ τὸν νομοθέτην· εἰ δὲ τῷ Σόλωνος, τί βελτίων ἦν Σόλων Σωκράτους; ἀποκρινάσθω μοι καὶ Πλάτων ὑπὲρ φιλοσοφίας, εἰ μηδεὶς αὐτὸν³ ἐπετάραξεν, μὴ Δίων φεύγων, μὴ Διονύσιος ἀπειλῶν, μὴ τὰ Σικελικὰ καὶ τὰ Ἰόνια πελάγη, ἄνω καὶ κάτω πρὸς ἀνάγκην διαπλεόμενα.

Κἂν ἐπὶ Ξενοφῶντα ἔλθω, βίον καὶ τοῦτον ὁρῶ μεστὸν πλάνης καὶ τύχης ἀμφιβόλου καὶ στρατιᾶς κατηναγκασμένης καὶ στρατηγίας ἀκουσίου καὶ φυγῆς εὐπρεποῦς. ταύτας τοίνυν φημὶ τὰς περιστάσεις διαφεύγειν ἐκεῖνον τὸν βίον, δι' ὃν καὶ Διογένης ὑψηλότερος ἦν καὶ Λυκούργου καὶ Σόλωνος καὶ Ἀρταξέρξου καὶ Ἀλεξάνδρου, καὶ ἐλευθερώτερος αὐτοῦ τοῦ Σωκράτους, οὐ δικαστηρίῳ ὑπαχθείς, οὐδὲ ἐν δεσμωτηρίῳ κείμενος, οὐδὲ ἐκ τῶν συμφορῶν ἐπαινούμενος.

³ αὐτὸν Heinsius, Dübner: αὐτὴν R

but if it is Solon's, how was Solon any greater than Socrates? I also want Plato to speak on behalf of philosophy, and to tell me whether nothing confounded him—not Dion's exile, nor Dionysius' threats, nor the Sicilian and Ionian seas that he was forced to traverse again and again.[22]

And if I turn to Xenophon, I see that his life too is full of wandering, dubious fortune, a campaign forced upon him, an unwilling generalship, and a retreat, albeit a dignified one. Such then are the external exigencies that I claim were avoided by his famous life that elevated Diogenes above Lycurgus, Solon, Artaxerxes,[23] and Alexander,[24] and made him more free than Socrates himself—for he was not hauled into court, confined in prison, or praised because of the misfortunes he faced.

[22] Plato's difficult dealings with Dion and Dionysius II of Syracuse, the subject of Pl. *Ep.* 7, are also cited at *Orr.* 15.9 and 34.9.

[23] Presumably, Artaxerxes II, whose luxurious life and first experience of thirst is described at *Or.* 34.6.

[24] Probably an allusion to the famous anecdote when Alexander asked Diogenes if he could do anything for him, and Diogenes asked him to stand aside and not block the sun, to which Alexander replied that if he were not Alexander he would be Diogenes. Cf. Plut. *Alex.* 14.

ORATION 37

INTRODUCTION

The importance of the liberal arts (τὰ ἐγκύκλια μαθήματα in the title), and especially of music and geometry, in pursuit of virtue and order within the state, was raised in numerous Platonic texts.[1] The oration opens by observing that in the *Republic* guardians were appointed to oversee training in music and gymnastics, while in the *Laws* music served to tame the citizens' passions and prepare them not only to withstand the rigors of war but also to quell any sedition in their souls (§1). Philosophy is not some trivial exercise in singing, playing instruments, or drawing geometric lines, but it seeks to secure obedience to law in the soul (§2). Philosophy is assisted by other arts in achieving proper order in a person, namely gymnastics, rhetoric, poetry, arithmetic, logic, geometry, and music (§3).[2] Setting aside the other arts, the speaker first takes up music and deplores its degeneration from the healthy, natural

---

[1] For example, music (*Resp.* 3.398c–403c and 4.424a–25a; *Leg.* Book 2, etc.); geometry (*Meno* 82b–85e). Discussions in the imperial period include Seneca, *Ep.* 88, and Philo, *De congressu eruditionis gratia*.

[2] Alcin. *Didasc.* 28.182.10–14 lists music, arithmetic, astronomy, geometry, and gymnastics.

music of yore, to its modern-day pandering to people's desire for pleasure. For example, the Dorians in Sicily abandoned their mountain music and became dissolute; the Athenians abandoned their rustic choruses and descended into civil disorder (§4). According to Pythagoras, the heavenly bodies produce a divine music that only the gods can hear. In the human realm, music and poetry temper the soul's passions and lead to political order (§5). The legends of Orpheus and Amphion moving trees and boulders with their lyre playing are allegories for music's ability to civilize human behavior and instill order in armies. The music of pipes led the Spartans in battle like a chorus; it aided the Athenians at Salamis (§6). Just as the ethical benefits of music are not appreciated by those seeking only entertainment, so geometry is only considered useful for surveying land and constructing things. Its true function, however, is to sharpen the soul's "vision" and allow it to contemplate the universe. Confining geometry to its practical applications is like sailing a ship only inside a harbor (§7). Athena, who built the first ship, says of geometry—also her contrivance—that it will convey a person up to the heavens and into the tranquil sea of reality, where contemplation is necessary if anyone is to achieve happiness (§8).

ORATION 37

Εἰ συμβάλλεται πρὸς ἀρετὴν τὰ ἐγκύκλια
μαθήματα

1. Σωκράτης ἐν Πειραεῖ διαλεγόμενος πολιτικοῖς ἀνδράσιν ἀναπλάττει τῷ λόγῳ, καθάπερ ἐν δράματι,
πόλεώς τε καὶ πολιτείας ἀγαθῆς εἰκόνα, καὶ τίθεται
νόμους καὶ παῖδας τρέφει καὶ φρουροὺς ⟨καθίστησι⟩[1]
τῇ πόλει, μουσικῇ καὶ γυμναστικῇ παραδοὺς τὰ τῶν
πολιτῶν σώματα καὶ τὰς ψυχάς, παραστήσας ἀμφοῖν
τοῖν μαθημάτοιν διδασκάλους ἀγαθούς, ἐκκρίτους,
ὥσπερ ἀγέλης ἡγεμόνας, φύλακας ὀνομάζων τοὺς
ἡγεμόνας, ὄναρ οὐχ ὕπαρ, ὡς δόξαι ἄν τινι τῶν
ἀγροικοτέρων, ξυνιστὰς πόλιν. ἀλλὰ γὰρ τῆς παλαιᾶς φιλοσοφίας ὁ τρόπος οὗτος ἦν, ἐοικὼς τοῖς
χρησμοῖς.

Εἰ δὲ βούλει, τὸν μὲν Σωκράτην ἐῶμεν· τὸν δὲ
Ἀθηναῖον παρακαλῶμεν ξένον ἀποκρίνασθαι ἡμῖν·
καὶ γὰρ αὖ καὶ τούτου ἀκούω ἐν Κρήτῃ διαλεγομένου
⟨ὑπὸ⟩[2] τοῦ Διὸς τοῦ Δικταίου τῷ ἄντρῳ Μεγίλλῳ τῷ

---

[1] suppl. Markland: lacunam stat. Trapp
[2] suppl. Russell: lacunam stat. Trapp

ORATION 37

Whether the liberal arts contribute
to virtue

1. When Socrates was conversing in the Piraeus with men interested in politics,[1] he fashioned in his dialogue, as in a drama, a representation of a good city with a good constitution. He made laws, educated the children, and established watchers over the city. He entrusted the bodies and souls of the citizens to the arts of music and gymnastics,[2] and appointed good instructors of both disciplines, who were carefully chosen, to act like leaders of a herd, and he called these leaders "guardians."[3] His creation of this city was theoretical, not actual, as some less sophisticated people might think, for such was the manner of early philosophy, one akin to oracular pronouncements.[4]

But with your permission, let us leave Socrates and summon instead the Athenian Stranger[5] to answer our questions. For I can hear him too conversing in Crete below the cave of Dictaean Zeus with Megillus from

---

[1] That is, in Plato's *Republic*.   [2] Pl. *Resp.* 2.376e: "gymnastics for the body and music for the soul."

[3] The education of the guardians begins at *Resp.* 2.374e.

[4] For the resemblance of philosophical tenets to oracles, see *Orr.* 11.6, 29.7, and 41.3.   [5] The interlocutor in Plato's *Laws*.

Λακεδαιμονίῳ καὶ Κλεινίᾳ τῷ Κνωσίῳ, πόλει Δωρικῇ
οἰκιζομένῃ τιθέντος νόμους, ἵνα πείθωνται τὸ Κρητῶν
γένος μουσικὴν εἰς τὰ τῆς ἀνδρείας ἐπιτηδεύματα
εἰσοικίσαι καὶ ἡμερῶσαι τὸν θυμὸν τῷ μέλει, ἵνα μὴ
κολοβὸς αὐτοῖς ἡ ἀρετὴ μηδὲ ἀτελὴς γίγνηται, πρὸς
τὸν μὲν ἔξω πόλεμον παρασκευάζουσα καρτερεῖν
καλῶς καὶ ἀνέχεσθαι πονουμένους καὶ ἀποθνήσκειν
μένοντας, πρὸς δὲ τὸν ἐν τῇ ψυχῇ τὸν στασιωτικὸν
μηδεμίαν παρασκευὴν πορισαμένη τοῖς αὑτῆς θρέμμασιν.

2. Πῶς τοῦτο λέγεις, ὦ ξένε Ἀττικέ; οὕτω τὸ ἀγαθὸν
ἡμῖν στενὸν καὶ γλίσχρον καὶ δύσληπτον καὶ ἄδηλον
καὶ πραγματείας πολλῆς ἐμπεπλησμένον, ὥστε οὐκ
ἂν αὐτοῦ τύχοιμεν ὅτι μὴ τερετίζοντες καὶ ψάλλοντες
καὶ τὰς ἐν γεωμετρίᾳ γραμμὰς ἄνω καὶ κάτω κατα-
γράφοντες καὶ τριβόμενοι ἐν τούτοις, ὥσπερ ἄλλο τι
ἐθέλοντες, ἀλλ' οὐκ ἄνθρωποι ἀγαθοὶ εἶναι, πρᾶγμα
κατὰ <μὲν>³ τὴν χρείαν ὑψηλὸν καὶ μέγα καὶ ἐγγύς
που τινὸς θείας⁴ ἀρετῆς, κατὰ δὲ τὴν κτῆσιν οὐ χαλεπὸν τῷ ἅπαξ ἐθελήσαντι εἶξαι τῷ καλῷ καὶ πρὸς τὰ
αἰσχρὰ ἀντιβλέψαι; ἀποκρίνεται ὁ Ἀθηναῖος ξένος
ὅτι καὶ πόλεως τὸ καλούμενον δὴ τοῦτο νόμος ἄνευ
πειθοῦς τῶν χρωμένων σύγγραμμά ἐστιν ἄλλως
κενόν· δεῖ δὴ αὐτῷ τοῦ δήμου πειθομένου ἑκόντος· ὁ
δὲ ἐν τῇ ψυχῇ δῆμος πολὺς καὶ ἔμπληκτος, ἀλλ' ἐπει-

³ suppl. Markland   ⁴ τινὸς θείας Davies²: τινὸς τῆς
χρείας R: τεῖνον τῆς θείας Koniaris: obel. Trapp

Sparta and Clinias from Cnossus, as he was making laws
for the founding of a Dorian city, so as to convince the
Cretans to introduce music into their cultivation of cour-
age, and to tame their passions with its melodies, thus
ensuring that their virtue would not be deficient or incomplete, if it prepared them to take a noble stand against an
external enemy, to endure physical hardship, and to die
standing their ground, but did not provide its trainees with
any preparation at all against the seditious elements within
their souls.[6]

2. What do you mean by this, Athenian Stranger? Is the
Good for us humans so narrow and petty, so obscure and
difficult to grasp, and fraught with so much study, that we
cannot attain it except by humming tunes and strumming
instruments, and by drawing geometric lines this way and
that, and by exhausting ourselves in these endeavors, as if
we were aiming at something other than becoming good
human beings, an achievement that when put into practice
is lofty, grand, and somewhat close to divine virtue,[7] and
not difficult for anyone to attain, once he is willing to yield
to what is good and face down what is shameful? The
Athenian Stranger replies that in the case of a city as well,
any so-called law without the obedience of its subjects is
an utterly useless regulation, for it must have the willing
obedience of the populace. Then too, the populace in the
soul is large and impulsive, but once it yields and consents

[6] See Pl. *Leg.* 1.626d–e for war within a person. The lengthy
discussion of music begins in *Leg.* 2.

[7] I have accepted Davies' conjecture of τινὸς θείας (divine)
for the corrupt τινὸς τῆς χρείας of manuscript R. For the relationship of divine and human virtue, see *Orr.* 35.2 and 38.5.

δὰν ἅπαξ εἴξας ὁμολογήσῃ τῷ νόμῳ καὶ ἕπηται ᾗ
αὐτὸς ἐπικελεύῃ, τοῦτο ἂν εἴη τὸ χρῆμα πολιτεία ψυχῆς ἡ ἀρίστη, ἣν καλοῦσιν οἱ ἄνθρωποι φιλοσοφίαν.
   3. Φέρε δή, νομοθέτου δίκην παρίτω φιλοσοφία,
ψυχὴν ἄτακτον καὶ πλανωμένην κοσμήσουσα καθάπερ δῆμον· παρακαλείτω δὲ ξυλλήπτορας ἐσομένας
αὐτῇ καὶ ἄλλας τέχνας, οὐ βαναύσους, μὰ Δία, οὐδὲ
χειρουργικάς, οὐδὲ οἵας συντελεῖν τὰ φαῦλα ἡμῖν·
ἀλλὰ τὴν μὲν τὸ σῶμα τῇ ψυχῇ παρασκευάσουσαν
ὄχημα εὐπειθὲς καὶ ἐρρωμένον τοῖς προστάγμασιν
ὑπηρετεῖν, γυμναστικὴν ταύτην ὀνομάζουσα, τὴν δὲ
ἄγγελον τῶν τῆς ψυχῆς διανοημάτων, ῥητορικὴν
ταύτην ὀνομάζουσα, τὴν δὲ

   ἀγαθὴν τιθήνην καὶ τροφὸν γνώμης νέας,

ποιητικὴν ταύτην ὀνομάζουσα, τὴν δὲ ἡγεμόνα τῆς
ἀριθμῶν φύσεως, ἀριθμητικὴν ταύτην ὀνομάζουσα,
τὴν δὲ καὶ λογισμῶν διδάσκαλον, λογιστικὴν ταύτην
ὀνομάζουσα, γεωμετρίαν δὲ καὶ μουσικήν, ξυνερίθω
τε καὶ ξυνίστορε φιλοσοφίας, τούτων νείμασα ἑκάστῃ
μέρος τοῦ πόνου.
   4. Καὶ περὶ μὲν τῶν λοιπῶν τάχα δὴ ἐξῆς διέξειμι·
νῦν δὲ δὴ μουσικῆς πέρι, τοῦ πρεσβυτάτου τῶν ἐν
ψυχῇ ἐπιτηδευμάτων, προχειρισάμενοι λέγωμεν τὰ
εἰκότα· ὡς ἔστιν καλὸν μὲν καὶ ἀνδρὶ ἑνὶ μουσική,
καλὸν δ' αὖ καὶ πόλει καὶ γένει ξύμπαντι, ᾧ τῶν θεῶν
μοῖρα μουσικὴν συνέβη ἐπιτηδευθῆναι. οὔτι τοι λέγω
τὴν δι' αὐλῶν καὶ ᾠδῆς καὶ χορῶν καὶ ψαλμάτων ἄνευ

to the law and follows wherever it commands, then the result will be the best constitution of the soul—one which men call philosophy.

3. So now let philosophy come forward like a lawmaker to bring order to a soul that is in disarray and adrift, just as it would for a populace. And let it summon other arts to assist it—not vulgar ones, by Zeus, nor manual ones, nor the kind that supply us with trivial things, but first of all the art that will prepare the body to be a vehicle for the soul, one that is obedient and vigorous in executing the soul's commands, the art that philosophy calls gymnastics; then the art that communicates the soul's thoughts, which philosophy calls rhetoric; then the art that is

a good nurse and nurturer of young minds,[8]

which it calls poetry; then the art that is the guide to the nature of numbers, which it calls arithmetic; then the art that is the teacher of reasoning, which it calls logic; and finally geometry and music, philosophy's two assistants and confidants, to each of which it has allotted a share in its overall task.

4. At some later time I may treat each of these other arts, but for now let us take up music, the most venerable of the practices in the soul, and give a proper account of it, showing how music is good not only for an individual person, but also for cities and entire nations that by divine dispensation happen to practice it. I am not talking here about the kind of music produced by pipe playing, singing,

---

[8] A verse from an unknown tragedy (fr. adesp. 305 *TrGF*).

λόγου ἐπὶ τὴν ψυχὴν ἰοῦσαν, τῷ τερπνῷ τῆς ἀκοῆς
τιμηθεῖσαν. ταύτην μὲν γὰρ ἔοικεν ἡ ἀνθρωπίνη ἀγα-
πήσασα πλημμέλεια, ἑπομένη τῷ ἡδεῖ φαινομένῳ,
νοθεῦσαι διὰ τοῦ ἔρωτος τούτου τὴν ἀκρίβειαν τῆς
μουσικῆς· τὸ γὰρ νῦν ἔχον ἐξίτηλος ἡμῖν γενομένη
οἴχεται, ἀποδυσαμένη τὸ αὑτῆς κάλλος, τὸ ὑγιὲς
ἐκεῖνο καὶ ἀρχαῖον, ἐξαπατῶσα ἡμᾶς καθαπερεὶ ἑταί-
ρας ἐπίχριστον οὐκ αὐτοφυὲς ἄνθος· καὶ εἰδώλῳ τινὶ
μουσικῆς ξυνόντες λανθάνομεν, αὐτὴν ἐκείνην τὴν
ἀληθῆ καὶ ἐκ τοῦ Ἑλικῶνος Μοῦσαν, τὴν Ὁμήρῳ
φίλην, τὴν Ἡσιόδου διδάσκαλον, τὴν Ὀρφέως μη-
τέρα, οὔτε ἔχοντες οὔτε εἰδότες.

Ἡ δὲ παρανομία, κατὰ σμικρὸν συμφορηθεῖσα
ἡμῖν, τὴν ψυχὴν εἰς τὸν ὄλισθον τοῦτον κατέσπασεν
καὶ ἰδίᾳ καὶ δημοσίᾳ· οὕτω Δωριεῖς μὲν οἱ ἐν Σικελίᾳ,
τὴν ὄρειον ἐκείνην καὶ ἀφελῆ μουσικὴν {οἴκοι}[5] καταλιπόντες ἣν ἐπὶ ἀγέλαις καὶ ποίμναις εἶχον, Συβαρι-
τικῶν αὐλημάτων ἐρασταὶ γενόμενοι καὶ ὄρχησιν
ἐπιτηδεύσαντες οἵαν ὁ αὐλὸς ἠνάγκαζεν Ἰώνων,
ἀφρονέστεροι μὲν τὸ εὐφημότατον, ἀκολαστότατοι δὲ
τὸ ἀληθέστατον ἐγένοντο· Ἀθηναίοις δὲ ἡ μὲν παλαιὰ
μοῦσα χοροὶ παίδων ἦσαν καὶ ἀνδρῶν, γῆς ἐργάται
κατὰ δήμους ἱστάμενοι, ἄρτι ⟨ἀπ'⟩[6] ἀμητοῦ καὶ
ἀρότου κεκονιμένοι, ᾄσματα ᾄδοντες αὐτοσχέδια· με-
ταπεσοῦσα δὲ ἡσυχῇ ἐπὶ τέχνην ἀκορέστου χάριτος

[5] del. Markland, Trapp
[6] suppl. Russell, Trapp

choruses, and string plucking, which comes to the soul with no rational content and is esteemed for delighting the ears. For it seems that discordant human nature has welcomed this kind of music in its pursuit of whatever seems pleasant, and has, through this passion, adulterated the purity of music. For as things stand now, this true music has faded away and disappeared from our midst. It has stripped off its proper beauty, that healthy, ancient beauty it had, and deceives us, like a courtesan's beauty that is not natural but merely applied. And without realizing it, we are now living with a mere semblance of music, and do not possess, or even recognize, that true Heliconian Muse,[9] who was Homer's friend, Hesiod's teacher, and Orpheus' mother.

This deviant form has gradually built up in us and has dragged our souls down a slippery slope in both our private and public lives. Thus it was that the Dorians in Sicily abandoned the simple mountain music they played while tending their herds and flocks, and fell in love with Sybaritic pipe playing, and took up the kind of dancing induced by the Ionian pipes, and thus became (to put it as politely as I can) less sensible, but (to tell the whole truth) utterly dissolute.[10] Then too, the ancient music for the Athenians consisted of choruses of boys and men, formed throughout their districts by farmers, still covered with dust from harvesting and plowing, singing impromptu songs. But when their music had gradually degenerated into an art that fed an insatiable appetite for entertainment on stage and in

---

[9] Calliope.   [10] The same example is cited at *Or*. 14.8. For the contrast between the "truly Greek" Dorian mode and the languid Ionian mode, see Pl. *La*. 188d and *Resp*. 3.398e.

ἐν σκηνῇ καὶ θεάτροις, ἀρχὴ τῆς περὶ πολιτείαν αὐτοῖς πλημμελείας ἐγένετο. ἡ δὲ ἀληθὴς ἁρμονία, ἣν ᾄδει μὲν ὁ μουσῶν χορός, ἐξάρχει δὲ αὐτῆς ὁ Ἀπόλλων ὁ μουσηγέτης, σῴζει μὲν ψυχὴν μίαν, σῴζει δὲ οἶκον, σῴζει πόλιν, σῴζει ναῦν, σῴζει στρατόπεδον.

5. Εἰ δὲ Πυθαγόρᾳ πειθόμεθα, ὥσπερ καὶ ἄξιον, καὶ μελῳδεῖ ὁ οὐρανός, οὐ κρουόμενος ὥσπερ λύρα, οὐδὲ ἐμπνεόμενος ὥσπερ αὐλός, ἀλλ᾽ ἡ περιφορὰ τῶν ἐν αὐτῷ δαιμονίων καὶ μουσικῶν σωμάτων, σύμμετρός τε οὖσα καὶ ἀντίρροπος, ἦχόν τινα ἀποτελεῖ δαιμόνιον· τῆς ᾠδῆς ταύτης τὸ κάλλος θεοῖς μὲν γνώριμον, ἡμῖν δὲ ἀναισθές, δι᾽ ὑπερβολὴν μὲν αὐτοῦ, ἔνδειαν δὲ ἡμετέραν. τοῦτό μοι δοκεῖ καὶ Ἡσίοδος αἰνίττεσθαι, Ἑλικῶνά τινα ὀνομάζων ζάθεον καὶ χοροὺς ἠγαθέους ἐν αὐτῷ, κορυφαῖον δὲ εἴτε Ἥλιον εἴτε Ἀπόλλωνα, εἴτε τι ἄλλο ὄνομα φανοτάτῳ καὶ μουσικῷ πυρί.

Ἡ δέ γε ἀνθρωπίνη καὶ περὶ τὴν ψυχὴν ἰοῦσα, τί ἂν εἴη ἄλλο ἢ παιδαγώγημα τῶν τῆς ψυχῆς παθημάτων, τὸ μὲν ἐξᾷττον αὐτῆς καὶ φερόμενον κατεπᾴδουσα, τὸ δὲ παρειμένον καὶ ἐκλελυμένον ἔμπαλιν ἐπαίρουσα καὶ παροξύνουσα; δεινὴ μὲν γὰρ ἐπελαφρῦναι οἶκτον, δεινὴ δὲ ἀμβλῦναι ὀργήν, δεινὴ δὲ ἐπισχεῖν θυμόν, ἀγαθὴ ἐπιθυμίαν σωφρονίσαι καὶ λύπην ἰάσασθαι καὶ ἔρωτα παραμυθήσασθαι καὶ συμφορὰν κουφίσαι, ἀγαθὴ καὶ ἐν θυσίαις παρα-

theaters, it marked the beginning of discord in their political life.[11] But the true harmony, which the chorus of the Muses sings, and which Apollo Musagetes directs, is what preserves an individual soul, a household, a city, a ship, and an army.

5. If we are to believe Pythagoras, as we should, the heavens too make music, though not plucked like a lyre or blown like a pipe. Instead, the revolutions of the divine and musical bodies in them, being symmetrical and balanced, produce a kind of divine sound.[12] The beauty of this song is known to the gods, but we humans cannot perceive it, because of divine superiority and our deficiency. This phenomenon, I believe, is what Hesiod alluded to, when he called a certain Helicon "most sacred"[13] and the choruses on it most holy—whether one calls their chorus leader Helios or Apollo, or gives some other name to that most radiant and harmonious fire.[14]

But when it comes to human music that revolves around the soul, what else can it be but a means of training the emotions of the soul, by soothing what is violent and impulsive in it, and conversely arousing and stimulating what is slack and weak? For music is skilled at lightening sorrow, blunting anger, and restraining passion, but is also good at curbing desire, healing pain, consoling lovesickness, and alleviating misfortune. It is a good attendant at sacrifices, a good companion at dinner, and a good com-

[11] For the degeneration of music and public life in Athens, see Pl. *Leg.* 3.700d–701b.   [12] The "music of the spheres" is briefly mentioned at Pl. *Resp.* 10.617b–c.   [13] Hes. *Theog.* 2.
[14] That is, the Sun (Helios), with which Apollo was commonly identified, as in *Orr.* 4.8 and 22.7.

στάτις καὶ ἐν δαιτὶ σύσσιτος καὶ ἐν πολέμῳ στρατηγός, δεινὴ δὲ καὶ ἐν ἑορταῖς εὐφρᾶναι καὶ ἐν Διονυ-
σίοις κωμάσαι καὶ ἐν τελεταῖς ἐπιθειάσαι, δεινὴ καὶ
πολιτείας ἦθος κεράσαι τῷ μέτρῳ· οὕτω Βοιωτοὺς
τοὺς ἀγροίκους αὐλὸς ἐπιτηδευόμενος ἡμέρωσεν καὶ
ποιητὴς Πίνδαρος συνῳδὸς τῷ αὐλῷ, καὶ Σπαρτιάτας
ἤγειρεν τὰ Τυρταίου ἔπη, καὶ Ἀργείους τὰ Τελεσίλ-
λης μέλη, καὶ Λεσβίους ἡ Ἀλκαίου ᾠδή· οὕτω καὶ
Ἀνακρέων Σαμίοις Πολυκράτην ἡμέρωσεν, κεράσας
τῇ τυραννίδι ἔρωτα Σμερδίου καὶ Κλεοβούλου κόμην
καὶ κάλλος⁷ Βαθύλλου καὶ ᾠδὴν Ἰωνικήν.

6. Τὰ δὲ τούτων ἀρχαιότερα ἔτι εἰ χρὴ λέγειν,
Ὀρφεὺς ἐκεῖνος ἦν μὲν Οἰάγρου παῖς καὶ Καλλιόπης
αὐτῆς, ἐγένετο δὲ ἐν Θρᾴκῃ ἐν τῷ Παγγαίῳ ὄρει·
νέμονται δὲ τοῦτο Θρᾳκῶν οἱ Ὀδρύσαι, ὄρειον γένος,
λῃσταὶ καὶ ἄξενοι· ἀλλ' εἵποντό γε Ὀδρύσαι ἑκόντες
ἡγεμόνι Ὀρφεῖ, καλῇ κηλούμενοι τῇ ᾠδῇ. τοῦτο ἄρα
δρῦς καὶ μελίας ἐλέγετο ἄγειν, εἰκαζόντων τὸ ἀγεννὲς
τοῦ τῶν κηλουμένων τρόπου ἀψύχοις σώμασιν.

Ἄλλος ἦν περὶ Βοιωτίαν κιθαριστὴς γενναῖος, οὐ
λίθους ὅδε, οἷον ὁ μῦθός φησιν, προσαγόμενος τῇ

---

⁷ κάλλος Markland: αὐλοὺς R: obel. Trapp, Koniaris

---

15 The Boeotians were formerly considered rustics (cf. e.g.,
"pigs" at Pind. *Ol.* 6.90 and fr. 83).

16 For ancient accounts of Telesilla (5th c. BC) and the mea-
ger fragments of her poetry, see Campbell, *Greek Lyric*, vol. 4
(LCL 461), 70–83.

mander in battle. It is skilled at providing merriment at festivals, revelry at the Dionysia, inspiration in the mysteries, and is also effective at tempering with its moderation the character of a state. Thus it was that pipe playing, and the odes that Pindar sang to its accompaniment, tamed the rustic Boeotians,[15] and the verses of Tyrtaeus roused the Spartiates, the lyrics of Telesilla roused the Argives,[16] and the songs of Alcaeus roused the Lesbians.[17] So too Anacreon tamed Polycrates to the benefit of the Samians, by tempering his tyranny with Smerdies' love, Cleobulus' hair, Bathyllus' beauty, and his Ionian song.[18]

6. If one needs to mention examples still more ancient than these, there was that famous Orpheus, the son of Oeagrus and of Calliope herself, who was born in Thrace on Mount Pangaeus, where the Thracian Odrysians lived, a mountain tribe of inhospitable bandits. Nonetheless, these Odrysians willingly followed Orpheus as their leader, when enchanted by his beautiful singing. Hence arose the legend that he could move oaks and ashes, because people compared the ignoble character of the men he enchanted to inanimate things.[19]

Another noble lyre player lived in Boeotia.[20] He did not really draw stones to himself with his artistry, as the story

[17] Alcaeus' political poems opposing the tyrants of Mytilene have not survived.

[18] For Anacreon's rivalry with Polycrates over Smerdies, see *Or.* 20.1; for his praise of these three boys, see *Or.* 18.9.

[19] For Orpheus leading oak trees with his lyre playing, cf. Ap. Rhod. *Argon.* 1.23–31.

[20] Amphion assembled boulders with his lyre playing to form the walls of Thebes; cf. Ap. Rhod., *Argon.* 1.735–41.

τέχνη (πῶς γὰρ ἂν γένοιτο ἐξ ᾠδῆς τεῖχος;), ἀλλ᾽ ὑπὸ
μέλει ἐμβατηρίῳ καὶ τακτικῷ συναγαγὼν εἰς φάλαγγα
τοὺς Βοιωτῶν νέους, τεῖχος ἄμαχον ταῖς Θήβαις περι-
έβαλλεν· οἷον τεῖχος καὶ Σπαρτιάταις ἐμηχανήσατο
Λυκοῦργος, ἐπιτάξας τοῖς νέοις αὐλὸν ἡγεμόνα ἐν
ταῖς μάχαις· οἱ δὲ ἐπείθοντο καὶ ἐπολέμουν ⟨ἐν⟩ χοροῦ νόμῳ. τοῦτον ἔχων καὶ Θεμιστοκλῆς τὸν αὐλὸν
εἰς τὰς ναῦς ἐνεβίβασεν τὰς Ἀθήνας, οἱ δὲ ὑπ᾽ αὐλῷ
οἱ μὲν ἤρεσσον, οἱ δὲ ἐμάχοντο, ἐνίκων δὲ ἄμφω, ξυν-
επήχουν δὲ καὶ αἱ θεαὶ τῷ χορῷ Ἐλευσινόθεν. ἐκεῖθεν
ἐπινίκια ἔστηκεν, ἐκεῖθεν τρόπαια Λακωνικὰ καὶ Ἀττικά, θαλάττια καὶ ἠπειρωτικά, μετ᾽ ἐπιγραμμάτων
καλῶν· τοῦτον τὸν χορὸν ἐνίκων μὲν Λακεδαιμόνιοι,
ἐδίδασκεν δὲ Λεωνίδης.

7. Καὶ τί δεῖ πλέω λέγειν, ἢ μουσικῆς πέρι ἀπομη-
κύνειν; ἀγαθὴ μὲν γὰρ εἰρήνης ξυνεργός, ἀγαθὴ δὲ
ἐν πολέμῳ παραστάτις, ἀγαθὴ δὲ ἐν πολιτείᾳ ξύνοι-
κος, ἀγαθὴ δὲ καὶ παίδων τροφός. ταχεῖα γὰρ τῶν
αἰσθήσεων ἡ ἀκοὴ καὶ ὀξέως ἐπὶ τὴν ψυχὴν τὰ γνω-
σθέντα ἀναπέμπουσα καὶ προσαναγκάζουσα συμ-
φθέγγεσθαι καὶ συνορμᾶν τοῖς αὑτῆς πάθεσιν. ὅθεν
ἄμουσοι ψυχαὶ καὶ ἐκμελεῖς, παντὶ τῷ ἡδεῖ φαινομένῳ
ἐνδιδοῦσαι, οὐδαμῶς ἄν ποτε γένοιντο μέτοχοι ὀρθοῦ

---

21 Perhaps a reference to the Sacred Band's impenetrable
phalanx, described in *Or.* 18.2.

22 In 480 BC, before the battle of Salamis.

goes, for how could singing build a wall? No, what he did do was surround Thebes with an impregnable wall, by using his tunes for marching and maneuvering to form the Boeotian youths into a phalanx.[21] Such too was the wall that Lycurgus contrived for the Spartiates, by stationing a pipe to command the young men in battle, who obeyed it and fought in the manner of a chorus. And Themistocles too took this same pipe with him when he embarked the people of Athens onto their ships.[22] At the pipe's direction some rowed, others fought, and both groups were victorious, while from Eleusis the goddesses also joined their voices with the chorus.[23] As a result, victory monuments were erected; as a result, trophies were set up in Laconia and Attica, proclaiming victories at sea and on land with their noble inscriptions. This was the choral competition won by the Lacedaemonians,[24] but it was Leonidas who trained their chorus.[25]

7. Why say more, or prolong our discussion of music? Music is a good coworker in peacetime, a good comrade in wartime, a good fellow citizen in a state, and a good nurse of children. For our sense of hearing is swift, and quickly conveys what it has apprehended to the soul, and compels it to resound and to move in concert with the sensations it transmits. That is why unmusical and discordant souls that surrender to whatever seems pleasant to them could never participate in proper melody. They call

[23] For the ritual cries, presumably of Demeter and Persephone, from Eleusis before the battle, see Hdt. 8.65.

[24] Presumably, at the Battle of Plataea in 479 BC.

[25] Leonidas set the example with his heroic stand at Thermopylae in 480 BC.

νόμου, μουσικὴν δὲ ὀνομάζουσιν τὴν αὐτῶν ἡδονὴν
δι᾽ ὁμοιότητα οὐ τοῦ τέλους, ἀλλὰ τῆς περὶ τὰ μέλη
πραγματείας· οἷον εἴ τις καὶ ἰατρικὴν καλοῖ τέχνην
ἀπεληλαμένην μὲν τοῦ ὑγιεινοῦ, περὶ δὲ τὰ αὐτὰ φάρμακα ἐξεταζομένην.

Οὕτως ἀμέλει καὶ γεωμετρίαν, τὸ γενναιότατον φιλοσοφίας μέρος, οἱ μὲν πολλοὶ φαῦλον καὶ ἐπὶ τῷ
φαύλῳ τέλει μέχρι τοῦ περὶ τὴν χρείαν ἀναγκαίου
δοκοῦντος προσίενται, διαμετρῆσαι γῆν καὶ ἀναστῆ-
σαι τειχίον, καὶ πᾶν ὅσον εἰς χειρουργίαν αὕτη συν-
τελεῖ δοκιμάζοντες, πρόσω δὲ οὐχ ὁρῶντες· ἡ δὲ οὐχ
οὕτως ἔχει—πολλοῦ γε καὶ δεῖ· οὐ γὰρ ἂν ᾠκεῖτο
χεῖρον ἡ γῆ, μὴ διαμετρουμένων αὐτὴν ἀκριβῶς
πενήτων γεωργῶν. ἀλλὰ τοῦτο μὲν εἴη ἂν {τι}[8] τῶν ἐν
γεωμετρίᾳ τὸ φαυλότατον· τὸ δ᾽ ἔργον αὐτό, ὥσπερ τι
ὀξυωπὲς τῆς διανοίας φάρμακον, ῥώμην αὐτῇ οὐκ
ἀγεννῆ παρασκευάζει πρὸς τὴν θέαν τῶν ὅλων. ἀθέα-
τοι δὲ οἱ πολλοὶ τῆς χρείας ταύτης, καθάπερ εἴ τις
ἠπειρώτης ἀνὴρ ναῦν ἰδὼν ἐν λιμένι, ἀγασθεὶς τοῦ
σοφίσματος ἔνδον τῇ νηῒ χρῷτο, πάντα κινῶν τὰ ὄργανα, τοῦτο οἰόμενος εἶναι τέλος τῆς νεώς.

8. Φαίη δ᾽ ἄν, οἶμαι, πρὸς αὐτὸν ἡ Ἀθηνᾶ, ἡ
εὑρέτις τοῦ ἔργου τούτου· "ὁρᾷς πέλαγος πλατὺ καὶ
ἄπειρον, κεχυμένον ὑπὲρ τῆς γῆς, συνάπτον αὐτῆς τὰ
τέρματα, ὧν πρόσθεν οὐδὲ ἀκοὴν εἴχετε οὐδὲ ἐλπίδα
τῆς θέας; ἑκάστῳ δὲ εἷς ἦν τόπος γνώριμος, ὥσπερ οἱ

[8] del. Reiske, Trapp

310

their own pleasure "music," not because music and pleasure have a similar purpose, but because they both involve melodies. It is like someone calling an art "medicine" that has nothing to do with health, but only proves to dispense the same drugs that medicine uses.[26]

In just the same way, most people consider geometry, the noblest part of philosophy, to be a trivial activity that leads to trivial ends, to the extent that its use seems necessary for surveying land and building a wall, and they also approve of everything it contributes to handicrafts, but they look no further. Yet that is not how geometry functions, in fact far from it! For the earth would be no less well inhabited, if needy farmers were not accurately surveying it into plots. No, such would constitute the most trivial use of geometry, whereas its proper function is to act like a drug that sharpens the vision of the mind and equips it with sufficient power to contemplate the whole universe.[27] Most people do not see this application, but act like some landlubber who sees a ship in a harbor, marvels at the contrivance, and puts the ship to use inside the harbor, operating all its tackle and thinking that this is the purpose of the ship.

8. I believe that Athena, the inventor of this creation,[28] would say to this person, "Do you see the broad and endless sea, which spreads over the earth and connects its distant destinations, which until now you have neither heard of, nor hoped to see? Each person used to know but

---

[26] That is, the art of an apothecary.   [27] For the power of geometry to turn the soul toward reality, cf. Pl. *Resp.* 7.526c–27c.

[28] For Athena's role in building the Argo, the "first ship," cf. Ap. Rhod. *Argon.* 1.18–19 and 526–27.

φωλεοὶ τοῖς ἑρπετοῖς· φιλία δὲ καὶ ἐπιμιξία καὶ κοι-
νωνία καὶ ἀμοιβὴ τῆς παρ' ἑκάστοις εὐπορίας, ἐκποδὼν ἦν ἕως ὑμῖν τὸ σόφισμα τοῦτο ἐμηχανησάμην
τὴν ναῦν. τοῦτό γε τὸ ὄχημα ἀράμενον ὄρνιθος δίκην
διαπτήσεται πανταχοῦ· εἰ δὲ ἀπιστεῖς, πείρᾳ μάθε."

Τοῦτο καὶ περὶ γεωμετρίας λέγει—τίς θεῶν; ἢ
ἐκείνη ἡ θεός, ἡ Ἀθηνᾶ λέγει· "ἐκεῖσε βλέψον· ὁρᾷς
τουτὶ τὸ ὑπὲρ κεφαλῆς θέαμα, τὸ καλόν, τὸ ποικίλον,
ἐληλαμένον περὶ γῆν ἐν κύκλῳ καὶ περὶ αὐτὴν ἑλιτ-
τόμενον, μεστὸν ἄστρων, ἥλιον φέρον, σελήνην ἔχον;
τοῦτο ὅ τι μέν ἐστιν οὐκ οἶσθα, δοκεῖς δὲ ὁρᾶν καὶ
εἰδέναι· ἀλλὰ ἐγώ σε, ὦ οὗτος, ἀνάξω κεῖσε ἠπειρώ-
την ὄντα, ὄχημά σοι πηξαμένη κοῦφον, παραδοῦσα
γεωμετρίᾳ· ἥ σε τὰ μὲν πρῶτα ἔνδον ἐν τῷ λιμένι
ὀχήσει, ἐθίζουσα ἀνέχεσθαι τῆς πορείας καὶ μὴ ἰλιγ-
γιᾶν πρὸς τὸ πέλαγος μηδὲ ἀποδειλιᾶν· {πρὸς τὸ
πέλαγος}[9] ἔπειτα ἀγαγοῦσα ἔξω τοῦ λιμένος εἰς καθαρὸν καὶ εὔδρομον τὸ τῶν ὄντων πέλαγος ἀνάξει,
κεῖσ' ,

> ὅθι τ' ἠοῦς ἠριγενείης
> οἰκία καὶ χοροί εἰσι καὶ ἀντολαὶ ἠελίοιο

καὶ σελήνης αὐγαὶ καὶ τῶν ἄλλων ἀκηράτων σωμάτων. ἕως δὲ ἀθέατος τούτων εἶ, μένεις εὐδαιμονίας
ἀμέτοχος, ἄμοιρος."

[9] omit. I, del. Trapp

one place, as reptiles know their lairs. Consequently, there was no opportunity for friendship, mingling with others, associations, or the exchange of each one's resources, until I created this contrivance for you called a ship. This conveyance will take off like a bird and fly everywhere,[29] and if you do not believe me, then give it a try and find out."

She says the same about geometry—and what goddess might that be? Why that same Athena, who says: "Look up there! Do you see this beautiful and varied spectacle above your head that encircles the earth and revolves around it, filled with stars, bearing the sun, and supporting the moon? You have no idea what it actually is, although you think you see and know it. But, O my landlubber friend, I shall take you up there. I shall build for you a light conveyance and will hand you over to geometry, which at first will convey you around the harbor to accustom you to tolerate the voyage without becoming dizzy or holding back in fear of the open sea. Then it will go forth from the harbor and take you up into the clear, tranquil sea of reality,[30] there

> where stands the home of early-rising Dawn
> and her dancing places, and the risings of the sun,[31]

and the rays of the moon and of the other uncorrupted bodies. But as long as you fail to behold these, you will remain without any share or portion of happiness."

[29] "Flying" alludes to the ship's use of sails.
[30] For the tranquil realm of truth, see *Orr.* 10.3 and 11.10.
[31] *Od.* 12.3–4, describing the location of Circe's island.

ORATION 38

INTRODUCTION

This oration complements the discussions in *Orr.* 27 ("Whether virtue is an art") and 34 ("That it is possible to benefit from adverse circumstances"), concerning the origin of virtue and the conditions that make it possible. *Or.* 27 argued that virtuous order in the soul comes through reason's control of the emotions; *Or.* 34 argued that adverse circumstances are necessary to test virtue. *Or.* 38 adds that divine help is needed to attain virtue,[1] not only by helping the soul to turn away from depravity to virtue but also by creating the hardships that make virtuous action possible.

The oration opens with three quotations from Homer illustrating the divine help given to Telemachus, Demodocus, and Phemius (§1). The examples of Hesiod and of Minos illustrate the divine origins of their particular skills (§2). The examples of Melesagoras, Epimenides, and Aris-

---

[1] At the end of the *Meno* (99e), Socrates tentatively concludes that "virtue is found to be neither natural nor taught, but is imparted to us by a divine dispensation" (trans. W. R. M. Lamb). The phrase "by divine dispensation" (θείᾳ μοίρᾳ) occurs five times in this oration and nowhere else in the corpus (though cf. *Or.* 37.4 τῶν θεῶν μοίρᾳ).

teas, who could not produce any teachers of their abilities, proved that their skills were due to divine dispensation (§3). Although Socrates valued knowledge and sought out teachers of various arts, he considered nature more fundamental to learning and implied that divinity played a role in his associations with young men. The question is then posed to Plato whether men can become good, that is virtuous, by divine dispensation and not just be good at some skill as in the aforementioned examples (§4). Reason itself answers that if these other skills are provided by divine inspiration, then *a fortiori* god would mete out virtue, which is more important than all of them (§5). Proof is offered that divinity,[2] in its perfection, self-sufficiency, and power, would dispense virtue. The question is how virtue comes to humans. It happens when a god helps to incline the good disposition of the soul toward virtue and away from depravity (§6). It was by divine dispensation that Odysseus was rescued on so many occasions by divinities, and also by divine dispensation that he was subjected to so many trials. It was Zeus himself who imposed the labors on his sons Heracles and Dionysus. Had Socrates relied on mere human skill, he would have adopted his father's trade of stonemason, but god determined that he take up virtue instead (§7).

---

[2] Divinity is variously rendered in this oration by *to theion*, *theos* and *to daimonion*.

ORATION 38

Εἰ γένοιτό τις θείᾳ μοίρᾳ ἀγαθός

1. Ὅμηρος μὲν πρὸς τὸν Τηλέμαχον διαλεγόμενος ἐν προσώπῳ Νέστορος οὑτωσὶ περὶ αὐτοῦ λέγει·

> οὐ γὰρ ὀίω
> οὔ σε θεῶν ἀέκητι γενέσθαι τε τραφέμεν τε·

ὁ δὲ αὐτὸς καὶ τοὺς ἀγαθοὺς ἅπαντας δίους καλεῖ, διότι ἦσαν, οἶμαι, οὐ κατὰ τέχνην ἀγαθοί, ἀλλὰ ἔργον Διός. ὑποπτεύω δὲ αὐτοῦ καὶ τὰ ἔπη ἃ περὶ τοῦ Δημοδόκου λέγει, ὅτι ἦν αὐτῷ πεποιημένα μὲν εἰς τὴν αὐτοῦ τύχην, ἀνακείμενα δὲ τῷ Δημοδόκῳ. ἔχει δὲ τὰ ἔπη ὧδέ πως·

> τὸν πέρι Μοῦσα φίλησε, δίδου δ᾽ ἀγαθόν τε
> κακόν τε·
> ὀφθαλμῶν μὲν ἄμερσε, δίδου δ᾽ ἡδεῖαν ἀοιδήν.

ἐγὼ δὲ αὐτῷ περὶ μὲν τῆς ᾠδῆς συντίθεμαι, περὶ δὲ

---

[1] *Od.* 3.27–28, actually spoken by Athena disguised as Mentor; it is correctly attributed at *Or.* 8.5.

316

ORATION 38

Whether one can become good by divine dispensation

1. When Homer speaks to Telemachus through the character of Nestor, he has this to say about him:

> for I do not think
> that you were born and raised without the care of the
> gods.[1]

The same poet also calls all his good characters "godlike," not, I think, because they were good through the exercise of skill, but through the work of Zeus.[2] I also suspect that the verses he speaks about Demodocus, although applied to Demodocus, were actually composed to refer to his own condition. They are as follows:

> The Muse loved him greatly, and gave him both good
> and evil:
> she took sight from his eyes, but gave him sweet
> song.[3]

I agree with Homer about his song, but disagree about his

---

[2] There is a play on "godlike" (δῖος) and "Zeus" (Διός). In a similar gambit, *Or.* 35.1 uses Homer's epithet of "godlike" to open its discussion of friendship.

[3] *Od.* 8.63–64.

τῆς συμφορᾶς οὐ συντίθεμαι· οὐ γὰρ μουσικὸν τὸ δῶρον. ἀπίθανος δὲ καὶ ὁ Δημόδοκος οὑτωσὶ περὶ αὑτοῦ λέγων·

αὐτοδίδακτος δ᾽ εἰμί, θεοὶ δέ μοι ὤπασαν ὀμφήν.

καὶ πῶς ἐσσί, ὦ βέλτιστε ἀοιδῶν, αὐτοδίδακτος, παρὰ θεῶν τὴν ὀμφὴν ἔχων, οἵπερ διδασκάλων ἀπται- στότατοι; ἀποκρίνεται ὁ Δημόδοκος ὅπερ ἂν τῶν πλουσίων οἱ πατρῷον λαβόντες κλῆρον πρὸς τοὺς χρηματιστὰς ἀποκρίναιντο, ὡς ἔστιν αὐτοῖς αὐτο- γενὴς ὁ πλοῦτος, οὐ παρ᾽ ἄλλων τέχνῃ καὶ πόνῳ συν- ενηνεγμένος.

2. Ἐπεὶ καὶ τὸν Ἡσίοδον τί οἰόμεθα, ποιμαίνοντα περὶ τὸν Ἑλικῶνα ἐν Βοιωτίᾳ, ᾀδούσαις ταῖς Μού- σαις ἐντυχόντα, ὀνειδισθέντα τῆς τέχνης τῆς ποιμε- νικῆς, παρ᾽ αὐτῶν λαβόντα δάφνης κλάδους, εὐθὺς ᾄδειν, γενόμενον ποιητὴν ἐκ ποιμένος, ὥσπερ φασὶν τοὺς κορυβαντιῶντας ἐπειδὰν ἀκούσωσιν αὐλοῦ ἐν- θουσιᾶν, τῶν προτέρων λογισμῶν ἐξισταμένους; πολ- λοῦ γε καὶ δεῖ. ἀλλὰ ᾐνίξατο, οἶμαι, ὁ Ἡσίοδος τὸ αὐτοφυὲς τῆς αὑτοῦ τέχνης, ἀναθέμενος αὑτοῦ τὴν αἰτίαν τῷ Μουσῶν χορῷ, ὥσπερ ἂν εἰ καὶ χαλκευτι- κὸς γενόμενός τις τέχνης ἄνευ ἀνετίθετο Ἡφαίστῳ φέρων τὸ αὐτόματον τῆς δημιουργίας. τί δὲ οἱ Κρῆτες; ἤ σοι οὐ δοκοῦσιν ὑπὸ βασιλεῖ τῷ Μίνῳ κοσμηθέντες

318

misfortune, because that is no gift a Muse would give. Demodocus too defies belief when he says of himself,

I am self-taught, and the gods gave me my voice.[4]

How can you, O best of singers, be self-taught, when you have received your voice from the gods, who are the most infallible teachers? Demodocus can only respond with the same answer that rich men who have inherited their fathers' fortunes might give to those who earn their own money, that their wealth is "self-made," rather than accumulated by the skill and hard work of others.

2. Then too, what about Hesiod?[5] Are we to believe that when he was tending his flock around Helicon in Boeotia and happened upon the Muses as they were singing, that they reproached him for plying his skill as a shepherd, and that when he accepted a laurel branch from them, he was transformed from a shepherd into a poet and immediately began to sing—just as they say that whenever Corybants[6] hear a pipe, they become possessed and abandon their former senses? Far from it! Instead, I believe that Hesiod alluded to the spontaneous origin of his own skill, when he attributed its cause to the chorus of the Muses, just as someone who has become a bronzesmith without technical training would attribute the spontaneous nature of his craftsmanship to Hephaestus. And what about the Cretans? Do you not think that because they had

---

[4] An adaptation of *Od*. 22.347–48, spoken, however, by Phemius the Ithacan bard. It is also quoted at *Or*. 10.5.

[5] The following account summarizes Hes. *Theog*. 22–34.

[6] Armed male dancers who worshipped Cybele. At Pl. *Ion* 534a, poets are compared to "Corybants out of their minds."

καλῶς, ἀγασθέντες τῆς ἀρετῆς, διδάσκαλον αὐτῷ ἐπιφημίσαι τὸν Δία· εἶναι μὲν αὐτόθι ἐν τῇ Ἴδῃ ἄντρον
Διός, φοιτῶντα δὲ τὸν Μίνω δι' ἐνάτου ἔτους, συγγι-
γνόμενον τῷ Διί, μανθάνειν παρ' αὐτοῦ τὰ πολιτικά.
οὗτοι Κρητῶν λόγοι.

3. Ἐγένετο καὶ Ἀθήνησιν ἀνὴρ Ἐλευσίνιος, ὄνομα
Μελησαγόρας· οὗτος οὐ τέχνην μαθών, ἀλλ' ἐκ νυμφῶν κάτοχος, θείᾳ μοίρᾳ σοφὸς ἦν καὶ μαντικός, ὡς
ὁ Ἀθηναίων λόγος. ἦλθεν Ἀθήναζε καὶ ἄλλος, Κρὴς
ἀνήρ, ὄνομα Ἐπιμενίδης· οὐδὲ οὗτος ἔσχεν εἰπεῖν
αὐτῷ διδάσκαλον, ἀλλ' ἦν μὲν δεινὸς τὰ θεῖα, ὥστε
τὴν Ἀθηναίων πόλιν κακουμένην λοιμῷ καὶ στάσει
διεσώσατο ἐκθυσάμενος· δεινὸς δὲ ἦν ταῦτα οὐ μαθών, ἀλλ' ὕπνον αὐτῷ διηγεῖτο μακρὸν καὶ ὄνειρον
διδάσκαλον.

Ἐγένετο καὶ ἐν Προκοννήσῳ ἀνὴρ φιλόσοφος,
ὄνομα Ἀριστέας· ἠπιστεῖτο δὲ αὐτῷ ἡ σοφία τὰ
πρῶτα, διότι μηδένα αὐτῆς διδάσκαλον προὔφερεν.
πρὸς οὖν δὴ τὴν τῶν ἀνθρώπων ἀπιστίαν ἐξεῦρεν λό-
γον· ἔφασκεν τὴν ψυχὴν αὐτῷ καταλιποῦσαν τὸ
σῶμα, ἀναπτᾶσαν εὐθὺ τοῦ αἰθέρος, περιπολῆσαι τὴν
γῆν τὴν Ἑλλάδα καὶ τὴν βάρβαρον καὶ νήσους πάσας καὶ ποταμοὺς καὶ ὄρη· γενέσθαι δὲ τῆς περιπο-
λήσεως αὐτῇ τέρμα τὴν Ὑπερβορέων γῆν· ἐποπτεύ-

---

7 Pl. *Leg.* 1.624b. Contrast *Or.* 6.7, where Minos is said to
have spent nine years with Zeus.

been well organized by King Minos and were in awe of his virtue, that they called Zeus his teacher, and claimed that there was a cave of Zeus there on Ida, which Minos visited "every ninth year"[7] to converse with Zeus and learn the art of politics from him? So say the Cretans.

3. There was also a man from Eleusis in Athens, whose name was Melesagoras.[8] As the Athenians tell it, he had been taught no skill, but his wisdom and prophetic ability resulted from divine dispensation, because he was inspired by Nymphs. And another man, a Cretan, came to Athens whose name was Epimenides. He too could not say who his teacher was, but was so skilled in divine matters, that by expiatory sacrifices he saved the city of Athens when it was afflicted with plague and civil strife. He was an expert at this without having been taught. Instead, he explained that a prolonged sleep and dream had instructed him.[9]

There was also a philosopher in Proconnesus whose name was Aristeas.[10] At first his wisdom was greeted with skepticism, because he could not produce any teacher of it. Therefore, to counter men's disbelief, he came up with an explanation. He said that his soul had left his body and had flown straight up into the ether, where it made a circuit of Greek and barbarian lands, along with all the islands, rivers, and mountains, and that the farthest limit of his soul's excursion was the land of the Hyperboreans. He

[8] Only Maximus mentions a prophet of this name.

[9] For an account of Epimenides' five-decades-long sleep and dream, see *Or.* 10.1.

[10] The travel of Aristeas' soul is mentioned at *Or.* 10.2.

σαι δὲ πάντα ἑξῆς νόμαια καὶ ἤθη πολιτικὰ καὶ
φύσεις χωρίων καὶ ἀέρων μεταβολὰς καὶ ἀναχύσεις
θαλάττης καὶ ποταμῶν ἐκβολάς· γενέσθαι δὲ αὐτῇ
καὶ τὴν τοῦ οὐρανοῦ θέαν πολὺ τῆς νέρθεν σαφε-
στέραν. καὶ ἦν πιθανώτερος λέγων ταῦτα ὁ Ἀριστέας
μᾶλλον ἢ Ἀναξαγόρας ἢ Ξενοφάνης ἐκεῖνος, ἤ τις
ἄλλος τῶν ἐξηγησαμένων τὰ ὄντα ὡς ἔχει· οὐ γάρ πω
σαφῶς ἠπίσταντο οἱ ἄνθρωποι τὴν ψυχῆς περιπόλη-
σιν, οὐδὲ οἷστισιν ὀφθαλμοῖς ἕκαστα ὁρᾷ, ἀλλὰ ἀτεχνῶς ἀποδημίας τινὸς ᾤοντο τῇ ψυχῇ δεῖν εἰ μέλλει
ὑπὲρ ἑκάστου φράσειν τὰ ἀληθέστατα.

4. Βούλει τοίνυν Ἀριστέαν μὲν καὶ Μελησαγόραν
καὶ Ἐπιμενίδην καὶ τὰ τῶν ποιητῶν αἰνίγματα τοῖς
μύθοις ἐῶμεν, ἐπὶ δὲ τοὺς φιλοσόφους τὴν γνώμην
τρέψωμεν, τουτουσὶ τοὺς ἐκ Λυκείου καὶ Ἀκαδημίας
τῆς καλῆς; οὐ γὰρ μυθολόγοι οὐδ᾽ αἰνιγματώδεις οὐδὲ
τερατείαν ἀσπαζόμενοι, ἀλλ᾽ ἐν δημοτικῇ λέξει τε καὶ
ἐν διανοίᾳ εἰθισμένῃ <. . .>[1] δὲ αὐτῶν τόν γε ἡγεμόνα
πρῶτον ὧδέ πως· ὅτι μὲν ἐπιστήμην τιμᾷς παντὸς
μᾶλλον, ὦ Σώκρατες, ἀκούομέν σου πολλάκις διατει-
νομένου, προξενοῦντος τοὺς νέους ἄλλον ἄλλῳ διδα-
σκάλῳ· ὅς γε καὶ εἰς Ἀσπασίας τῆς Μιλησίας παρα-

---

[1] lacunam stat. Reiske, Trapp

---

[11] A similar description of a soul's (Homer's) peregrinations is
at *Or.* 26.1.

said that it surveyed, without exception, all the customs, forms of governance, kinds of terrain, variations of climate, inundations of the sea, and outflows of rivers. He added that the view his soul had of the heavens was much clearer than any from down below on earth.[11] Aristeas was more convincing with this explanation than was Anaxagoras or that famous Xenophanes,[12] or anyone else who expounded on the nature of reality. For the people did not yet have a clear understanding of a soul's peregrinations, nor what kind of vision enabled it to see everything, but they simply believed that the soul had to make some kind of travel abroad, if it was to give the truest account of each thing.

4. So with your permission, may we now dismiss Aristeas, Melesagoras, Epimenides, and the poets' hidden meanings with their myths, and turn our attention to those philosophers who come from the Lyceum and the noble Academy?[13] For they do not narrate myths, or speak in riddles, or embrace miraculous tales, but ⟨employ⟩ ordinary language and familiar concepts. And first ⟨let us question⟩ their leader along these lines: We often hear you insisting, Socrates, that you value knowledge above all else, as you recommend a different teacher for each of the young men. Indeed, you urge Callias to send his son to visit Aspasia the Milesian, a man to a woman's house, and

[12] Anaxagoras was indicted for his scientific theories and went into exile from Athens. *Or.* 16.1–4 provides a fictive account of his inability to convince the Clazomenians that his philosophical endeavors were worthwhile. It is unclear why Xenophanes of Colophon (late 6th c. BC) is included.

[13] That is, Socrates (Lyceum) and Plato (Academy).

κελεύῃ Καλλίᾳ τὸν υἱὸν πέμπειν, εἰς γυναικὸς ἄνδρα,
καὶ αὐτὸς τηλικοῦτος ὢν παρ' ἐκείνην φοιτᾷς· καὶ
οὐδὲ αὕτη σοι ἀρκεῖ διδάσκαλος, ἀλλ' ἐρανίζῃ παρὰ
μὲν Διοτίμας τὰ ἐρωτικά, παρὰ δὲ Κόννου τὰ μου-
σικά, παρὰ δὲ Εὐήνου τὰ ποιητικά, παρὰ δὲ Ἰσχομά-
χου τὰ γεωργικά, παρὰ δὲ Θεοδώρου τὰ γεωμετρικά.
καὶ ταῦτα μέν σου τὰ εἴτε οὖν εἰρωνεύματα εἴτε καὶ
ἀνδρίσματα ἐπαινῶ, ὅπως ἄν τις αὐτῶν ἀποδέχηται.

Ἀλλ' ἐπειδὰν ἀκούω σου πρὸς Φαῖδρον διαλεγομένου ἢ Χαρμίδην ἢ Θεαίτητον ἢ Ἀλκιβιάδην, ὑποπτεύω σε μὴ πάντα ἐπιστήμῃ νέμειν, ἀλλ' ἡγεῖσθαι
τοῖς ἀνθρώποις πρεσβύτερον εἶναι διδάσκαλον τὴν
φύσιν· καὶ τοῦτο εἶναι ὅπερ οὑτωσὶ φαύλως ὑπεῖπάς
που ἐν τοῖς λόγοις, θείᾳ μοίρᾳ δεδόσθαι σοι πρὸς
Ἀλκιβιάδην ὁμιλίαν, καὶ πάλιν αὖ Φαῖδρον καλεῖς
τὴν θείαν κεφαλήν, καὶ περὶ Ἰσοκράτους που κατεμαν-
τεύσω ἐν τοῖς λόγοις νέου ὄντος κομιδῇ. τί ταῦτά σοι
ἐθέλει, ὦ Σώκρατες;

Εἰ βούλει, σὲ μὲν ἐῶ, τὸν δὲ ποιητὴν τῶν λόγων
τουτονὶ τὸν ἐξ Ἀκαδημίας φίλον μέτειμι· ὁ δ' ἡμῖν
δεομένοις μάλα ἀποκρινέσθω, εἰ καὶ θείᾳ μοίρᾳ γένοιντ' ἂν ἀγαθοὶ ἄνδρες, αὐτὸ τοῦτο, ἄνδρες ἀγαθοί·
οὐ ποιηταὶ λέγω, ἵνα μὴ προφέρῃς τὸν Ἡσίοδον, οὐδὲ

---

14 Cf. Pl. *Menex.* 235e–36b; Xen. *Mem.* 2.6.36 and *Oec.* 3.14.
15 Diotima (Pl. *Symp.* 201c–12a); Connus (Pl. *Euthd.* 272c–
d); Evenus (Pl. *Phd.* 60c–61c); Ischomachus (Xen. *Oec.* 15.5–
20.26); and Theodorus (Pl. *Tht.* 147d–48b).

you yourself, even at your age, go to study with her.[14] Yet
even she does not prove to be a sufficient teacher for you,
so you garner instruction on love from Diotima, on music
from Connus, on poetry from Evenus, on farming from
Ischomachus, and on geometry from Theodorus.[15] And I
applaud these efforts of yours, whether they are meant
ironically or sincerely, however anyone takes them.

But when I hear you conversing with Phaedrus, Charmides, Theaetetus, or Alcibiades, I suspect that you do not
attribute everything to learned knowledge, but that you
consider nature to be a more fundamental teacher for
humans. And this is what you suggested in passing somewhere in your conversations, when you said, "my association with Alcibiades was a gift of divine dispensation,"[16]
and then when you called Phaedrus "divine one,"[17] and
when, at one point in your conversation, you uttered a
prophecy about Isocrates, although he was very young at
the time.[18] What do you mean by this, Socrates?

If you are willing, I shall let you go and turn to that
friend of yours from the Academy who composed these
conversations,[19] and have him answer our pressing inquiry, whether by divine dispensation good men can become good men in the strict sense. I do not mean poets,
so do not put forward Hesiod; nor prophets, so do not

---

[16] Adapted from Aeschin. *Alc*. fr. 53, 5–6 [Giannantoni] =
Aristid. *Or*. 2.61: "But in fact my belief was that it was by divine
dispensation that I had been given the ability to do this for Alcibiades" (trans. Trapp). Cf. [Pl.] 1 *Alc*. 105e, where Socrates says
that god determined when he should converse with Alcibiades.

[17] Pl. *Phdr*. 234d (*tēs theias kephalēs*).

[18] Pl. *Phdr*. 278e–79b.   [19] That is, Plato.

μάντεις, ἵνα μὴ τὸν Μελησαγόραν λέγῃς, οὐδὲ καθάρ-
ται, ἵνα μὴ διηγήσῃ Ἐπιμενίδην· ἀλλὰ ἀφελὼν ἑκάστου τὸ τῆς τέχνης ὄνομα, τὴν ἀρετὴν προσθείς, ᾗ²
ἂν ἄνθρωποι ἀγαθοὶ τὰ ἀνθρώπων ἔργα, οἶκόν τε
οἰκονομεῖν δεξιῶς καὶ ἐν πόλει πολιτεύεσθαι καλῶς,
περὶ ταύτης φαθί, εἰ γένοιτ᾽ ἄν τινι ἄνευ τέχνης θεόσ-
δοτος. ἢ καὶ σὲ κατὰ χώραν ἐάσω, ἀποκρίνεται δὲ ὁ
λόγος αὐτὸς αὑτῷ, ὡς ἀνὴρ ἀνδρί, ἀπαυθαδιζόμενος
ὧδέ πως;

5. "Ὦ σχέτλιε, τί ταῦτα ληρεῖς, ὃς ἡγεῖ τὸ καλλιστεῦον τῶν ἀνθρωπίνων ἀγαθῶν παρὰ μὲν ἀνθρώπου
τέχνης τάχιστα ἥξειν, ἐκ δὲ θείας ἀρετῆς ἀπορώτατα;
καίτοι μαντικὴν καὶ τελεστικὴν καὶ ποιητικὴν καὶ
καθάρσεις καὶ χρησμῳδίας ξυλλήβδην ἅπαντα οὐκ
ἂν εἴποις ἀντάξια εἶναι τῆς ἀρετῆς· εἶτα ἐκεῖνα μὲν
ἡγῇ θείᾳ τινὶ ἐπινοίᾳ ψυχαῖς ἀνθρωπίναις ἀνακίρνα-
σθαι, τὸ δὲ τούτων σπανιώτερον, τὴν ἀρετήν, ἔργον
εἶναι τέχνης θνητῆς; ἢ πολλοῦ ἄξιον νομίζεις τὸ
θεῖον, πρὸς μὲν τὰ φαῦλα καλῶς καὶ ἀφθόνως παρ-
εσκευασμένον, πρὸς δὲ τὰ κρείττω ἄπορον.

"Οὔπω λέγω, ὡς εἴπερ ἐκείνων ἕκαστον τελεσιουρ-
γεῖται ὁ θεός, ἀνάγκη καὶ τὸ κρεῖττον· οὐ γάρ, ὥσπερ
ὁ χαλκευτικὸς οὐκ ἂν τέκτονα ἐκδιδάξαι, οὐδὲ ὥσπερ
ὁ γεωργὸς κυβερνητικῆς ἄπειρος καὶ ὁ κυβερνήτης

---

² ᾗ Markland, Dübner: καθ᾽ ἣν Scaliger: ἣν ἂν R: ἣν ἂν obel.
Koniaris

speak of Melesagoras; nor purifiers, so do not tell me about Epimenides. But take the name from each of their skills and substitute virtue, by means of which men may become good at human endeavors, namely at managing a household capably and engaging in civic affairs honorably,[20] and speak instead about this virtue and say whether anyone can receive it as a gift from the gods without recourse to expertise. Or should I let you go as well, and reason will answer for itself, frankly as man to man, in the following manner?

5. "You fool! Why are you spouting this nonsense? Do you really think that the finest of all human goods[21] can come to men immediately from human skill, but only with utmost difficulty from divine virtue? Yet you would not claim that the arts of divination, initiation, poetry, purification, and prophecy, even if all are taken together, are as valuable as virtue. Do you then believe that those arts are instilled in human souls by some divine inspiration, but that virtue, which is rarer than these, is the product of human expertise? Apparently you consider divinity to be greatly esteemed for providing trivial things readily and in abundance, but lacking the means to provide the more important ones.

"I say not, on the grounds that if god brings about each of those things, then he must also bring about the more important one, for god is not restricted to the confines of a single art. He is not like a bronzesmith who could not train a carpenter, or a farmer who knows nothing of navi-

---

[20] For the doublet of managing households and engaging in civic affairs, cf. Pl. *Prt.* 318e–19a and *Or.* 6.5: "households are well managed, the city is well governed." [21] That is, virtue.

ἰατρικῆς, ἄλλος ἄλλης ὁ μὲν ἔμπειρος τέχνης, ὁ δὲ
ἄπειρος τῆς αὐτῆς, οὕτως καὶ ὁ θεὸς ἐν περιγραφῇ
μένει τέχνης μιᾶς· ἀλλ' εἴπερ τι παρ' ἐκείνου ἔλθη,
πρὸς μὲν ἀνθρωπίνης ψυχῆς δύναμιν τέχνης ἂν εἴη
μέτρον, πρὸς δὲ θείας ἐπιστήμης παρασκευὴν μόριον
τοῦ ὅλου. ὅρα δὴ μή σοι θεός, ᾗ τὰ τοιαῦτα δύναται
κληρουχεῖν καὶ νέμειν, πολὺ τούτων πρότερον ἀρετὴν
νέμειν καὶ δύναιτο καὶ ἐθέλοι.

6. "Οὑτωσὶ δὲ αὐτὸ σκέψαι· τὸ θεῖον πάντως †που†[3]
τίθεσαι τελεώτατον καὶ αὐταρκέστατον καὶ ἰσχυρότα-
τον, ὡς εἴ τι ἀφέλοις, λυμανεῖ τῷ ὅλῳ. εἰ γὰρ μὴ
τέλεον, οὐκ αὔταρκες· εἰ δὲ οὐκ αὔταρκες, οὔπω τέλεον·
εἰ δὲ μή<τε>[4] αὔταρκες μήτε τέλεον, πῶς ἰσχυρόν;
αὔταρκες δὲ ὂν καὶ τέλεον καὶ ἰσχυρόν, κατὰ μὲν τὴν
τελεότητα τὰ ἀγαθὰ βούλεται, κατὰ δὲ τὴν αὐτάρ-
κειαν ἔχει, κατὰ δὲ τὴν ἰσχὺν δύναται. βουλόμενος δὲ
δὴ καὶ ἔχων καὶ δυνάμενος, κατὰ τί μὴ δῷ; ὁ μὲν γὰρ
ἔχων οὐ διδούς, οὐ βούλεται· ὁ δὲ βουλόμενος οὐκ
ἔχων, οὐ δύναται· ὁ δὲ ἔχων καὶ βουλόμενος, πῶς οὐ
δύναται; οὐκοῦν εἴπερ ἔχει τἀγαθά, τὰ τελεώτατα
ἔχει, τελεώτατον δὲ ἡ ἀρετή· δίδωσιν τοίνυν ὃ ἔχει·
ὥστε οὐ δέος μὴ ἄλλο τι ἀγαθὸν εἰς ἀνθρώπους ἔλθη,
μὴ παρὰ θεοῦ ὁρμηθέν.

3 obel. Koniaris: ποι R: που Trapp: πῃ Dübner
4 suppl. Markland, Trapp

22 For divine perfection, cf. Pl. *Resp.* 2.381b–c and Alcin.
Didasc. 10.164.31–33.

gation, or a helmsman who knows nothing of medicine, and so on, with one person knowledgeable in one art and another person ignorant of it. But if anything does come from god, then with respect to the capabilities of the human soul, it would constitute a discrete measure of expertise, but with respect to the resources of divine knowledge, it would constitute but a part of the whole. So, consider whether god, insofar as he is capable of dispensing and distributing such things as these, would much sooner be able and willing to distribute virtue than any of them.

6. "Consider the issue in this way. You surely believe that divinity is in every way entirely perfect,[22] self-sufficient, and powerful, such that if you remove anything at all, you will damage the whole. For if divinity is not perfect, then it is not self-sufficient; and if it is not self-sufficient, then it is by no means perfect. If divinity is neither self-sufficient nor perfect, then how could it be powerful? But since it is self-sufficient, perfect, and powerful, then in terms of its perfection it wishes good things; in terms of its self-sufficiency it possesses them; and in terms of its strength it has the power to give them. If then it has the will, the resources, and the power, what would prevent it from giving them? He who possesses them but does not give them, wishes not to do so. He who wishes to give them but does not possess them, lacks the power to do so. But he who both possesses them and wishes to give them, how can he not do so? Therefore, if he possesses good things, he possesses the most perfect things, and the most perfect thing is virtue. Consequently, he gives what is in his possession, so there can be no fear that any other good comes to humans except what originates from god.

"Ἀλλὰ μὴν ⟨εἰ⟩⁵ οὐδέν ἐστιν ἄλλο ἀνθρώποις ἀγαθόν, ὃ μὴ παρὰ θεῶν ἔρχεται, τίν' οὖν τρόπον ἀρετὴ
παρὰ θεοῦ ἔρχεται; πέφυκεν τὸ ἀνθρώπινον πᾶν ἐξ
ἀρχῆς δίχα, τὸ μὲν εἰς ἀρετῆς ἐπιτηδειότητα, τὸ δὲ
εἰς μοχθηρίας· ὧν ἡ μὲν μοχθηρία ἐνδεὴς τοῦ κολάζοντος, ἡ δὲ ἀρετὴ τοῦ σώζοντος. μοχθηρὰ μὲν γὰρ
φύσις τυχοῦσα ἐπιστάτου χρηστοῦ, νόμου καὶ ἔθους,
τὸ ἄλυπον τῷ πλησίον περιεβάλετο καὶ πλεονεκτεῖ
οὐκ ἐν μοίρᾳ ἀγαθῶν, ἀλλ' ἐν ἐλαττώσει βλάβης· αἱ
δὲ ἄρισται ψυχῆς φύσεις ἀμφισβητήσιμοι, ἐν μεθορίᾳ τῆς ἄκρας ἀρετῆς πρὸς τὴν ἐσχάτην μοχθηρίαν
καθωρμισμένοι, δέονται ξυναγωνιστοῦ θεοῦ καὶ ξυλ-
λήπτορος τῆς ἐπὶ θάτερα τὰ κρείττω ῥοπῆς καὶ χει-
ραγωγίας. ὁ μὲν γὰρ ἐπὶ τὰ αἰσχρὰ ὄλισθος αὐτοφυοῦς ἀσθενείας ἔργον, ἣ καὶ τὰς ἐπιεικεῖς ψυχὰς
κολακεύουσα διὰ ἡδονῶν καὶ ἐπιθυμημάτων εἰς τὰς
αὐτὰς ὁδοὺς ταῖς μοχθηραῖς συγκαθέλκει.

7. "Ἀκούσῃ γοῦν τοῦ Διὸς αὐτοῦ λέγοντος,

ὦ πόποι, οἷον δή νυ θεοὺς βροτοὶ αἰτιόωνται·
ἐξ ἡμέων γάρ φασι κακ' ἔμμεναι· οἱ δὲ καὶ αὐτοὶ
σφῆσιν ἀτασθαλίῃσιν ὑπὲρ μόρον ἄλγε' ἔχουσιν.

⁵ suppl. Reiske, Dübner, Trapp

"But if there is no other good for men that does not come from the gods, then in what way does virtue come from god? From its very beginning, the entire human race has a dual nature, having on the one hand a predisposition for virtue, and on the other for depravity.[23] Of these two, depravity needs something to restrain it, while virtue needs something to safeguard it. For when depraved nature finds a good overseer in the form of law and custom, it secures freedom from distress for its neighboring part,[24] and what it gains is no share of goodness, but instead a reduction of harm. On the other hand, the best natural dispositions of the soul are fought over, being situated in the middle ground between the utmost virtue and extreme depravity, and they need a god as a comrade in arms and a helper to incline them to the better side and lead them there. For the proclivity to shameful things is the result of innate weakness, which entices even good and reasonable souls with pleasures and desires, and drags them down the same paths that depraved souls take.

7. "You will certainly hear Zeus himself saying,[25]

O my, how mortals blame the gods,
for they say that evils come from us, but they
    themselves
by their own misdeeds suffer pains beyond what is
    fated.[26]

[23] For this dual disposition of the human soul, see *Orr.* 27.5, 34.4, and 41.5.
[24] That is, for the good disposition of the soul.
[25] That is, when speaking about depraved men.
[26] *Od.* 1.32–34, also quoted at *Or.* 41.4.

περὶ δὲ τῶν ἀγαθῶν ἀνθρώπων οὐκ ἀκούσῃ τοιοῦτον
οὐδὲν λέγοντος, οὐδὲ ἀπωθουμένου τὴν αἰτίαν, οὐδὲ
ἀποτιθεμένου τὴν φροντίδα, ἀλλ᾽ αὐτὸ τοὐναντίον·

πῶς ἂν ἔπειτ᾽ Ὀδυσῆος ἐγὼ θείοιο λαθοίμην,
οὗ πέρι μὲν πρόφρων κραδίη καὶ θυμὸς ἀγήνωρ
ἐν πάντεσσι πόνοισι, φιλεῖ δέ ἑ Πάλλας Ἀθήνη;

τίς οὖν οὐκ ἂν εἴποι τὸν Ὀδυσσέα ἀγαθὸν εἶναι θείᾳ
μοίρᾳ, οὗ μέμνηται μὲν ὁ Ζεύς, κήδεται δὲ ἡ Ἀθηνᾶ,
ἡγεῖται δὲ ὁ Ἑρμῆς, ἔραται δὲ Καλυψώ, σῴζει δὲ ἡ
Λευκοθέα; εἰ δὲ ἀγαθὸς ἦν, ὥσπερ ἦν, διότι

πολλῶν δ᾽ ἀνθρώπων ἴδεν ἄστεα καὶ νόον ἔγνω

καὶ

πολλὰ δ᾽ ὅγ᾽ ἐν πόντῳ πάθεν ἄλγεα ὃν κατὰ
θυμόν,

πῶς οὐ θείᾳ μοίρᾳ αὐτῷ συνηνέχθη τὰ γυμνάσια, ἀφ᾽
ὧν ἀγαθὸς καὶ ἦν καὶ ἔδοξεν, περιστήσαντος αὐτῷ
τοῦ δαιμονίου ἀνταγωνιστὰς πολλούς, τῶν μὲν βαρβάρων τὸ Τρωϊκόν, τοῦ δὲ Ἑλληνικοῦ τοὺς ἀρίστους
Παλαμήδη καὶ Αἴαντα, τῶν δὲ οἴκοι τοὺς ἰσχυρο-
τάτους καὶ ἀκολαστοτάτους, Κυκλώπων τὸν ἀγριώτα-
τον, Θρᾳκῶν τοὺς ἀξενωτάτους, φαρμακίδων τὴν δει-

---

27 *Il.* 10.243–45, spoken by Diomedes, not Zeus.
28 He gives him moly on Circe's island; cf. *Orr.* 26.9 and 29.6.
29 She buoys him up at sea; cf. *Orr.* 11.10, 22.1, and 26.9.

But you will not hear him saying any such thing about good men, nor disavowing their blame, nor abandoning his concern for them, but just the opposite:

> Then how could I forget godlike Odysseus,
> whose heart and proud spirit are zealous beyond all
>   others
> in all kinds of trials, and Pallas Athena loves him?[27]

Who then would deny that Odysseus was good by divine dispensation, when Zeus remembers him, Athena cares for him, Hermes guides him,[28] Calypso loves him, and Leucothea saves him?[29] If he was good, as indeed he was, because

> he saw the cities of many men and learned their ways,

and because

> in his heart he suffered many pains on the sea,[30]

then how could these physical trials, through which he proved his goodness and gained his reputation, not have been amassed against him by divine dispensation, when divinity surrounded him with so many adversaries? From the barbarians there was the Trojan army, from the Greek camp there were the champions Palamedes and Ajax,[31] and at home there were the most powerful and dissolute men;[32] there was the most savage Cyclops, the most inhospitable Thracians,[33] the most dangerous witch,[34] and the

---

[30] *Od.* 1.3–4, also quoted at *Or.* 41.4.

[31] Odysseus' rivalries with Palamedes and Ajax were the subject of the *Cypria* and many tragedies.

[32] The suitors.   [33] The Ciconians.   [34] Circe.

νοτάτην, θηρίων τὴν πολυκεφαλωτάτην, θάλατταν
πολλήν, χειμῶνα χαλεπόν, συνεχῆ ναυάγια, προσ-
αναγκάσαντος ἀλᾶσθαι καὶ πτωχεύειν, ῥάκη ἀμπι-
σχόμενον καὶ μετὰ ταῦτα αἰτοῦντα ἀκόλους, παλαί-
οντα, λακτιζόμενον, παροινούμενον; ὧν ἕκαστον αὐτῷ
διὰ φιλίαν θεὸς προὔβαλλεν, οὐχ ὁ Ποσειδῶν ὀργι-
ζόμενος,

ὅτι οἱ υἱὸν φίλον ἐξαλάωσεν,

οὐδὲ ὁ Ἥλιος μηνιῶν τῶν βοῶν (μὴ τοσαύτη μήτε
Ποσειδῶνα ἔχοι φιλία πρὸς ἄνθρωπον ἄγριον καὶ
παῖδα ἄξενον, μήτε τὸν Ἥλιον πτωχεία καὶ φειδὼ
βοῶν)· ἀλλὰ γὰρ τοῦ Διὸς ταῦτα ἦν τὰ προστάγ-
ματα.

"Ἦ γὰρ οὐχ οὗτός ἐστιν ὁ καὶ τὸν Ἡρακλέα τὸν
αὑτοῦ παῖδα μὴ ἐάσας ἀργὸν καὶ τρυφῶντα, ἀλλὰ
ἐξελκύσας τῶν ἡδονῶν, καὶ εἰς μὲν ἐκείνας τὸν Εὐρυ-
σθέα ἐμβαλών, τῷ δὲ Ἡρακλεῖ ἐπιστήσας κάπρους
καὶ λέοντας καὶ δυνάστας καὶ τυράννους καὶ λῃστὰς
καὶ ὁδοὺς μακρὰς καὶ γῆν ἔρημον καὶ ποταμοὺς
ἀπόρους; ἢ νύκτα μὲν ἠδύνατο ποιῆσαι ὁ Ζεὺς τρι-
πλῆν ἐκ μιᾶς, ὃν δὲ ἐν τῇ νυκτὶ ταύτῃ ἐποιήσατο, τῶν
{δὲ}[6] τοῦ βίου πόνων οὐκ ἠδύνατο ἐξελέσθαι; ἀλλ' οὐκ
ἤθελεν· οὐ γὰρ θέμις Διὶ βούλεσθαι ἄλλο τι ἢ τὸ

6 del. Trapp

beast with the most heads,[35] as well as the vast sea, harsh storms, and frequent shipwrecks, while divinity compelled him to be a vagabond and a beggar, to put on rags and then beg for pieces of bread, to wrestle,[36] and be kicked and maltreated by drunkards. But it was out of affection that god subjected him to each of these trials. It was not Poseidon, angry with him

because he had blinded his dear son,[37]

nor Helios enraged because of his cattle[38] (may Poseidon never have such affection for a savage man and murderous son, or Helios be so needy and thrifty with his cattle!) No, these were the commands of Zeus.

"And was it not he who also did not allow his own son Heracles to live an idle and pampered life? Did he not tear him away from pleasures by inserting Eurystheus into their midst,[39] and thus pit Heracles against boars, lions, rulers, tyrants, bandits, long journeys, deserts, and impassable rivers? Or was Zeus able to turn one night into three,[40] but unable to rescue the son he fathered on that night from his lifelong labors? No, he did not wish to do so, because it is not right for Zeus to will anything other

---

[35] Scylla.   [36] Actually, box (with Irus the beggar).

[37] *Od.* 11.103 (slightly adapted). Poseidon's son is Polyphemus the Cyclops.

[38] For Helios' anger, see *Od.* 12.374–88.

[39] Zeus allowed Eurystheus to impose Heracles' incessant labors, thus keeping him away from pleasures.

[40] A reference to Heracles Triesperus (he of the three nights), when Zeus prolonged the night in which he impregnated Alcmene; cf. Apollod. 2.4.8.

κάλλιστον. οὕτως ἦν καὶ ὁ Ἡρακλῆς ἀγαθὸς καὶ Διόνυσος καὶ ὁ Ὀδυσσεύς. καὶ ἵνα μὴ πόρρω σε ἀπάγω
τῶν ἐν ποσίν, τὸν Σωκράτην αὐτὸν οἴει γενέσθαι
τέχνῃ ἀγαθόν, ἀλλ' οὐ θείᾳ μοίρᾳ; ἢ κατὰ μὲν τὴν
τέχνην ἐγένετο ἂν λιθοξόος, παῖς παρὰ πατρὸς λαβὼν τὸν κλῆρον, κατὰ δὲ τὴν τοῦ θεοῦ χειροτονίαν
τὴν μὲν τέχνην διώσατο, τὴν δὲ ἀρετὴν ἐλάμβανεν;"

than what is best. This is how Heracles, Dionysus,[41] and Odysseus became good. And so as not to take you too far from the case at hand, do you think that Socrates himself became good through skill and not by divine dispensation? Or rather is it that as a matter of skill he would have become a stonecutter by inheriting his father's trade,[42] but that by the god's choosing he rejected his skill, and took up virtue instead?"

[41] Dionysus traveled far and wide and faced much opposition in spreading his worship. He is similarly paired with Heracles in *Or.* 32.7.

[42] His father, Sophroniscus, was a stonemason (or sculptor); cf. Diog. Laert. 2.18 and *Or.* 39.5.

ORATION 39

INTRODUCTION

This is the first of a pair of orations debating whether there is a hierarchy of goods or only one Good. It adopts a Stoicizing position that only the Good (*to agathon*) exists, which is indivisible and cannot be augmented or diminished. It opens by rejecting Homer's criticism of Glaucus for exchanging his gold armor for Diomedes' bronze armor, because the exchange was made for the sake of friendship, thus making the material values irrelevant. So it is that business transactions are based on changing values, whereas the Good is stable and does not change (§1). The unity of the Good is analogous to the balance of health, to the harmony of a chorus, to the unified rowing on a trireme, and to the unity of an army (§2). When the good of these enterprises is disrupted, they break down into conflicting elements. Then again, there are many stages of a journey, but only the destination matters. Life is like a journey, whose destination is an initiation into the Good. The way is extremely difficult, and only very hardy souls can reach it (§3).[1] Such so-called goods as health, wealth, beauty, and honors are valued on the basis of plea-

[1] This example will be countered in *Or.* 40.4, where the stages have value by encouraging the traveler to press on.

sure, not on the basis of good things, and pursuing them is to sin against the divine and profane the initiation into the Good. As in the case of the road to the Good, where it is the destination that is truly good, not the places on the way, the heavens surpass all the lower parts of the universe and have a size and beauty that cannot be altered (§4). It is because of human weakness that the unity of the divine is mistakenly divided up into various named deities with specific spheres of activity, analogous to our naming different segments of the one sea. Likewise, the Good is one single, consistent thing. Who would prefer such "goods" as the wealth of Callias, the beauty of Alcibiades, the esteem of Pericles, or the reputation of Nicias to the goodness of Socrates, who was ugly, lowborn, disreputable, condemned, and executed? Apollo certainly cast his vote for Socrates (§5).

ORATION 39

Εἰ ἔστιν ἀγαθὸν ἀγαθοῦ μεῖζον·
ἐν ᾧ ὅτι οὐκ ἔστιν

1. Οὐδὲ τοῦ Ὁμήρου ἔγωγε ἀποδέχομαι τῷ Λυκίῳ
Γλαύκῳ μεμφομένου, ἀμείβοντι ὅπλα χρυσᾶ πρὸς τὰ
τοῦ Διομήδους χαλκᾶ ὄντα καὶ ἐννεάβοια ἑκατομ-
βοίων ἀλλαττομένῳ. χρηματιστὴς γὰρ ἂν τοῦτό γε
αἰτιάσαιτο ἐν δίκῃ,

ἀρχὸς ναυτάων οἵ τε πρηκτῆρες ἔασιν,
φόρτου τε μνήμων . . .
κερδέων θ' ἁρπαλέων,

μή τί γε ἀνὴρ ποιητικὸς καὶ ἀξιῶν μαθητὴς εἶναι τῆς
Καλλιόπης, ᾗ μηδὲν θέμις μήτε ἐπαινεῖν τῶν αἰ-
σχρῶν, μήτε ψέγειν τῶν καλῶν. εἰκὸς δέ που τὸν
Γλαῦκον, εἴπερ ἦν Ἱππολόχου τοῦ Βελλεροφόντου τοῦ
Σισύφου τοῦ Αἰόλου, ἀγαθῶν ἁπάντων, ἐντυχόντα ἀν-

---

[1] Cf. *Il.* 6.119–236. Homer's "reproach" is at 6.234: "Zeus took
away Glaucus' wits." This episode is also discussed at *Orr.* 32.5,
35.3, and 40.1.

ORATION 39

Whether there exists one good greater than another.
That there does not

1. Even though it is Homer, I for one cannot accept his reproach of Lycian Glaucus for exchanging his gold armor for Diomedes' bronze armor and accepting what was worth nine oxen for what was worth a hundred.[1] To be sure, a businessman might well find fault with such a transaction, and rightly so, if he is

a captain of sailors who are merchants,
with his mind set on his cargo . . .
and his greedy profits,[2]

but certainly not a poet who claims to be a student of Calliope,[3] for she is not permitted to praise anything shameful or blame anything good. It was perfectly reasonable for Glaucus (since he was the son of Hippolochus, son of Bellerophon, son of Sisyphus, and son of Aeolus, all good

[2] *Od.* 8.162–64, spoken sarcastically by Euryalus the Phaeacian to taunt Odysseus.

[3] Homer never mentions Calliope, who only later became associated with epic poetry. Pl. *Phdr.* 259d associates Calliope (and Urania) with philosophy. She is also cited as Homer's Muse at *Orr.* 1.2, 26.1, 32.8, and 40.6.

341

δρὶ ἐχθρῷ δοκοῦντι κατὰ τὴν τοῦ πολέμου τύχην,
φίλῳ δὲ κατὰ τὴν τῶν πατέρων ξενίαν, ξυμβαλλόμε-
νον φιλίαν αὖθις καὶ ἀνακαλούμενον τὴν προγενῆ
οἰκειότητα, συμμετρήσασθαι τῷ καιρῷ καὶ μὴ τῇ
ἀξίᾳ τῶν ὅπλων τὴν ἀλλαγήν, μὴ λογισμοὺς συν-
τιθέντα χρυσοῦ καὶ χαλκοῦ καθάπερ οἱ ἐκ Λήμνου
οἰνιζόμενοι,

ἄλλοι μὲν χαλκῷ, ἄλλοι δ᾽ αἴθωνι σιδήρῳ
ἄλλοι δὲ ῥινοῖς, ἄλλοι δ᾽ αὐτοῖσι βόεσσι.

Μέχρι μὲν γὰρ τῆς χρείας τῆς ἐν ποσὶν ἔχει λογισμοὺς ἡ ἀντίδοσις, καὶ τὸ πλέον πρὸς τοὔλαττον τῷ
ἀντιστασίῳ ἐν τοῖς ἀνομοίοις κατὰ τὴν τιμὴν ἐξετά-
ζεται· κἂν ἐγκεκαλυμμένος γοῦν τις γνοίη ὅτι τὸ
τάλαντον τῶν δέκα μνῶν πολλαπλάσιον καὶ ἡ δραχμὴ
τοῦ ὀβολοῦ τιμαλφεστέρα· καὶ ἐν κτήσει γῆς {καὶ}[1]
κατὰ τὸν Ἡρόδοτον οἱ μὲν γεωπεῖναι ὀργυίαις διαμε-
τροῦνται τὴν γῆν, οἱ δὲ τούτων ἀμφιλαφέστεροι στα-
δίοις, οἱ δὲ τούτων πολὺ γεωργικώτεροι σχοίνοις,
καθάπερ οἱ Αἰγύπτιοι· καὶ ἐν κτήσει θρεμμάτων πο-
λυκτεανώτερος τοῦ Πολυφήμου ἦν ὁ Δάρδανος,

τοῦ τρισχίλιοι ἵπποι ἕλος κάτα βουκολέοντο.

[1] del. Reiske, Trapp, Koniaris

---

[4] Glaucus' genealogy is detailed at *Il.* 6.152–211.
[5] *Il.* 7.473–74.   [6] A talent is worth sixty minas; a drachma
is worth six obols.

men),[4] when encountering a man who seemed to be his enemy because they happened to meet in battle, but who was actually a friend because of their forefathers' hospitality, to renew their friendship and revive their forefathers' intimacy, and thus to assess the value of the exchange by the occasion, not by the worth of the armor, and not calculate the value of gold and bronze, like men purchasing wine from Lemnos,

> some for bronze, some for gleaming iron,
> some for hides, and some for live cattle.[5]

For as far as everyday business goes, exchanges are subject to calculations, and when they involve goods of dissimilar value, "more" and "less" is determined by the market price of each. And obviously, even someone with his eyes covered would know that a talent is worth many times more than ten minas, and that a drachma is worth more than an obol.[6] Then too, when it comes to land ownership, Herodotus reports[7] that poor farmers measure their land in arm spans, those with larger estates in stades,[8] while far more successful farmers measure theirs in schoeni,[9] as the Egyptians do. And in ownership of livestock, Dardanus possessed many more animals than Polyphemus, for

> his three thousand mares pastured in the
>   marshland.[10]

[7] Hdt. 2.6.2.
[8] Approximately two hundred meters.
[9] Long lengths of rope used to measure miles.
[10] *Il.* 20.221.

343

Ἀλλ' ἐπειδάν τις τὰς χρείας παρωσάμενος ἀντεξε-
τάζῃ αὐταῖς τὰ ἀγαθά, εὕροι ἄν, οἶμαι, ταύτας μὲν
καιρῷ καὶ νόμῳ καὶ ἡδοναῖς καὶ ἔθεσιν καὶ τύχαις,
ἄνω καὶ κάτω εἰς τιμὴν καὶ ἀτιμίαν μεταβαλλομένας,
τὸ δὲ ἀγαθὸν ἑδραῖον, βέβαιον, ἀκλινές, ἰσόρροπον,
κοινόν, ἀνέμητον, ἄφθονον, ἀνενδεές, μήτε αὔξησιν
χωροῦν μήτε ἐνδείας ἀνεχόμενον. τό τε γὰρ αὐξόμε-
νον προσθήκῃ αὔξεται· ἀλλ' εἰ μὲν ἀγαθὸν ἀγαθῷ
προσελήλυθεν, οὐδὲν μᾶλλον τῇ προσθήκῃ νόει ἀγαθὸν τὸ ἀγαθόν, ἦν γὰρ ἀγαθὸν καὶ πρότερον· εἰ δὲ
οὐκ ἀγαθὸν ἦν τὸ προσελθὸν εἰς αὔξησιν, δεινὸν λέγεις εἰ ἔσται τι ἀγαθὸν μεῖζον προσθήκῃ κακοῦ· τό
τε ἐνδεὲς ἐλλείψει ἐνδεές· ἀλλ' εἰ μὲν τοῦ ἀγαθοῦ
ἀπουσίᾳ ἐνδεῖ τὸ ἀγαθόν, <οὐκ ἦν ἀγαθὸν>[2] ὁπότε
ἐνδεῖ· εἰ δὲ ἑτέρῳ ἐνδεῖ καὶ μὴ τῷ ἀγαθῷ, οὐ λυπεῖ
τὸ ἀγαθὸν ἡ ἔλλειψις.

2. Τί δὲ οὐχὶ καὶ ταύτῃ σκοπεῖς τὸ λεγόμενον;
καλεῖς τι ὑγείαν σώματος (τί δὲ οὐ μέλλεις;), καλεῖς
δὲ καὶ νόσον; φέρε οὖν διαλαβὼν ἑκάτερον φαθί. οὐχ
ἡ μὲν ὑγεία μέτρον τί ἐστιν τῆς τῶν σωμάτων εὐαρ-
μοστίας, ἐπειδὰν ὁμολογήσῃ τῇ πρὸς τὸ ἄριστον
κράσει τἀναντία, πρὸς ὕδωρ πῦρ καὶ γῆ πρὸς ἀέρα
καὶ ἑκάτερον αὖθις αὖ πρὸς ἑκάτερον, καὶ πάντα πᾶ-

---

[2] suppl. Scaliger, edd.

---

[11] This elaborates a Stoic formulation. Cf. Diog. Laert. 7.101:
"They [Hecaton and Chrysippus] hold that all goods are equal

344

But when someone sets aside business transactions and instead makes good things the basis of comparison, he will find, I think, that the former change their value up and down as circumstances, laws, pleasures, customs, and chance dictate, whereas the Good is stable, steadfast, unwavering, constant, accessible to everyone, indivisible, abundant, lacking nothing, and leaving no room for increase or tolerating any deficiency.[11] For in general, anything that increases does so because of some addition, but if good is added to good, do not think that the good becomes any more good because of the addition, since it was good before. But if what is added to increase it was not good itself, then it is preposterous for you to claim that something will become a greater good by the addition of anything evil. In general, anything deficient lacks something, but if the good is deficient because good is absent, then it was not good when it was deficient. But if it lacks something other than the good, then the lack does not impair its goodness.

2. Why not view the argument in the following way as well? Is there something you call bodily health? Of course. And something you call sickness? Well then, take each one in turn and tell me this. Is not health a certain due measure of concord in bodies, when the opposing elements consent to form the best possible mixture, fire with water, earth with air, and everything else with everything else

and that all good is desirable in the highest degree and admits of no lowering or heightening of intensity" (trans. R. D. Hicks). Similar attributes of the Good (*to agathon*) are cited at *Or*. 29.7. See also Pl. *Phlb*. 20c–d, where the Good is said to be perfect (*teleon*) and sufficient (*hikanon*).

MAXIMUS OF TYRE

σιν; ἔστιν οὖν ὅπως ποικίλον τι σοὶ ἡ ὑγεία ἔσται καὶ
παντοδαπόν, οὐχὶ δὲ ἁπλοῦν καὶ ὁμολογημένον; ἐπειδὰν γὰρ μέτρον εἴπῃς, στάσιν λέγεις· οὐδὲν γὰρ τῶν
συμμέτρων μεταχωρεῖν φιλεῖ ἐφ᾽ ἑκάτερα, ἀλλ᾽ εἰσὶν
αὐτῶν ἀκριβεῖς οἱ ὅροι.

Ἡ δ᾽ αὖ νόσος τί ἄλλο ἐστὶν ἢ διάλυσις καὶ τα-
ραχὴ τῆς ἐν σώματι ἐκεχειρίας, ἐπειδὰν αὖθις συμ-
πεσόντα ἀλλήλοις τὰ τέως ἡρμοσμένα πολεμῇ καὶ
ταράττῃ, καὶ λυμαίνηται ὑπ᾽ αὐτῶν τὸ σῶμα κλονού-
μενόν τε καὶ σπαραττόμενον καὶ σειόμενον; ἔστιν οὖν
ὅπως τὸν πόλεμον τοῦτον ἡγήσῃ ἁπλοῦν καὶ ἕνα; ὀλί-
γου μέντ᾽ ἂν ἦν ἡ ἰατρικὴ ἀξία. νῦν δὲ τὸ πολυμερὲς
καὶ πολύφωνον τοῦ τῶν σωμάτων πολέμου, ἃς καλοῦμεν νόσους, ἐγέννησεν τέχνην παντοδαπὴν καὶ μεστὴν ὀργάνων ποικίλων καὶ πολλῶν φαρμάκων καὶ
σιτίων καὶ διαιτημάτων.

Κἂν ἐπὶ μουσικὴν ἔλθῃς, τὸ μὲν ἡρμοσμένον κἀνταῦθα ἕν, οὔτε κρεῖττον αὐτὸ αὐτοῦ γιγνόμενον οὔτε
ἔλαττον· τὸ δὲ ἀνάρμοστον πολὺ καὶ παντοδαπὸν καὶ
διῃρημένον. οὕτω καὶ χορὸς ὁμολογήσας μὲν εἰς ὁμο-
φωνίᾳ· μὴ ὁμολογῶν δέ, σχίζεται καὶ διαχεῖται καὶ
σκεδάννυται καὶ πλῆθος γίγνεται. οὕτω καὶ τριήρης
ἐρεσσομένη ὑπ᾽ αὐλῷ τὴν πολυχειρίαν συνάπτει τῇ
ὁμοιότητι τῆς εἰρεσίας· ἐὰν δὲ ἀπαλλάξῃς τὸν αὐλόν,
διέλυσας αὐτῆς τὴν χειρουργίαν. οὕτω καὶ ὑφ᾽ ἡνιόχῳ
ἅρμα εὐθύνεται κοινῷ δρόμῳ καὶ θυμῷ ἑνί· ἐὰν δὲ
ἀφέλῃς τὸν ἡνίοχον, ἐσκέδασας τὸ ἅρμα. οὕτω καὶ
στρατόπεδον συντάττεται ὑπὸ συνθήματι ἑνί· ἐὰν δὲ

and all with all? Can you then possibly consider health to be something varied and diverse, rather than simple and stable? I ask because when you speak of due measure you imply stability, for nothing that attains due measure tends to move one way or the other, because its boundaries are sharply defined.

And as for disease, what else is it but a dissolution and disturbance of the truce within the body, when the elements that were previously in harmony once again attack one another, make war, cause mayhem, and wreck the body as it is stricken, riven, and shaken by them? Can you then possibly think that this war is something simple and single? If that were so, the practice of medicine would be of little value.[12] But in reality, the complex war of competing voices in our bodies that we call disease, has produced an art that is multifaceted and replete with intricate instruments and many different medicines, diets, and regimens.[13]

And if you turn to music, here too harmony is a single entity and becomes neither more or less than itself, whereas disharmony is multiple, varied, and divided up. Similarly, a chorus in agreement is a single harmonious whole, whereas one without agreement splits up, disperses, scatters, and becomes a multitude. So too, a trireme being rowed in time to a pipe combines the many hands of its crew into unified rowing, but if you remove the pipe, then you break up the work of their hands. Similarly, under the guidance of a charioteer, a chariot is driven straight on a common course with a single impetus,

[12] Because it would find a simple cure.   [13] The complexity of medicine is also described at *Orr.* 4.2 and 28.1.

ἀφέλῃς τὸ σύνθημα, διέλυσας τὴν φάλαγγα εἰς πλήθους φυγήν.

3. Τί τοίνυν ἀγαθὸν σωμάτων; ὑγίεια· κακόν; νόσος.
ἓν μὲν ἡ ὑγίεια, πολλαὶ δὲ αἱ νόσοι. τί ἐν μουσικῇ τὸ
ἀγαθόν; ἁρμονία· ⟨κακόν; ἀναρμοστία·⟩[3] ἓν μὲν τὸ
ἡρμοσμένον, πολλὴ δὲ ἡ ἀναρμοστία. καὶ ἐν χορῷ ἓν
μὲν ἡ ὁμολογία, παντοδαπὸν δὲ ἡ διαφωνία· καὶ ἐν
τριήρει ὁ μὲν αὐλὸς ἕν, πολλὴ δὲ ἡ ἀπείθεια· καὶ ἐν
ἅρματι ἡνιόχου τέχνη, ἓν μὲν τοῦτο, παντοδαπὸν δὲ
ἡ ἀτεχνία. τί δὲ ἐν φάλαγγι φυλακὴ συνθήματος; ἓν
μὲν τοῦτο, παντοδαπὴ δὲ ἡ ἀναρχία. ἐν μὲν οὖν τῇ
τοῦ ἑνὸς φύσει ὑπερβολὰς καὶ ἐνδείας οὐχ ὁρῶ· στάσιμος γὰρ αὕτη καὶ μηδένα ἀνεχομένη δρόμον μήτε
εἰς φυγὴν μήτε εἰς δίωξιν.

Ὅταν δὲ εἰς πλήθους ἀριθμὸν ἐμπέσω, δύναμαι
τότε διαμετρεῖσθαι τὰς φύσεις· καὶ γὰρ ὁδοῦ μακρᾶς
τὸ μὲν τέρμα ἕν, πολλαὶ δὲ αἱ ἀποστάσεις. ἐὰν ἐπὶ
Βαβυλῶνα ἴῃς, πλησιαίτερος μὲν τοῦ Ἀρμενίου ὁ Ἀσσύριος καὶ τοῦ Λυδοῦ ὁ Ἀρμένιος καὶ τοῦ Ἴωνος ὁ
Λυδὸς καὶ τοῦ νησιώτου ὁ Ἴων· ἀλλ' οὐδεὶς ἐν Βαβυλῶνι οὔπω, οὐχ ὁ Ἀσσύριος, οὐχ ὁ Ἀρμένιος, οὐχ ὁ
Λυδός, οὐχ ὁ Ἴων, οὐχ ὁ νησιώτης. κἂν ἐπ' Ἐλευσῖνα
ἴῃς, Πελοπόννησος αὕτη, εἶτα Ἰσθμός, εἶτα Μέγαρα·

---

[3] suppl. Trapp Heinsium secutus

---

14 Cf. Xen. Oec. 8.3–8 for the same examples of order and
disorder in a chorus, army, and trireme. Thuc. 7.44 provides a

but if you take away the charioteer, then you cut loose the chariot. Similarly, an army is kept in order by one watchword, but if you take away the watchword, then you break up the phalanx into a fleeing multitude.[14]

3. What then is the good for bodies? Health. And the bad? Disease. Health is a single thing, whereas diseases are many. What is the good in music? Harmony. And the bad? Disharmony. Harmony is a single thing, whereas disharmony becomes a multitude. In the case of a chorus, unison is a single thing, whereas discord takes many forms. In the case of a trireme, the pipe is single, but disobedience becomes a multitude. In the case of a chariot, the charioteer's expertise is a single thing, whereas the absence of expertise takes many forms. And what is good in the case of a phalanx? Keeping the watchword. It is one single thing, whereas anarchy takes many forms. Therefore in the nature of unity I detect neither excess or deficiency, for it is stable and tolerates no sudden movement either in flight or pursuit.

But whenever I come across a number of entities, I am then able to distinguish their different natures. For example, on a long journey the destination is a single place, but there are many stages along the way. If you are going to Babylon, an Assyrian is closer to it than an Armenian, an Armenian closer than a Lydian, a Lydian closer than an Ionian, and an Ionian closer than an islander. None of these is yet in Babylon, not the Assyrian, Armenian, Lydian, Ionian, or islander. And if you are traveling to Eleusis, first is the Peloponnesus, then the Isthmus, and then

famous example during the Sicilian Expedition of the mayhem caused by soldiers not knowing the watchword.

ἀλλὰ ἀμύητος εἶ, κἂν ἐν Μεγάροις ᾖς, ὁμοίως τῷ Πε-
λοποννησίῳ· μέχρι μήπω τῷ ἀνακτόρῳ προσελήλυ-
θας, ἀμύητος εἶ.

Νόμιζε δὴ καὶ τὸν βίον ὁδόν τινα εἶναι μακρὰν ἐπ'
Ἐλευσῖνα ἢ Βαβυλῶνα ἄγουσαν, τέρμα τε δὴ τῆς
ὁδοῦ τὰ βασίλεια αὐτὰ καὶ ἀνάκτορα καὶ τὴν τελετήν·
ὑπὸ δὲ πλήθους ὁδοιπόρων μεστὴν τὴν ὁδὸν θεόντων,
ὠθιζομένων, καμνόντων, ἀναπαυομένων, κειμένων, ἐκ-
τρεπομένων, πλανωμένων· πολλαὶ γὰρ αἱ παρατριβαὶ
καὶ ἀπατηλαί, ὧν αἱ μὲν πολλαὶ ἐπὶ κρημνοὺς καὶ
βάραθρα ἄγουσιν, ⟨αἱ δὲ⟩[4] ἐπὶ τὴν Σειρήνων, αἱ δὲ
ἐπὶ τοὺς Λωτοφάγους, αἱ δὲ ἐπὶ τὸν Κιμμερίων δῆμον·
μία δέ πού τις στενὴ καὶ ὄρθιος καὶ τραχεῖα καὶ οὐ
πολλοῖς πάνυ ὁδεύσιμος ἐπ' αὐτὸ ἄγει τὸ τῆς ὁδοῦ
τέρμα, ἣν μόγις καὶ μετὰ πραγμάτων σὺν πολλῷ
πόνῳ καὶ ἱδρῶτι ἀνύουσιν καματηραὶ καὶ ἐπίπονοι
ψυχαί, καὶ ἐπιθυμοῦσαι τοῦ χωρίου καὶ ἐρῶσαι τῆς
τελετῆς, καταμαντευόμεναι αὐτῆς τὸ κάλλος· ἐπειδὰν
δὲ ἀφίκωνται ἐκεῖ, παυσάμεναι τοῦ πονεῖν, παύονται
τοῦ πάθους. τίς γὰρ ἄλλη τελετὴ μυστικωτέρα καὶ τίς
ἄλλος τόπος σπουδῆς ἄξιος; ταύτην ἔχει τοῖς ἀνθρώποις τὴν χώραν τὸ ἀγαθόν, ἣν τοῖς ἀμυήτοις Ἐλευσὶν
ἔχει· μυήθητι, ἐλθέ, ἐπίβηθι τοῦ χωρίου, λάμβανε τὰ
ἀγαθά, καὶ οὐ ποθήσεις ἄλλο μεῖζον.

4 suppl. Davies[2], Dübner, Trapp

Megara, but even if you are in Megara, you are not yet an initiate, any more than the Peloponnesian is. For until you actually enter the *anaktoron*,[15] you remain uninitiated.[16]

Consider life too as a long road,[17] so to speak, leading to Eleusis or to Babylon, and having as its destination the palace itself[18] and the *anaktoron* and its initiation. Because of the large number of travelers, the road is crowded with people running, jostling, toiling, resting, lying down, leaving the road, and wandering off, for there are many seductive byways, most of which lead to cliffs and chasms— some to the island of the Sirens, others to the Lotus-Eaters, others to the country of the Cimmerians. There is, however, a single path, one that is narrow, steep, and rough, which very few can travel, that leads to the road's final destination. Scarcely with much trouble, toil, and sweat do hardworking and long-suffering souls reach the end of this path, those that long for the place and crave the initiation, because they divine its beauty. And when they finally do arrive there, they cease from their labor and rest from their suffering. What other initiation is more mystical, and what other place is worthy of such effort? The Good has the same significance for men in general that Eleusis holds for the uninitiated. Come and be initiated, set foot on this ground, take hold of these goods, and you will desire nothing greater.

[15] The temple where the Eleusinian mysteries were conducted.

[16] A starting point such as Tyre could suit both journeys.

[17] The road of life with its many pitfalls is a favorite analogy of Maximus; cf. *Orr.* 1.3, 8.7, 14.1, and 34.2.

[18] That is, the royal palace in Babylon.

4. Ἐὰν δὲ τὸ ἀγαθὸν ἐπονομάζῃς τῇ τῶν μὴ ἀγαθῶν φύσει, ὑγιείας σωμάτων καὶ εὐμορφίας, καὶ περιβολὴν χρυσοῦ καὶ ἀργύρου, καὶ δόξαν προγόνων καὶ τιμὴν πολιτικήν, πράγματα ἡδοναῖς μᾶλλον ἢ ἀγαθοῖς μετρεῖσθαι πεφυκότα, ἐξαγορεύεις τὰ μυστήρια, πλημμελεῖς περὶ τὸ θεῖον. τοιούτων ἀγαθῶν μεταλαβεῖν ποθεῖς οἵων καὶ Ἀλκιβιάδης μυστηρίων, μεθύων δᾳδοῦχος καὶ ἐκ συμποσίου ἱεροφάντης καὶ ἐν παιδιᾷ τελεστής. ἀγαθὸν δὲ ἀγαθοῦ ἀπορρητότερον οὐκ ἂν εὕροις μᾶλλον ἢ κάλλος κάλλους ὡραιότερον· ἐὰν γάρ τι τούτων ἀφέλῃς, οὐκ ἔτι καλὸν ⟨τὸ μήπω καλὸν⟩[5] οὐδὲ ἀγαθὸν τὸ μήπω ἀγαθόν.

Οὐχ ὁρᾷς τὸν ὑπὲρ κεφαλῆς τοῦτον οὐρανὸν καὶ τὰ ἐν αὐτῷ ἄστρα καὶ τὸν ὑπ᾽ αὐτῷ αἰθέρα καὶ τὸν ὑπὸ τούτῳ ἀέρα καὶ τὴν ὑπ᾽ αὐτῷ θάλατταν ⟨καὶ τὴν ὑπὸ ταύτῃ γῆν⟩;[6] διαμέτρησον αὐτῶν τὰς φύσεις· τοῦτο γῆς μέρος τοῦ ὅλου πλατὺ καὶ πολυτρόφον καὶ δενδροφόρον καὶ ζῳοτρόφον· ἀλλ᾽ ἐὰν πρὸς τὴν θάλατταν ἐξετάζῃς, ἔλαττον θαλάττης, καὶ θάλαττα ἀέρος ἔλαττον, ⟨καὶ ἀὴρ αἰθέρος,⟩[7] καὶ αἰθὴρ οὐρανοῦ. μέχρι τούτου τὰ μέρη πρόεισιν ὑπερβάλλοντα καὶ ὑπερβαλλόμενα· ἐὰν δὲ ἔλθῃς ἐκεῖ, στήσεται ὁμοῦ

5 suppl. Davies[2], Trapp
6 suppl. Markland, Trapp
7 suppl. Trapp

4. If, however, you bestow the name of "good" on things that are not naturally good, things like physical health and comeliness, ornaments of gold and silver, famous ancestors, and political honors, things that are naturally suited to be measured in terms of pleasures rather than in terms of goods, you are profaning the mysteries and sinning against the divine. The kind of goods you yearn to partake in are like the mysteries conducted by Alcibiades as a drunken torchbearer and hierophant from a drinking party, playing the role of an initiating priest.[19] But you will not find one true good more sacred than another, or one beauty lovelier than another, for if you take anything away from these, then ‹that which falls short of being beautiful› ceases to be beautiful, as does good that falls short of being good.

Do you not see these heavens above your head, and the stars within them, and the ether beneath them, the atmosphere beneath that, and sea below it, ‹and the earth underneath that›? Then compare their dimensions. The earth's portion of the whole universe is indeed broad and fertile, and it supports many plants and animals, but if you compare it to the sea, it is less extensive, while the sea is less extensive than the atmosphere, ‹the atmosphere less than the ether,› and the ether less than the heavens. Up to this point these portions will form a progression, with each surpassing the previous one, and in turn being surpassed by the next. But once you reach that point, the increasing magnitude together with its beauty will come

<hr/>

[19] An allusion to Alcibiades' alleged profanation of the mysteries before the Sicilian Expedition in 415 BC. Cf. Thuc. 6.53 and 60–61, and Plut. *Alc.* 19.

τῷ μεγέθει καὶ τὸ κάλλος. τί γὰρ ἂν εἴη οὐρανοῦ
ὡραιότερον; τί ἄστρων περιλαμπέστερον; τί ἡλίου ἀκμαιότερον; τί σελήνης εὐτροφώτερον; τί τῶν ἄλλων
χορῶν εὐτακτότερον; τί τῶν θεῶν αὐτῶν τιμιώτερον;

5. Κινδυνεύουσιν δὲ οἱ ἄνθρωποι καθάπερ τοῖς ἀγαθοῖς, οὕτω καὶ τοῖς θεοῖς ζυγοστατεῖν τὰς τιμάς. τίς
οὗτος; Ζεύς· ἀρχέτω. τίς οὗτος; Κρόνος· δεδέσθω.
Ἥφαιστος· χαλκευέτω. Ἑρμῆς· ἀγγελλέτω. Ἀθηνᾶ·
ὑφαινέτω. {ὡς Πελοποννησίοις ἐπέσθωσαν.}[8] ἀγνοοῦ-
σιν γάρ, οἶμαι, ὡς θεοῖς πᾶσιν εἷς νόμος καὶ βίος καὶ
τρόπος, οὐ διῃρημένος οὐδὲ στασιωτικός· ἄρχοντες
πάντες, ἡλικιῶται πάντες, σωτῆρες πάντες, ἰσοτιμίᾳ
καὶ ἰσηγορίᾳ συνόντες τὸν πάντα χρόνον· ὧν μία μὲν
ἡ φύσις, πολλὰ δὲ τὰ ὀνόματα. ὑπὸ γὰρ ἀμαθίας
αὐτῶν τὰς ὠφελείας τὰς πάντων ἑκάστοις ἐπονομάζο-
μεν, ἄλλος ἄλλῃ κλήσει θεοῦ· καθάπερ καὶ τὰ μέρη
τῆς θαλάττης, Αἰγαῖον τοῦτο, Ἰόνιον ἐκεῖνο, Μυρτῶον
ἄλλο, Κρισαῖον ἄλλο· ἡ δ᾽ ἐστὶν μία, ὁμογενὴς καὶ
ὁμοπαθὴς καὶ συγκεκραμένη· οὕτω καὶ τἀγαθόν, ἐν
ὃν καὶ ὅμοιον αὐτῷ καὶ ἴσον πάντοθεν, ὑπὸ ἀσθενείας
τῆς πρὸς αὐτὸ καὶ ἀγνωσίας ταῖς δόξαις διαιρούμεθα.

[8] del. Paccius, Davies[2], Dübner: obel. Koniaris: lacunam stat.
Trapp

[20] As Trapp (1997a, 312n21) points out, "mention of the subordinate elements in the cosmos seems to suggest the existence
of just the hierarchy of beauty—and thus also, by analogy, of
Goods—that Maximus at this point is seeking to deny."

to a halt. For what could be more lovely than the heavens, more radiant than the stars, more intense than the sun, more nourishing than the moon, more beautifully arranged than the choruses of the other heavenly bodies, and what more esteemed than the gods themselves?[20]

5. It seems that humans try to apportion honors to different gods just as they do to different goods. Who is this? Zeus: let him reign. Who is this? Cronus: let him be imprisoned. Hephaestus: let him forge bronze. Hermes: let him convey messages. Athena: let her weave . . .[21] That is because they are unaware, I believe, that all the gods share one law, one existence, and one way of life, which is not divided up or split into factions, because all of them are rulers, all have the same age, all are tutelary, and all live together with equal status and equal rights for all time. They have one nature, although they bear many names. Because of our ignorance concerning them, we assign the benefits that come from all of them to individual gods, giving each one a different divine name,[22] just as we do with segments of the sea. This part is the Aegean, that one the Ionian Sea, another is the Myrtoan Sea, and yet another is the Crisaean, whereas the sea itself is a single entity with the same properties and same behavior, all blended together. The same is true of the Good. It is one single thing, consistent with itself and the same throughout, but because of our weakness with respect to it and our ignorance, we divide it up in our minds.

[21] The corrupt text has "as, let them accompany Peloponnesians." Hobein proposed that the Dioscuri were at issue, but the text makes no sense.

[22] Cf. Diog. Laert. 7.147 (*SVF* 2.1021) for the Stoic view that god is one, but we assign various names to his powers.

Πλουτεῖ Καλλίας, μακάριος τῶν ἀγαθῶν· ἀλλὰ
Ἀλκιβιάδης Καλλίου ὡραιότερος. ἀντιθῶμεν τἀγαθά,
πλοῦτον κάλλει· ποῖον αὐτῶν ἑκατόμβοιον; ἐννεά-
βοιον ποῖον; πότερον ἑλώμεθα; πότερον εὐξώμεθα;
οὐκοῦν ὁ μὲν Φοῖνιξ καὶ ὁ Αἰγύπτιος τὸ Καλλίου ἀγαθὸν εὔξεται, ὁ δὲ Ἠλεῖος καὶ ὁ Βοιώτιος τὸ Ἀλκιβιάδου; εὐγενὴς Παυσανίας, ἀλλ᾽ ἐνδοξότερος Εὐρυβιά-
δης. ἀντιθῶμεν εὐδοξίᾳ γένος· τίς κρατεῖ; τίνι δῶμεν
τὰ νικητήρια φέροντες; Σωκράτης πένης, Σωκράτης
αἰσχρός, Σωκράτης ἄδοξος, Σωκράτης δυσγενής, Σωκράτης ἄτιμος. πῶς γὰρ οὐκ αἰσχρὸς καὶ ἄτιμος καὶ
δυσγενὴς καὶ ἄδοξος καὶ πένης ὁ τοῦ λιθοξόου, ὁ
σιμός, ὁ προγάστωρ, ὁ κωμῳδούμενος, ὁ εἰς δεσμωτήριον ἐμβαλλόμενος, ἀποθνήσκων ἐκεῖ, ἔνθα καὶ Τι-
μαγόρας ἀπέθανεν; ὦ τῆς ἐρημίας τῶν ἀγαθῶν· ὀκνῶ
γὰρ εἰπεῖν πλῆθος κακῶν. τί τούτοις ἀντιθῶμεν; τί
φῶμεν; παράβαλε τοῖς ἀνταγωνισταῖς τὸν Σωκράτην
ἐν κτήσει ἀγαθῶν· οὐχ ὁρᾷς ἡττώμενον ἐν πλούτῳ
Καλλίου, ἐν σώματι Ἀλκιβιάδου, ἐν τιμῇ Περικλέους,

Callias is rich and blessed with good things, but Alcibiades is more handsome than Callias. Let us then compare these two goods, wealth and beauty. Which one is worth a hundred oxen, and which nine? Which should we choose, which pray for? So then will a Phoenician and an Egyptian pray for Callias' kind of good, and an Elean and a Boeotian pray for Alcibiades' kind of good?[23] Pausanias is wellborn, but Eurybiades is more reputable.[24] Let us compare good birth and reputation. Which is superior? To which do we award the crown? Socrates is poor, Socrates is ugly, Socrates is undistinguished, of low birth, and held in low esteem. For how could he not be ugly, undistinguished, of low birth, held in low esteem, and poor, when he was the son of a stonemason,[25] with a flat nose and a pot belly, mocked by comic poets, thrown into prison, and executed in the same place where Timagoras was put to death?[26] Oh, what a dearth of good things (for I am loath to call it a multitude of bad things)! What shall we compare them to? What are we to say? Go ahead and compare Socrates to his adversaries by how many so-called good things they possess. Can you not see that Socrates comes off worse than Callias in wealth, than Alcibiades in physi-

---

[23] Phoenicians and Egyptians represent merchants; the Eleans and Boeotians (Thebans) represent admirers of masculine beauty; cf. *Orr.* 18.2 and 20.8.

[24] Pausanias, the Spartan king victorious at Plataea in 479 BC was later disgraced; Eurybiades commanded the victorious allied fleet at Salamis in 480 BC.

[25] Sophroniscus; see *Or.* 38.7.

[26] Timagoras was condemned for bribery in 367 BC; cf. Plut. *Artax.* 22.

ἐν δόξῃ Νικίου, ἐν θεάτρῳ Ἀριστοφάνους, ἐν δικαστηρίῳ Μελήτου; μάτην ἄρα αὐτῷ ὁ Ἀπόλλων τὰ νικητήρια ἔδωκεν, μάτην ἐπεψηφίσατο;

cal advantages, than Pericles in esteem, than Nicias in reputation, than Aristophanes in the theater, and than Meletus in the courtroom? Was it then all in vain that Apollo awarded him the crown, in vain that he cast his vote for him?[27]

[27] For Apollo's endorsement of Socrates as the wisest man, see Pl. *Ap.* 21a and *Or.* 3.1. Trapp (1997a, 313n23) points out that with this final paragraph, "we are back (as in §4) with a sequence of merely *apparent* goods that in fact, in comparison with the true Good, are not goods at all. The two points, that the Good is one and without degrees, and that so-called 'goods' of body and fortune are separated from it by an unbridgeable gap, have not themselves been kept properly separate in Maximus' exposition."

ORATION 40

INTRODUCTION

This is a response to the previous oration with its Stoic insistence that the Good is a single thing that does not admit of degrees. It opens with Glaucus defending his unequal exchange of arms on the same grounds of friendship as was argued in *Or.* 39.1 but quickly turns to Odysseus, who, in his praises, endorsed various kinds of goods. If the Stoic view that beauty does not admit degrees is accepted (as argued at *Or.* 39.4), then Paris, by choosing Aphrodite, convicted Athena and Hera of being ugly (§1). Likewise, Homer praises the beauty of Artemis over that of her Nymphs and Agamemnon's over that of Menelaus. Since Nireus was second to Achilles in beauty, that would make him no more handsome than Thersites. Furthermore, there is a clear hierarchy of military virtue in Homer, from Achilles to Sthenelus (§2). There are also degrees of virtue and intelligence, as in the case of Andromache and Penelope and Agamemnon and Nestor. Health too is no simple matter, as was claimed at *Or.* 39.2, but admits many degrees. Three factors, benefit, possibility, and truth, must be considered in determining if one good can surpass another (§3). Benefit: allowing stages of ascent to the Good encourages seekers to make progress in their pursuit, whereas restricting the Good to excellence alone destroys their hopes of ever attaining it. Possibility: all things are tested by comparison with their likes. If the Good has no good against which to be measured, then there will be no standard to measure any particular good (§4). Truth: happiness (*eudaimonia*) consists of a harmonious hierarchy of soul, body, and fortune, with soul in command, the body obeying, and fortune intervening (§5). Inequality and hierarchy are evident everywhere: among the senses, the gods, families, and individuals. The Stoic representative is reinvoked and slyly asked whether he considers wealth a good or an evil, or if it is somewhere in between. If it is the latter, then it belongs either in the Stoic category of "indifferent" or in that of "preferred." He may keep it as indifferent rather than good, but with a slight change of name it becomes preferred and still retains its value (§6).

ORATION 40

Εἰ ἔστιν ἀγαθὸν ἀγαθοῦ μεῖζον·
ἐν ᾧ ὅτι ἔστιν

1. Ἀλλ' ἐπεὶ τὸν Ὅμηρον αἰτιᾷ, μεμφόμενον τῷ Γλαύκῳ τῆς ἀμοιβῆς, πότερα καὶ σοὶ ὑπὲρ τοῦ Ὁμήρου ἀπολογητέον, ἢ Ὁμήρῳ ὑπὲρ τοῦ Γλαύκου; τούτῳ, νὴ Δία· τιμητέος γάρ μοι καὶ πρὸ τῶν ἄλλων Ὅμηρος, μή τί γε πρὸ δικαστοῦ σου. ὧδε τοίνυν ὁ Γλαῦκος λέγει·

"Εἰ μέν τι, ὦ Ὅμηρε, ἢ ἔλαττον ἦν ἀγαθὸν ἀγαθοῦ, ἢ ἔλαττον μείζονος, εἰκότως ἄρα σοι εἶχεν αἰτίαν ὁ Ζεὺς ὡς τὰς φρένας μοι λυμαινόμενος· ἐν δὲ χρυσοῦ καὶ χαλκοῦ ἀλλαγῇ μήπω πάνυ αἰτιάσῃ μήτε τὸν Δία μήτε ἐμέ· οὐδὲν γὰρ οὔτε τῷ λαβόντι χρυσὸς πλέον, οὔτε τῷ ἀλλαξαμένῳ ὁ χαλκὸς ἔλαττον· ἀλλὰ ἀμφοτέροις καλῶς ἔχει ἑκάτερα, ἐν τῷ ἀνίσῳ τῆς ὕλης ἰσοστασίῳ τῇ γνώμῃ δοθέντα."

Καὶ ὁ μὲν Γλαῦκος ἡμῖν ἀπίτω ἐκποδών· ἡκέτω δὲ ὁ Ὀδυσσεὺς ὁ τούτου σοφώτερος, ἀποδειξόμενος ἡμῖν

ORATION 40

Whether there exists one good greater than another. That there does

1. Well, since you[1] blame Homer for reproaching Glaucus over the exchange of his armor, should I address a defense of Homer to you, or a defense of Glaucus to Homer? The latter, by Zeus! For I must value Homer above other judges, to say nothing of a judge like you. So here is what Glaucus has to say:

"If this were a case, Homer, either of one good being less than good, or of one good being less than a greater good, then it would be reasonable for you to blame Zeus for impairing my wits.[2] But in an exchange of gold and bronze, do not at all blame either Zeus or me, for gold brings no advantage to the one receiving it, nor bronze disadvantage to the one exchanging gold for it, because the exchanges are satisfactory for both parties, since the equality of the goodwill with which they are given compensates for the inequality of the materials."

At this point let Glaucus leave us, and let Odysseus come forward, who is wiser than he, to give us his own

[1] That is, the Stoic representative in the previous oration.
[2] *Il.* 6.234: "Zeus took away Glaucus' wits."

τὴν αὐτοῦ γνώμην, ἣν περὶ ἀγαθῶν κτήσεως ἔχει. ἢ
γὰρ οὐχ οὗτός ἐστιν ὁ μακαρίζων μὲν τὸν Ἀλκίνου
οἶκον τῆς εὐφροσύνης καὶ τῆς ᾠδῆς, συνευχόμενος δὲ
τῇ Ναυσικάᾳ ὁμόφρονα αὐτῇ ξυστῆναι γάμον, εὐδαι-
μονίζων δ' αὖ τῆς ἀθανασίας τὴν Καλυψώ; οἶμαι δὲ
αὐτόν, εἰ καὶ παρ' ἄλλον τινὰ ἀφίκετο τῶν οὐ κατ'
ᾠδὴν καὶ κατὰ δαῖτα εὐδαιμόνων, οὐδὲ τῶν μακαρίων
κατὰ ἁρμονίαν γάμου, ἀλλὰ τὰ ἔτι τούτων μείζονα
ἀγαθὰ κεκτημένων, εἰπεῖν ἂν καὶ περὶ ἐκείνων τὰ
εἰκότα.

Ἐπεὶ δὲ καὶ τὸ κάλλος μοι προφέρεις ὡς ἐν μέτρῳ
ἑνὶ τὴν χώραν ἔχον, φέρε καὶ περὶ τούτου σοι βραχέα
ἄττα ἀποκρίνωμαι. δοκεῖς γάρ μοι, γενόμενος ἐν
χώρᾳ τοῦ Τρωϊκοῦ ποιμένος, ἀφικομένου παρά σε
Ἑρμοῦ πομπῇ Διός, ἄγοντος θεὰς τρεῖς πρὸς δικα-
στήν σε, προστάττοντος βραβεῦσαι περὶ κάλλους
αὐταῖς, ἡσθεὶς τῇ Ἀφροδίτῃ, καθάπερ ἐκεῖνος, κατα-
δικάσαι ἂν αἶσχος τῆς Ἥρας καὶ τῆς Ἀθηνᾶς· εἰ γὰρ
ἓν μὲν τὸ ἐν κάλλει καλόν, κρατεῖ δὲ ἐκ τῶν τριῶν μία,
ἀνάγκη τὰς ἡττωμένας αἰσχρῶς ἔχειν.

2. Μὴ σύ γε, ὦ δικαστῶν εὐδαιμονέστατε, ἀλλὰ
φειδὼ ἔχε ὀνομάτων αἰσχρῶν, καὶ ἠρέμα κάτιθι ἐκ
τῶν ἄκρων ἐπὶ τὰ ἔσχατα, ἵνα μὴ τὸν Ὅμηρον αὖθίς
σοι προφέρω λευκώλενον τὴν Ἥραν λέγοντα καὶ ῥο-
δόπηχυν τὴν Ἠὼ καὶ τὴν Ἀθηνᾶν γλαυκῶπιν καὶ ἀρ-

---

3 *Od.* 9.2–11.   4 *Od.* 6.180–85.

opinion on the possession of goods. After all, was it not he
who called the palace of Alcinous blessed for its merriment and song,[3] and who joined with Nausicaa in praying
for her to make a harmonious marriage,[4] and who called
Calypso fortunate because of her immortality?[5] I am of the
opinion that if he had come to some other host from the
ranks of people whose happiness did not consist of song
and feasting, nor were blessed with harmonious mar-
riages, but who possessed goods still greater than these,
he would have spoken appropriately about them too.[6]

And since you also cite beauty to me as something
admitting only one degree,[7] come then, let me answer you
with some brief remarks about this as well. It seems to me
that if you had been put in the position of the Trojan
shepherd,[8] and Hermes had come to you on a mission
from Zeus, bringing three goddesses for you to judge, and
ordered you to rank them for their beauty, and if you were
as thrilled with Aphrodite as he was, then you would have
convicted Hera and Athena of ugliness. For if, in the
sphere of beauty, only one thing counts as beautiful, and
if only one goddess of the three can win, then the losers
must necessarily be ugly.

2. Do not do this, most fortunate judge! Hold back
from ugly appellations and descend gradually down a scale
from highest to lowest, lest I cite Homer to you again,
when he calls Hera white-armed, Dawn rosy-armed,

[5] *Od*. 5.215–18.
[6] That is, Odysseus would have endorsed varieties and grada-
tions of good.   [7] As argued at *Or*. 39.4: "that which falls
short of being beautiful ceases to be beautiful."
[8] Paris; cf. *Il*. 24.25–30.

γυρόπεζαν τὴν Θέτιν καὶ Ἥβην καλλίσφυρον· ὧν
οὐδεμιᾶς ἀφαιρήσεις τὸ κάλλος, κἂν ἐν μέρει ᾖ, εὔ-
φημός γε ἐθέλων εἶναι τὰ θεῖα καὶ ἥκιστα πλημ-
μελής.

Ἀκούεις δ᾽ αὐτοῦ διηγουμένου χορὸν ἀγρευτικόν,
παιζούσας ἐν ὄρει τὰς νύμφας ἐξηγουμένης τῆς Ἀρ-
τέμιδος·

πασάων δ᾽ ὕπερ ἥ γε κάρη ἔχει ἠδὲ μέτωπα,

φησίν, καὶ

ῥεῖα δ᾽ ἀριγνώτη πέλεται, καλαὶ δέ τε πᾶσαι.

ἦ που καταγελᾷς τοῦ Ὁμήρου προτιμῶντος μὲν νυμφῶν κατὰ κάλλος Ἄρτεμιν; ἀκούεις δὲ αὐτοῦ καὶ περὶ
Μενελάου κάλλους τοιαυτὶ λέγοντος, ὅτε ἔφη τρωθέν-
τος ῥυῆναι τὸ αἷμα κατὰ τοῦ μηροῦ, ἔπειτα εἰκάζει τὸ
τοῦ μηροῦ κάλλος γυναικὸς τέχνῃ ἐλέφαντα χραινού-
σης φοίνικι, ἵπποις εἶναι παρήιον·

τοῖοί τοι, Μενέλαε, μιάνθην αἵματι μηροὶ
εὐφυεῖς,

φησίν, καὶ κνῆμαι καὶ σφυρά.

Τοῦ δὲ Ἀγαμέμνονος αὖθις αὖ ἐπαινῶν τὸ κάλλος
οὐκ ἐδεήθη εἰκόνος Λυδίας ἢ Καρικῆς, οὐδὲ ἐλέφαν-
τος ὑπὸ γυναικὸς βαρβάρου φοίνικι ἐξηνθισμένου,

---

9 Cf. *Il.* 1.195 (Hera), 1.477 (Dawn, actually, "rosy-fingered"),
1.206 (Athena), 1.538 (Thetis), and *Od.* 11.603 (Hebe).

Athena gray-eyed, Thetis silver-footed, and Hebe fair-ankled.[9] You are not going to deprive any of these goddesses of their beauty, even if it is just a portion, if you wish to speak respectfully of divinities and offend them as little as possible.

You can also hear him describing a woodland band of Nymphs sporting in the mountains, led by Artemis, who, he says,

holds her head and brow high above them all,

adding,

and easily stands out, although all are beautiful.[10]

Are you really going to scoff at Homer for granting Artemis precedence in beauty over Nymphs? Then too you can hear him saying similar things about Menelaus' beauty, when he tells how blood ran down his thigh when he was wounded, and then goes on to compare the beauty of his thigh to the skilled work of a woman dyeing ivory with crimson to make a cheekpiece for horses. He says,

for thus were your shapely thighs, Menelaus, stained with blood,[11]

and adds, "your shins and ankles too."

But then, when he praises Agamemnon's beauty, he does not need a comparison drawn from Lydia or Caria,[12] nor of ivory decorated with crimson by a foreign woman,

[10] *Od.* 6.107–8.

[11] *Il.* 4.146–47.

[12] That is, the nationalities of the women dyers cited in the Homeric simile at *Il.* 4.142.

ἀλλὰ εἰκάζει αὐτοῦ τῷ Διὶ τὴν κεφαλὴν καὶ τὰ ὄμ-
ματα· ᾧ καὶ δῆλον ὡς καλλίων ὁ Ἀγαμέμνων ἦν· τῷ
μὲν γὰρ ἦν τὸ κάλλος περὶ τὴν κεφαλὴν καὶ τὰ ὄμ-
ματα, τῷ δὲ ἀμφὶ τοὺς μηροὺς καὶ τὰ σφυρά· ὁ δὲ τὰ
κρείττω καλός, καλλίων· ὁ δὲ τὰ ἥττω καλός, οὔπω
μὲν αἰσχρός, καλὸς δὲ ἧττον. τί δέ; ἐν τῷ στρατοπέδῳ
τῷ Ἑλληνικῷ οὐ διέφερεν μὲν ὥρᾳ ὁ Ἀχιλλεύς, εἶχεν
δὲ τὰ δεύτερα ὁ Νιρεύς; δικαστῇ δέ σοι, ἀπολειπόμε-
νος ὁ Νιρεὺς τοῦ Ἀχιλλέως οὐδὲν ἦν διαφέρων τοῦ
Θερσίτου.

Καὶ ἵνα μὴ περὶ κάλλους σοι μόνον διαλέγωμαι,
οὐκ ἀμφισβητεῖ τῷ Ἀχιλλεῖ περὶ ἀνδρείας ὁ Αἴας,
οὐδὲ τῷ Αἴαντι ὁ Διομήδης, οὐδὲ τῷ Διομήδει ὁ Σθέ-
νελος, οὐδὲ τῷ Σθενέλῳ ὁ Μενεσθεύς· ἀλλ᾽ οὐδεὶς διὰ
τοῦτο τὴν ἀρετὴν ἀφαιρεῖ τοῦ Μενεσθέως διὰ τὸν
Σθένελον, οὐδὲ τοῦ Σθενέλου διὰ τὸν Διομήδην, οὐδὲ
τοῦ Διομήδους διὰ τὸν Αἴαντα, οὐδὲ τοῦ Αἴαντος διὰ
τὸν Ἀχιλλέα· ἀλλ᾽ ἔστιν κἀνταῦθα ἡ ὁδὸς τῆς ἀρετῆς
οὐ διαπηδῶσα τὰς διὰ μέσου φύσεις, ἀλλὰ κατιοῦσα
ἠρέμα ἀπὸ τῶν ἀρίστων ἐπὶ τοὺς καταδεεστέρους.

3. Καὶ ἵνα ποτὲ ἀπαλλαγῶμεν τῶν σωμάτων οἷς
ἀναμέμικται ἡ ῥώμη καὶ τὸ κάλλος, εἰ τὴν Ἀνδρομά-
χην τῇ Πηνελόπῃ ἀντεξετάζοις, οὐχὶ σώφρων μὲν
ἑκατέρα καὶ φίλανδρος, προτιμήσεις δὲ τὴν Πηνελό-
πην, οὐχ ὅσα γυναικὸς βαρβαρικῆς Ἑλληνίδα, ἀλλὰ
τῷ περιόντι κατὰ τὴν ἀρετὴν τὸ πλεῖον νέμων; συμ-
βουλεύει δὲ καὶ ὁ Νέστωρ τῷ Ἀγαμέμνονι· ἆρ᾽ ἀνοήτῳ

but instead compares his head and eyes to Zeus,[13] which makes it clear that Agamemnon was the more beautiful one, because his beauty was that of his head and eyes, whereas Menelaus' was that of his thighs and ankles. He who is beautiful in more important respects is more beautiful, whereas he who is beautiful in less important respects is by no means ugly, but only less beautiful. Tell me this: Was not Achilles preeminent in the Greek army for his youthful beauty, while Nireus took second place?[14] Then in your judgment, Nireus' inferiority to Achilles made him no better than Thersites.[15]

And so as not to limit my discussion with you to beauty alone, when it comes to bravery Ajax cannot contend with Achilles, nor Diomedes with Ajax, nor Sthenelus with Diomedes, nor Menestheus with Sthenelus. Yet no one uses this as a reason to deprive Menestheus of his virtue because of Sthenelus, or Sthenelus because of Diomedes, or Diomedes because of Ajax, or Ajax because of Achilles. No, here too is a progression of virtue that does not leap over intermediate examples, but descends gradually from the best ones to the inferior ones.

3. And finally, moving on from bodies, wherein strength and beauty are combined, if you were to compare Andromache with Penelope, both being chaste and affectionate wives, will you not give precedence to Penelope, not because she is Greek and the other woman a barbarian, but because you place greater emphasis on superiority in virtue? Also, Nestor indeed gives advice to Agamemnon,

13 *Il*. 2.478: "his eyes and head like Zeus."
14 *Il*.2.673–74: "Nireus, the most handsome man . . . after Achilles."   15 *Il*. 2.216: "the ugliest man who came to Troy."

φρόνιμος; ἢ οὐκ ἂν ἐθελήσαις τὸν τῶν Πανελλήνων
βασιλέα, τὸν διογενῆ καὶ λαῶν ποιμένα, καθυβρίσαι
δυσφήμῳ αἰτίᾳ; ἀλλὰ καὶ ὡς ἐδέησεν αὐτῷ φρονίμῳ
ὄντι φρονιμωτέρου συμβούλου, τοῦ Νέστορος.

Πείθω δέ σε οὐδέν τι μᾶλλον περὶ τῶν ἀρετῶν
διαλεγόμενος, τὰ ὅμοια τοῖς ὁμοίοις, τῷ ἀνίσῳ κατὰ
τὴν μετουσίαν, εἰς ὑπεροχῆς καὶ ἐλαττώσεως μοῖραν
παραβαλεῖν ἐθέλων; ὅς γε καὶ τὴν ὑγίειαν ἡγεῖ
ἁπλοῦν τι εἶναι. τὸ δέ ἐστιν ἁπλοῦν παντὸς ἧττον· αἱ
γὰρ τῶν σωμάτων φύσεις πολὺ τῶν τῆς ψυχῆς ἀμφι-
λαφέστεραι εἰς ὑγίας μέτρον· καὶ αὐτὸ τοὐναντίον, ὁ
μὲν διώκων ἀκρότητα ἐν ὑγιεινῷ διώκει πρᾶγμα φεῦ-
γον, καὶ οὔτε Ἀσκληπιῷ οὔτε Χείρωνι ἐξ ἐπιδρομῆς
ἁλώσιμον· ὁ δὲ ἐν τῷ ἀνίσῳ τοῦ ἐφικτοῦ τὸ ληφθὲν
ἀγαπῶν, εὐγνωμονέστερος μὲν πρὸς τὴν τέχνην, οὐκ
ἀνέλπιστος δὲ πρὸς τὴν ἀκρότητα.

Οὕτω τοι κἀπὶ τοῖς ἀγαθοῖς ἔχει. τριῶν γὰρ ὄντων
οἷς ἄν τις διαιτήσαι τὸ παρὸν τουτὶ σκέμμα, ἑνὸς μὲν
τείνοντος ἐπὶ τὸ ἀληθὲς αὐτό, δευτέρου δὲ ἐπὶ τὸ
δυνατόν, τρίτου δὲ ἐπὶ τὸ ὠφέλιμον, καθ' ἕκαστον
τούτων σκεψώμεθα, ἀνατρέψαντες αὐτῶν τὴν ἀκολου-
θίαν, ἀπὸ τοῦ ὠφελίμου ἀρξάμενοι· μήπω γὰρ δυνατὸν ἔστω μηδὲ ἀληθὲς τὸ λεγόμενον, ὡς ἔστιν ἀγαθὸν
ἀγαθοῦ μεῖζον, ἀλλὰ ἴδωμεν αὐτοῦ τὸ ὠφέλιμον·

---

[16] As argued in *Or.* 39.2: "Can you then possibly consider
health to be something varied and diverse, rather than simple and
stable?"

but is this really a case of a prudent man advising an utter fool? Or would you prefer not to insult the king of all the Greeks, who is Zeus-born and the shepherd of his people, with such a slanderous accusation? For in spite of being prudent himself, he nonetheless needed a more prudent adviser in Nestor.

Do you find me no more convincing, when in discussing virtues I choose to compare things that are similar by using their unequal participation in the quality at issue to demonstrate the degree of their superiority or deficiency? Probably not, since you consider even health to be a simple matter![16] But in fact, health is less simple than most anything, for the constitutions of bodies offer far more variation in attaining a degree of health than do those of the soul, and contrary to your position, anyone seeking perfection in health is in pursuit of a fleeing thing that neither Asclepius nor Chiron can overtake and capture. Thus, when confronted with the diverse degrees of attainable health, he who is content with what he has obtained not only is more thankful for medicine, but also does not despair over perfection.

The same also holds true for good things. There are three factors that should be considered if anyone is to resolve the present investigation. The first pertains to the truth itself, the second to possibility, and the third to benefit. So let us examine each one, beginning in reverse order with the question of benefit. Let us not yet determine whether our proposition—that there exists one good greater than another—is either possible or true, but instead consider its benefit. For it may be the case that many

πολλὰ γάρ που καὶ τῶν οὔτε ἀληθῶν οὔτε δυνατῶν
ὠφέλησεν πιστευθέντα.

4. Οὐχ ὁ μὲν εἰς ἀκρότητα[1] ἄγων τὸ ἀγαθὸν καὶ
περιγράφων αὐτοῦ τὴν οὐσίαν ἐν τῷ ἀρίστῳ μόνῳ,
διέσκαψεν καὶ διετείχισεν τὴν ἐλπίδα τῶν πολλῶν τῆς
ἐπ' αὐτὸ ὁδοῦ; ὁ δὲ ὑποβάθρας διδοὺς καὶ ἀναπαύλας
διὰ μέσου καὶ ἀναγωγὰς πολλάς, προὔπεμψεν πόρρω
πάνυ ὡς τευξόμενον τοῦ μετρίου, παρεμυθήσατο δὲ τῇ
ἐπιτυχίᾳ τὸν προελθόντα ἤδη ὡς προσελευσόμενον[2]
τῷ ἀρίστῳ, ἀνεκήρυξεν δὲ τὸν ἀφικόμενον εἰς τὸ
ἄκρον ὡς ἐν ἀγαθοῖς ἄριστον· ὁ δὲ ἕτερος τῶν λόγων
οὐχὶ τὸν μὲν ἀριστέα ἐν δειλοῖς στεφανοῖ, τὸν δὲ
ἰσχυρὸν ἐν ἀσθενεστάτοις, καὶ τὸ ὅλον ἀνταγωνιστὰς
τοῖς ἀρίστοις οὐ δίδωσιν, οὐδὲ ἐλέγχει τὰς ἀρετὰς ἐν
τοῖς ὁμοίοις;

Καὶ τοῦ μὲν ὠφελίμου παύομαι, τὸ δὲ δυνατὸν ἤδη
σκοπῶ. χρυσὸν μὲν τὸν διαφέροντα ἐλέγχει χρυσὸς
ἥττων, οὐ μόλιβδος, καὶ ἄργυρον ἄργυρος καὶ χαλκὸν χαλκός· καὶ πάντων ἁπλῶς γίγνονται αἱ ἐξετάσεις ἐν τῇ παραβολῇ τοῦ ὁμοίου μὲν κατὰ τὴν οὐσίαν
ἀνομοίου δὲ κατὰ τὴν ὑπεροχήν. τὸ δὲ ἀγαθὸν εἰς τὰ
κακὰ αὐτὰ ἐμβαλὼν οὕτως ἐξετάζεις· καὶ πῶς οὐ φα-
νεῖταί σοι τὸ σμικρότατον τῶν ἀγαθῶν ἐν χώρᾳ τοῦ
ἀρίστου; ὡς γὰρ ἐν νυκτὶ φῶς ἐκ πυρὸς τοῦ δι' ἡμέρας

---

[1] εἰς ἀκρότητα Koniaris, Trapp: ἰσοκράτης τὰ R
[2] προσελευσόμενον Trapp praeeunte Davies[2]: προσεληλυ-
θότα Markland, Koniaris: προεληλυθότα R

things prove to be beneficial without being either true or possible, simply by being believed.

4. Does not the man who places the Good at the summit of perfection and confines its essence to excellence alone, thereby dig trenches and build walls that block most people's hopes of making their way to it? But he who provides stepping stones, places to rest along the way, and many stages of ascent, sends the traveler much further on his way with the prospect of attaining a measure of success, encourages the one who has made progress with his success thus far into hoping that he will reach that excellence, and then proclaims the one who does arrive at the summit as the best among good men.[17] But does not the other proposition[18] crown the champion among cowards and the strong man among utter weaklings, and on the whole deprive the best men of worthy opponents and not even test the virtues against their likes?

So much for benefit. I shall now take up possibility. The quality of gold is tested by comparing it against less pure gold, not against lead, and likewise silver against silver and bronze against bronze. And as a general rule all substances are appraised by comparison with what is similar in essence but dissimilar in degree of superiority. Yet the way you evaluate the Good is by casting it among things that are wholly evil.[19] How then will the most insignificant of goods not seem to you to rank as the best? For just as light from a fire at night is brighter than one appearing in day-

[17] This counters the "road of life" analogy of Or. 39.3 that stressed the difficulty of ever reaching the Good.

[18] That is, that only the Good is truly good.

[19] That is because Stoic doctrine admitted only one Good.

φανέντος ἀκμαιότερον ὑπὸ πολλοῦ τοῦ περικεχυμένου
σκότους ἐλεγχόμενον, ἐν δὲ ἡλίῳ τὸ αὐτὸ ἀμυδρὸν καὶ
ἀσθενὲς πρὸς ἀνταγωνιστὴν ἰσχυρότερον· οὕτως ἀμέλει καὶ τὸ ἀγαθὸν τοῖς μὲν κακοῖς συνεξεταζόμενον,
καὶ τὸ τυχόν, ἄριστον καὶ μέγιστον καὶ ἐξοχώτατον,
ὡς ἐν πολλῷ ζόφῳ μικρὸν ζώπυρον, ἐν πολλῇ νυκτὶ
ὀλίγον φῶς· ἐὰν δὲ παράσχῃς αὐτῷ πρὸς τὰ ὅμοια
δρόμον καὶ ἅμιλλαν, τότε ὄψει τὸ ἄριστον ὄντως· νῦν
δὲ συγχεῖς τὴν κρίσιν καὶ ταράττεις.

Οὐχ ὁρᾷς καὶ τὴν σελήνην, ἄστρον ἀμφίβιον πρὸς
νύκτα καὶ ἡμέραν, ἐν μὲν νυκτὶ λαμπράν, μετὰ δὲ
ἡλίου ἀμαυράν; οὐκοῦν ἐν ἡμέρᾳ ἥλιος κρατεῖ, τὸ ἄριστον καὶ ἀκμαιότατον τῶν ἐν οὐρανῷ σωμάτων, ἐν δὲ
νυκτὶ σελήνη κρατεῖ, τὸ ἀσθενέστατον. καὶ τοίνυν καὶ
τὸ ἀγαθόν, ἐὰν μὲν εἰς νύκτα καὶ ζόφον καὶ ἀφέγ-
γειαν κακῶν ἐμβάλῃς, κρατεῖ τὸ ἀμαυρότατον· ἐὰν δὲ
παραθῇς ἀγαθὰ ἀγαθοῖς, ἀνάγκη κρατεῖν τὰ περιλαμ-
πέστερα.

5. Παύομαι τοῦ δυνατοῦ, καὶ ἐπὶ τὸ ἀληθὲς μέτειμι.
τὸν γὰρ τοῦ ἀνθρώπου βίον ἆρα ἄλλο τι ἡγητέον ἢ
διαγωγὴν ζωῆς συγκεκραμένην ἐκ ψυχῆς καὶ σώματος καὶ τύχης; ἐκ δὲ τῆς τούτων ἁρμονίας κραθέντων
καλῶς, ἑκάστου εἰς τὸ ἀκρότατον τῆς ἑαυτοῦ ῥώμης
ἀφιγμένου, τὸ ἄθροισμα τοῦτο εὐδαιμονίαν κλητέον·
ἀρχούσης μὲν τῆς ψυχῆς, στρατηγοῦ δίκην, ὑπηρε-
τοῦντος δὲ τοῦ σώματος, στρατιώτου δίκην, συνερ-

light because it is set against the deep darkness that sur-
rounds it, while in sunlight the same light appears dim and
weak against a more powerful opponent; in just the same
way, when any good, even a trifling one, is measured
against evils, it is best, biggest, and preeminent, like a tiny
spark in deep darkness or a little light in the depths of
night. But if you make it run and compete against like ri-
vals, then you will see what is truly best. But as it is, you
are confusing and confounding the assessment.

Do you not see that the moon, a star that appears both
at night and during the day, is bright at night, but dim in
sunlight? Accordingly the sun, the best and mightiest of
the heavenly bodies, is supreme during the day, while the
very weak moon is supreme at night. So too of the Good:
if you cast it into the night, shade, and darkness of evils,
the weakest good is supreme, but if you place good things
side by side with other good things, the brighter ones
necessarily prevail.

5. So much for possibility. I shall now turn to truth. Can
we conceive of human life as anything other than a passage
through existence, wherein soul, body, and fortune are
combined?[20] When these three elements are properly and
harmoniously blended, and each has reached the peak of
its own strength, then this combination must be called
happiness.[21] When the soul is in charge like a general, and
the body obeys it like a soldier, and fortune lends support

[20] This tripartite division of goods is Platonic; cf. esp. *Grg.*
467e and *Euthd.* 279a–c.

[21] This is the Aristotelian position. For happiness consisting
of the combination of external goods and those of the soul and
body, cf. Arist. *Eth. Nic.* 1.8–10, 1098b9–1101a21.

γούσης δὲ τῆς τύχης, ὅπλων δίκην· ἐξ ὧν ἁπάντων τὸ
νικᾶν ἔρχεται. ἐὰν δὲ ἀφέλῃς τὴν τύχην, τὸν στρατιώτην ἐξοπλίζεις· κἂν τὸν στρατιώτην ἀφέλῃς, ἀπο-
χειροτονεῖς τὸν στρατηγόν· τιμιώτερον δὲ καὶ στρα-
τιώτης ὅπλων καὶ στρατιώτου στρατηγός. ἐὰν δὲ
δυοῖν θάτερον, ἢ τὸν στρατηγὸν τιμῶν τὰ λοιπὰ ἀτι-
μάσῃς, τί χρήσεται ὁ στρατηγὸς τῇ τέχνῃ; ἢ καὶ
ταῦτα εἰσάγων ἰσοτιμίαν νέμῃς, τί χρήσεται τέχνη
τῷ στρατηγῷ; ἀρχέτω ψυχή, στρατευέτω τὸ σῶμα,
συναγωνιζέσθω ἡ τύχη· πάντα ἐπαινῶ, πάντα δέχο-
μαι, ἀλλὰ τὴν ἰσοτιμίαν αὐτῶν ἀφαιρῶ.

Οὐχ ὁρᾷς καὶ τὸν ἐν θαλάττῃ πλοῦν, ἔνθα ὁ μὲν
κυβερνήτης ἄρχει, ὡς ψυχὴ σώματος· ἡ δὲ ναῦς ἄρχεται, ὡς ὑπὸ ψυχῆς σῶμα· τὰ δὲ πνεύματα ἐπιρρεῖ,
ὡς ταῖς ἀρεταῖς ἡ τύχη; ἐὰν δὲ χειμὼν ἐπιγένηται, καὶ
μένῃ μὲν ἡ ναῦς, μένῃ δὲ ὁ κυβερνήτης, ἐλπὶς σωτηρίας, †κἂν οἴχηται ἡ ναῦς ὀρθά, ἢ καταδύσεται†[3] διὰ
τῆς τέχνης· ἐὰν δὲ ἀπὸ τοῦ κυβερνήτου ἄρξῃ καὶ ἐκεῖνον ἀφέλῃς, ἀχρεῖος μὲν ἡ ναῦς κἂν μένῃ, ἀχρεῖος δὲ
ἡ ἐπιρροὴ τῶν πνευμάτων κἂν φέρῃ. καὶ διὰ τοῦτο ἐν
μὲν θαλάττῃ καὶ νηὶ καὶ πλῷ τιμιώτατον ὁ κυβερνήτης, καὶ μετὰ τοῦτον ἡ ναῦς, καὶ μετὰ ταύτην ἡ
ἔξωθεν ἐπικουρία· ἐν δὲ τῷ τοῦ βίου τούτῳ δρόμῳ
τιμιώτατον μὲν ἡ ψυχή, μετὰ δὲ ταύτην τὸ σῶμα, καὶ

[3] obel. Trapp

376

like the soldier's weapons, then victory results from the combination of them all. But if you take away fortune, you disarm the soldier; and if you take away the soldier, you deprive the general of his command. At the same time, the soldier is more important than his weapons, and the general than the soldier. You then have two options. If you grant the general his importance and deprive the rest of any, what use will the general have for his expertise? Or, if you include all three and grant them equal status, then what use will expertise have for the general? Let the soul be in charge, let the body be a soldier, and let fortune fight on their side. That way I approve of them all, and I accept them all, but I deny them equal status.

Do you not also observe sailing on the sea, where the helmsman is in command as the soul commands the body, and the ship is under his command as the body is under the soul's, and the winds blow on it, as fortune does on the virtues? And if a storm intervenes, as long as the ship remains intact and the helmsman remains in charge, there is hope of survival . . .[22] through his expertise. But if you begin by removing the helmsman, the ship is useless even if it remains intact, and the blowing winds are of no use, even if they propel the ship along. That is why, for a ship sailing on the sea, the helmsman is the most important element, and after him the ship, and after it assistance from outside. And on our journey of life, the soul is the most important element, then comes the body, and thirdly fortune, and the goods pertaining to the more important

---

[22] The corrupt text has not been convincingly emended. Trapp translates the text of the manuscript as "even if the ship goes straight down or sinks."

τρίτον ἡ τύχη· τὰ δὲ τοῦ τιμιωτέρου ἀγαθὰ τῶν ἧττον
τιμίων τιμιώτερα.

6. Ἐγὼ καὶ τῶν αἰσθήσεων τὴν ἰσοτιμίαν ἀφαιρῶ.
τυφλὸς ἦν Ὅμηρος, ἀλλ᾽ ἤκουεν τῆς Καλλιόπης· κω-
φὸς ἦν Ἄτυς, ἀλλ᾽ ἑώρα τὸν ἥλιον. μετάθες τὰς συμ-
φοράς· ἀκουέτω Ἄτυς μὴ ὁρῶν, βλεπέτω Ὅμηρος μὴ
ἀκούων· Ἄτυϊ μὲν οὐκ ᾄσεται ἡ Καλλιόπη, Ὁμήρου
δὲ οὐκ ἀφαιρήσεις τὴν διδάσκαλον; ἐγὼ καὶ τῶν θεῶν
τὴν ἰσοτιμίαν ἀφαιρῶ· πείθομαι γὰρ Ὁμήρῳ λέγοντι·

τριχθὰ δὲ πάντα δέδασται, ἕκαστος δ᾽ ἔμμορε
τιμῆς·

τιμῆς οὐκ ἴσης, οὐδὲ γὰρ ἀρχῆς ἴσης· οὐ γὰρ ἴση ἡ
νομὴ οὐρανοῦ πρὸς θάλατταν καὶ θαλάττης πρὸς Ἅι-
δην· θεὸς δὲ ὁμοίως καὶ Κρόνου παῖς καὶ Ἅιδης καὶ
Ποσειδῶν καὶ Ζεύς· καὶ γὰρ Λύσανδρος Σπαρτιάτης,
ἀλλὰ Ἀγησίλαος Ἡρακλείδης. ἐγὼ δὲ κατὰ τὰς ἀρετὰς καὶ τὰ γένη προτιμῶ. οὐ γὰρ ὁ μὲν πωλοδάμνης
εὐγενείας ἱππικῆς ἐρᾷ,

ἧς Τρωΐ περ εὐρύοπα Ζεὺς
δῶχ᾽ υἷος ποινὴν Γανυμήδεος, οὕνεκ᾽ ἄρισται
ἵπποι ἔσαν,

---

23 Cf. Hdt. 1.34.2, where it is actually Atys' unnamed brother
who is deaf and dumb.   24 That is, hearing takes precedence for a blind person; seeing, for a deaf one.

25 As argued at *Or.* 39.5: "[They] all live together with equal
status and equal rights for all time."

element are more important than those belonging to the less important elements.

6. I also deny that the senses are of equal importance. For Homer was blind, but he could hear Calliope; Atys was deaf,[23] but he could see the sun. Change these misfortunes and let Atys hear but not see, and let Homer see but not hear. Then won't Calliope sing to Atys, and won't you deprive Homer of his teacher?[24] I also deny that the gods are of equal status,[25] for I believe Homer when he says,

> everything was divided three ways, and each received his status.[26]

But this was not an equal status, for their domains were not equal: the sky is not an equal share compared to the sea, nor the sea compared to Hades, even though Hades, Poseidon, and Zeus are all alike gods and sons of Cronus. Then too, Lysander was a Spartiate, but Agesilaus a Heraclid.[27] I also give precedence to families on the basis of their virtues. For doesn't a horse trainer love horses of good stock,

> . . . which wide-browed Zeus once gave to Tros
> in recompense for his son Ganymede, because they
> were
> the finest mares,[28]

[26] *Il.* 15.189, spoken by Poseidon concerning the division of the universe among Zeus, Poseidon, and Hades. In this speech (*Il.* 15.185–99), Poseidon is in fact claiming equal status to Zeus.

[27] That is, he traced his ancestry to Heracles.

[28] *Il.* 5.265–67.

ὁ δὲ θηρευτὴς εὐγενείας σκυλάκων ἐρᾷ; φιλάνθρωπος
δὲ καὶ φιλοθρέμμων τοῦ ζῴου τούτου οὐκ ἐξετάσεις⁴
τὰ γένη; λέγων οὐκ Ἀρτοξέρξην τὸν Ξέρξου (δειλόν
μοι γένος λέγεις) οὐδὲ Ἱππίαν τὸν Πεισιστράτου (πο-
νηρόν μοι γένος λέγεις) οὐδὲ Κροῖσον τὸν Ἀλυάττου
(ἀσθενὲς λέγεις)· ἐὰν δὲ Λεωνίδαν λέγῃς καὶ Ἀγη-
σίλαον, γνωρίζω τὴν ἀρετὴν καὶ μέμνημαι τοῦ Ἡρακλέους καὶ ἐπαινῶ τὴν εὐγένειαν.

Εἴθε μοι καὶ τὸ Ἀριστείδου γένος ἦν Ἀθήνησιν,
εἴθε τὸ Σωκράτους· ἐτίμησα ἂν τούτους ὡς Ἡρακλείδας, ὡς Περσείδας, ὡς Εὐπατρίδας. ἢ ποταμῶν μὲν
ῥεύματα ⟨ἐπαινεῖς⟩,⁵ ἐὰν καθαρὰ ἐκ πηγῶν ἔλθῃ, καὶ
φυτὰ ἐπαινεῖς, κἂν γηράσκῃ μὲν αὐτῶν τὰ σώματα,
μένῃ δὲ τὰ σπέρματα· εὐγένειαν δὲ ἀνθρωπίνην οὐκ
ἐπαινέσεις, ἐὰν ἀρξαμένη ἀπὸ τῆς ἀρετῆς ὡς ἐκ πη-
γῆς καθαρᾶς γνήσιος μένῃ, ἀνεπίμικτος μένῃ;

Καὶ μέχρι μὲν ταύτης ἀνδρίζῃ, καὶ ἀξιόπιστος εἶ
λέγων· ἐὰν δέ σου καὶ περὶ πλούτου πυνθάνωμαι, τί
φῇς; ποῖ τὸ πρᾶγμα τάττεις; ἐν ποίῳ χορῷ; λέγε γυ-

---

⁴ ἐξετάσεις Koniaris: ἐξετάσει R
⁵ suppl. Hobein, Trapp, Koniaris

---

29 Artoxerxes I (variant of Artaxerxes) was Xerxes' son.
Artoxerxes II is the subject of *Orr.* 34.6 and 36.6.

30 Hippias, who succeeded his father as tyrant of Athens, was
exiled in 510 BC.

31 Croesus' defeat by Cyrus the Great (ca. 546 BC) marked
the end of the Lydian dynasty that began with Gyges; he is also
mentioned at *Orr.* 5.2, 11.6, 13.5, 22.5, 32.9, and 34.4–5.

and doesn't a hunter love puppies of good stock? And as a lover of man who takes delight in raising this creature, will you not scrutinize its breeds? Not, however, by speaking of Xerxes' son Artoxerxes[29] (you tell me of a cowardly breed), nor Pisistratus' son Hippias[30] (you bring up a wicked breed), nor Alyattes' son Croesus (you mention a weak one).[31] But if you speak of Leonidas and Agesilaus, then I recognize their virtue, and am reminded of Heracles, and I praise their noble lineage.[32]

If only there were a bloodline of Aristides[33] in Athens, if only one of Socrates! I would have honored them as I do the Heraclids, Perseids, and Eupatrids.[34] Do you[35] praise rivers, if their waters come fresh from their sources, and praise plants whose seeds remain fertile even when their stalks grow old, and yet you do not praise human nobility, even if it arises from virtue, as if from a pure spring, and remains clear and unpolluted?

Thus far you act bravely and what you say is plausible. But if I question you about wealth, what is your response? Where do you rank this asset? In what category? Speak

[32] Both are Heraclids. The two appear at *Orr.* 19.5, 22.5, and 23.2.

[33] The fifth-century BC politician known as "The Just," also cited at *Orr.* 6.5, 22.5, and 27.6.

[34] Legendary families in Sparta, Corinth, and Athens.

[35] I follow Trapp's interpretation (1997a, 321n28) that the "you" is the Stoic proponent addressed in §§1–3, and that the speaker goes on to tease him "with his school's perceived difficulties and consequent equivocation over wealth and all other 'preferred indifferents.'"

μνῇ τῇ κεφαλῇ, τὰς τῆς ψυχῆς φωνὰς λέγε· τί φῇς
τὸν πλοῦτον; κακόν; τί οὖν ἐρᾷς; ἀγαθόν; τί οὖν φεύ-
γεις;

ἡ γλῶττ᾽ ἐπώμοσ᾽, ἡ δὲ φρὴν ἀνώμοτος;

ἀλλ᾽ οὐδέτερον ἡγεῖ, οὐκ ἀγαθόν, οὐ κακόν, ἀλλ᾽ ἐν
μεθορίᾳ καὶ χώρᾳ μέσῃ; τήρησον αὐτὸ ἀδιάφορον,
μὴ προέλθῃς περαιτέρω, μὴ ὑπερβῇς τοὺς ὅρους. ἂν
δὲ ὑπαλλάξας τὸ ὄνομα ἀγαθὸν μὲν μὴ καλῇς, προηγμένον δὲ καλῇς, τὴν μὲν φωνὴν μετέβαλες, τὴν δὲ
τιμὴν δίδως.

frankly with your head uncovered³⁶ and tell what your soul says. What do you say about wealth? Is it an evil? Then why do you love it? Is it a good? Then why do you shun it?³⁷ Is this a case of

my tongue swore, but my mind is not under oath?³⁸

Or rather do you think that it is neither a good nor an evil, but occupies a position somewhere in between? Then keep it as "indifferent" and go no further; stay within your limits. If, however, you slightly change its name and while not calling it a good, you call it "preferred," then you change the word, but still grant it value.³⁹

---

³⁶ A reference to Socrates covering his head when saying something shameful, at Pl. *Phdr.* 237a.

³⁷ For Stoic views of wealth as either indifferent (ἀδιάφορον) or useless (ἀνωφελές), cf. Plut. *Stoic. rep.* 1047e–48c and *Comm. not.* 1069c and 1065a.

³⁸ The notoriously unethical statement by Hippolytus at Eur. *Hipp.* 612.

³⁹ See Diog. Laert. 7.105–7 for a discussion of the Stoic categories of indifferent (ἀδιάφορον) and preferred (προηγμένον), and the status of wealth as a "preferred indifferent."

ORATION 41

INTRODUCTION

This final (incomplete) oration investigates the origin of good and evil. The Platonic tenet that the gods are responsible only for good things[1] is elaborated in §§1–2, leaving the rest of the oration to deal with the more difficult subject, the origin of evils. It opens with an anecdote (not known elsewhere) that when Alexander the Great visited the oracle of Zeus Ammon, the only question he asked the god was where the Nile arose. He therefore missed an opportunity to ask for an oracle that would benefit all humanity (§1). The speaker therefore seeks such an oracle from Zeus as to the origin of human goods, but declares that it really is unnecessary, because as "the father and creator"[2] his good works are abundantly clear in his governance of the universe, as his mind (*nous*) permeates all creation. Zeus' nod in Homer alludes to his being the creator of everything, so both Homer and Plato confirm that all good things come from the gods (§2). But when it comes to ascertaining the origin of evils, an oracle really is necessary, so that question is posed to the gods in gen-

[1] See *Orr*. 5.1 and 13.8. The title reflects this tenet ("Since god brings about good things").

[2] The appellation alludes to Pl. *Ti*. 28c.

eral, amplified by an impassioned litany of all the terrible
things that beset humans throughout their lives (§3). If it
is granted that heaven is free of evils and that only good
things flow from it, then evils on earth must come from
two inherent imperfections: the attributes (*pathos*) of
matter and the freedom (*exousia*) of the human soul. With
regard to physical materials, a craftsman is not responsible
for the by-products of materials he uses, such as sparks
from an anvil, because he looks to the crafting of the
whole. Likewise, what we see as destruction in the physical world happens for the preservation of the whole, as
illustrated by Heraclitus' "way up and down" (§4). Human
superiority over all other creatures is secured by its possession of reason and its life in communities based on law,
justice, and friendship. But to secure its inferiority to the
divine, god mounted man's immortal soul, like a charjo-
teer, on a human body, with the freedom either to control
the team or to give in to depravity.[3] To keep the chariot on
course, the charioteer must restrain the conflicting impulses of the four horses pulling it toward lust, pleasure,
sloth, or recklessness (§5). The oration breaks off at this
point.

[3] This adaptation of the chariot analogy at *Phdr*. 246a–56b is
typical of Maximus' creative refashioning of familiar Platonic im-
ages and analogies.

ORATION 41

Τοῦ θεοῦ τὰ ἀγαθὰ ποιοῦντος,
πόθεν τὰ κακά

1. Φασὶ τὸν Μακεδόνα Ἀλέξανδρον, ἀφικόμενον εἰς
Ἄμμωνος, προσειπόντος αὐτὸν τοῦ Ἄμμωνος παῖδα,
πιστεῦσαι τῷ θεῷ κατὰ τὴν Ὁμήρου φήμην, πατέρα
αὐτὸν θεῶν καὶ ἀνθρώπων ὀνομάζοντος· ἀποδεξάμε-
νος δὲ τοῦ μαντείου ἄλλο μὲν ἠξίωσεν οὐθὲν τὸν πατέρα μετὰ τοῦτο ἐρέσθαι, οὐ περὶ τῆς Δαρείου φυγῆς,
οὐ περὶ τῆς μελλούσης μάχης, οὐ περὶ τῆς Ἑλλάδος
κακουμένης, οὐ περὶ τῆς Ἀσίας κυκωμένης· ἀλλ᾽
ὥσπερ αὐτῷ τῶν ἄλλων καλῶς ἐχόντων, ἠρώτα τὸν
θεὸν περὶ τοῦ Νείλου, ὁπόθεν ὁρμηθεὶς ἐπὶ Αἰγύπτου
κάτεισιν. πάνυ γοῦν αὐτῷ τοῦτο ἓν ἔδει πρὸς εὐδαιμονίαν καὶ μαθόντι εἶχεν ἂν καλῶς· οὐδ᾽ εἰ, μὰ Δία,
πρὸς τῷ Νείλῳ τὸν Ἴστρον ἔγνω, ἢ τὸν Ὠκεανὸν
αὐτόν, εἴτε τίς ἐστιν ποταμοῦ φύσις περὶ πᾶσαν γῆν
εἰλουμένου, εἴτε ἀρχαὶ τῆς δεῦρο καὶ πηγαὶ θαλάττης,

ORATION 41

Since god brings about good things,
where do evil things come from?

1. They say that when Alexander the Macedonian came to the oracle of Ammon and Ammon called him "son," he believed the god on the word of Homer, who called him "father of gods and men."[1] But once he received this oracle, he then saw fit to ask his father only one thing. It did not concern the flight of Darius,[2] nor the impending battle,[3] nor trouble in Greece, nor turmoil in Asia. No, acting as if these other affairs were going perfectly well for him, he asked the god where the Nile originated for its downward flow to Egypt.[4] Obviously he needed to know this single thing for his happiness to be complete, and, having learned it, all would go well for him! No, by Zeus, it wouldn't, not even if, in addition to the Nile, he had learned about the Ister, or about the Ocean itself— whether its nature is that of a river winding around the entire earth, or if it is the origin and source of our sea, or

---

[1] *Il.* 1.544, etc. Zeus and Ammon were regularly conflated as Zeus-Ammon. Alexander visited the oracle in 332 BC.
[2] Darius III fled after the Battle of Issus (333 BC).
[3] The Battle of Gaugamela (331 BC).
[4] There is no other account of his asking this question.

εἴτε λίμνη ὑποδεχομένη τὰς ἡλίου καταδύσεις καὶ σελήνης, εἴτε ἄλλο τι, οἷον οἱ ποιηταὶ καταμαντεύονται· ἐξὸν τοὺς μὲν ποταμοὺς ἐᾶν ῥεῖν, ὁπόθεν αὐτοὺς ἀφῆκεν <ὁ θεός>,[1] αὐτὸν δὲ ἐπὶ Ἄμμωνα ἀφικόμενον, ἢ ἐπὶ τὴν Θεσπρωτῶν γῆν καὶ τὴν ἐκεῖ δρῦν, ἢ ἐπὶ τὸν Παρνασσὸν καὶ τὴν Πυθοῖ χρησμῳδίαν, ἢ ἐπὶ τὸν Ἰσμηνὸν καὶ τὴν ἐκεῖ φωνήν, ἢ ἐπὶ Δῆλον καὶ τοὺς ἐκεῖ χορούς, ἢ εἴ που ἄλλο τι μαντεῖον ἦν φθεγματικὸν τῆς Ἑλλάδος ἢ τῆς βαρβάρου γῆς, δεῖσθαι τοῦ Διὸς καὶ τοῦ Ἀπόλλωνος ἐπιδοῦναι χρησμὸν ἕνα κοινὸν καὶ δημόσιον τῷ πάντων ἀνθρώπων γένει. ἢ γὰρ ἂν κοινωφελεστέραν θεωρίαν ἐστείλαντο οἱ ἄνθρωποι τήνδε μᾶλλον ἢ Δωριεῖς περὶ Πελοποννήσου μαντευόμενοι, ἢ Ἀθηναῖοι περὶ Ἰωνίας πυνθανόμενοι, ἢ Κορίνθιοι περὶ Σικελίας ἀνερωτῶντες.

2. Φέρε μιμησάμενοι τοὺς θεωροὺς ἐκείνους τοὺς κοινούς, τοὺς ὑπὲρ τοῦ γένους ἐπὶ τὰ μαντεῖα σταλέντας, ἐρώμεθα τὸν Δία, τίς τῶν ἀνθρωπίνων ἀγαθῶν πατὴρ καὶ χορηγός, τίνες ἀρχαί, τίνες πηγαί, πόθεν ὁρμηθέντα ῥεῖ; ἢ τούτων μὲν πέρι οὐθὲν δεῖ τὸν θεὸν ἐνοχλεῖν, αἰσθανομένους τῆς χορηγίας καὶ ὁρῶντας τὴν αἰτίαν καὶ συνιέντας τὴν πηγὴν καὶ τὸν πατέρα καὶ ποιητὴν εἰδότας, τὸν οὐρανοῦ ἁρμοστήν, τὸν ἡλίου καὶ σελήνης ἀγωγέα, τὸν κορυφαῖον τῆς τῶν

---

[1] suppl. Davies[2], Trapp: <ὁ Ζεὺς> suppl. Paccius: <ὁ θεὸς> ante αὐτοὺς suppl. Hobein

if it is a lake that receives the sun and moon when they set, or if it is some other thing that poets divine it to be.[5] And yet he could simply have let the rivers flow from wherever god sends them forth, and gone to Ammon, or to the land of the Thesprotians and its oak tree,[6] or to Parnassus and its oracle at Pytho, or to the Ismenus and its prophetic voice,[7] or to Delos and its choruses, or to any other oracle that spoke to people in Greece or in foreign lands, and ask Zeus and Apollo to deliver one common, public oracle for the entire human race. For this would have been a mission of more universal benefit for humans to undertake than when the Dorians sought an oracle about the Peloponnesus, when the Athenians inquired about Ionia, or the Corinthians asked about Sicily.[8]

2. Come, let us imitate those public ambassadors sent to oracles on behalf of the human race and pose these questions to Zeus. Who is the father and provider of human goods? What are their origins and sources? From where do they arise and flow? Or is there no need at all to trouble the god about this, since we are well aware of this provision, see its cause, understand its source, and know for ourselves "the father and creator,"[9] the governor of the heavens, the director of the sun and moon, the conductor

---

[5] Encircling the earth (*Il.* 18.607–8), source of all seas (*Il.* 21.195–97); resting place for the setting sun (Stesichorus, fr. 185 PMG).

[6] That is, to Dodona with its prophetic oak; cf. *Or.* 8.1.

[7] Apollo's oracle was by the Ismenus River near Thebes.

[8] Three colonizations approved by the oracle at Delphi.

[9] An adaptation of Pl. *Ti.* 28c, ποιητὴν καὶ πατέρα (creator and father); variations occur at *Orr.* 2.10 and 11.9 and 12.

ἄστρων περιφορᾶς καὶ δινήσεως καὶ χορείας καὶ
δρόμου, τὸν ὡρῶν ταμίαν, τὸν πνευμάτων οἰκονόμον,
τὸν ποιητὴν θαλάττης, τὸν δημιουργὸν γῆς, τὸν ποταμῶν χορηγόν, τὸν καρπῶν τροφέα, τὸν ζώων γεν-
νητήν, τὸν γενέθλιον, τὸν ὑέτιον, τὸν ἐπικάρπιον, τὸν
πατρῷον, τὸν φυτάλιον, οὗ ὁ νοῦς ἀρραγὴς ὢν καὶ
ἄτρυτος καὶ ἐπὶ πάσας ἐξικνούμενος φύσεις ἀμηχάνῳ
τάχει, ὡς προσβολὴ ὄψεως, πᾶν κοσμεῖ ὅτου ἂν ἐπα-
φήσηται, καθάπερ καὶ αἱ παρ' ἡλίου ἀκτῖνες προσπε-
σοῦσαι τῇ γῇ λαμπρύνουσιν αὐτῆς τὸ καταληφθὲν
πᾶν.

Τίς δέ ἐστιν ὁ τῆς ἐπαφῆς ταύτης τρόπος, ἐγὼ μὲν
εἰπεῖν οὐκ ἔχω, ᾐνίξατο δὲ αὐτὴν ἠρέμα Ὅμηρος·

ἦ καὶ κυανέῃσιν ἐπ' ὀφρύσι νεῦσε Κρονίων.

ὁμοῦ δὲ τῷ Διὸς νεύματι γῆ ξυνέστη καὶ ὅσα γῆς
θρέμματα, καὶ θάλασσα ξυνέστη καὶ ὅσα θαλάττης
γεννήματα, καὶ ἀὴρ ξυνέστη καὶ ὅσα ἀέρος φορήματα,
καὶ οὐρανὸς ξυνέστη καὶ ὅσα ἐν οὐρανῷ κινήματα.
ταῦτα ἔργα τῶν Διὸς νευμάτων· μέχρι τούτων ἀδεής
εἰμι χρησμῳδίας, καὶ Ὁμήρῳ πείθομαι καὶ πιστεύω
Πλάτωνι καὶ οἰκτείρω τὸν Ἐπίκουρον.

3. Ἐὰν δὲ εἰς τὰς τῶν κακῶν ἐννοίας παρέλθω,
πόθεν ταῦτα παρέδυ δεῦρο; τίνες αἱ τῶν κακῶν πηγαὶ
καὶ γενέσεις; πόθεν ἀρξάμενα ἔρχεται; ἐξ Αἰθιόπων,

---

10 *dēmiourgos*.   11 As Trapp (1997a, 325n11) points out,
"the whole description of the divine Mind in this paragraph could

of the revolutions, movements, dances, and courses of the stars, the keeper of the seasons, the regulator of the winds, the creator of the sea, the craftsman[10] of the earth, the provider of rivers, the nourisher of crops, the begetter of living things—the god of birth, rain, and fertility, the god of families, and the fostering god, whose mind is indestructible and untiring; it pervades all nature with incredible speed like the glance of an eye, and brings order and beauty to everything it touches, just like the rays from the sun when they fall on the earth and illuminate every part of it they reach.[11]

I myself cannot explain the nature of this touch, but Homer subtly alluded to it, when he said,

the son of Cronus spoke and nodded his dark brow.[12]

At this nod of Zeus the earth came into being with all its progeny, as did the sea with everything born in it, and the air with all that is borne on it, and heaven with all that moves in it. These are the work of Zeus' nods.[13] Thus far I do not need any oracle, for I believe Homer and I trust Plato, and I pity Epicurus.[14]

3. But when I turn to the consideration of evils, these questions arise. Where did they come from to steal into this world? What are the sources and origins of evils? Where do they start out from? From Ethiopia like the

in theory be applied as well to the Stoics' immanent divinity as to the transcendent God of Platonism."

[12] *Il.* 1.528, etc.

[13] Zeus' nods are similarly allegorized at *Or.* 4.8.

[14] Typical scorn for the godless materialist; see *Orr.* 4.8–9, 25.4, and 30.2–3.

ὡς ὁ λοιμός; ἐκ Βαβυλῶνος, ὡς ὁ Ξέρξης; ἐκ Μακε-
δονίας, ὡς Φίλιππος; οὐ γὰρ ἐξ οὐρανοῦ, μὰ Δία, οὐκ
ἐξ οὐρανοῦ·

φθόνος γὰρ ἔξω θείου χοροῦ ἵσταται.

ἐνταῦθα τοίνυν, ἐνταῦθά μοι δεῖ χρησμῳδίας· ἐρώμεθα τοὺς θεούς· "Ζεῦ καὶ Ἄπολλον, καὶ ὅστις ἄλλος
θεὸς μαντικὸς καὶ κηδεμὼν τῆς τῶν ἀνθρώπων ἀγέλης, δεομένοις εἴπατε, τίς κακῶν ἀρχή; τίς αἰτία; πῶς
φυλαξώμεθα; πῶς λάθωμεν;

οὐ γάρ τις νέμεσις φυγέειν κακόν, οὐδ᾽ ὑπαλύξαι.

ἢ οὐχ ὁρᾶτε ὅσα τὰ δεινὰ εἰς τὰς ἀνθρωπίνας κῆρας
ἐμπεπτωκότα περὶ γῆν στρέφεται, παντοίων στόνων
καὶ ὀδυρμῶν ἐμπιμπλάντα τὴν γῆν; στένει μὲν τὸ ἀνθρώπου σῶμα τὰς ἐπιτετειχισμένας αὐτῷ νόσους ὀδυ-
ρόμενον καὶ τὸ ἀκροσφαλὲς τῆς σωτηρίας καὶ τὸ
ἄδηλον τοῦ βίου. τίς γὰρ ἡλικίας καιρὸς ἀνυπεύθυνος
ἀνθρωπίνῳ σώματι; ὃ γενόμενον μὲν εὐθὺς καὶ ἀπο-
σπασθὲν ἐκ μητέρων, ὑγρὸν καὶ ἰλυῶδες καὶ διαρ-
ρέον, ὀδυρμῶν καὶ κινυζημάτων ἀνάπλεων· προϊὸν δὲ
καὶ εἰς ὥραν ἀναφυόμενον, ἔμπληκτον καὶ ἀκρατές·
κἂν εἰς ἥβην προέλθῃ, ὑπὸ φλεγμονῆς ἀκατάσχετον·
κἂν εἰς γῆρας ἔλθῃ, κατὰ βραχὺ νεκρούμενον καὶ

---

15 In the repeated phrase "not from heaven," Trapp detects
an echo of Dem. 8.26, when Demosthenes says that Philip's resources did not come "from heaven."

plague? From Babylon like Xerxes? From Macedonia like Philip? Certainly not from heaven, by Zeus, not from heaven,[15]

> for Envy stands outside the divine chorus.[16]

Here, then, here I do indeed need an oracle. So let us ask the gods: "Zeus and Apollo, and any other oracular god who cares for our human herd, tell us, we beg of you, what is the origin of evils? What causes them? How can we guard against them? How can we avoid them?

> for there is no shame in fleeing evil . . . or eluding it.[17]

Or do you not see all the terrible things that assault our human defects[18] and roam about the earth, filling the land with groans and lamentation of all sorts? The human body groans as it laments the diseases that besiege it, the precariousness of its survival, and the uncertainty of its life. For what stage of life is free from the demands of the human body? As soon as it is born and pulled from its mother's womb, all wet and slimy and leaking, it is full of howling and whimpering. In time, if it develops into childhood, it is impulsive and intemperate. If it matures to adolescence, its fiery passions make it uncontrollable, and if it reaches old age, it gradually dies away and is extin-

---

[16] Pl. *Phdr.* 247a.

[17] *Il.* 14.80 + 12.327.

[18] Maximus seems to play on κῆρες as "defects" (cf. Pl. *Leg.* 11.937d) and the Homeric κῆρες, "fates of death," as at *Il.* 12.326–27: "myriad fates of death stand close by, which no mortal can escape or elude."

ἀποσβεννύμενον· ἐνδιαίτημα τῇ ψυχῇ ἀχρειότερον,
δυσάρεστον, δύστηνον, δύσεργον, οὐκ ὄμβρων ἀνεχόμενον, οὐ πνευμάτων, οὐχ ἡλίου, μεμφόμενον ταῖς
ὥραις τοῦ οὐρανοῦ καὶ ἀντιστρατηγοῦν τῷ Διί· χειμὼν οὗτος, ἀμπέχεται· θέρος τοῦτο, ἀναψύχει· πληρω-
θὲν μὲν κενώσεως, κενωθὲν δὲ πλησμονῆς ὀρεγόμε-
νον· Εὐρίπου καὶ ἀμπώτεως δίκην μηδέποτε ἑστός,
μηδέποτε ἀτρεμοῦν, ἀκόρεστον, ἀκατάσχετον, ἀδηφά-
γον, ἐνδεὲς ἀμπεχόνης, δεόμενον ὑποδημάτων, ἀλειμ-
μάτων, φαρμάκων, λουτρῶν. ἓν σῶμα θεραπεύουσιν
χεῖρες πολλαὶ καὶ τέχναι πολλαί· χιλίας δὲ ἵππους
ἱπποφορβὸς εἷς, καὶ τοσαῦτα μῆλα ποιμὴν εἷς, καὶ
τοσούτους βοῦς βουφορβὸς εἷς. καὶ οὐδὲ τὰ τοσαῦτα
ἱκανά· τίς γὰρ ἀνθρωπίνη μηχανὴ λοιμοῦ προσβολὰς
ἀλέξασθαι, ἢ ἀνασχεῖν ὄμβρους ἐξ οὐρανοῦ καταφε-
ρομένους, ἢ στῆσαι γῆν σειομένην, ἢ σβέσαι πῦρ ἐκ
γῆς ἀνιστάμενον; ὁρᾷς τὸν δρόμον καὶ τὴν διαδοχὴν
τῶν κακῶν καὶ τὴν συνέχειαν τῶν κινδύνων·

οὐδὲν ἀκιδνότερον γαῖα τρέφει ἀνθρώποιο.

κἂν ἐπὶ τὴν ψυχὴν ἔλθῃς, κἀκεῖ ὄψει ὄχλον νοση-
μάτων τῇ ψυχῇ ἐπιχεόμενον· ἐὰν λύπην ἀπώσῃ, φόβος ὑπορρεῖ· ἂν ἀπέλθῃ φόβος, ὀργὴ ἀνίσταται· ἂν
παύσηται ὀργή, φθόνος ἔπεισιν· παρὰ πόδας τὰ δυσχερῆ, ἐν γειτόνων τὰ κακά, ἀνοχὴ δὲ ἀκριβὴς οὐδεμία."

4. Τί ἂν οὖν πρὸς ταῦτα ἀποκρίναιτο ὁ Ζεὺς ἢ ὁ

uished. As a habitation for its soul, the body is of little
use: it is peevish, miserable, sluggish, unable to endure
rain, wind, or sun, constantly complaining about the seasons sent from the sky and battling against Zeus.[19] Winter
comes and it wraps itself up; summer comes and it cools
itself off. When it is full, it longs to be empty; when empty,
it longs to be full. Like the Euripus[20] and the ebb and flow
of tides, it is never stable, never still, but is insatiable,
uncontrollable, voracious, in need of clothing, and requir-
ing shoes, ointments, medicines, and baths. Many hands
and much expertise minister to just one human body, even
though one trainer suffices for a thousand horses, one
shepherd for as many sheep, and one cowherd for as many
cows. And yet, even that much attention is insufficient, for
what human devices are there to ward off the attacks of a
plague, or to hold back the rains pouring from the sky, or
to stop an earthquake, or to extinguish lava spewing up
from the earth? You see around you the circulation and
succession of evils and the constant series of dangers, for

the earth breeds nothing more feeble than man.[21]

And if you turn to the soul, here too you will see a horde
of diseases assailing it. If you stave off sorrow, fear seeps
in; if fear goes away, anger arises. If anger ceases, envy
takes its place. Troubles are at hand, evils are nearby, and
there is no sure respite whatsoever."

4. What answer might Zeus, Apollo, or any other pro-

19 That is, Zeus as the god of weather.
20 For these straits as a symbol of instability, see *Or.* 5.6.
21 *Od.* 18.130, Odysseus speaking to Amphinomus.

Ἀπόλλων, ἤ τις ἄλλος μαντικὸς θεός; ἀκούσωμεν το
ὑποφήτου λέγοντος

ἐξ ἡμέων γάρ φασι κάκ' ἔμμεναι· οἱ δὲ καὶ αὐτοὶ
σφῆσιν ἀτασθαλίῃσιν ὑπὲρ μόρον ἄλγε' ἔχουσι

τίς οὖν ἡ τῆς ἀτασθαλίης αἰτία; οὐρανοῦ καὶ γῆς δι
οἷν ἑστίαιν τὴν μὲν ἄμοιρον ἡγητέον κακῶν, τὴν δ
ἐξ ἀμφοῖν ἐπιμεμιγμένην, ᾗ τὰ μὲν ἀγαθὰ ἐπίρρυτ
ἐκ τῆς ἑτέρας, τὰ δὲ κακὰ ἐξ αὐτοφυοῦς μοχθηρία
ἀνίσταται. διττὴ δὲ αὕτη, ἡ μὲν ὕλης πάθος, ἡ δ
ψυχῆς ἐξουσία.

Ῥητέον δὲ δὴ τὰ πρῶτα ὑπὲρ τῆς προτέρας. ὕλη
ὁρᾷς ὑποβεβλημένην δημιουργῷ ἀγαθῷ, ἧς τὸ μὲ
κοσμηθὲν ἥκει παρὰ τῆς τέχνης, εἰ δέ τι ἀκρατῶ
ἑαυτῶν τὰ ἐν γῇ ἔχοντα πάσχει πλημμελές, ἀναίτιό
μοι τὴν τέχνην τίθει· βούλησις γὰρ οὐδεμία τεχνίτο
ἄτεχνος, οὐδὲ γὰρ νομοθέτου ἄδικος· ὁ δὲ θεῖος νοῦ
ἀνθρωπίνης τέχνης εὐστοχώτερος. καθάπερ οὖν ἐ
ταῖς τῶν τεχνῶν χειρουργίαις τὰ μὲν ἡ τέχνη προη
γουμένως δρᾷ, στοχαζομένη τοῦ τέλους, τὰ δὲ ἔπετα
τῇ χειρουργίᾳ, οὐ τέχνης ἔργα ἀλλ' ὕλης πάθη, σπι

---

22 Homer.

23 *Od.* 1.33–34, Zeus speaking, also cited at *Or.* 38.7.

24 Craftsman recalls Zeus as *dēmiourgos* of the earth in §2.

25 That is, an artist cannot be blamed for imperfections in h
materials, or a lawmaker for infringements of his laws. Chrysip
pus the Stoic argued that divinity could not be held responsibl

phetic god have for this? Let us hear what their inter-preter[22] has to say:

> For men say that evils come from us, but they
> themselves
> by their own misdeeds suffer pains beyond what is
> fated.[23]

What, then, is the cause of this misbehavior? Of the two habitable realms, heaven and earth, we must believe that the former is free of evils, while the latter contains a mixture of both good and evil, where the good things flow down from the former, whereas the evils arise in the latter from its inherent imperfections. These imperfections are of two kinds: the ones derive from the properties of matter, and the others from the freedom of the soul.

I must therefore speak first of the material component. What you see around you is matter that has been subjected to the work of a good craftsman.[24] The element of order in it has come about through his skill, but if the things on earth undergo any discord through their own lack of control, then please do not hold his skill responsible, because it is by no means an artisan's intention to lack skill, any more than a lawmaker's to be unjust,[25] and the divine mind is surer in its aim than human skill. Now just as in the exercise of handicrafts, the skill itself accomplishes some things on purpose as it aims for its proper end, while other things follow from that handiwork which are not the effects of the skill itself, but are by-products of the material,

for impiety any more than a law for illegality (Plut. *Stoic. rep.* 1049e).

θῆρές τε ἐξ ἄκμονος καὶ ἐκ βαύνου αἰθαλώσεις, καὶ
ἄλλο ἐξ ἄλλης πάθος, ἀναγκαῖον μὲν τῇ ἐργασίᾳ, οὐ
προηγούμενον δὲ τῷ τεχνίτῃ· οὕτως ἀμέλει καὶ ὅσα
περὶ γῆν πάθη γίνεται, ἃς καλοῦμεν κακῶν ἀνθρωπίνων ἐμβολάς, ἐνταῦθα ἡγητέον ἀναίτιον {καὶ}[2] τὴν
τέχνην, εἶναι δὲ ταῦτα τῆς τοῦ ὅλου δημιουργίας
ὥσπερ τινὰς ἀναγκαίας καὶ ἑπομένας φύσεις.

Ἃ δὲ ἡμεῖς καλοῦμεν κακὰ καὶ φθοράς, καὶ ἐφ' οἷς
ὀδυρόμεθα, ταῦτα ὁ τεχνίτης καλεῖ σωτηρίαν τοῦ
ὅλου· μέλει γὰρ αὐτῷ τοῦ ὅλου, τὸ δὲ μέρος ἀνάγκη
κακοῦσθαι ὑπὲρ τοῦ ὅλου. λοιμώττουσιν Ἀθηναῖοι,
σείονται Λακεδαιμόνιοι, ἡ Θετταλία ἐπικλύζεται, ἡ
Αἴτνη φλέγεται. καὶ πότε Ἀθηναίοις ἀθανασίαν ὁ
Ζεὺς ὑπέσχετο; ἐὰν γὰρ ἀπέλθῃ ὁ λοιμός, Ἀλκιβιάδης ἐπὶ Σικελίαν οὐκ ἄγει; πότε Λακεδαιμονίοις ὑπέσχετο γῆν ἄσειστον; πότε Θετταλοῖς γῆν ἄκλυστον;
πότε Σικελιώταις γῆν ἄπυρον; μόρια ταῦτα σωμάτων.
ὁρᾷς οὖν τὰ πάθη, ἃ σὺ μὲν καλεῖς φθοράν, τεκμαι-
ρόμενος τῇ τῶν ἀπιόντων ὁδῷ, ἐγὼ δὲ σωτηρίαν, τεκ-
μαιρόμενος τῇ διαδοχῇ τῶν μελλόντων. μεταβολὴν
ὁρᾷς σωμάτων καὶ γενέσεως ἀλλαγήν,

ὁδὸν[3] ἄνω καὶ κάτω,

2 del. Markland, Trapp   3 ὁδὸν Markland, Trapp: ὁδῶν R

26 For the same argument (concerning providence) that the
part is subordinate to the whole, see *Or.* 5.4.
27 The same examples are used at *Or.* 5.4.

such as sparks from an anvil, soot-filled smoke from a furnace, and other such by-products of other materials, that are necessitated by the work being done but not intended by the artisan—in just the same way all those events come to pass that we call onslaughts of human evils, and here too we must believe that the skill is blameless, and that these effects are, as it were, the necessary and natural consequences of the crafting of the whole.

That which we call evil and destruction, those things which make us lament, are what the artisan calls the preservation of the whole. His concern is for the whole, and the part must necessarily suffer damage on behalf of the whole.[26] The Athenians suffer plague, the Lacedaemonians are shaken by earthquakes, Thessaly is inundated, Aetna erupts.[27] So when did Zeus promise the Athenians immortality? For even if the plague goes away, does not Alcibiades lead them against Sicily?[28] When did he promise the Lacedaemonians a land without earthquakes? When did he promise the Thessalians a land without inundations? When did he promise the Sicilians a land without volcanic eruptions? These are but parts of larger bodies. And so you see these events, which you call destruction, because you are judging by how things go away, but which I call preservation, judging by the succession of what will come. What you see is an alteration of physical bodies and a change of things coming into being,

the way up and down,[29]

[28] The Athenians lost thousands of citizens in the expeditions against Sicily.   [29] An adaptation of Heraclit. fr. D 51 L-M (B 60 D-K): ὁδὸς ἄνω κάτω μία καὶ ὠυτή (the way up and down: one and the same).

κατὰ τὸν Ἡράκλειτον· καὶ αὖθις αὖ

> ζῶντας μὲν τὸν ἐκείνων θάνατον,[4] ἀποθνήσκον-
> τας δὲ τὴν ἐκείνων ζωήν.

> ζῇ πῦρ τὸν γῆς θάνατον καὶ ἀὴρ ζῇ τὸν πυρὸς
> θάνατον· ὕδωρ ζῇ τὸν ἀέρος θάνατον, γῆ τὸν
> ὕδατος.

διαδοχὴν ὁρᾷς βίου καὶ μεταβολὴν σωμάτων, και-
νουργίαν τοῦ ὅλου.

5. Ἴθι δὴ καὶ ἐπὶ τὴν τῶν ἄλλων ἀρχήν, τὴν αὐτο-
φυῆ, ἣν ἡ ψυχῆς ἐξουσία κυΐσκει τε καὶ τελεσφορεῖ,
ᾗ ὄνομα μοχθηρία· αὐτὸ τοῦτο

> ἑλομένου αἰτία, θεὸς ἀναίτιος.

ἐπεὶ γὰρ ἔδει γῆν γενέσθαι μὲν ἔγκαρπον καὶ ζωοτρό-
φον καὶ πολυθρέμμονα, ἔχειν δὲ ἐν ἑαυτῇ κακὰ ἔνδον
καθειργμένα ἐξεληλαμένα τοῦ οὐρανοῦ, εἰς τὸν δεῦρο
τόπον ἐμίγη θεὸς πολλὰς καὶ παντοδαπὰς ζῴων κλη-
ρουχίας, δίχα αὐτῶν τὴν πρώτην φύσιν διελόμενος·
τὴν μὲν εἶναι παντοδαπὴν ἐν τοῖς βίοις καὶ ποικίλην
τοῖς σώμασιν, ἄλογον, ἄφρονα, ἀλληλοφθόρον, ἀνόητον θεοῦ, ἀρετῆς ἄμοιρον, ὑπ' αἰσθήσεως ἐφημέρου
βοσκομένην καὶ δημαγωγουμένην, ἰσχυρὰν μὲν τῷ

---

[4] θάνατον Heinsius, Trapp: βίον R

according to Heraclitus; and again,

> they live the others' deaths and die the others' lives.[30]

> fire lives earth's death, and air lives fire's death; water lives air's death, and earth lives water's death.[31]

What you see is the passing on of life, the alteration of bodies, and the renewal of the whole.

5. Turn now to the source of the other evils, the one innate in us, which is conceived and brought to birth by the very freedom of the soul. This source is called depravity, the very thing where

> the responsibility is the chooser's; god is blameless.[32]

Since it was necessary for the earth not only to bear plants, sustain creatures, and support many species, but also to have confined within it evils that had been banished from heaven, god mingled together many different kinds of colonies of creatures in this realm of ours, having divided them into two primary natures. The one nature is that of creatures living all sorts of lives and endowed with various bodies, lacking in reason and intelligence, mutually destructive, with no concept of god or participation in virtue, nurtured and guided by immediate sensations, having

---

[30] Heraclit. fr. D 70 L-M (B 62 D-K). The first part of the fragment is quoted at *Or.* 4.4: θεοὶ θνητοί, ἄνθρωποι ἀθάνατοι (gods mortal, humans immortal). [31] A variation of Heraclit. fr. D 100 L-M (B 76 D-K). [32] Pl. *Resp.* 10.617e, spoken by Ur before the selection of souls.

σώματι, ἀμήχανον δὲ τῷ λογισμῷ· τὴν δὲ ἑτέραν αὖ
τὴν ἀνθρωπίνην ἔμπαλιν ὁμογενῆ καὶ ξύννομον καὶ
μίαν, ἀσθενῆ μὲν τῷ σώματι, ἄρρηκτον δὲ τῷ λόγῳ,
συνετὴν θεοῦ, πολιτείας μέτοχον, κοινωνίας ἐρῶσαν,
δίκης καὶ νόμου καὶ φιλίας γεγευμένην.

Ἔδει δὲ ἄρα τὸ γένος τοῦτο κρεῖττον μὲν εἶναι τῆς
ἐν γῇ πάσης ἀγέλης, ἔλαττον δέ, οἶμαι, θεοῦ. τὴν δὲ
ἐλάττωσιν αὐτοῦ οὐδὲ θάνατος ἄρα παρέξεσθαι ἔμελ-
λεν· ὃν γὰρ καλοῦσιν οἱ πολλοὶ θάνατον, αὐτὸ τοῦτο
ἦν ἀθανασίας ἀρχὴ καὶ γένεσις μέλλοντος βίου, τῶν
μὲν σωμάτων τῷ αὐτῶν νόμῳ καὶ χρόνῳ φθειρομένων,
τῆς δὲ ψυχῆς ἐπὶ τὸν αὑτῆς τόπον καὶ βίον ἀνακα-
λουμένης. τοῦτον δὴ τῆς ἀνθρωπίνης ἐνδείας πρὸς τὸ
θεῖον ἐξεῦρεν θεὸς τρόπον· ἐπιθεὶς τὴν ψυχὴν γηΐνῳ
σώματι ὡς ἡνίοχον ἅρματι, παραδοὺς τὰς ἡνίας τῷ
ἡνιόχῳ ἀφῆκεν θεῖν, ἔχουσαν μὲν παρ' αὐτοῦ ῥώμην
τέχνης, ἔχουσαν δὲ καὶ ἀτεχνίας ἐξουσίαν. ἡ δὲ ἐπειδὰν ἐπιβῇ ἅρματος καὶ λάβηται τῶν ἡνιῶν, ἡ μὲν
εὐδαίμων καὶ μακαρία ψυχὴ καὶ μεμνημένη τοῦ ἐπὶ
τὸ ὄχημα αὐτὴν ἐμβιβασαμένου θεοῦ καὶ ἡνιοχεῖν
προστάξαντος, ἔχεται τῶν ἡνιῶν καὶ ἄρχει τοῦ ἅρματος καὶ κολάζει τὰς τῶν ἵππων ὁρμάς· οἱ δέ εἰσιν
ἀτεχνῶς παντοδαποί, ἄλλος ἀλλαχοῦ θεῖν διωρμημέ-
νοι, ὁ μὲν αὐτῶν ἀκόλαστος καὶ ἀδηφάγος καὶ ὑβριστής, ὁ δὲ θυμώδης καὶ ἰτητικὸς καὶ ἔμπληκτος, ὁ δὲ

strong bodies, but incapable of reasoning. In contrast, human nature is that of a single, homogeneous species living together, weak in body but invincible in reason, knowing god, participating in government, loving community, and experienced in justice, law, and friendship.

This race therefore needed to be superior to any herd of animals on earth, but obviously inferior to god. Its inferiority, however, was not going to be secured even by death, for the very thing most people call death turns out to be the beginning of immortality and the genesis of future life, when bodies perish in their own ways over the course of time and the soul is summoned back to its proper place and existence. So, god devised the following means to render humans inferior to divinity. He mounted the soul on an earthly body like a charioteer on a chariot.[33] He gave the reins to this charioteer and set it free to run, since he gave it the power of skill, but also the freedom not to use that skill. And whenever it mounts the chariot and takes the reins, the happy and blessed soul that preserves its recollection of the god who placed it on the chariot and ordered it to drive holds the reins tight, controls the chariot, and checks the impulses of the horses. But they are of all different kinds, with each one straining to run in a different direction—one being licentious, gluttonous, and lustful; another headstrong, reckless, and impulsive; an-

[33] The following is a free adaptation of Plato's "chariot analogy" at *Phdr*. 246a–56b. Plato's two-horse chariot (biga), drawn by one good horse and one unruly one, has become a four-horse chariot (quadriga) with four unruly horses.

MAXIMUS OF TYRE

νωθὴς καὶ ἐκλελυμένος ‹καὶ . . .›,[5] ὁ δὲ ἀνελεύθερος
καὶ σμικρόφρων καὶ ταπεινός. †αυτουη†[6] ἅρμα ἐστα-
σιασμένον ταράττει τὸν ἡνίοχον· κᾆτα ἢν μὴ[7] κρα-
τήσῃ αὐτοῦ, κατὰ τὴν τοῦ δυναστεύοντος ἵππου
ῥύμην ἄξαν φέρεται, νῦν μὲν τῷ ἀκολάστῳ ἵππῳ πᾶν
τὸ ἅρμα ξυμφερόμενον αὐτῷ ἡνιόχῳ ἐπὶ ὕβρεις καὶ
παροινίας καὶ λαγνείας καὶ ἄλλας οὔτε εὐσχήμονας
οὔτε εἰλικρινεῖς ἡδονάς, νῦν δὲ τῷ θυμικῷ ἐπὶ κακώ-
σεις παντοδαπὰς ‹. . .›[8]

Μαξίμου · Τυρίου
Φιλοσοφούμενα
÷ ÷ + ÷ ÷
τέλος

[5] lacunam stat. Renehan, Trapp
[6] obel. Trapp, Koniaris: οὕτως U
[7] μὴ Markland, Trapp: μὲν R
[8] lacunam stat. Markland, Trapp, Koniaris

other dull, sluggish, ⟨and . . .⟩,[34] another slavish, small-minded, and cowardly. . . .[35] the chariot's disorder confounds the charioteer, and then, if he fails to gain control of it, it is carried headlong by the force of whichever horse proves most powerful. At one time, the entire chariot, together with its charioteer, is carried along by the licentious horse to acts of violence, drunkenness, lechery, and other indecent and impure pleasures; at another time, it is drawn by the hotheaded horse to all kinds of mischief . . .[36]

Maximus of Tyre's
Philosophical Works
end here

[34] A third quality is lacking.
[35] No emendation has made sense of the letters αυτουη.
[36] The rest is missing. A later hand seems to indicate that the manuscript copy ends here.

INDEX OF PROPER NAMES

INDEX OF NAMES

408

INDEX OF QUOTATIONS

Only verbatim (or near verbatim) quotations are listed.

INDEX OF QUOTATIONS

INDEX OF QUOTATIONS